The Career Advisor Series offers three Healthcare Career Directories to cover the whole spectrum of jobs in this crucial and fast-growing field:

Healthcare Career Directory—Nurses and Physicians covers:

Critical Care Nurse

Long-Term Care Nurse

Neurosurgeon

Nurse Practitioner

Oncology Nurse

Pathologist

Pediatrician

Psychiatrist

Specialty Nurse

Surgeon

Traveling Nurse

Healthcare Career Directory—Allied Health Professions is designed to cover licensed health workers, other than physicians, nurses, and public health professionals, who provide one-on-one services to patients, including:

Dietitian

Environmental Health Specialist

Health Services Administrator

Medical Illustrator

Medical Photographer

Mortician

Occupational Therapist

Optometrist

Physical Therapist

Rehabilitation Therapist

Respiratory Therapist

and others!

Healthcare Career Directory—Medical Technicians is designed to cover medical technologists and technicians, other than physicians and nurses, including:

Blood Bank Technician

Dental Hygienist

EEG/EKG Technician

Emergency Medical Technician

Laboratory Technician

Medical Records Technician

Nuclear Medicine Technician

Radiology Technician

Surgical Technician

and more!

HEALTHCARE

CAREER DIRECTORY
—Nurses and Physicians

Visible Ink Press proudly presents the second edition of the acclaimed *Healthcare Career Directory—Nurses and Physicians*, first published by the Career Press. The hallmark of this volume, part of VIP's Career Advisor Series, remains the essays by active professionals. Here, industry insiders describe opportunities and challenges in all categories of nursing and medicine, including:

- Pediatrics
- Neurology
- Pathology
- Nurse practitioner
- Critical care nursing
- Traveling nursing
- Surgery
- Psychiatry
- Specialty nursing
- Oncology nursing
- Long-term nursing

Careers in allied health and medical technology will be covered in two future volumes of the Career Advisor Series.

In fully up-to-date articles, they describe:

- What to expect on the job
- Typical career paths
- What they look for in an applicant
- How their specialty is unique

New Edition Provides Greatly Enhanced Job Hunting Resources

Once this "Advice from the Pro's" has given you a feel for healthcare careers, the *Directory* offers more help than ever before with your job search strategy:

- **The Job Search Process** includes essays on determining career objectives, resume preparation, networking, writing effective cover letters, and interviewing. With worksheets and sample resumes and letters. **NEW:** Resumes are now targeted to the realities of healthcare.

- **Job Opportunities Databank** provides details on hundreds of hospitals and companies that hire at entry-level. **NEW:** More companies are listed, and information on internships that they offer is now included.

- **Career Resources** identifies sources of help-wanted ads, professional associations, employment agencies and search firms, career guides, professional and trade periodicals, and basic reference guides. **NEW:** Resource listings are greatly expanded, and now include detailed descriptions to help you select the publications and organizations that will best meet your needs.

New Master Index Puts Information at Your Fingertips

This edition is more thoroughly indexed, with access to essays and directory sections both by subject and by organization name, publication title, or service name.

CAREER ADVISOR SERIES

HEALTHCARE

CAREER DIRECTORY
— Nurses and Physicians

A Practical, One-Stop Guide to Getting a Job as a Doctor or Nurse

2ND EDITION

Bradley J. Morgan, Editor
Joseph M. Palmisano, Associate Editor

VISIBLE INK PRESS

DETROIT • WASHINGTON, D.C. • LONDON

CAREER ADVISOR SERIES

HEALTHCARE
CAREER
DIRECTORY—
Nurses and Physicians

2nd Edition

A Practical, One-Stop Guide to Getting a Job as a Doctor or Nurse

Published by **Visible Ink Press** ™
a division of Gale Research Inc.
835 Penobscot Building
Detroit, MI 48226-4094

ISBN 0-8103-9437-5

Art Director: Cynthia Baldwin
Cover and Interior Design: Mary Krzewinski
Career Advisor Logo Designs: Kyle Raetz

Printed in the United States of America

Contents

PART ONE

Advice from the Pro's

1 Why Medicine?

Dr. James S. Todd, Executive Vice President, American Medical Association

The leading medical association in the United States makes a strong argument for considering a career in medicine. **1**

2 Pediatricians, More Than Just "Baby Doctors"

Frederick Kassab, M.D.

Explains how the role of the pediatrician continues to expand to treat an array of health problems that are now affecting children. **5**

3 Diseases of the Brain, Nerve, and Muscle: The Challenge of Neurology

Dr. Walter J. Koroshetz, Department of Neurology, Massachusetts General Hospital, Boston, MA

Intrigued by the biological basis of human behavior? Then consider working within the field of neurology. **9**

4 Pathology as a Career in Medicine

Intersociety Committee on Pathology Information

Pathology, which is the study of disease, offers more career paths than any other medical specialty. **13**

v

PART TWO

The Job Search Process

PART THREE

Job Opportunities Databank

PART FOUR

Career Resources

PART FIVE

Master Index

Acknowledgments

The editor would like to thank all the "pro's" who took the time out of their busy schedules to share their first-hand knowledge and enthusiasm with the next generation of job-seekers. A special thanks to Kathleen M. Daniels, Assistant Director of the Career Planning and Placement office at the University of Detroit Mercy, who provided much needed help with the job search section.

Thanks are also owed to the human resources personnel at the companies listed in this volume and to the public relations staffs of the associations who provided excellent suggestions for new essays. Lisa Levin of the American Medical Association deserves special mention.

Introduction

A 1992 *New York Times* article reported that college graduates were facing the toughest job market the United States has seen in twenty years. An ongoing series by the *Detroit Free Press* tracked the progress of six University of Michigan graduates; despite beginning their job search months before graduation day, only one of the six had landed that elusive first job one month after graduation.

Clearly, job-hunting in the 1990s is a challenging and demanding proposition, one that benefits from assistance at each step. *Healthcare Career Directory—Nurses and Physicians,* formerly published by the Career Press, was developed to provide job-seekers with all the help they need to break into the rewarding world of medicine as a nurse or physician. It provides a comprehensive, one-stop resource for carrying out a successful job search, including:

- Essays by professionals that provide practical advice not found in any other career resource
- Job search guidance designed to help you get in the door in a hospital or other professional setting
- Job and internship listings from leading hospitals, medical corporations, and pharmaceutical firms in the United States
- Information on additional career resources to further the job hunt
- A Master Index to facilitate easy access to the *Directory*

The *Directory* is organized into four parts that correspond to the steps of a typical job search—identifying your area of interest, refining your presentation, targeting employers, and researching your prospects.

Sidebars located throughout the *Directory* are intended to amplify the text or provide a counterpoint to information presented on the page. They'll help you build a context for your career and job-search efforts by bringing you discussions of trends in the book publishing industry and the business world, labor statistics, job-hunting techniques, and predictions about our future worklife. These and other tips and tidbits were gleaned from a wide range of sources—sources you can continue to draw upon for a broader understanding of your chosen field and of the job-search process.

Advice from the Pro's: An Invaluable Tool

Instead of offering "one-size-fits-all" advice or government statistics on what the working world is like, the *Healthcare Career Directory* goes into the field for first-hand reports from experienced professionals working in all segments of nursing and medicine. This

"Advice from the Pro's" is offered by people who know what it's like to land that first job and turn it into a rich and rewarding career. Learn about:

- the changing role of the pediatrician from Frederick Kassab, M.D.
- the challenges of neurology from Dr. Walter J. Koroshetz, Department of Neurology, Massachusetts General Hospital, Boston, MA
- what it takes to make it as a surgeon from Robert E. Hermann, M.D., Senior Surgeon, Past Chairman, Department of General Surgery, Cleveland Clinic Foundation
- and eight other areas of specialization, including:

Pathology	Nurse practioner
Psychiatry	Oncology nursing
Specialty nursing	Critical care nursing
Long-term nursing	Traveling nursing

The essays cover the most important things a job applicant needs to know, including:

- What academic training and professional development paths offer the best preparation
- Specific skills that are needed
- What employers look for in an applicant
- Typical career paths
- Salary information

The Job Search Process: Making Sense of It All

What is the first thing a new job-hunter should do?

What different types of resumes exist and what should they look like?

What questions are off-limits in an interview?

These important questions are among the dozens that go through every person's mind when he or she begins to look for a job. Part Two of the *Healthcare Career Directory*, **The Job Search Process**, answers these questions and more. It is divided into five chapters that cover all the basics of how to aggressively pursue a job:

- **Getting Started: Self-Evaluation and Career Objectives.** How to evaluate personal strengths and weaknesses and set goals.
- **Targeting Prospective Employers and Networking for Success.** How to identify the organizations you would like to work for and how to build a network of contacts.
- **Preparing Your Resume.** What to include, what not to include, and what style to use. Includes samples of the three basic resume types and worksheets to help you organize your information.
- **Writing Better Letters.** What letters should be written throughout the search process and how to make them more effective. Includes samples.
- **Questions for You, Questions for Them.** How to handle an interview and get the job.

Job Opportunities Databank: Finding the Job You Want

Once you're ready to start sending out those first resumes, how do you know where to start? **The Job Opportunities Databank**, Part Three of the *Directory*, includes listings for more than 200 hospitals, health services companies, and pharmaceutical firms in the United States that offer entry-level jobs. These listings provide detailed contact information and data on the organizational profile, hiring practices, benefits, and application procedures—everything you need to know to approach potential employers. And since undergraduate internships play an increasingly important role in the career research and employment process, information on the internship opportunities offered by the companies listed is also included.

For further information on the arrangement and content of the Job Opportunities Databank, consult "How to Use the Job Opportunities Databank" immediately following this introduction.

Career Resources: A Guide to Organizations and Publications in the Field

Need to do more research on the specialty you've chosen or the hospitals you'll be interviewing with? Part Four of the *Directory*, **Career Resources**, includes information on the following:

- Sources of help-wanted ads
- Professional associations
- Employment agencies and search firms
- Career guides
- Professional and trade periodicals
- Basic reference guides

Listings now contain contact information and descriptions of each publication's content and each organization's membership, purposes, and activities, helping you to pinpoint the resources you need for your own specific job search.

For additional information on the arrangement and content of Career Resources, consult "How to Locate Career Resources" following this introduction.

New Master Index Speeds Access to Resources

A Master Index leads you to the information contained in all four sections of the *Directory* by citing all subjects, organizations, publications, and services listed throughout in a single alphabetic sequence. The index also includes inversions on significant keywords appearing in cited organization, publication, and service names. For example, the "American Medical Association" would also be listed in the index under "Medical Association; American." Citations in the index refer to page numbers.

New Information Keeps Pace with the Changing Job Market

This new edition of *Healthcare Career Directory* has been completely revised and updated. New essays in the Advice from the Pro's section were contributed by leading professionals in the healthcare industry on subjects of particular interest to today's job seekers. The best essays from the previous edition were reviewed and completely updated as needed by the original authors (a small number of essays from the earlier edition have been reassigned to Career Advisor volumes devoted to allied health and medical technology careers, making roon for additional specialty coverage here). All employers listed in the Job

Opportunities Databank were contacted by telephone or facsimile to obtain current information, and Career Resources listings were greatly expanded through the addition of selected material from other databases compiled by Gale Research Inc.

Special Thanks

Thanks to the many people at Visible Ink Press and Gale who helped to shape this book: Katherine Gruber and Linda Hubbard, whose guidance and skill made my job easy; Karen Hill, who kept the big picture in sight; Jennifer Mast and her staff; Diane Dupuis for her technical expertise; and the staff of the Sourcebooks team for their superior skill and assistance.

Comments and Suggestions Welcome

The staff of the *Healthcare Career Directory—Nurses and Physicians* appreciates learning of any corrections or additions that will make this book as complete and useful as possible. Comments or suggestions for future essay topics or other improvements are also welcome, as are suggestions for careers that could be covered in new volumes of the Career Advisor Series. Please contact:

Career Advisor Series
Visible Ink Press
835 Penobscot Bldg.
Detroit, MI 48226-4094
Phone: 800-347-4253
Fax: (313)961-6815

Bradley J. Morgan

How to Use the Job Opportunities Databank

The **Job Opportunities Databank** comprises two sections:

Entry-Level Job and Internship Listings
Additional Companies

Entry-Level Job and Internship Listings

Provides listings for more than the 200 hospitals, health services companies, and pharmaceutical firms in the United States. Entries in the **Job Opportunities Databank** are arranged alphabetically by company name. When available, entries include:

- **Company name.**
- **Address and telephone number.** A mailing address and telephone number are provided in every entry.
- **Fax and toll-free telephone number.** These are provided when known.
- **Business description.** Outlines the organization's activities.
- **Corporate officers.** Lists the names of executive officers, with titles.
- **Number of employees.** Includes the most recently provided figure for total number of employees. Other employee-specific information may be provided as well.
- **Average entry-level hiring.** Includes the number of entry-level employees the organization typically hires in an average year. Many organizations have listed "Unknown" or "0" for their average number of entry-level jobs. Because of current economic conditions, many could not estimate their projected entry-level hires for the coming years. However, because these organizations have offered entry-level positions in the past and because their needs may change, we have continued to list them in this edition.
- **Opportunities.** Describes the entry-level positions that the organization typically offers, as well as the education and other requirements needed for those positions.
- **Benefits.** Lists the insurance, time off, retirement and financial plans, activities, and programs provided to employees, if known.
- **Human resources contacts.** Lists the names of personnel-related staff, with titles.

- **Application procedure.** Describes specific application instructions, when provided by the organization.

Many entries also include information on available undergraduate internship programs. Internship information provided includes:

- **Contact name.** Lists the names of officers or personnel-related contacts who are responsible for the internship program.
- **Type.** Indicates the type of internship, including time period and whether it is paid, unpaid, or for college credit. Also indicates if an organization does not offer internships.
- **Number available.** Number of internships typically offered.
- **Number of applications received.** Total number of applications received in a typical year.
- **Application procedures and deadline.** Describes specific application instructions and the deadline for submitting applications.
- **Decision date.** Final date when internship placement decisions are made.
- **Duties.** Lists the typical duties that an undergraduate intern can expect to perform.
- **Qualifications.** Lists the criteria a prospective applicant must meet to be considered for an undergraduate internship.

Additional Companies

Covers those companies and hospitals that elected to provide only their name, address, and telephone number for inclusion in the *Directory*. Entries are arranged alphabetically by organization name.

How to Locate
Career Resources

The **Career Resources** chapter contains six categories of information sources, each of which is arranged alphabetically by resource or organization name. The categories include:

▼ **Sources of Help-Wanted Ads**

- **Covers:** Professional journals, industry periodicals, association newsletters, placement bulletins, and online services that include employment ads or business opportunities. Includes sources that focus specifically on healthcare, as well as general periodical sources such as the *National Business Employment Weekly.*
- **Entries include:** The resource's title; name, address, and telephone number of its publisher; frequency; subscription rate; description of contents; toll-free and additional telephone numbers; and facsimile numbers.
- **Sources:** *Job Hunter's Sourcebook* (published by Gale Research Inc.) and original research.

▼ **Professional Associations**

- **Covers:** Trade and professional associations that offer career-related information and services.
- **Entries include:** Association name, address, and telephone number; membership; purpose and objectives; publications; toll-free or additional telephone numbers; and facsimile numbers. In some cases, the publications mentioned in these entries are described in greater detail as separate entries cited in the Sources of Help-Wanted Ads, Career Guides, Professional and Trade Periodicals, and Basic Reference Guides categories.
- **Sources:** *Encyclopedia of Associations* (published by Gale Research Inc.) and original research.

▼ **Employment Agencies and Search Firms**

- **Covers:** Firms used by companies to recruit candidates for positions and, at times, by individuals to pursue openings. Employment agencies are generally geared towards filling openings at entry- to mid-level in the local job market, while executive search firms are paid by the hiring organization to recruit professional and managerial candidates, usually for higher-level openings. Also covers temporary employment agencies because they can be a method of identifying and obtaining regular employment.

Includes sources that focus specifically on healthcare, as well as some larger general firms.

- **Entries include:** The firm's name, address, and telephone number; whether it's an employment agency, executive search firm, or temporary agency; descriptive information, as appropriate; toll-free and additional telephone numbers; and facsimile number.
- **Sources:** *Job Hunter's Sourcebook.*

▼ Career Guides

- **Covers:** Books, kits, pamphlets, brochures, videocassettes, films, online services, and other materials that describe the job-hunting process in general or that provide guidance and insight into the job-hunting process in healthcare.
- **Entries include:** The resource's title; name, address, and telephone number of its publisher or distributor; name of the editor or author; publication date or frequency; description of contents; arrangement; indexes; toll-free or additional telephone numbers; and facsimile numbers.
- **Sources:** *Professional Careers Sourcebook* and *Vocational Careers Sourcebook* (published by Gale Research Inc.) and original research.

▼ Professional and Trade Periodicals

- **Covers:** Newsletters, magazines, newspapers, trade journals, and other serials that offer information to healthcare professionals.
- **Entries include:** The resource's title; the name, address, and telephone number of the publisher; the editor's name; frequency; description of contents; toll-free and additional telephone numbers; and facsimile numbers. Publication titles appear in italics.
- **Sources:** *Professional Careers Sourcebook, Vocational Careers Sourcebook,* and original research.

▼ Basic Reference Guides and Handbooks

- **Covers:** Manuals, directories, dictionaries, encyclopedias, films and videocassettes, and other published reference material used by healthcare professionals.
- **Entries include:** The resource's title; name, address, and telephone number of the publisher or distributor; the editor's or author's name; publication date or frequency; description of contents; toll-free and additional telephone numbers; and facsimile numbers. Publication titles are rendered in italics.
- **Sources:** *Professional Careers Sourcebook, Vocational Careers Sourcebook,* and original research.

Advice from the Pro's

CHAPTER ONE

Why Medicine?

**James S. Todd, Executive Vice President,
American Medical Association**

If you are considering a career in medicine, chances are someone has tried to dissuade you. Perhaps you have heard horror stories about long hours, malpractice suits, medical school debt, and reimbursement hassles. If you read the newspaper, you have most likely seen foreboding stories about the future of the medical profession and the advent of health care reform that will inevitably decrease doctors' salaries. Given these headaches, it is not unreasonable to ask, why should anyone go into medicine?

While I can't deny that medicine, like any other career, has its share of pressure, I can think of no other profession that provides a higher degree of personal satisfaction and societal respect. It is an exciting, rewarding career that combines intellectual challenge and the ability to make a difference in the quality of life.

In choosing medicine, you are not choosing a single career track, but rather opening yourself up to a myriad of options. Physicians are in demand almost everywhere. While many choose clinical practice, many others are at work in the research arena. They are developing new, medical technologies, such as diagnostic scanners and artificial organs, and seeking treatments for life threatening diseases, such as AIDS and cancer.

Some of the most outstanding physicians share their skills and wisdom through teaching, while other doctors work for health insurance corporations, pharmaceutical manufacturers, government service and corporate health and safety programs. Plus, there are a variety or medical specialties and practice options to match your interests and preferred style of work.

There has never been a more exciting time to become a physician. Medicine is in the midst of a scientific and technological revolution, which is helping doctors to unlock more of the secrets of how the body functions and adding to their ability to prevent, diagnose, and treat disease.

The boom in new technology and biomedicine is nothing short or spectacular.

Physicians have taken great strides in molecular biology, genetics, and neuroscience. Advances are being made in implants, miniaturization, artificial organs, and new biomaterials, and we have only begun to see the potential impact imaging and robotics will have on invasive procedures. Already, these discoveries have contributed to significant breakthroughs in our ability to treat cancer and heart disease, and we are making progress in our search for a cure or vaccine for AIDS.

Changes and Challenges for the Future

As we prepare to enter a new decade, you may wonder what the medical profession will be like in the 21st century. Fundamentally, much of medicine will remain the same. Physicians will still be involved in providing medical care to patients. They will still be educators and scientists and patient advocates. But, at the same time, the medical profession is already beginning to undergo profound changes, some of which present new challenges and opportunities for physicians.

One very positive change is the growing number of women entering the field. In 1965, only 10 percent of the entrants to medical school were women. In 1991, that figure increased to almost 40 percent. These women are not only making major contributions to their field, but are also helping to change the lifestyle of medicine for both themselves and their male peers.

While medicine will remain a demanding profession requiring longer hours than most, the effort to balance practice and family has led to a number of career options that provide greater flexibility in work hours. For example, many doctors have joined group practices or organizations, such as HMOs, that provide backup coverage and assure time off for rest, family responsibilities, leisure pursuits, and professional renewal. In fact, many new practice organizations allow physicians to develop their own work schedules to fit their specific needs.

Health care reform is another event that will inevitably spur changes in the medical profession. Throughout the nation, there is broad consensus that the need to widen access to services and contain the spiraling cost of health care delivery is urgent. Yet, we continue to struggle with the best way to accomplish these goals. Numerous proposals have emerged from the political arena, the medical profession, and the insurance industry, but we have yet to agree on a solution.

Regardless of the health system reform plan we choose, however, it is clear that access to health care will mean a greater emphasis on primary care and preventative medicine. Health care reform is also likely to spur fundamental changes in practice patterns. Some recent trends that will likely continue include: the rise in managed care organizations such as PPOs and HMOs; shorter hospital stays, and an increase in outpatient procedures.

Finally, the rapid aging of the population will alter the practice of medicine dramatically. Today, the "over-85" group is the fastest growing segment of the population. By the year 2000, it is estimated that there will be 35 million Americans over the age of 100. Fueled by the current explosion of knowledge and technology, it

Top Ten Best Jobs

Based on earnings, security, prestige, satisfaction, outlook, and 14-year growth
1. Biologist
2. Geologist
3. **Physician**
4. College math professor
5. High school principal
6. Sociologist
7. Pharmacist
8. Urban planner
9. Civil engineer
10. Veterinarian
Source: *Money*

will not be uncommon in the next century to have five family generations, all alive and well. This aging population will demand that doctors, regardless of specialty, become applied geriatricians.

Training for the 21st Century

Most prospective medical students have many questions about medical school and how it will help them prepare for the challenges they will face as practicing physicians. As the training ground for our future physicians, medical schools are responding to the demands posed by the changing profession. Students are learning new techniques that were unheard of just a few years ago.

In addition to teaching the latest technological methods, however, medical schools are taking strides to assure that newly trained physicians remain in touch with the human aspects of medicine. Courses in ethics and the doctor/patient relationship are increasingly included in medical school curricula. As outpatient procedures become more and more common, medical schools have attempted to provide more educational experience in ambulatory care settings.

Of course, the cost of medical school and the prospect of incurred debt is a concern to almost all prospective students. There is no question that medical school is expensive and that most medical students borrow at least a portion of the money they need to finance their education. However, there are numerous options for loans and scholarships that may minimize your potential debt. Keep in mind, too, that a medical education is an investment that keeps returning dividends throughout your life.

Medicine isn't for everyone. It demands hard work, long hours, intelligence, discipline, maturity, and unflagging commitment. But, if you are intrigued by new challenges, new technologies, and never-ending opportunities to care for people and serve society, nothing else comes close.

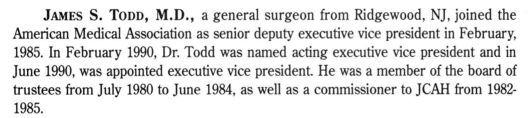

JAMES S. TODD, M.D., a general surgeon from Ridgewood, NJ, joined the American Medical Association as senior deputy executive vice president in February, 1985. In February 1990, Dr. Todd was named acting executive vice president and in June 1990, was appointed executive vice president. He was a member of the board of trustees from July 1980 to June 1984, as well as a commissioner to JCAH from 1982-1985.

Born in 1931, Dr. Todd graduated cum laude from both Harvard College and Harvard Medical School. He interned and served his residency in surgery at Columbia Presbyterian Medical Center, becoming chief resident in 1963. He is a diplomate of the American Board of Surgery and a fellow of the American College of Surgeons. From 1977 through 1985, he was chairman of the Board of the New Jersey State Medical Underwriters, Inc., and is a past president of the Physician Insurers Association of America.

Dr. Todd has been a director of the Institute of Society, Ethics, and the Life

Sciences (Hastings Center) and is a member of the Overseers Committee to Visit the Harvard Medical School. His service to the community includes: Committee to Establish Guidelines for the Care of Comatose Patients, State of New Jersey, 1977; recipient of the Edward J. Ill Distinguished Physician Award of the New Jersey Academy of Medicine in 1980 and the Distinguished Service Award of the New Jersey Hospital Association.

He has served as trustee and chairman of the Board of Trustees of the Medical Society of New Jersey, chairman of the New Jersey Delegation to the AMA House of Delegates, and chairman of the Ad Hoc Committee to Review the AMA's Principles of Medical Ethics.

Dr. Todd has published numerous articles dealing with health care and professional liability in various journals.

CHAPTER TWO

Pediatricians: More than Just "Baby Doctors"

Fred D. Kassab, M.D.

Most pediatricians that I have met knew that they wanted to be pediatricians early in their medical training. I have come to understand that caring for children from infancy through young adulthood requires more than just a fondness for children. It also provides experience and satisfaction unattainable in any other field of medicine.

Entering the Field of Pediatrics

Like all other fields of medicine, pediatrics requires a four-year postgraduate medical degree (either an M.D. or a D.O.). American medical schools all have specific undergraduate entrance requirements in subjects such as general sciences, mathematics, and humanities, which are available through college or university counseling departments. However, it is certainly possible, and even helpful, in gaining medical school admission to major in a non-science field in college, so long as the entrance requirements are met. Several factors are weighed when considering a candidate's application to medical school, including the undergraduate grade point average and the results of standardized medical school entrance exams. Without a doubt, any community service, volunteer, or research experience is beneficial.

Medical school is comprised of two years of basic medical sciences, followed by two years of clinical training in the healthcare setting. Much of the clinical training involves the daily care of hospitalized patients, often for 24 hours or more at a stretch. During the second two years, medical students begin to explore the diverse fields of medicine and determine which directions they will pursue. It is at this point that one decides to become a pediatrician, rather than, say, a surgeon, radiologist, gynecologist, or ophthalmologist. Just prior to graduation, medical students are informed of the residency program that they will enter, based on an intensive

5

application and interview process, which has taken place over the preceding six months.

Aside from a few months of pediatric training during medical school, the residency in pediatrics represents the bulk of a pediatrician's experience and education in the care of ill children.

The Pediatric Residency

Depending on the medical specialty, a residency lasts between three and five years and is based at a specific hospital or medical center. The pediatric residency is three years of long hours and hard work, and usually requires working 24- to 36-hour shifts every three to four nights for the majority of the residency. This is the first time that one is paid for being a pediatrician. But like all specialties, the pay is low when the actual number of hours worked—often reaching 80 to 100 hours per week—is considered. Most residents are paid between $20,000 and $30,000 their first year, depending on the particular residency program, and receive yearly incremental pay raises. As a resident graduates to her or his second or third year, (s)he increasingly assumes the role of teacher or supervisor of junior pediatric residents and medical students.

During the pediatric residency, one learns to care for children of all ages with every type of illness of all severities. A pediatric resident becomes skilled at handling such diverse situations as resuscitating and treating premature infants no bigger than one's hand, or caring for a 17-year-old who has fallen unconscious into a swimming pool after drinking too much alcohol. Children born with heart, kidney, or other organ defects are frequently cared for by pediatric residents, as are children with serious infections, cancer, or paralysis from neck injuries. On the lighter side, a resident establishes a continuity clinic, where he or she learns to care for healthy children in an outpatient setting, doing routine physicals, giving immunizations, and teaching healthcare maintenance.

Best Hospitals for Pediatrics

Ranked by physicians in 16 specialties
1. Children's Hospital of Boston
2. Children's Hospital of Philadelphia
3. Johns Hopkins Hospital
4. Childrens Hospital of Los Angeles
5. Rainbow Babies and Childrens Hospitals (University Hospitals of Cleveland)

Source: *U.S. News and World Report*

From Residency Onward

For me and others entering the field of general pediatrics, the formal pediatric training ended with our residency. However, many pediatricians continue their training in pediatric *sub*-specialties for two to three years following residency, which is termed a **fellowship.** Pediatric fellowships involve patient care and research in specific disorders affecting children. These include neonatology (the care of newborns, including premature infants), pediatric cardiology (the heart and circulatory system), pediatric neurology (the brain and nervous system), pediatric hematology (the blood), pediatric oncology (cancer and tumors), pediatric gastroenterology (the digestive system), and pediatric nephrology (the kidneys), to name a few.

Some **pediatric subspecialists** have private subspecialty practices in community settings, but many are employed at hospitals and medical centers which allow them to pursue research interests, as well as participating in patient care. Many pediatric subspecialists see patients by referral only and may not have a general pediatrics practice of their own. Someone choosing to be a pediatric subspecialist might have a greater interest in being on the "cutting edge" of medical research—developing new or improved treatments or expanding the understanding of health conditions—rather than day-to-day health care of children.

As a **general pediatrician,** I am considered a *primary care provider.* This means that I provide the majority of well and illness care to a specific group of children. I establish care with newborns in the hospital nursery, performing their first of many physical exams and teaching the new parents about caring for a brand new infant at home. I *round* on these babies first thing in the morning before seeing patients in the office. I then continue outpatient care of these children throughout childhood in my office.

A typical day in the office of a general pediatrician consists of seeing healthy children of all ages for routine physicals, intermixed with urgent visits of sick or injured children and follow-up visits of children with ongoing or chronic conditions. Behavioral and developmental problems such as bedwetting, temper tantrums, or attention deficit disorder (hyperactivity) are also commonly part of a pediatrician's daily schedule. Administering medications, dressing wounds, suturing lacerations, and splinting or casting fractured bones are some of the daily procedures that general pediatricians may perform. Those children who are seriously ill must be admitted to the hospital, where a pediatrician will round on them daily and supervise their inpatient care until they are discharged home.

For children with special health care needs, or those with complicated or uncommon health problems, the general pediatrician will coordinate assessment and therapy by one or more pediatric subspecialists. This system allows the general pediatrician to care for and supervise the development of children from birth through adolescence, while also providing means to participate in the care of her or his patients' illnesses of any severity, ensuring continuity of care.

Career Opportunities

Compared to other healthcare specialties, there is a relative abundance of primary care (i.e., pediatric or family practice) positions nationwide, with particular needs in rural and inner-city areas. This is in part due to the lower income of primary care providers compared to other specialties. There is a wide range of incomes by pediatricians, in general between $60,000 and $150,000 per year. Income depends partially on the type of practice one chooses and seniority in the field. For example, one might make less money employed at a Health Maintenance Organization (HMO), where one is paid a salary, and the office, equipment, etc., are owned and operated by a board of directors. This frees the pediatrician from many administrative responsibilities and spreads after-hours patient care, such as emergency room visits and phone calls from parents, over a large group of pediatricians. This is in contrast to a solo private practice, where the pediatrician may own and operate a much smaller scale office, increasing his or her income by increasing productivity. In this scenario, after hours responsibilities are assumed by the solo practitioner, or may be divided among several other private pediatricians in a specific geographical area. Group pediatric practices fall somewhere between the HMO and solo private practice.

Pediatrics for the Future

A pediatrician has always been more than just a "baby doctor." However, health problems which didn't exist a generation ago are now affecting today's children, such as the survival of increasingly small premature infants with their associated physical and emotional problems, pediatric AIDS, drug-addicted babies, and rampant adolescent sexual activity with its associated teenage pregnancy and/or sexually transmitted diseases. The role of the pediatrician is ever-expanding and is crucial to children's healthy development into adulthood, now more than ever. As this trend continues, the need for more skilled general and subspecialty pediatricians will undoubtedly increase. Without caring and dedicated pediatricians, the health of the future is at risk.

▼

DR. FRED D. KASSAB received his bachelor of arts degree at Kalamazoo College, MI, where he double-majored in French and health sciences. Dr. Kassab received his M.D. at Wayne State University in Detroit, MI, and went on to do his pediatric residency at the University of Michigan in Ann Arbor, MI. Born in Detroit, MI, he currently lives in Seattle, WA, working as a general pediatrician in an HMO and loves it!

CHAPTER THREE

Diseases of the Brain, Nerve, and Muscle: The Challenge of Neurology

Dr. Walter J. Koroshetz, Department of Neurology, Massachusetts General Hospital, Boston, MA

Neurology is an intellectual internal medicine specialty that deals with disorders of the human brain, spinal cord, peripheral nerves, and muscles. It is one of the most exciting and fast-paced of the medical specialties. In the United States, 15 to 20 percent of patients seek medical care due to a neurologic problem, and new research continuously improves a doctor's ability to treat these problems.

Practicing neurologists are responsible for diagnosis, treatment, and rehabilitation, while **academic neurologists** also train new neurologists. Both use modern scientific methods to better understand and treat human neurologic illness. Some neurologists specialize in the neurologic disorders of children.

If you are fascinated with the biological basis of human behavior, you would enjoy working within the field of neurology. Many of those who go on to study neurology are first attracted through the study of psychology, biology, chemistry, and biophysics, though the field includes students from the entire range of scholastic endeavors.

The Role of a Neurologist

The neurologist cares for persons with a variety of disorders. Patients come to neurologists with a myriad of complaints; some have pain, others weakness of an arm or a leg, some with loss of memory. The neurologist functions as a medical Sherlock Holmes, trying to deduce from the story of the patient's illness and abnormalities uncovered during examination what is wrong with the brain, nerves, or muscles. This diagnostic process has been aided to some extent by the recent ability to produce great images of the brain and spinal cord. Neurology, however, remains an art. It requires precision in diagnosis and care in treatment. No test is superior to the skilled opinion of the experienced neurologist. A good neurologist has special understanding of how the brain and nerves work. A great neurologist probably develops the most advanced kind of understanding of human behavior. However, neurology, is only secondarily an intellectual pursuit. The neurologist's first and primary duty is to advocate for the patients, both for their health and also for their social rights. Because patients with damage to the brain, nerve, and muscle are so disabled by their problems, it takes an especially caring person to stick with the neurologic patient through their tough times. Dr. Anne Young, one of the world's finest neurologist, works with hundreds of poor Venezuelan families afflicted by a tragic hereditary brain degeneration, Huntington's disease. Dr. Douglas Buchanan, a great neurologist, once said to me, "If you can see yourself helping a patient who becomes slowly, but completely, paralyzed over years, then you can be sure that you can be a neurologist." Because neurology patients often have brain injury, they require greater guidance from their physicians as well as from other health care professionals. Neurology is a challenge!

The Best Hospitals for Neurology

Ranked by physicians in 16 specialties
1. Mayo Clinic
2. Massachusetts General Hospital
3. Johns Hopkins Hospital
4. Cleveland Clinic
5. Columbia-Presbyterian Medical Center
6. University of California, San Francisco
7. UCLA Medical Center
Source: *U.S. News and World Report*

The Education of a Neurologist

A neurologist's work requires tremendous skill and training. A neurologist in the United States must first graduate from an accredited medical school with either an MD or DO degree. Graduates of non-United States or non-Canadian medical schools must pass the examinations administered by the Educational Commission for Foreign Medical Graduates (ECFMG).

Medical students who pursue a career in neurology must enroll in a three-year accredited neurology residency program, including supervised neurology experience in both hospital and clinical care settings. Educational conferences and research training are also part of a neurology residency.

If you decide to specialize in adult neurology, you will be required to complete one year of internship with a minimum of eight months in internal medicine. If your interests lie more in child neurology, specializing in this category requires two years in a general pediatric residency, or one year each in internal medicine and pediatrics, or one year in research and one year in pediatrics. Residents in child urology then spend at least one year in adult and two years in a pediatric neurology service.

Career Paths

Upon completing your education and residency training, you may wish to further your education by applying for a fellowship, or you can accept a position in patient care or choose to teach and do research in an academic position.

If you opt for clinical practice, you will have daily contact with those patients with neurological disorders. One of the benefits of such a decision is your ability to help patients directly.

Many neurologists have major subspecialty expertise and care for patients with particular subclasses of disease, such as muscular weakness, epilepsy, brain tumors, behavioral disorders, memory disorders, movement disorders, stroke and neuro-visual disorders, or they may specialize in neuro-rehabilitation or neurogenetics.

Recent neurologic advances now allow the accurate diagnosis and treatment of many severely disabling disorders considered unapproachable 20 years ago. Researchers have unlocked more mysteries of the brain in the past five to ten years than in the past 300 years. Breakthroughs in understanding and treatment of other nervous system illnesses are imminent, making neurology one of the most dynamic fields in medicine. Indeed, Congress and the President declared the 1990s the "Decade of the Brain" to encourage even more progress in brain science and the treatment of brain diseases.

Many neurologists choose to stay in the academic environment, teaching other doctors about neurology and its many subspecialties and conducting research. Research neurologists spend much of their time advancing the knowledge of neurology by actively seeking therapies, cures, and answers that continue to challenge neurologists about the diseases they must deal with.

Career Outlook

The demand for neurologists should continue to be good and, perhaps, even increase as the importance of the brain in connection with the rest of the human body becomes even more significant and more understood. Practicing neurologists can often be expected to conduct such diagnostic tests as electrical studies of muscle and nerve function, brain wave analysis, and brain imaging. Those neurologists who join a clinical practice can often expect to be offered a partnership based upon productivity.

In fact, practicing neurologists continue to demand and receive some of the highest salary and compensation packages among the cognitive medical specialties.

Salaries

Practicing neurologists beginning their careers can often expect salaries topping $100,000, but often range from $70,000 to $120,000, with the deciding factors being specialization and location. The harder it is to get a neurologist to settle in a particular area, the more clinics and research organizations are willing to pay to hire a neurologist. Academic neurologists are paid considerably less, but usually care for fewer patients than private practitioners.

The Rewards of Practicing Neurology

The practice of neurology is especially exhilarating. It affords the neurologist unique insights into the function of the human nervous system, from movement and sensation to thought and creativity. Neurologists are major contributors to many of the most recent advances in the neurosciences and continuously strive to convert new basic science knowledge into better therapies for patients with diseases of the nervous system.

DR. WALTER J. KOROSHETZ was born in Brooklyn, NY, and attended Xaverian High School and Georgetown University. He majored in biology and minored in physics and mathematics. He then attended the University of Chicago Medical School. After medical school, he did one year of internship and residency at the University of Chicago Hospital and one year of medical residency at the Massachusetts General Hospital. He then trained in neurology at the Massachusetts General Hospital. His time is now spent caring for patients with stroke and Huntington's disease, teaching young doctors and medical students, and investigating new treatments to halt cell death in the nervous system. He is an assistant neurologist at the Massachusetts General Hospital, an assistant professor at Harvard Medical School, and a member of the American Academy of Neurology.

CHAPTER FOUR

Pathology as a Career in Medicine

Intersociety Committee on Pathology Information

Pathology is a medical specialty which provides the scientific foundation for medical practice. The pathologist works with all other medical specialties, using the tools of laboratory medicine to provide information essential to problem solving in clinical practice.

All pathologists share a fascination with the process of disease, its scientific meaning, its logic, its mystery, its intellectual challenge. Pathologists practicing in hospital laboratories have access to the knowledge gained from the examination and treatment of large numbers of patients. As consultant physicians, they apply this knowledge to assist in diagnostic and therapeutic problem solving for individual patients. As medical scientists, they make contributions that advance the understanding of disease. As teachers, they impart this understanding to their medical colleagues, to house staff and to students.

The study and practice of pathology are limited only by the curiosity and imagination of the pathologist. No other medical specialty requires such broad knowledge of both the basic sciences and clinical medicine or offers such a rich variety of opportunities for career development and practice. The pathologist probes deeply to identify the visible and quantifiable changes that characterize different diseases in the cells, fluids and life processes of the body. Such findings are fundamental to medical diagnosis, patient management and research.

Many pathologists are generalists concerned with all facets of disease that can be examined in the laboratory. Others specialize. Anatomic pathologists concentrate on abnormal morphology; clinical pathologists obtain and interpret laboratory data as needed for diagnosis and patient care.

There are pathology specialties concerned with every category of disease. Among them are: blood banking/transfusion medicine, cardiovascular pathology, comparative pathology, cytopathology, dermatopathology, environmental pathology, forensic pathology, gastrointestinal pathology, geographic pathology, gynecologic/

obstetrical pathology, hematopathology, immunopathology, neuropathology, ophthalmic pathology, orthopedic pathology, pediatric pathology, pulmonary pathology and renal pathology.

New instruments that allow the viewing and sampling of formerly inaccessible areas of the body provide these subspecialists with material for study and interaction with the clinical subspecialists. In the community hospital setting, pathologists tend to be generalists, in the university environment and large metropolitan medical centers, subspecialists.

The Pathologist in Patient Care

Pathologists participate in day-to-day care of hospital patients by providing and interpreting laboratory information to help solve diagnostic problems and to monitor the effects of therapy. The delicate management of patients with acute leukemia, AIDS, cancer and other complex disorders frequently depends in part on the pathologist's medical knowledge and scientific skill. With new and highly complex tests multiplying in recent years, many clinicians rely on the pathologist for guidance and direction in use of the clinical laboratory. This is especially true in community hospital practice.

Pathology Has It All

Surveys show that medical students who choose pathology as a career are often drawn by the opportunities it offers to combine patient care, teaching and research. Many have been inspired by the example and encouragement of an individual teacher of pathology. Pathology has a special appeal to those who enjoy solving disease-related problems, using technology based in such fundamental biologic sciences as biophysics, molecular biology and molecular genetics.

The surgical pathologist is responsible for rendering the diagnosis on all tissues removed from the patient. The pathologist is often called as a consultant during the operative procedure to interpret the gross findings and make a frozen section diagnosis. Each diagnosis is made in collaboration with the patient's physician after full consideration of the clinical history and the results of other laboratory tests. This places pathologists in a central position in patient care, since their diagnoses form the underpinning for future therapy.

Cytopathology, which makes possible disease detection by the study of individual cells, is assuming increasing importance in modern patient care. Originally introduced in the detection of female genital cancer—the "Pap smear"—cytopathology now concerns itself with all organ systems.

Together with clinicians and radiologists, pathologists now obtain cells from such deep-seated diseases as tumors in the lung or breast by fine-needle aspiration. Such diagnosis can often spare the patient major surgery. In addition, single cells can be analyzed chemically and functionally by the new techniques of flow cytometry, in which chemical and immunologic reagents can be combined with physical techniques to measure a variety of cell populations.

The autopsy provides unique insights into the natural history of disease and the influence of therapy on disease processes. After an autopsy, the pathologist assumes the role of educator by sharing the findings with the patient's physician. Together, they search for the lessons in each case that will benefit future patients.

Autopsy findings are often discussed with various specialists in hospital mortality conferences, and sometimes with families directly. Information gained at autopsies is frequently used as the basis for scientific presentations involving both pathologist and clinician. Autopsy data are used extensively as a quality-control measure; current studies show a consistent 30 percent discrepancy rate between clinical diagnoses and actual findings at autopsy.

The autopsy's value is dramatized when the pathologist is called to determine the exact cause of death in legal cases and to present the findings as an officer of the court. Pathologists who are specially trained and certified in forensic pathology serve as full-time medical examiners for states or large cities. Their postmortem studies of violent and unexplained deaths are valuable sources of information about public health and safety.

The clinical pathologist is responsible for the clinical laboratories which cover hematology, clinical chemistry (including toxicology), microbiology (including immunology) and the blood bank. These activities involve the pathologist in direct patient care as a consultant.

In the clinical hematology laboratory, for example, pathologists review all abnormal blood smears. They may also obtain bone marrow specimens from patients. By examining the smear and histological sections of marrow, the pathologist can provide definitive diagnosis of diseases such as leukemia. The pathologist also serves as consultant on special hematologic problems, such as those related to bleeding disorders.

Functioning as an immunohematologist, the pathologist in most hospital settings is in charge of the blood bank, with responsibility for procurement and processing of all needed blood and blood products. This involves supervising the technical personnel in typing, cross-matching and antibody identification, in preparation of component therapy, and in therapeutic and donor pheresis, among other procedures. The pathologist is trained to monitor the use of blood within the hospital, to trace the causes of any transfusion reactions, and to serve as a consultant in planning appropriate therapy.

In clinical chemistry, the pathologist selects testing methods and equipment, and supervises the technical staff in performance of tests, use of instruments, and maintenance of a strict system of quality control. Toxicology is often part of the clinical chemistry service, involving the pathologist in therapeutic drug monitoring and detection of illicit drugs and poisons.

The ability to evaluate the immune system in the clinical laboratory has developed rapidly and heavily involves the pathologist. In addition to traditional testing for immune responses to various agents of disease, the pathologist now uses the tools of immunology to assess the ability of patients to protect themselves from various environmental factors, to tolerate a transplanted organ, and to respond to such internal threats as cancer. Immunologic testing now extends to all specialties and crosses all laboratory boundaries, furnishing exciting new opportunities for pathologists.

Quality control and quality assurance are major concerns in all clinical laboratories. The pathologist's responsibility for these activities extends to all aspects of an individual patient's laboratory needs. Quality assurance aims to provide prompt, efficient specimen collection and rapid availability of test results to the treating physician. Such duties require extensive use of computers, ranging from those that are part of laboratory instruments to those that deal with the data generated within the laboratory and, finally, to the computer facility central to the operation of the entire institution. Pathologists have played major roles in the development and utilization of such comprehensive information systems.

Abnormal results are clearly identified on the laboratory reports, and the pathologist communicates with the patient's physician when there are unusual or unexpected results that require follow-up. This is of special concern when life-threatening critical values are found, requiring immediate response.

Clinical pathologists are responsible for the production of large volumes of laboratory data. They are continually seeking ways to achieve greater accuracy, precision, specificity and sensitivity of laboratory tests. Also prominent among their concerns are:

- new test development,
- monitoring of therapeutic drug levels,
- rapid identification of toxic and infectious agents,
- reducing test costs to patients,
- increased physician awareness of the clinical relevance of test results,
- appropriate utilization of laboratory-generated information.

The Pathologist as Teacher

One of the greatest appeals of a pathology career is the opportunity to teach. No other medical specialty has as many different opportunities in education. Pathologists generally play a major role in the conferences held by the clinical services of all hospitals, large and small.

Pathologists teach medical students, residents in pathology and the clinical services, graduate students in basic science departments, and students in medical technology and nursing educational programs. Pathologists teach at the bedside, in the laboratory, behind the microscope, in the lecture hall, in the classroom, in workshops and seminars—wherever medical and allied health personnel are being trained. In medical school, pathology is a required basic science, and additional pathology courses can be taken as electives.

Pathologists are closely involved in the continuing medical education of practicing physicians. Their participation is sometimes as teacher, often as pupil. Skills are sharpened by attending workshops and seminars at regional and national meetings, in which diagnostic applications of new basic science findings and technology are presented.

In community hospitals where the pathology laboratory performs tests on nearly every patient, the pathologists are usually on the premises full time and have a broad view of all patient problems. Other specialists call on them not only for formal teaching conferences but also for consultation on individual patients and for guidance on the application and usefulness of newly available tests.

The Pathologist in Research

The pathologist-investigator seeks new understanding of the basic nature of disease as a first step toward devising better ways to identify, control and prevent it. To test new ideas about the origins and mechanisms of disease, the pathologist in research uses the sophisticated technologies of modern molecular biology, biochemistry, immunology, cell biology and pathology. These tools and methods include cell culture, biochemical analysis, electron microscopy, immunological and molecular genetic techniques, computer modeling and use of animal models.

In many cases, the normal must be unraveled in order to understand the abnormal. Biological mechanisms in particular must be understood at a molecular level, because it is a defect in the normal processes that may lead to disease.

Comparison of the composition of the cell surfaces of normal and neoplastic cells, for example, may help identify the components necessary to inhibit or prevent the spread of cancer cells. Discovery that the chemical mediator of insulin action is generated from the plasma membrane and controls phosphorylation may help explain insulin-resistant diabetes with post-receptor defects and lead ultimately to more effective therapy.

The range of problems under study by research pathologists is enormous. Environmentally induced disease is a timely area of interest, because pathologists have unparalleled facilities and training for tracing a newly recognized disease to its origin. Pathologists have figured prominently in recognition of pulmonary disease among miners, asbestos and textile workers; of liver cancer from prolonged contact with vinyl chloride and aflatoxin; of nerve disorders and sterility from exposure to certain pesticides and toxic wastes, and of diseases produced by drugs used to treat various illnesses.

> **N**obel Prize winners have included pathologists who used their understanding of pathologic processes to make significant contributions to medicine. Baruj Benacerraf was honored in 1980 with two other scientists for work on genetically determined structure on the cell surface that regulate immunological reactions. Other Nobel Laureate pathologists have included Karl Landsteiner, George Whipple, Howard Florey, Alexander Flemming and MacFarlane Burnet.

The diagnosis and treatment of infectious disease remain a major challenge for the contemporary physician. Despite sophisticated diagnostic techniques, these diseases often escape detection during life. The pathologist plays a key role in improving diagnosis through discovery of new infectious agents and better application of such modern methods of diagnosis as magnetic resonance imaging (MRI). Examples are the unraveling of the role of retroviruses in AIDS and the utility of MRI in the diagnosis of multiple sclerosis.

Graduate Medical Education

Medical school graduates currently need four to five years of residency training to prepare for a career in pathology. Accredited training programs in several hundred hospitals throughout the United States and Canada offer diverse types of training and opportunities for special study. During training, the resident usually works in all activities of a pathology department.

Most pathology residents train in both anatomic (AP) and clinical pathology (CP), although it is possible to train in just one branch. The fifth year of training needed for combined anatomic and clinical pathology certification can be entirely clinical, entirely research or a combination of the two.

Successful completion of a residency training program and passage of an objective written and practical examination fulfill the American Board of Pathology's requirements for certification in anatomic or clinical pathology or both. As in other medical disciplines, Board certification is not an absolute requirement for practice, but it is highly prized as evidence of professional competence.

There are also opportunities for subspecialization. Anatomic pathology can lead to certification in *forensic pathology, neuropathology, cytopathology* or *dermatopathology.* Clinical pathology includes the certifiable subspecialties of *medical microbiology, chemical pathology, hematology, blood banking/transfusion medicine* and *immunopathology.* A basic certificate from the American Board of Pathology in anatomic pathology, clinical pathology or both, plus one or two years of appropriate training or experience are prerequisites for taking the Board's Special Competence examination in each of these subjects.

Career Options

Although 75 percent of pathologists practice in the community hospital setting, many other options exist.

Community hospital practice offers the opportunity to play a part in the clinical decision-making of physicians in all medical specialties on the hospital staff. As laboratory director, the pathologist is involved with hospital administration and strategic planning, as well as providing patient service, consultation and teaching. This combination of administrative and clinical expertise places the pathologist in a bridging position between medical and administrative staffs of the hospital.

Hospital pathologists often operate laboratories that also serve the office practices of their community's physicians. With the growth of ambulatory care, pathologists may practice in more nonhospital settings such as their own private offices, clinics and other health care facilities.

The nation's medical schools attract the second largest group of pathologists—about 3,000—often those who want more extensive teaching opportunities than those available in the community setting, with time to carry on research at either the basic or applied level. Here, too, there is opportunity to develop an administrative bent. Pathologists often serve as deans and associate deans and on national professional and research bodies.

Independent laboratories have assumed an increasing role as a practice site for pathologists. Many of these laboratories are part of major national medical industries; others are more confined geographically or may be purely local.

Forensic pathologists typically work in municipal, state, and federal agencies to determine the facts about unattended, unexplained and violent deaths.

The military need for pathologists is a significant one; they also work in government agencies, such as the National Institutes of Health, Armed Forces Institute of Pathology, and Food and Drug Administration. In addition, freestanding research institutes and private industrial enterprises such as drug companies have pathologists on staff.

The best available data suggest a continuing need for pathologists in all sectors in the future.

▼

The **INTERSOCIETY COMMITTEE ON PATHOLOGY INFORMATION** disseminates information about the medical practice and research achievements of pathology. It also produces career information, including the brochure in which this essay originally appeared, and the annual *Directory of Pathology Residency Training Programs* listing residency programs in the United States and Canada, post-sophomore fellowships for medical students, and postgraduate fellowships in specialty areas of pathology. The Committee consists of one representative of each of the major pathology association in the United States: the American Society of Clinical Pathologists, the American Society for Investigative Pathology, the Association of Pathology Chairmen, the College of American Pathologists, and the U.S. and Canadian Academy of Pathology.

Additional information is available from:

Intersociety Committee on Pathology Information (ICPI)
4733 Bethesda, Ave., Ste. 700
Bethesda, MD 20814
(301)656-2944

CHAPTER FIVE

What Does It Take to Be a Surgeon

Robert E. Hermann, M.D., Senior Surgeon and Past Chairman, Department of General Surgery, Cleveland Clinic Foundation

Surgery has a great deal of appeal to students considering the practice of medicine. Surgeons deal directly with medical problems and have the opportunity to correct that problem by their operative procedure with immediate results within days. It is a direct approach with an opportunity to use your hands and technical ability as well as your mind and judgement. Frequently, the problem may be a mechanical or structural one, such as a hernia, a fracture, a leaking heart valve, an intestinal obstruction, a malignant tumor; a biologic dysfunction, such as a duodenal ulcer; or a metabolic problem, such as an islet cell tumor of the pancreas which secretes too much insulin.

The variety of surgical careers which are available in the specialty of surgery include: gastrointestinal surgery, plastic surgery, vascular surgery (surgery of blood vessels), cardiothoracic surgery (surgery of the heart and chest), pediatric surgery (surgery of children), endocrine surgery (surgery of glands), orthopedic surgery (surgery of bones and joints), urology (kidney and bladder surgery), neurologic surgery (surgery of the brain and nervous system), otolaryngology (surgery of the ear, nose, and throat), gynecology (surgery of female organs), hand surgery, trauma and burn surgery (surgery of injuries), surgical oncology (surgery of cancer), and transplantation surgery (surgery of transplanted organs). Surgery is thus a dynamic field, constantly changing and enlarging with many opportunities to specialize.

Personality Traits of Surgeons

Surgeons as a group like to get things done. They enjoy working with their hands and the opportunity they have to go directly into the body, to see "inside" where vital processes happen, and to correct problems directly.

Medical students who choose surgery as a career also have identifiable attitudes and personality traits. They appear to be "thing" oriented rather than "idea" oriented.

They are realists, have good memories for facts and details, and are frequently good at handling tools and machinery. They tend to have a capacity to handle difficult situations without great distress, to be confident, often somewhat unsophisticated, sometimes crude, easily pleased, and free of jealousy. They often have athletic ability.

Surgeons must have the ability to make a decision promptly and decisively. The personality of a surgeon must be one that is prepared to deal with crises, to stay calm and maintain composure under stress, and to tolerate long hours of intense concentration, often working into the late hours of the night. A career in surgery is demanding and time-consuming. Students considering a career in surgery should ask themselves whether these demands will fit in with their other plans for a satisfying life. For those who gain personal satisfaction from serving others, from making sick people well, who enjoy responsibility, and are able to make decisions, surgery offers many rewards and much satisfaction.

The Education of Surgeons

High school or college students interested in medicine should obtain a basic foundation in the biological sciences: biology, chemistry, and physics. Verbal skills and the ability to relate to other people are also important; English, social science, the humanities, sociology, and history contribute to a well-rounded academic background. As high school students choose their college, they should investigate the opportunities provided by that college in biological science and the success rate of students who have graduated from this college in obtaining acceptance to medical school. Some colleges have a combined program, a special six- or seven-year combined bachelor and medical degree program, whereby undergraduate and medical school curriculum are integrated. At the present time, these programs are available in approximately 22 medical schools.

The competition for admission into a top-notch college and medical school remains intense, and it is important that students achieve the best grades possible during their undergraduate years. Extracurricular activities are also important, including sports activities, service clubs or groups, school newspapers, and musical organizations. All of these contribute to students' understanding of other people, to the enrichment of their personal lives, and to their ability to relate to and work with other people.

Although the majority of students interested in medicine major in one of the sciences in college, almost half of premedical students major in other areas such as English, social science, economics, or humanities. Students interested in medicine should obtain a list of the basic, required courses necessary for acceptance into medical school and should take those courses early during their years in college.

The Medical College Admission Test (MCAT) should be taken approximately 12-15 months before the students plan to enter medical school. This test has four sections: biological sciences, physical sciences, verbal reasoning, and a writing sample. Each section is scored independently. The MCAT examination measures specific knowledge of scientific concepts and principles, it evaluates problem solving and logical reasoning, as well as critical thinking skills that are considered important for the practice of medicine. In considering students for acceptance into medical school, most medical school admissions committees look at grades in college, MCAT scores, letters of recommendation, and the skills and experience students have obtained through extracurricular activities.

Medical School

During medical school, students spend the first two years reviewing basic laboratory studies in biology, chemistry, anatomy, microbiology, physiology, pharmacology, epidemiology and biostatistics, and pathology. During the second year and the last two years of medical school, clinical subjects are begun with courses in physical diagnosis, medical ethics, and basic clerkships in medicine, surgery, obstetrics and gynecology, pediatrics, neurologic sciences, and psychiatry. For students interested in a career in surgery, it is important to obtain a strong background in all aspects of medicine and to obtain excellent basic medical information and skills, prior to making a decision for surgery. By the third year of medical school, most students begin to identify their career goals. The senior year is often a predominately elective year, and students interested in surgery frequently take elective rotations in general surgery or some of the surgical specialties, to further evaluate or confirm their interest in a career in surgery.

Choosing a Residency

During the latter part of the junior year and early part of the senior year, medical students begin to think about residency training. The National Resident Matching Program (NRMP) and the Accreditation Council for Graduate Medical Education (ACGME) of the American Medical Association both publish directories which list all hospital residency programs in the medical and surgical specialties. There are approximately 285 residency training programs in surgery in the United States, with approximately 4,000 first-year positions available each year.

Most students, after reviewing the list of hospital residency programs, will choose to visit four to ten hospitals to interview for a residency position. At that time, they meet the residency program director, the chairman of the surgical department, some of the surgeons on the faculty, and some of the residents in training at the hospital to learn their views about that residency program. After visiting the various hospitals of their choice, the students list these hospitals in their order of preference with the NRMP. The hospitals also rank the senior students who have interviewed with them. Both then submit their rank list to the NRMP. The NRMP then matches the students' rank list with that of the hospital through a computerized matching program.

The results of this "match" are then released in late February or early March of each year, identifying where students have been selected into their residency training program. Approximately 60% of senior medical students will achieve the residency position of their first choice; another 25% will receive the residency position of their second or third choice. For those few students that do not "match" and for those hospitals that have not filled their residency through the NMRP, phone calls to or from the various hospitals place this small group of students into a hospital residency program.

Residency Training

Residency training in general surgery requires five years of hospital experience as a minimum. The final two years are those of senior responsibility and the final or last year is the year of chief residency. Some programs require six years and a few require seven years of surgical training. Often, one or more years are taken in the middle of the residency training program for a research period, outside of the regular training program.

During those five or more years of surgical training, residents are given increasing responsibility in diagnosis, decision making, and in operative responsibility. Young surgical residents begin to assist in surgery, learn the principles of surgical operative procedures, and then gradually perform more and more of the operative procedure itself. In their senior and final years, they perform the operation in its entirety under the supervision of a senior surgeon or faculty member. By the time of their graduation from the residency program, they should have achieved all of the skills necessary to practice in their surgical specialty.

For surgeons that specialize in other areas, such as orthopedics, otolaryngology, neurologic surgery, or urology, one or two basic years of general surgery are obtained, prior to an additional three or four years in the surgical specialty. Some specialties require full training (five years) in general surgery, prior to going into that specialty. These specialties include cardiovascular surgery, peripheral vascular surgery, pediatric surgery, colon and rectal surgery, and surgical oncology.

During the years of surgical residency training, young surgeons learn from their teachers, from the many patients they treat, and from a variety of textbooks which are available for surgeons. Examinations are given under the supervision of the American Board of Surgery or by one of the other twelve surgical boards. At the completion of their surgical training, a two-part examination is given, first a written examination and then an oral examination in their surgical specialty. When these examinations have been passed, the young surgeon is fully accredited or "certified" by the American Board of Surgery or by the appropriate specialty board. With this certification, they may obtain hospital privileges to practice in the location of their choice anywhere in the United States.

A Career in Surgery

In most surveys, surgeons score high in personal satisfaction with their career. They work hard, but they obtain great satisfaction and personal gratification from the opportunities they have to directly treat and cure surgical illness. Moreover, they have the respect of their peers in the medical profession and are generally held in high regard by their colleagues. Finally, their earning capacity is among the highest of all physicians. Personal satisfaction, respect of colleagues, and monetary reward more than make up for the stress and strain of a surgeon's busy life.

Surgery requires a commitment to a lifetime of learning. The field of surgery constantly changes with the introduction of new techniques and new procedures. Most surgeons continue their personal education by attending medical meetings and conferences, postgraduate courses, and by observing and discussing surgical problems with their colleagues. There are many surgical organizations, most notably the American College of Surgeons, which provide postgraduate education for practicing surgeons throughout the United States and the world. Other societies and groups, such as the Central Surgical Association, Western Surgical Association, Southern Surgical Association, Society for Surgery of the Alimentary Tract, Society of Surgical Oncology, Society of Thoracic Surgeons, American Academy of Orthopedic Surgeons, American Urological Association, etc., provide opportunities and collegial experiences for practicing surgeons to keep up with their specialty and to continue to offer their patients modern, expert surgical care. If you have what it takes to be a surgeon, it is a rewarding and satisfying career.

▼

ROBERT E. HERMANN, M.D., is senior surgeon and past chairman of the Department of General Surgery at the Cleveland Clinic Foundation. He was born and raised in Highland, IL, the son of a family doctor. He received an A.B. degree from Harvard University and his M.D. from Washington University School of Medicine, St. Louis. He obtained his residency training at University Hospitals of Cleveland and was appointed to the faculty of Case Western Reserve University School of Medicine, where he is now clinical professor of surgery. He joined the staff of the Cleveland Clinic in 1962 and was chairman of the Department of General Surgery for 23 years.

Dr. Hermann is a member of approximately 30 professional societies, has served as a director of the American Board of Surgery, and as a member of the Residency Review Committee for Surgery. He is past president of the Association of Program Directors in Surgery and the Society for Surgery of the Alimentary Tract, and is past chairman of the Board of Governors of the American College of Surgeons. He has published approximately 250 scientific papers and book chapters, and is the author of two books on surgery.

CHAPTER SIX

Random Thoughts on Surgery, Decision Making, and Life's Expectations

Donald Trunkey, M.D., Professor and Chairman, Department of Surgery, Oregon Health Sciences University

Career choice decision making is a dynamic process and evolves as one gains new experiences. The first and maybe most critical decision is the initial one that makes a person decide on medicine as a career. In my case, I broke my arm when I was in the seventh grade playing football. That evening, my father took me to the general practitioner's office, where a very difficult reduction of my fracture was accomplished after approximately three hours. Over the next eight weeks, I became close friends with this general practitioner, and he became an excellent role model of community and personal values. Before the cast on my arm came off, I had decided that I wanted to be a physician.

The next career decision comes during medical school, when most students decide on a specialty or branch of medicine they wish to pursue. My role models in medical school were all internists and, although I enjoyed the diagnostic aspects of internal medicine, I was not really satisfied with the treatment component of this specialty. Treatment in internal medicine seems incomplete and frustrating because of prolonged courses on various pharmacological regimens. The solution became obvious—surgery almost invariably provides instant personal gratification and patient gratification, since the treatment is essentially instantaneous. I also found that surgery seemed to suit my personality. I am comfortable making decisions even during an emergency, when one has limited information on which to base that decision. Surgery satisfies my need to work with my hands and offers the satisfaction one gets from making somebody better with their own skills, Although not unique to surgery, the bond between surgeon and patient is truly rewarding. Surgery combines the intellectual challenge of diagnosis with a sense of completeness in therapy.

Surgical Residency

Surgical residency typically is 5-6 years long. Surgical specialty training such as cardiopulmonary surgery, pediatric surgery, plastic surgery, and vascular surgery requires an additional 2-3 years. Physicians who want to specialize in orthopedic surgery, neurosurgery, or urology usually take only 1-2 years of general surgery followed by 4-6 years of specific specialty training. A typical resident makes 25,000-30,000 dollars per year.

During general surgery residency, the training is progressively complex. During the first two years, the emphasis is on preoperative assessment and postoperative care, particularly critical care. Operative care is introduced during the first year of residency, usually with minor operations, such as hernia repair and appendectomy. As the resident progresses, the operations become more complex. By the time the resident is in his or her final year (chief resident), they are qualified to do most operations independently and require direct supervision only in the most complex procedures.

Most surgery residencies try to limit the hours worked each week to 80. Unfortunately, this is sometimes difficult to achieve. One of the principles in surgery is the concept of commitment by the surgeon to the patient once surgical treatment is recommended. Thus, once the surgeon has operated on the patient, he or she is committed to follow them through their postoperative care, including postoperative complications and the need for further surgery. Fortunately, most patients do very well, but when complications occur they can be time-consuming. Anyone contemplating a career in surgery should appreciate that the training can be arduous, since one is learning new knowledge, the art and skills of surgery.

Career Paths

I have made subsequent career decisions since becoming a general surgeon. I have special interests within general surgery, which include trauma surgery, surgical critical care, and vascular surgery. I have a particular interest in trauma surgery, since it is a disease that primarily affects young people. I am biased, but I believe it is one of the most rewarding areas of medicine. The trauma surgeon is literally putting Humpty Dumpty back together again. To take a severely injured young person, resuscitate them from shock, repair their injuries, and care for them through what is often a very stormy postoperative period, is truly gratifying. In my opinion, it is one of the few areas in medicine where a physician can actually make the difference between life and death.

Surgical critical care is an intellectual challenge, since one is caring for the sickest patients in the hospital. I usually do this for one week each month. In order to fulfill this commitment, I must keep up-to-date on all aspects of medicine, including specialties outside of surgery.

Vascular surgery is of interest to me because of its technical challenges. Although the surgery of blood vessels does not usually make a difference between life and death, it can make a major difference in the patients' quality of life.

Another career decision I have made is to remain in academic medicine. This may have been one of the most difficult decisions I have faced. The lure of private practice in a community hospital is very attractive, since one becomes part of the community and you know your patients and their families far more intimately than is possible in a large teaching hospital. Like the general practitioner who I tried to emulate, there is a bond between community and physician. Academic practice is an intellectual challenge. The rewards come from working with students and residents and passing your knowledge and skills on to them.

Work Schedules

A surgeon who practices in a community hospital typically puts in a 65-70 hour workweek. Their relationship to other surgeons could be very loose and simply represent shared office space and night call, or more formal, including partnerships, specialty surgeon groups, and multi-specialty groups. Some surgeons work for Health Maintenance Organizations, such as Kaiser, for salary and a more controlled workweek. A typical starting salary would be $120,000.

Most surgeons working in a community setting have patients referred to them by primary care specialties, such as family practice or internal medicine. The patient usually has already been evaluated by the physician and is perceived to have an illness that requires surgical treatment. The surgeon will do his or her own evaluation and recommend surgery, if indicated. This type of practice constitutes the "elective" practice. In addition, the surgeon usually takes call at night and selected days when they may be called to the emergency room for emergencies, such as appendicitis or accidents.

Surgeons do have time for leisure activities and many have very interesting hobbies or avocations. I enjoy making wine with friends. However, all doctors must set aside time for learning, which might include attending postgraduate courses. Medicine is a very dynamic profession that is constantly changing as new knowledge becomes available. The surgeon must keep up with this knowledge and new operative techniques. "Doctor" is a latin word (docere) which means to teach. Consequently, a doctor must continue to learn.

Jobs that Pay the Most

1. Physician
2. Financial Planner
3. Dentist
4. Veterinarian
5. Airline Pilot
6. Stockbroker
7. Lawyer
8. Lobbyist
9. Ad Executive
10. Purchasing Manager

Source: *Money*

Almost all surgeons become involved with their community. Their contact with patients and community leaders invariably puts them in leadership positions. Surgeons tend to be gregarious, outspoken, and have strong opinions, which add to their leadership potential. Surgeons are not timid! Since they are often in difficult positions during complex care, they have to be decisive.

My typical workweek averages 80-85 hours. I usually spend at least one night a week in the hospital taking trauma call. I do not consider these hours a burden, nor do I really consider what I do as work, since I enjoy it so much. Surgeons don't put in the longest workweek. (Couples who work in "mom and pop" grocery stores or individuals who own gas stations probably put in longer hours than I do.) Individuals who wish to be physicians often do so because they have independent natures, and medicine allows one to express this independence. Time cannot be a consideration when a physician makes a commitment to a patient to take them through an illness or injury. I do not believe that my long hours have been a detriment to my family, since the time I spend with them is quality time and the values I ascribe to maybe an inspiration to them as well.

As an academic surgeon, I receive a salary and this would typically average $180,000 a year. Salaries are also an option in private practice, particularly if one is working for a health maintenance organization or a large medical center. Fee for service is still a viable option, and incomes would typically be $150,000-$225,000 a year for a general surgeon. Specialty surgeons within general surgery make a little bit more. These incomes are very handsome by any standard, yet typically represent $38 per hour. It must be stressed that financial reward pales in comparison to the personal gratification that comes from caring for a critically ill or injured patient.

▼

DONALD D. TRUNKEY, M.D. was born and raised in farm country in Eastern Washington: the Palouse Country. Early work included farm work, mining, hod carrying, carpentry, sheet rocking, and building contracting. He attended Washington State University for his undergraduate degree and the University of Washington Medical School. Uncertain about medicine or surgery as a career, he chose to do a rotating internship with Dr. Bert Dunphy at the University of Oregon. After one month on the surgical service, there was no question on what career to pursue. Following his internship, he spent two years in the United States Army as a general medical officer in Germany.

Upon completion of his military duties, be rejoined Dr. Dunphy at the University of California, San Francisco, where his general surgery training was completed. During this period of time, he spent one year in the Organ Preservation Laboratory with Dr. Folkert Belzer. Following his general surgery training, he spent an additional year with Dr. Tom Shires at Southwestern Medical Center in Dallas, Texas, where he was involved in a National Institutes of Health special fellowship in trauma. Following completion of his fellowship, he returned to the University of California, San Francisco, where he became very involved in the care of trauma patients. He was chief of the Burn Center at San Francisco General Hospital and also had an extensive interest in elective vascular surgery and non-cardiac thoracic surgery. He established a laboratory to study mechanisms of shock at the cellular level with a special interest in myocardial performance following shock, lung injury, and cellular immune mechanisms following injury.

In 1978, he became chief of surgery at San Francisco General Hospital and more recently, he has assumed the chairmanship at Oregon Health Sciences University Department of Surgery. His intent is to build a general surgery residency based on all the primary components of general surgery. His own special interest remains trauma surgery.

CHAPTER SEVEN

Psychiatry:
An Opportunity to Ease Human Suffering

**Theresa Anna Yuschok, M.D.,
Duke University Medical Center**

Cartoons stereotype the bearded psychiatrist scribbling notes behind a couch. The field has changed a lot since Freud. Psychotherapy techniques are broader. More women have entered the field. A variety of other medical treatments are available, such as ECT and medications. A choice of practice options are open. A career in psychiatry may take many forms and appeal to many types of people.

Medical School

As in Freud's day, however, medical school is required to practice psychiatry, a medical specialty. In the four-year college degree, one may major in any art degree or science, psychology, if you'd like. But pre-medical science classes are required in chemistry, physics, and biology. (If the science classes are intimidating, other careers in the mental health fields such as psychologist, social worker, or psychiatric nurse may be more appealing).

Medical school requires another four years of study. The first two years include more science classes and laboratory work, such anatomy, dissection of the human body, and histology—examining the cell structure of each organ. Medicine is a lot to learn—memorizing every artery, muscle, and nerve and how each works. The third year is spent out of the classroom and in the hospital wards. Students rotate through each specialty experiencing delivery rooms, as well as the psychiatric wards. This year reinforces the book learning with patient care. By the end of the third year, most medical students have chosen a specialty and apply for further training in a residency program.

Residency Training

The post-graduate residency training takes four years including neurology and medicine during the first "internship" year. Residents are paid $25,000. They work long hours with "on-call" (overnight) duties every three to six nights during the first two years. They work in the hospitals using stethoscopes and expanding skills from medical school. They also acquire new skills in psychotherapy, psychopharmacology and electroconvulsive therapy (ECT).

Psychotherapy is a complex art learned by observing senior psychiatrists interviewing patients, the resident discussing patient sessions with a supervisor, reading, or attending conferences, and sometimes experientially through a group meeting or hiring a psychotherapist for oneself. Some programs offer special training in group therapy, family therapy, substance abuse treatments, and behavioral therapy.

Psychiatrists also learn to prescribe medications for mental illnesses, such as depression and schizophrenia. Although other professionals may be licensed to do psychotherapy, the psychiatrist has the prescription pad and ECT, and the psychologist interprets tests such as Rorschach "ink blots" and personality testing.

Career Paths

After residency training, a variety of practice options are available. As a relatively young specialty, psychiatry attracts academic researchers. Funding is available to find cures or at least more effective treatment for schizophrenia, Alzheimer's disease, mood disorders, and other mental illnesses. This is an exciting time when much will be discovered during our lifetime. The research may include animals which are used for models of behaviors and diseases.

Some psychiatrists work independently or with a group. The practice may be office-based or hospital-based. Others work for salaries in state mental health centers, HMOs, state hospitals, or VAMCs. Most psychiatrists begin their practice with a variety of roles, including a part-time salaried position, a private office, and perhaps a teaching affiliation. It is easy to work part-time with a choice of hours and this appeals to those starting a family. Starting incomes range from $60,000 to $120,000 full time.

Further training choices include child psychiatry, forensics in prisons or courtroom, geriatrics, consultation-liaison with other medical specialties, or psychoanalysis. (Yes, the couch still exists). Child psychiatry may be the best choice—a scarcity of practitioners is predicted compared to expected need.

Psychiatrists are privy to a full range of human suffering, which can be quite stressful. Empathy, genuine caring for human beings and their struggles, is needed, but one must be able to also be an objective "participant observer" and not become overly involved or overwhelmed. The specialty can be fulfilling for those interested in the human condition and helping people with the tools of medication, communication, support, and insight.

THERESA ANNA YUSCHOK, M.D. practices psychiatry at Duke University Medical Center, Durham, NC. In addition to seeing patients for medication therapy and psychotherapy, she does group and family therapy, teaches residents and medical students at Durham Veterans Administration Medical Center, serves on committees, and has administrative duties. She graduated from a small town high school, enrolled in Northwestern University's Honors Program in Medical Education, and graduated from Northwestern University Medical School in Chicago in 1986. She did her residency training for four years at Duke University Medical Center and then continued on staff in 1990. She belongs to the American Psychiatric Association and the American Group Psychotherapy Association. In her free time, she enjoys playwriting and poetry.

CHAPTER EIGHT

If You Think You Want to Be a Nurse

Diane Mancino, M.A., R.N., C.A.E., Deputy Executive Director, National Student Nurses' Association, Inc.

A career as a registered professional nurse brings many rewards, recognition, and personal satisfaction. Once you earn the title of R.N., doors open and challenges and opportunities found in no other profession become available to you. Exciting nursing specialties and practice settings can accommodate a broad spectrum of personal interests and prospects for advancement. And, nursing positions are available in every geographic location in the world.

But it all starts in school!

A prerequisite for becoming a nursing student is an interest in people and service. The profession of nursing is centered around maintaining and enhancing health, as well as providing professional care to individuals with impaired health. Nursing also involves teaching people about how to maintain health, how to care for sick family members, how to locate healthcare services, and how to use the latest medical and technological advances to treat acute and chronic illnesses.

Management and coordination of nursing and healthcare services is part of every nursing position from staff nurse to executive vice president of a healthcare facility. In today's highly technical healthcare environment, nurses combine patient contact with the tools of technology, so that the highest quality care is provided.

Do You Have What It Takes?

In addition to an interest in people and service, good verbal and written communication skills, a sound academic standing, a commitment to alleviate human suffering, an ability to think and respond quickly in emergency situations, and good interpersonal skills are essential for success in the nursing profession.

An honest personal assessment of your abilities is the obvious first step if you're considering a nursing career. If you are uncertain about your ability to work with sick people, consider "testing the waters"—become a volunteer or nurse's aide in a hospital or long-term care facility to see if you are comfortable in these settings. Watch and listen closely to what goes on—the "normal" daily routines and the equally "normal" emergencies—around the hospital.

At the end of the day, if you feel gratified and energized by your interactions, chances are you will like nursing. If the patients and/or the role of the healthcare providers makes you uncomfortable or fails to stimulate your interest, consider another career.

You're Ready to Proceed

Once you have decided that nursing is for you and that you have the characteristics and academic ability to succeed in nursing school, you will need to select the nursing program that best suits your needs. To become a registered professional nurse, you must complete a two-, three-, or four-year nursing education program and successfully pass a state board examination for licensure.

Most Advertised Products/Services in Nursing Journals

Ranked by 1990 share of ad dollars
1. Employment
2. Classified
3. Malpractice Insurance
4. Procardia XL
5. U.S. Air Force
6. Tubex injector
7. Army Reserve
8. Navy Reserve
9. Public Health
10. Pub-Mosby

Source: *Medical Marketing & Media*

Choosing the Right Program

Deciding on a nursing education program is an important decision, and you will need to be fully informed of the advantages and disadvantages of each potential route into the profession. Your decision will be based on your career goals, economic situation, the amount of time you can dedicate to your education, family responsibilities, and the availability of nursing programs.

If you are a high school student, seek advice from your guidance counselor. But be careful—many high school guidance counselors do not know very much about nursing and may try to steer you off in another direction. If you are already a high school graduate (perhaps you are looking for a new career), seek guidance from a professional career counselor. Aptitude testing to determine if your interests and skills match your career choice is also a good idea. The public library has books on nursing careers and several organizations have career resources available for free or for a nominal charge.

Talk to the Professionals

Talk to nurses who have graduated from the various nursing programs and ask them to share their experiences. Your local nurses' association can help you to network with graduate nurses. Explore as many resources as possible so that you are fully informed and can make a knowledgeable decision.

Choosing the Right School

Once you have decided on the type of program you wish to enter, obtain bulletins from several schools. See if you meet the entrance requirements, find out how to apply (note deadlines), and, if possible, plan a visit to the school to meet with faculty and nursing students. Many schools of nursing have open houses for prospective students. It is important that the school of nursing you choose is the right one for you. Here are some questions to consider when choosing a nursing school:

- How long is the program?

- Is there a waiting list to get in?

- What credential will I receive upon graduation?

- Do I meet the entrance requirements? If not, what does the school have available to help me meet the requirements (i.e., remedial courses)?

- What is the tuition, and is financial aid available?

- What other costs will I have to incur (i.e., books, uniforms, lab fees, equipment)?

- Is the school accredited by the National League for Nursing? (This criteria is particularly important if you plan to further your education beyond your basic nursing program.)

- What are the expectations of the program (i.e., what grade point average must I maintain to stay in)?

- What is the passing rate on the state board exam for students graduating from this program?

- What are the credentials of the instructors and professors who teach in the program?

- Are professors readily available for academic and other counseling?

- What are the time demands of the program (for lecture as well as for clinical experience)?

- Where are the sites for clinical experience located and is transportation provided?

- What is the philosophy of the nursing program (i.e., do they base their teaching on a specific nursing theory)?

- Where do the graduates from this program work, and what kinds of nursing positions are they qualified for after passing the state board licensing exam?

- What assistance is provided to ensure my passing the state board licensure exam (i.e., assessment through testing and counseling)?

- Is job placement assistance provided?

- What is the composition of the student body? Are they mostly recent high schoolgraduates or older, second-career students or a mixture of both?

- Is child care available?

- Is there a mechanism for student governance and involvement in the decision-making process in affairs relating to student's rights and responsibilities?

- Is there an honor society for nursing students in the school?

- Is there a chapter of the National Student Nurses' Association at the school?

- Will this program enable me to fulfill my career goals?

Once you have been accepted into the nursing school, be prepared to work hard. Passing grades are not easy to achieve since the program you choose must prepare you to pass the state board exam for licensure. Knowing how to study and how to take exams is an advantage for every student, but is absolutely essential for the nursing student. From the onset, develop good study habits and keep up with reading assignments—it will be difficult to catch up once you fall behind.

You're on Your Way

"Pinning" and graduation day may mark the beginning of an exciting career. The choices are unending. Most nurses advise new graduates to spend at least one year working in a hospital on a general medical-surgical unit, but if you know the area of specialization that you wish to pursue...go for it! Most hospitals will train new graduates to work in the specialty area of their choice. The pages ahead will describe some of the specialty practice areas in nursing as well as the educational options available to those considering a nursing career.

I hope you join us!

Diane J. Mancino, M.A., R.N., C.A.E., is the deputy executive director of the National Student Nurses' Association (NSNA), an association in New York City for nursing students who are studying to become registered nurses.

Ms. Mancino has a baccalaureate degree from the State University of New York at Buffalo; a master's degree in nursing from New York University; and is currently a doctoral candidate at Teachers College, Columbia University. She has worked in many areas of nursing including: intensive, coronary, and emergency nursing; instructor in an associate degree nursing program; and public health nursing. Over the past ten years, Ms. Mancino has worked closely with nursing student leaders in the NSNA.

Make Nursing a "Special" Choice

**Teresa Cervantez Thompson, Ph.D., R.N., C.R.R.N., Vice-President,
Rehabilitation Institute of Michigan**

Nursing provides a wide array of opportunities for those who wish to pursue this profession of caring. Once an individual has elected to become a nurse, the working world is open, and jobs will come looking for you.

From the needs of the newborn infant to those of the senior citizen, there are a multitude of nursing job opportunities available, each addressing the healthcare needs of humanity. Nurses are active in the prevention of illness in clinics, industry and public health care; the care of patients in emergency and intensive-care situations; general hospital nursing care; in long-term care settings; and in the home. Nurses work with clients who are well or have congenital problems; with patients who have acute illnesses, accidents, or chronic diseases; and with people who are dying.

This broad spectrum of healthcare presents the registered nurse with a lifetime of opportunities and challenges. Some nurses choose to be generalists and not identify with any one area of nursing. On the other hand, many nurses choose to work in the one area of nursing practice which best fits their knowledge, interest, personality, and professional goals and develop their career within that practice.

A Number of Choices

In the United States, there are more than 100 different nursing specialties. The reason for this ever-growing number is the constant advancement of knowledge and the degree of specificity with which we can address the variety of healthcare problems. The National Federation of Nursing Specialty Organizations (NFSNO), a federation of 38 nursing specialty organizations, describes specialty nursing as a practice area of nursing which focuses on a specific disease, organ/system, or setting; has a scope of practice; and clinical knowledge and skills which guides nursing actions in those areas. Other descriptions of specialty practice focus on patient age, acuity, technology, and nursing roles.

To illustrate, there are disease-related nursing specialties, such as oncology (focusing on cancer), organ/system related specialties, such as neuroscience nursing (focusing on the nervous system), or setting-related specialties, such as intensive-care or critical-care nursing. Each specialty focuses on a particular patient/client population and develops the standards of knowledge and expertise required within the scope of this nursing practice.

The Motivating Force

Working with people is what many nurses cite as their motivating force for entering nursing in the first place. All areas of specialty nursing practice will offer exposure to people and require certain people skills, though in different ways and to different degrees.

Working with a team of healthcare professionals who have diverse backgrounds but common goals creates a stimulating work environment. Working with a team is also given as a reason for going into nursing. There are many areas of healthcare in which a team approach to care is common.

Certification

The individual registered nurse working in specialty practice may formalize the recognition of his or her knowledge through a certification examination. Examinations are offered by the specialty nursing certification boards and testing agencies. These boards are usually directly or indirectly linked to the specialty nursing organizations or the American Nurses Association. The usual requirement is that the registered nurse be active in the practice of the specialty for an established period of time, pass an examination, and meet other stated requirements.

The desire to help others is yet another motivating force which brings people into nursing and, once again, the opportunity to help is pervasive within nursing. What draws a nurse into one specialty within nursing probably includes all the preceding reasons and one or more sets of experiences, interests, or skills that point to a particular specialization.

Entering Specialty Practice Nursing

Specialty nursing does not usually require formal advanced education or preparation beyond becoming a registered nurse. Specialty nursing preparation comes from the experiences and ongoing development of the nurse. In most instances, registered nurses gain their specialty knowledge through on-the-job staff development programs, continuing education, self-study, and clinical practice experience. The decision to identify with a specialty—or not—is an option for each individual nurse.

There are areas of specialty practice in which formalized education *is* required, such as nurse midwifery and nurse anesthesiology, which also have additional licensure requirements.

Rehabilitation Nursing as an Example

The description to this point seems quite formal. Perhaps an illustration of the specialty practice in which I am involved will give you an idea of just what it means to work in a specialty of nursing.

I am a rehabilitation nurse, which means I work with individuals who have been born with or acquired some physical, communicative, or cognitive disability. I also work with their families. The goal is to assist the patient to become as independent as possible.

What would lead one to choose this specialty? Perhaps it is exposure to young friends with disabilities such as muscular dystrophy or cerebral palsy; maybe it is caring for an elderly relative or neighbor who had a stroke, or watching a young athlete with a disability "just do it" in his exercise work out on a television advertisement.

Whatever the attraction, specialty nursing brings with it the idea and the reality that the nurse can make a difference in someone's life. To the rehabilitation nurse, the difference to be made is in *every* aspect of a patient's life, because disability is not something anyone plans for or expects. Any disability will affect how people think about themselves, how they relate to others, and how others relate to them for the rest of their lives. The extent to which a disability becomes a handicap is where rehabilitation intervention is key.

What It's All About

Rehabilitation is the process by which persons with disabilities are assisted to reach their optimal level of function within their capacity. Rehabilitation is provided in hospital settings, out-patient therapy settings, in the home, in nursing homes, and in schools, for patients ranging from the newborn to elderly. Whether the patient is a child born with a missing arm, a middle-aged man or woman who's had a stroke, a worker who has an industrial accident, or an elderly person coping with the problems of a deteriorating body function, he or she will need to learn how to gain or relearn the skills necessary to be as independent as possible. Together, the patient and the team of rehabilitation professionals work to ensure that patients learn about, compensate for, or adjust to their physical impairments. The rehabilitation nurse often functions as the patient's coach, fan, and cheerleader as he or she moves along the difficult road involving the mind, body, and will, learning and adjusting to the changes brought about by altered abilities.

In the hospital setting, the rehabilitation nursing staff is there around the clock and can help patients adapt all aspects of their personal care to their current abilities. The nurse teaches a family *how* to assist and *when* assistance is appropriate, as well as providing support and counsel when it is not. Watching, encouraging, and assisting men and women to learn to care for themselves with an artificial leg, a paralyzed arm, or limited speech is an exciting challenge. Knowing that the patients can resume their family roles—(and in many instances, their work roles)—because of the rehabilitation efforts is a rewarding experience. Once a patient is discharged from a hospital setting, there are rehabilitation nurses in the private sector who manage his or her ongoing rehabilitation course and deal with vocational and medical management.

This is just the example of my own experience. Each specialty has its own scenario of how nursing can make the difference. It is the fit between the nurse and the specialty which brings about the success of both.

Career Advancement

All nursing practice allows for movement into management, clinical, or education positions. Depending on the direction desired, each of these three areas may require certification. Further education—beginning with a Bachelor's degree, if not initially obtained—is required for advancement in many areas.

Moving into Management

In management, a nurse may move to a **nurse manager** position at the hospital unit level after a minimum of two years (but usually after three to five years). From that point, he or she may move to a **director of nursing** or **chief nursing officer** position—the titles vary depending on the structure of the institution. An advanced degree is preferred to move beyond the nurse manager level in almost all areas of nursing.

Clinical Ladders

For a nurse to move ahead in the clinical nursing area, some hospitals have clinical ladders that allow the nurse to apply for recognition and responsibility at a higher level. Some ladders recognize certification and further education as part of the criteria for advancement. Each level of the career ladder has a wage factor as part of its recognition.

Within the clinical advancement options are two which are recognized as requiring advanced education. They are the **nurse practitioner** and the **clinical nurse specialist.** The latter is a nurse with advanced knowledge in nursing practice and a Master's degree.

Education

The education track for nurses includes the academic institution route or the hospital route. The academic route has the same requirements that any college or university instructor or professor would have—advanced education at a Master's level and/or doctorate depending on the institution. In the hospital setting, there are **preceptor** and staff development positions which are used to orient and provide continuing education for the nursing staff to the nursing specialty. The preceptor is a staff nurse who helps to teach the newly employed registered nurse the day-to-day aspects of the practice specialty.

Entrepreneurial Opportunities

There are also entrepreneurial opportunities for nurses within specialty nursing practice, including consulting and private practice within their specialty. Case management is a prime example of a rehabilitation nursing opportunity for nurse entrepreneurs. The range of possibilities is unlimited, as are the opportunities for financial success.

In summary, nursing is a full-employment opportunity. The decision to move into specialty practice provides a career path with unlimited opportunities. There is potential to move in educational, managerial, clinical, and entrepreneurial directions within each specialty. For each nurse, the choice is based on how he or she elects to make the difference.

▼

TERESA C. THOMPSON, Ph.D., R.N., C.R.R.N., has worked as a staff nurse, head nurse, clinical nurse specialist, nurse practitioner, director of nursing, and administrator in geriatric and rehabilitation nursing. She has obtained certificates in Rehabilitation, Gerontology, as an Adult Nurse Practitioner, and in Administration.

In addition to being vice president of hospital services at the Rehabilitation Institute of Michigan, and adjunct professor at Wayne State University's College of Medicine and School of Medicine, Ms. Thompson is active in a number of nursing and rehabilitation organizations. She is past president of the National Federation of Specialty Nursing Organizations and the Association of Rehabilitation Nursing.

A registered nurse diploma graduate from Good Samaritan Hospital School of Nursing (Cincinnati, OH), Ms. Thompson continued to pursue further education while working in health care. A Bachelor's, a Master's degree in nursing, and a Ph.D. were earned at Wayne State University (Detroit, MI).

CHAPTER TEN

Nurse Practitioners: An Expanded Role in the Healthcare Marketplace

Ann M. Thrailkill, MSN, FNP, C.S.,
Palo Alto Veteran's Administration Medical Center

"Thank you, Doctor! You saved my life!"

Nurse practitioners frequently receive compliments like this from grateful patients, whom are quickly reminded that they are *not* physicians, but **nurse practitioners.**

Only to be told, "Yes, but you'll always be *my* doctor!"

Patients are not the only ones to be unfamiliar with this special nursing role.

What Is a Nurse Practitioner?

This special breed of nurses has been in existence for over twenty-five years. The role was developed to provide care to underserved, sometimes rural populations that were not receiving health care due to a shortage of physicians. Since that time, the role has expanded to all healthcare sites and serves all patient populations. Nurse practitioners work in rural and urban settings—hospitals, out-patient clinics, physicians' offices, health departments, nursing homes, VA facilities, schools, colleges, industrial settings, prisons, HMOs, and their own private practices—in all 52 states.

Education and License

Nurse practitioners are registered nurses (RNs) with advanced formal education that has prepared them in a specialty area to maintain and promote health in a certain population of people. Most nurse practitioners have a master's degree in nursing and are certified by the national professional organization. (In the past, some were prepared in a one-year certification program after receiving their RN degree. A few of these certificate programs still exist throughout the country, though they are rapidly disappearing.) Nurse practitioners practice under the rules and regulations of the

Nurse Practice Act of the state in which they work and are licensed independently to practice as experts in their field. Many states allow nurse practitioners to prescribe certain medicines.

Specialty Areas

Nurse practitioners provide primary care in a large number of specialty areas, such as school/college health, women's health (OB/GYN), pediatric/adolescent health, geriatrics, family health, adult health, occupational health, and psychiatric/mental health. **Nurse-midwives** and **nurse anesthetists** are also listed as advanced practice nurses in most states.

What Do Nurse Practitioners Do?

Nurse practitioners work in collaboration with physicians and other healthcare team members to provide quality, comprehensive primary care to children and adults of all ages. Specifically, they:

- Obtain medical histories and perform physical examinations;
- Diagnose and treat common health problems;
- Diagnose, treat, and monitor chronic diseases;
- Order and interpret lab work and X-rays;
- Prescribe medications and other treatments;
- Provide family planning, prenatal care, well baby and child care, and health maintenance care for adults;
- Conduct patient and family education and counseling programs; and
- Provide appropriate referral to physicians and other health team members when necessary.
- Manage care of clients by coordinating and utilizing resources in an appropriate manner.

Salaries

Depending on the region of the country, years of experience, educational preparation, and whether one is certified, nurse practitioner salaries range from $28,000 (starting) to $70,000.

New federal legislation also allows most practitioners to be reimbursed by Medicare, Medicaid, and by some private insurances. The beauty of this career is that you have a wide range of choices of specialization from a very narrow focus, such as neonatal nurse practitioner (premature birth), to a broad specialization, such as family nurse practitioner.

Jobs are usually plentiful, part- *and* full-time jobs are available, hours can be flexible, and it is a career choice that lasts a lifetime. It is often a second-career choice due to many creative college tracts being developed at some universities. These programs allow people with bachelor degrees in other areas to become an RN and a nurse practitioner in three years.

A Rewarding Career

Students considering this choice of an exciting career should be committed to wanting to help others to help themselves. They should be creative, risk-takers, and self-starters with an interest in health and science courses.

As a nurse practitioner, not only will you be a clinical provider, but also a health educator, a researcher, and often an administrator of a health program. It is recommended that you obtain a degree in nursing (BSN) and have at least one year of experience as an RN before completing a two-year master's program with preparation as a nurse practitioner. It is also recommended that you work in some type of health settings during the summers—a hospital, clinic, nursing home, or physician's office—so you're comfortable in a clinical setting.

If it stimulates you, arouses your curiosity and interest, and you seek out more responsibility, then go for it! Good luck in your pursuit of a most challenging, stimulating, and rewarding career that will fulfill all personal needs for a lifetime!

▼

ANN THRAILKILL is currently coordinator of the Women's Health Clinic, women veterans coordinator, and nurse practitioner in ambulatory care at the Palo Alto Veteran's Medical Center. She is also chair of the Council of Nurses in Advanced Practice of the American Nurses Association, former chair of the Nurse Practitioner Interest Group in San Francisco, and has served four years as the ANA Cabinet on Nursing Practice and as immediate past chair of ANA Board on Certification.

Ms. Thrailkill has also chaired the Council of Advanced Nurse Practitioners in Florida and was instrumental in the early development of state rules and regulations for NP practice and for developing groundwork for prescribing privileges in certain states.

Ms. Thrailkill had two articles published in the December 1990 issue of the *American Academy of Nurse Practitioner Journal* pertaining to NPs in the San Francisco area. For many years, she has precepted graduate NP students at her clinical sites.

CHAPTER ELEVEN

Choosing a Career in Oncology Nursing

**Pearl Moore, RN, MN, Executive Director,
Oncology Nursing Society**

"I believe that working in oncology is the best of all worlds for a nurse. It is the profession for me—where I can give to society while feeling professionally fulfilled. Sometimes it's fun, other times it's sad, but always it is rewarding."

Jeanette M. Ceglio, RN, BEd, OCN

They can be seen in every setting—the emergency room, the operating room, the critical care unit, the office, and the home. They care for every age group and treat varying stages of the disease. They are knowledgeable about the latest treatments and procedures as they make a difference each day in the lives of their patients. These nurses are oncology nurses, and they are in demand.

Within the next decade, the incidence of heart disease is expected to take a back seat to cancer as the leading cause of death. This change will not only have a rippling effect on the need for these oncology nursing specialists, but it will impact even nurses working in a general practitioner's office, charging them to be cognizant of cancer risk factors and signs and symptoms of the disease.

Areas of Specialization

From the oncology nursing specialty stems a diversity of subspecialty areas and roles in which nurses can practice. Marie Whedon, RN, MSN, OCN, Hematology/Oncology Clinical Nurse Specialist at Dartmouth-Hitchcock Medical Center in Lebanon, NH, practices in the area of medical oncology, a longstanding and evolving subspecialty.

Medical oncology nurses are often involved in administering chemotherapy since a majority of cancer patients will receive chemotherapy at some point during their treatment. Whedon believes that it is "a nursing art to assist these patients through their treatment" and she adds that "patients are grateful and remember the particular nurse who gave them therapy."

Whedon says that now that they understand side effects and can control them better, administering the therapy is a much more satisfying and rewarding experience for the nurse.

Roberta Strohl, RN, MN, OCN, Clinical Nurse Specialist in Radiation Oncology at the University of Maryland at Baltimore says that approximately 50-60% of cancer patients receive radiation during the course of their treatment. As a radiation oncology nurse, she deals predominately with symptom management, assessing side effects, and patient education. Patient education typically involves teaching the patients how to minimize their side effects and distilling fears and misconceptions about radiation therapy.

Strohl is challenged by the fact that she "sees so many patients a day— sometimes more than 100. It is up to us to quickly assess the changes in the physical and emotional status of each patient." She also has to deal with shrinking resources in the community, such as transportation and social services that are available for patients.

To Strohl however, the rewards of "getting to know the patients and their families while helping them cope with a very difficult treatment" outshine any challenges she may encounter.

Although bone marrow transplantation is considered to be experimental for most diseases, it is often the only hope for cure for many patients. In fact, the number of long-term disease-free survivors has increased leaving an expanding need for skilled oncology nurses to care for not only the marrow transplant recipient, but their donors and families. These nurses must be able to draw upon oncology, critical care, psychosocial, research, and ambulatory care nursing skills.

Best Hospitals for Cancer Treatment

1. University of Texas (M.D. Anderson Cancer Center)
2. Memorial Sloan-Kettering Cancer Center
3. Dana-Farber Cancer Institute
4. Mayo Clinic
5. Stanford University Hospital

Source: *U.S. News and World Report*

According to Rosemary Ford, RN, BA, BS, Clinical Practice Program Director at Fred Hutchinson Cancer Research Center in Seattle, WA, the bone marrow transplant nurse coordinates both the complex therapy and a multidisciplinary team. During the acute phase especially, the nurse's assessment skills are crucial.

Although these nurses are challenged by a high mortality rate, a young patient population, and experimental therapies, "they truly make a difference in the patient's day-to-day experience," says Ford.

Moving from the real high-tech end of the oncology nursing spectrum to the more high-touch end is the role of the hospice nurse, who eases the patient and family through the terminal phase of the disease.

Maryanne Fello, RN, MEd, Director of Cancer Services at Forbes Health Systems in Pittsburgh, PA, says that hospice is really nurse-directed and nurse-driven in that patients that are receiving hospice care have elected to have supportive care in the face of terminal illness. Therefore, hospice nurses are the coordinators and providers of the care that is given. "The nurse is the captain of the team when it comes to hospice," says Fello.

Hospice nursing can involve either bringing professional support to the terminally ill patient and family in the home, hopefully for the whole death experience, or providing nursing interventions in the inpatient care setting. "Hospice gives nurses the chance to shine and use all the skills they learned in school," says Fello.

Today, hospice care is focused outside of the hospital which is the trend for all health care, particularly oncology. In fact, Fello believes that between 80-90% of oncology care goes on outside the four walls of the hospital. As a result, hospice opportunities are abundant.

These areas discussed only touch upon the array of opportunities that are available for oncology nurses. Other areas of practice include prevention and early detection, HIV/AIDS, biotherapy and advanced nursing research, among others. The influence of outside factors, such as an increase in providing treatments in the outpatient setting and the use of chemotherapeutic agents in the physician's office, will expand the oncology nursing role in the home and community.

Education

Educational preparation for a career in oncology nursing can range from attending a two-year associate degree, a three-year diploma program or a four-year bachelor of science degree program. Many oncology nurses continue their education by pursuing a master's and a doctorate degree.

The oncology content that is offered in each nursing school varies. To gain experience in oncology, students should request a clinical rotation on an oncology unit, choose oncology as an elective, and perhaps, do an independent study practicum with an oncology nurse as a preceptor.

Because of a growing recognition for the need for education beyond what is taught in programs, most oncology units provide extensive orientation programs. Once experienced, nurses will often choose to demonstrate their oncology nursing knowledge base by becoming certified. To earn the credential, Oncology Certified Nurse (OCN), the nurse must have a specific amount of experience as an oncology nurse and the candidate must pass a written examination.

Oncology Nursing Society (ONS)

As the number of these oncology specialists surged, it was obvious that a national professional organization for oncology nurses needed to be established as a resource for educational and peer support. In 1975, the Oncology Nursing Society (ONS) was established with 250 interested nurses. Now, more than 17 years later, the membership has swelled to more than 22,500 members from around the world. In the process, more than 161 chapters were formed around the country to provide similar support at the local level.

ONS realized that as membership in the organization grew, so did the interests of its oncology nurse members. Sensitive to these varying needs, ONS established Special Interest Groups (SIGs) to provide national networking in an identified subspecialty or interest area, such as hospice, bone marrow transplant, radiation, HIV/AIDS, among others. To date, there are 28 formal SIGs.

In addition to the educational and networking opportunities available through chapters and SIGs, ONS members receive a subscription to the Society's official journal, the *Oncology Nursing Forum* and to the newsletter, the *ONS News*. Members also enjoy reduced rates on publications developed by the Society.

"In a profession that is so marked by change, staying updated on the latest treatments and approaches to oncology nursing is paramount," said ONS President Carol Curtiss, RN, MSN, OCN, and Oncology Manager/Consultant for Franklin Medical Center in Greenfield, MA.

Each year, ONS hosts an Annual Congress which attracts more than 5,500 of its members. Participants learn the latest in their specialty through instructional and abstract sessions, roundtable discussions, poster presentations, and educational and commercial exhibits. To complement the Annual Congress, ONS offers a Fall Institute each year to address clinically relevant, "hot" topics at both the advanced and basic levels.

Apart from its role of disseminating the latest information, ONS uses the strength of its collective voice to respond to health and legislative issues. For example, the issue of pain management has been a recent concern for oncology nurses. In support of pain interventions, ONS has come out with a powerful position paper on cancer pain, identifying it as a major responsibility of the profession.

Other issues, such as those that surround HIV-related illnesses, cancer rehabilitation, and the care of the elderly with cancer, are also being addressed through the voice of ONS.

"ONS is here to respond to the concerns of our members. Knowing the challenges they face each day, we realize how important it is that their educational and professional needs are met," says Curtiss.

▼

PEARL MOORE, RN, MN, is the executive director of the Oncology Nursing Society and the affiliated organizations, the Oncology Nursing Foundation and the Oncology Nursing Certification Corporation. She earned both a bachelor of science in nursing degree and a master's in nursing degree from the University of Pittsburgh in 1968 and 1974, respectively. Active nationally and internationally, Moore currently serves as the chairperson of the Nursing Project Committee of the International Union Against Cancer. Formerly, Moore was the coordinator of the Brain Tumor Study Group at Montefiore Hospital in Pittsburgh.

CHAPTER TWELVE

Critical Care Nursing:
Making the Critical Difference

S. Ann Evans, Past President,
American Association of Critical-Care Nurses

Critical care nursing is the profession for the `90s. It is the most exciting and dynamic specialty in nursing and in health care today. Critical care nurses are registered nurses (RNs) who have been specially educated to work in intensive or critical care units in hospitals with the most seriously ill patients—and their families.

In critical care, there are numerous options for an exciting and satisfying job. Critical care units are hospital-based, but you can also work in emergency rooms or helicopters, with patients following surgery, transplants, head injuries, or other trauma, with premature infants or children, with patients with heart problems—and the list goes on.

Making important decisions about life and death situations is something a lot of people avoid. Such people wouldn't make good critical care nurses. Critical care nurses consciously choose to be the first line of defense in times of health crisis. As such, they're among the most valuable, respected, well-paid, and in-demand professionals in health care.

Choosing a career in critical care nursing isn't a small decision. But if you love a challenge, care about people, are equally good at math, science, and helping people work through problems, then you may be a candidate.

What Critical Care Nurses Do

When the man who just had open heart surgery suddenly goes into cardiac arrest, it's a critical care nurse who immediately responds to save his life.

When the elderly lady with pneumonia must be connected to ventilation equipment to support her life, it's a critical care nurse who helps her overcome her fear. The nurse also explains the treatment to the patient and family, and operates the sophisticated, high-tech equipment which helps the patient breathe, and monitors her condition.

When a person is dying, it's the critical care nurse who consoles the family and helps them make the difficult decisions about life support and organ donation.

Critical care nurses work with patients and their families at some of the most vulnerable times of their lives. Patients are in critical care because they require constant monitoring and around-the-clock observation and testing. Critical care nurses are the primary caregivers to these patients 24 hours a day, seven days a week, and they must be prepared to handle any emergency or crisis that may arise in a caring, compassionate fashion. They do all this by combining special talents of acute observation with the skill and ability to manipulate sophisticated technology so they can intervene on a patient's behalf at a moments notice.

Only the critical care nurse sees every "bleep" on the heart monitor.

Only the critical care nurse is close enough to notice a slight change of color in the skin, or to hear the soft call for water.

Only the critical care nurse sees the family every day, answering their difficult and fearful questions.

**Largest
Medical/Surgical
Publications**

Ranked by estimated advertising revenues
1. *JAMA*
2. *Medical Economics*
3. *New England Journal of Medicine*
4. *American Medical News*
5. *Postgraduate Medicine*
6. *Diversion*
7. *Patient Care*
8. *American Family Physician*
9. *Emergency Medicine*
10. *Hospital Practice*
Source: *Medical Marketing & Media*

A Vital Part of the Team

Critical care nurses work side by side with physicians and surgeons from a wide variety of medical specialties. They also work with other important members of the health care team such as psychologists, physical therapists, respiratory therapists, and social workers.

Because nursing is separate and distinct from medicine, the nursing diagnosis of a patient is vital and not duplicated by other members of the team. Nurses are specially educated to make their diagnosis considering the patient as a whole person, not just as a disease or illness. Consequently, the nurse will often be the person who brings together a complete analysis of the patient using information from all of the other members of the team.

Nurses are the bedside managers of all care and services a patient receives that are vital to the well-being of the patient. Having the whole view of the patient is critical at the bedside.

Always at the Bedside

Because of the serious condition of the patient in an ICU (intensive care unit), a critical care nurse is generally assigned only one or two patients to care for at a time. In most cases, two or more nurses might care for a single patient, providing constant assessments of the patient's condition and around-the-clock monitoring. In this role, critical care nurses are part high-tech wizard, part patient advocate, part loving friend, part psychologist, and part diagnostician.

The High-Tech Wizard

Operating a hospital's highly sophisticated life support and monitoring equipment is second nature to a critical care nurse, and computers are a regular part of the daily work. Some of the high-tech equipment a critical care nurse might operate include cardiac and blood gas monitors; ventilation and humidification systems; bedside monitors that allow the nurse to be in touch with one patient while at another's bedside; computers that connect departments such as the pharmacy and the laboratory; and many others. Even thermometers are electronic these days.

The critical care nurse is such an expert at operating these systems that they are often called on by the hospital to help decide which equipment to buy. Sometimes the nurse investigates the equipment by attending trade shows where manufacturers display new and improved systems.

Patient Advocate and Educator

The patient and his or her family's needs are the critical care nurse's primary concern. Because of nurses' special whole patient view, they are in a position to be patient advocates. This involves explaining patient's rights, interpreting the sometimes complex language of health care for the patient and family, and explaining what the patient can expect as a result of medication or treatments. This vital advocate role requires knowledge, patience, compassion, and skill in personal interaction. The critical care nurse is the link between the highly organized procedures of the healthcare environment and the very real human being in the hospital bed, so good communication skills are essential.

The critical care nurse is also a patient educator, helping patients understand their illness and the treatments they are receiving. It is important for people to understand what happened to them in critical care and what they need to do to return to health and how to prevent further illness or injury.

Employment Opportunities

Very few professions provide such certain employment as critical care nursing. In fact, a good critical care nurse can generally pick and choose from positions at hospitals or with nursing registries that provide hospital staffing anywhere in the country.

Critical care nurses are in great demand for several reasons. The obvious one, of course, is that people always need healthcare. But more importantly, the need for critical care is growing. It is estimated that by the year 2000, hospitals will almost exclusively admit patients who require intensive monitoring. This makes critical care nurses the key to a hospital's ability to serve the community. For some time now there has been a nursing shortage, and while the overall shortage is easing, the availability of critical care nurses can barely keep up with the growing need. One thing is certain, critical care nurses will always be needed and valued professionals.

Employee benefits for critical care nurses are generally excellent, providing for paid vacations and holidays, retirement plans, medical/dental/optical plans and more.

Salaries vary according to the individual hospital. Entry-level salaries in 1992 were $32,000 or more; salaries for experienced nurses can go beyond $60,000.

Critical care nurses with certification (see education section below) receive special bonuses or additional salary in some hospitals. A critical care specialty puts nurses in an excellent position to qualify for a variety of advanced positions.

Critical care nursing is a very flexible career. While critical care nurses are needed on a 24 hour a day, seven day a week basis, there are many creative scheduling options available so nurses can combine an active personal and work life. For example, nurses working on an advanced degree can work only on weekends, keeping their weekdays free for school. Part-time and full-time work is also available.

Educational Requirements

To become a critical care nurse, you have to be licensed as a registered nurse (RN). To become licensed, you will need a high school diploma with college preparatory programs. In some cases, a GED equivalency diploma may be accepted if the student has passed required high school courses such as chemistry and algebra. Then you will major in nursing in one of the three programs listed below:

- A bachelor of science degree in nursing (BSN) offered by four-year colleges and universities.

- An associate degree given by a two-year junior or community college.

- A diploma from a program in nursing offered by some hospitals and private schools of nursing requiring two to three years of study.

To prepare yourself for critical care nursing, concentrate on courses like biology, chemistry, math, psychology, biochemistry, and computer science. To really take advantage of the incredible opportunities in critical care nursing which will be available in the next decade, most hospitals and other nursing experts recommend that you pursue a BSN degree. This degree will give you far more options for advancement and increased salary in the years ahead.

After you complete these educational requirements, most hospitals suggest that the new nurse spend a year in general medical-surgical nursing before entering critical care. However, some hospitals have shortened the required period in order to bring much-needed critical care nurses into practice more quickly. Comprehensive orientation, however, is vital both to the nurse and patient.

Once you've entered a critical care orientation program, you'll spend from two weeks to six months in classroom and clinical instruction. This program will focus on the physical assessment of critical care patients, anatomy and physiology reviews, and interpretation of the information on critical care monitors.

But once in the critical care unit, your educational responsibilities are just starting. To remain current with the rapidly expanding field, critical care nurses receive continuing education for ongoing study. In fact, many critical care nurses, particularly those interested in advanced clinical specialties, management, research, and teaching, eventually study for master's and doctorate degrees.

Some critical care nurses receive a special mark of recognition for their knowledge by seeking CCRN certification in critical care. A CCRN certification exam is available for critical care nurses working with critically injured adults, children, or infants. This credential, which is highly valued by many hospitals, is granted by the AACN Certification Corporation after a nurse has passed a challenging examination.

Opportunities for Growth and Advancement

Critical care nurses have endless opportunities to expand their knowledge and their contribution to the profession. Some chances for career growth come at the bedside. Others are in related areas.

You might, for example, become a clinical specialist in a particular field like heart surgery. Or specialize in taking care of critically ill babies and children. Flight nurses work with mobile units that air transport accident and emergency victims. Home healthcare is also a growing area, allowing critical care nurses to use their skills caring for the patient in the home. Working with organ transplant patients is yet another specialty within critical care.

Just as the world needs critical care nurses, it also needs nurses to teach them. Nursing education is a field you can choose by either teaching in universities and/or hospital-sponsored continuing education programs.

After taking care of patients at the bedside, you may consider becoming a nurse manager or administrator. In such a position, you'll help to establish nursing procedures as well as hospital policies, and manage the day-to-day operations of critical care departments. Hospitals are complex healthcare corporations. Working as a nurse administrator offers opportunities to develop and utilize a broad range of management skills such as budgeting, planning, negotiation and day-to-day supervision.

Nursing research is another exciting option for critical care nurses with a great love of science and the necessary advanced academic degrees. Funded by special grants and scholarships, these important pioneers develop and test ways to give even better care to critically ill patients and their families.

The Worldwide Profession

You're right in thinking that critical care nursing is the most personal job possible. The caring relationship which develops between critical care nurses and their patients, many of whom cannot speak or even open their eyes, is as important to healing as any high-tech instrument or medicine. It is also very personally rewarding for the nurse.

At the same time, critical care nursing is a worldwide network. From the fast-paced world of an ICU, critical care nurses are stepping forward to affect health care nationally and internationally. The worldwide demand for critical care is making nursing research vitally important. Nurses are meeting with their peers to plan the future, taking on decision-making positions in health care organizations, speaking before Congress and other government agencies to help shape health policy, and are relied on by manufacturers to guide technological developments. Organizations like the American Association of Critical-Care Nurses give critical care nurses an opportunity to meet, learn, and plan together with other nurses at the local, national, and global level. So you see, critical care nursing can take you anywhere.

The Profession that Uses All of You

So if you're looking for a profession that uses all of you, from your most personal feelings to your most critical judgment, from your ability to master small details to your ability to make decisions under pressure, then critical care nursing may be for you. It's a profession that asks you not to be bored in tedious situations and not to panic in crises. It needs you to care without being swept away; to be a great team player and an independent thinker; to sometimes be heroic without always being thanked.

In return, critical care nursing will give you challenging, certain employment and the chance to be a key player in one of the true professions of the 21st century. It's an opportunity to make a critical difference for you and all the patients and families you will care for.

It is truly the profession with a future.

▼

S. ANN EVANS has been a critical care nurse for over twenty years. She has worked across the country (including Alaska) as a staff nurse in critical care, flight nursing, post anesthesia and coronary care; as a nursing educator in a hospital, a community college and a university; and as a nursing administrator of a coronary care unit and an emergency air transport program.

Currently, Ms. Evans is the executive director of the Heart Institute at Tallahassee Memorial, Inc. and an adjunct assistant professor at the University of Florida and Florida State University Schools of Nursing. She is also a past president of the American Association of Critical-Care Nurses, the world's largest specialty nursing organization.

Ms. Evans received her BS in nursing from Florida State University in 1971 and an MBA and MS from the University of Alaska, Anchorage, in 1981 and 1986, respectively. She has been certified as a CCRN and is currently certified a CNAA (Nursing Administrator Advanced).

CHAPTER THIRTEEN

Choosy People Choose Long-Term Care

**Florence L. Huey, Editor,
American Journal of Nursing**

The drama of 911, the life-and-death decisions made in a flash, make the adrenalin surge. But after the crisis, the care begins. All too often—as in the fire victim left burned, the accident victim left comatose, or the stroke victim left paralyzed—there is no "cure" and the care becomes long-term, lasting months or years.

Every person who struggles back from a long-term injury or illness progresses with the caring, coaching, and encouragement of specially prepared personnel working in nursing homes, rehabilitation centers, and home-care agencies.

What Is Long-Term Care?

Long-term care is the sleeper where progress is measured in weeks and months instead of hours and days. It is also the area of healthcare where human contact and spirit make the greatest difference.

Ms. Jones may not believe she can walk without falling after her hip fracture has been repaired, but you can coach and cheer her, believing in her until she becomes strong enough to believe in herself. Long-term care is not just helping people, it is helping people help themselves. In long-term care, you use everything you ever learned, and try to teach it to others so they can learn to care for themselves.

Long-term care is about choices. First is the choice of where on the career ladder you will enter—and how far you plan to climb. The variety of services a person recovering from an illness requires creates a variety of job opportunities.

Homemaker

At the most basic level in home-care is the *homemaker,* who does light housework, shopping, and some cooking. Formal education is not required for the minimum wage position. Typically, the homemaker is assigned by the home-care agency to provide a client with four to eight hours of service, one to five days a week.

In nursing facilities, positions are available in the housekeeping department, but these are not considered healthcare positions, and any interactions with the patients are outside of the job description.

Nursing Assistant

In nursing facilities and in home-care agencies that do not provide homemakers, the first step on the healthcare career ladder is the *nursing assistant* or *nurses' aide.* The person provides basic nursing care—helping patients move about, bathe, dress, and toilet—and alerts the nurse to the first sign of any health problem.

A high school diploma is not required for a nursing assistant's position, but it helps. For both home-care and nursing facilities, nursing assistants are required by federal law to complete a training program of at least 75 hours. Some states require longer training programs. Many of the larger nursing facilities and home-care agencies conduct their own training programs or pay for their nursing assistants to attend outside programs. Federal law also requires that nursing assistants pass a state examination and be listed on a registry of certified nursing assistants.

Before signing up and paying to take a nursing assistant training course, contact your state department of health to be sure the program meets the state's requirements. Also, price shop, as many private training programs may charge more than, for example, a public vocational school. Nursing assistants usually work eight- to 12-hour shifts and earn slightly more than the minimum wage.

If you decide to enter long-term care as a nursing assistant, but don't plan to stop there, ask potential employers about tuition reimbursement. Try to select a facility or agency that will pay for nursing school.

Practical Nurse

If you become a *practical nurse,* you will earn twice as much as nursing assistants do, or about $12 an hour to start. Many local vocational and high schools offer 12- to 18-month courses that enable the graduate to take the state licensing exam to become a licensed practical (LPN) or vocational nurse (LVN). As an LPN or LVN, you will work under the direction of a professional registered nurse (RN) and supervise the activities of nursing assistants.

Registered Nurse

You can enter long-term nursing care as a *registered nurse* or work your way up to it. RNs earn $15 or more an hour depending on education, experience, and position. You must have a high school diploma or equivalency to enter an RN program. You can study for an associate in arts degree in nursing at a two-year community college or a baccalaureate degree in nursing at a four-year university. From a four-year RN program, you can go on to obtain a master's or even a doctorate in nursing. At the master's level, you can become a clinical specialist in, for example, geriatric nursing, or you can specialize in nursing administration.

After you complete your RN program, you must take the state licensing exam in order to call yourself an RN. At the staff nurse level, home-care RNs generally make visits lasting no more than two hours to each client. In these visits, they give injections, care for wounds, monitor people receiving stomach tube feedings, and so forth—or teach the client and his family to do these tasks. They also supervise the care given by nursing assistants. From staff nurse, an RN in home-care can be promoted to head nurse, supervisor, and eventually, director of nursing.

In nursing facilities, staff nurses usually supervise six to eight nursing assistants who give most of the basic care. RN and LPN staff nurses give the more complex care and periodically assess patients' progress toward recovery.

In the past, LPNs could advance in nursing facilities from staff nurse to head nurse, supervisor, and eventually director of nursing. Federal law, however, now requires that a director of nursing be an RN.

You would be wise, therefore, to plan on becoming an RN if you enter long-term care with long-range career plans. Holding an RN license also is ideal preparation for entrepreneurs who would like to eventually own or operate a home-care agency or nursing home.

Working for a Home-Care Agency

If you choose to work in home-care, you will probably be employed by a home-care agency, of which there are more than 8,000 across the country. The typical home-care agency employs about 25 full-time and 50 part-time registered and practical nurses, aides, and homemakers. You'll find home health agencies advertised in the Sunday paper and also listed in the telephone book's Yellow Pages. Though most of the home-care agencies are independently owned and operated, about 25 nationwide companies operate large chains of home-care agencies.

Patient Population

About 70% of the patients served in home-care are elderly. About a third have Alzheimer's disease. In these cases, the family is as much your patient as the person afflicted with the disease, for you must help the family to understand the progress of the disease and how to cope with it. Two-thirds of the elders cared for at home have chronic physical problems—difficulty walking, dressing, bathing—or a disease, such as heart, lung, or nerve, for example, Parkinson's disease, that makes it difficult for them to move around.

The three in 10 younger patients include infants who need to be watched to prevent crib death, children with cancer receiving intravenous drugs, and young adults with AIDS.

For-Profit Home-Care Agencies

You'll earn the highest salary if you choose to work for a for-profit home-care agency, as opposed to a government or nonprofit agency. Below are the average hourly salaries for employees in for-profit home-care agencies:

Registered Nurses	*$15*
Licensed Practical Nurses	*$11*
Homemakers/Aides	*$5*
Therapists	
Occupational	*$33*
Physical/Respiratory	*$35*
Speech Pathologist	*$32*

Working for Long-Term Care Institutions

If you choose to work in a long-term care institution, you'll have about 19,000 facilities to choose from. Most have fewer than 100 patients and equally small staffs. As with home-care agencies, however, there are a few nationwide companies operating multi-state chains. Working for a large chain can offer flexibility in moving from one state to another while maintaining seniority and job security.

Nursing Homes

Nursing homes today are vastly different from the nursing homes of a few years ago, plagued with scandals and charges of staff neglect and abuse. Nursing homes are now required by federal law to have more registered and licensed nurses. Plus, aides are required to complete formal training, be registered with the state, and continue their education with courses, usually provided by the nursing home, every year. States have also set up ombudsman programs to safeguard the rights of nursing home patients and investigate any charges of misconduct. All in all, while some of the old stereotypes linger, the image of nursing homes and the staff that work there is changing for the better. Only the most capable are sought now.

Patient Population

While a few patients are young adults who are paralyzed or comatose after an accident, most are over 65 years old. Many have memory disorders, but countless others have sharp minds in fragile bodies. A warm smile buys you a piece of living history as, for example, a 90-year-old recalls events you have merely read about.

Salaries

If you thrive on working independently, you'll love the opportunities in a nursing home. Alas, nursing home salaries have not kept pace with the challenges. As in home-care agencies, the highest payers now are for-profit facilities, but even here the pay is often less than home- care agencies offer. The average hourly salaries in for-profit nursing facilities are:

Registered Nurses	*$12*
Licensed Practical Nurses	*$9*
Nurses' Aides	*$5*

If you think nursing home-care could be your spot, however, take heart. Right now the United States Congress is considering bills that would raise salaries for nursing home staff.

Whatever You Choose

Long-term care—whether in home-care agencies or nursing facilities—offers the opportunity to really make a difference in the lives of patients and families trying to cope with prolonged illness or injury. And you make that difference every day. Last, but not least, working in long-term care means you'll never look for jobs—the jobs will come looking for you.

▼

FLORENCE L. HUEY, R.N., M.A., has practiced nursing in a variety of settings, including a nursing home (which today might be called a nursing facility). Ms. Huey is editor of the *American Journal of Nursing* and was formerly the editor of *Geriatric Nursing, American Journal of Care for the Aging,* a publication that counts many home-care and nursing home personnel among its subscribers.

CHAPTER FOURTEEN

On the Road Again: Becoming a Traveling Nurse

**Bruce Male, President, CEO and Founder,
TravCorps Corporation**

For many years, registered nurses, LPNs, and nursing aides had a single work schedule—regular, eight-hour shifts in the hospital of their choice. Innovation was slow in coming to the American work force, but when clerical workers started working as "temporaries" through agencies, things started to change for everyone.

The first departure from the traditional nursing career in hospitals and nursing homes came when an enterprising RN retired from floor nursing and initiated a service that enabled her nurse friends to work some extra shifts, doing "special or private duty" nursing for specific patients in the hospital, an extra that the patient—not the hospital—paid for. Thus began, some 30 to 40 years ago, the supplemental staffing or temporary nurse industry, which has become both more complex and infinitely larger—to the tune of several billion dollars in yearly revenue involving some 2,000 or more companies.

The Traveling Nurse Concept Is Born . . .

Even with thousands of temporary agencies—from small one- or two-person entities to mega-sized corporations—using literally hundreds of thousands of nurses, by the mid-1970s, hospitals *still* needed more nurses.

In 1978, Traveling Nurse Corps, (TravCorps), which I founded, developed another alternative to "traditional nursing" employment, which we first presented to Tulane University Medical Center in New Orleans. Tulane was unhappy recruiting nurses from and losing nurses to other local hospitals. They were also not getting the supply or quality of RNs they required from local registries, so they agreed to be the "test site" for 12 brave TravCorps nurses from all over the country who accepted short-term (eight to 13 weeks) "assignments" at Tulane.

The concept was to develop a system that would enable a nurse from one part of the country to travel to and work on a short-term basis at a hospital in another location. The immediate benefits to the nurse were that all round-trip expenses were paid for, housing provided, and a job waiting. It also gave the nurse an unprecedented opportunity to live in a new community and work in a new hospital environment, *without* making any type of long-term commitment.

The hospital also benefitted by getting an experienced, well-qualified nurse whom they would never have known about otherwise (since she came from a location outside of their normal recruiting area).

Since the nurses had committed to eight or 12 weeks of working a steady schedule, the hospital also vastly improved its continuity of patient care, since the "registry" nurses normally did no more than one to three consecutive shifts at the same institution.

. . . And Grows into an Industry

A Growing Field

lthough TravCorps was the innovator of the traveling nurse concept, there are now some 60 to 80 agencies that claim to offer similar traveling nurse services. Some are one-person operations with a telephone and a small classified ad in a nursing journal, others are companies with substantial staffs of 100 with the resources, client hospitals, benefits, and desire to offer the interested nurse traveling opportunities throughout the U.S.

The traveling nurse concept turned out to be a booming success. Hospitals recognized the benefits of having traveling nurses, the least of which was the lower program cost that helped with their departmental budgets. They also realized that the quality of traveling nurses was equal to their own staff and that as a "captive audience," so to speak, traveling nurses could possibly be recruited to the permanent staff.

Since 1978, at least 3,000 or more hospitals—ranging in size from major, metropolitan teaching institutions in all 50 states to small, community hospitals have used traveling nurses in every area of nursing practice, from the ICU to the operating room, even in nursing research. These hospitals use "travelers" for maternity leaves, seasonal fluctuations in patient census, openings of new patient wings and units, and situations caused by the still-chronic nursing shortage.

There have also been literally thousands of nurses who have followed the original 12 adventurous nurses into the realm of travel nursing. The traveling nurse concept and the industry it generated have become successful enough to enable an estimated five to ten thousand nurses to take one or several eight to 13 week short-term assignments per year in locations encompassing just about every major city and small town in the country.

Nurses work on either the hospital's payroll or the agency's, receiving excellent salaries and significant travel reimbursements. In addition, housing is usually free (depending on the agency) and often in beautiful, corporate-style, one- or two-bedroom apartments. Travelers also receive a variety of other benefits designed for both recruitment and retention purposes, ranging from cash bonuses and free Club Med vacations to totally free healthcare insurance.

Is Being a Traveling Nurse for You?

Traveling to a new part of the country, living and working in new areas, having the time and freedom to explore the local countryside, culture, and sporting activities—the many "poster-like" traveling nurse ads that predominate in the nursing journals make it all sound pretty wonderful.

Are they accurate?

Can you *really* do all that and earn money *too*?

The answer is absolutely, YES! However, there *are* some caveats. (*Nothing's* perfect!) For instance, when you arrive at a new hospital, you *are* an "outsider," new to both the city and the workplace. You can view (and deal) with this reality in one of two ways, much as you can view a partial glass of water as either half-full or half-empty. If you view the glass as half-empty, the initial and numerous *unknowns* may be too intimidating, and you will not be happy. If the glass is half *full,* you should be able to look at your new environment, cultural, social, and professional surroundings in a totally objective manner and appreciate both the positive and negative aspects of each.

Get Out Your Guidebooks

As a "typical" traveler, you *will* probably spend a lot of your off-work time doing everything there is to do within a 500-mile radius of your "temporary home." Nurses on assignment in the Northwest take trips to Canada or Alaska, while those in California, Arizona, or Colorado are constantly exploring every major and minor national park in that area. And there are many. Nurses who choose an assignment in Hawaii work either in Honolulu or Maui, but typically travel to and spend time on every Hawaiian island often. (Can you blame them?) Those taking assignments in the South, Northeast, Midwest, etc. take advantage of their new homes and visit all areas of interest, whether it's Cape Cod, plantation homes, Disney World, Mardi Gras, etc.

And Get Ready to Network

There's another side to traveling—the people side. Without even trying, you will get to meet and know an incredible number of people, far more than you would had you stayed in your present job, even if you took annual vacations. And I'm not referring to just patients, although nursing in different regions of the country obviously involves treating people from every type of cultural background. You meet and get to know new nursing colleagues, other travelers, neighbors, and countless others who are also biking, hiking, touring, and enjoying the sights when and where you are.

This kind of "world class interfacing" has a rich silver lining, too: networking.

It should be obvious by now that an experienced traveler has progressed past the typical "bound" address book to the "loose leaf" style out of necessity. It means that she has a network of friends, associates, professional colleagues, and contacts that literally spans the country and beyond. The possibilities not only become proportionate to the number of people you meet and get to know, but they add to the excitement and challenge of being a traveling nurse.

Expanding Your Knowledge of Nursing

Ask any traveling nurse who has completed three or more assignments and she will undoubtedly tell you that the experience of working in a variety of nursing environments in a wide range of geographic locations with an incredible assortment of other nurses who have been educated and trained in nursing schools all over the country is, if nothing else, a very broadening and wonderful experience! You will be exposed to methodologies and techniques that, had you stayed in your "hometown hospital" or even changed employers once or twice, you *still* would probably not have experienced. You will inevitably become a more confident nursing professional, one whose broad-based skills as an experienced and successful traveler will be sought after and make you more valuable to the hiring institution.

The Drawbacks and Caveats

Is being a traveling nurse all peaches and cream, all sweetness and light? Absolutely not. This isn't a perfect world, nor is travel nursing without its pitfalls and problems. The most common one is coming to grips with the first-time traveler's expectations.

Every nurse contemplating this adventure concentrates on the travel aspect, the fun aspect, the "no-involvement-in-the-hospital-politics" aspect—not necessarily some of the realities of this job. Remember: It *is* a job, *not* a working vacation. You usually work the night or the evening shifts, weekends (on a schedule identical to the permanent staff), and have to put up with all the inconveniences and quirks of moving into a new apartment, many times with a new traveler roommate and, once again, getting used to all of the above.

Other realities are similar to those you might encounter in your current job as a nurse on the permanent staff of a hospital: a difficult head nurse, uncooperative peers, a change in procedure you weren't aware of and don't like, an inadequate number of nurses or aides, too-high patient load, or "ticky-tacky" regulations, like no sneakers or colored uniforms, etc.

Not necessarily thrilling, but definitely reality. And if all of these day-to-day attributes do not jibe with how you pictured life as a traveling nurse, then you become disappointed, disillusioned (perhaps), even angry (sometimes).

What overcomes this is patient understanding, the right attitude on your part (and that of your agency coordinator or contact person), and a desire to make your assignment a success.

How to Be a Successful Traveler

Is travel nursing for everyone?

No, not really. In order to be successful as a traveling nurse, you must have the type of personality that enables you to easily adapt to a variety of different circumstances and changes, both professionally and socially. You've got to be a relatively assertive, though not extremely aggressive, individual. You should have a strong desire to "try something new" because you either feel stagnant in your nursing career, social life, or both. You've got to be willing to be flexible in all sorts of situations, especially with your choice of hospital and geographic location since the recession has, to some degree, limited the availability of certain traveling assignments in specific areas of the country where unemployment is high. This not universal, however, and *does not* affect nurses with any type of critical care experience. And you must, absolutely *must,* have the spirit of adventure. Age is not a factor in travel nursing, nor is gender, race, or cultural heritage.

But becoming a traveling nurse is not for everyone. The nurse who insists that the method she learned at "her hospital back home" is better than the one being used at her "assignment institution" isn't going to enjoy life as a traveler. And her employer won't "enjoy" her, either.

The nursing aspects of a traveling nurse's "life on the road" aren't the only ones demanding flexibility. Getting used to a new roommate, new landlord, or new boss on the unit—or all three every 13 weeks!—may demand some serious people skills! Knowing what to do in a strange town when your car breaks down or how to be successfully assertive without being aggressive or obnoxious are just a few of the attributes that a person must bring to the table, along with his or her nursing skills.

Although travel nursing has been around for over 14 years, the number of nurses who have participated in this rewarding and unusual form of nursing employment are still relatively few in comparison to the 2.1 million "universe" of American nurses. But the number is growing rapidly, because hospitals are demanding more travelers to match their fluctuating census and lower their costs over that of registries.

Because more nurses are telling their peers about this new, positive alternative to the "traditional" way of working—staying in the same job, on the same shift, doing the same thing, day after day—you can expect that traveling nurses will become a major factor in how hospitals staff their floors, units, and departments.

▼

Before founding TravCorps, **BRUCE MALE** was the New England branch manager for a healthcare electronics and distribution firm and technical sales representative for a scientific instrumentation company. He also has been a medical technologist, a medical research assistant at Tufts New England Medical Center, and a research technician at the Veterans Administration Hospital in Boston.

Male received a master's degree in health sciences from Northeastern University and a bachelor's degree in biology and chemistry from Tufts College. He is a member of the American Hospital Association, National and Massachusetts Associations of Personnel Consultants, Small Business Association of New England, Malden Chamber of Commerce, and The Executive Committee.

Male is an avid photographer and collector of photographic art and classic cars. He also spends much of his free time cross-country skiing or fly fishing in Maine. He resides in Andover, Massachusetts, with his wife, Leslie Chapper Male, who is executive vice president and chief operating officer of TravCorps.

THE JOB
SEARCH
PROCESS

CHAPTER FIFTEEN

Getting Started: Self-Evaluation
and Career Objectives

 etting a job may be a relatively simple one-step or couple of weeks process or a complex, months-long operation.

Starting, nurturing and developing a career (or even a series of careers) is a lifelong process.

What we'll be talking about in the five chapters that together form our Job Search Process are those basic steps to take, assumptions to make, things to think about if you want a job—especially a first job in some area of healthcare. But when these steps—this process—are applied and expanded over a lifetime, most if not all of them are the same procedures, carried out over and over again, that are necessary to develop a successful, lifelong, professional career.

What does all this have to do with putting together a resume, writing a cover letter, heading off for interviews and the other "traditional" steps necessary to get a job? Whether your college graduation is just around the corner or a far distant memory, you will continuously need to focus, evaluate and re-evaluate your response to the ever-changing challenge of your future: Just what do you want to do with the rest of your life? Whether you like it or not, you're all looking for that "entry-level opportunity."

You're already one or two steps ahead of the competition—you're sure you want to pursue a career in healthcare. By heeding the advice of the many professionals who have written chapters for this *Career Directory*—and utilizing the extensive entry-level job, organization, and career resource listings we've included—you're well on your way to fulfilling that dream. But there are some key decisions and time-consuming preparations to make if you want to transform that hopeful dream into a real, live job.

The actual process of finding the right company, right career path and, most importantly, the right first job, begins long before you start mailing out resumes to potential employers. The choices and decisions you make now are not irrevocable, but this first job will have a definite impact on the career options you leave yourself. To help you make some of the right decisions and choices along the way (and avoid some of the most notable traps and pitfalls), the following chapters will lead you through a series of organized steps. If the entire job search process we are recommending here is properly executed, it will undoubtedly help you land exactly the job you want.

If you're currently in high school and hope, after college, to land a job in healthcare, then attending the right college, choosing the right major, and getting the summer work experience many agencies look for are all important steps. Read the section of this *Career Directory* that covers the particular field and/or job specialty in which you're interested—many of the contributors have recommended colleges or graduate programs they favor.

If you're hoping to jump right into any of these fields without a college degree or other professional training, our best and only advice is—don't do it. As you'll soon see in the detailed information included in the **Job Opportunities Databank,** there are not that many job openings for students without a college degree. Those that do exist are generally clerical and will only rarely lead to promising careers.

The Concept of a Job Search Process

As we've explained, a job search is not a series of random events. Rather, it is a series of connected events that together form the job search process. It is important to know the eight steps that go into that process:

1. Evaluating yourself

Know thyself. What skills and abilities can you offer a prospective employer? What do you enjoy doing? What are your strengths and weaknesses? What do you want to do?

2. Establishing your career objectives

Where do you want to be next year, three years, five years from now? What do you ultimately want to accomplish in your career and your life?

3. Creating a company target list

How to prepare a "Hit List" of potential employers—researching them, matching their needs with your skills and starting your job search assault. Preparing company information sheets and evaluating your chances.

4. Networking for success

Learning how to utilize every contact, every friend, every relative, and anyone else you can think of to break down the barriers facing any would-be healthcare professional. How to organize your home office to keep track of your communications and stay on top of your job campaign.

5. Preparing your resume

How to encapsulate years of school and little actual work experience into a professional, selling resume. Learning when and how to use it.

6. Preparing cover letters

The many ordinary and the all-too-few extraordinary cover letters, the kind that land interviews and jobs.

7. Interviewing

How to make the interview process work for you—from the first "hello" to the first day on the job.

8. Following up

Often overlooked, it's perhaps the most important part of the job search process.

We won't try to kid you—it is a lot of work. To do it right, you have to get started early, probably quite a bit earlier than you'd planned. Frankly, we recommend beginning this process one full year prior to the day you plan to start work.

So if you're in college, the end of your junior year is the right time to begin your research and preparations. That should give you enough time during summer vacation to set up your files and begin your library research.

Whether you're in college or graduate school, one item may need to be planned even earlier—allowing enough free time in your schedule of classes for interview preparations and appointments. Waiting until your senior year to "make some time" is already too late. Searching for a full-time job is itself a full-time job! Though you're naturally restricted by your schedule, it's not difficult to plan ahead and prepare for your upcoming job search. Try to leave at least a couple of free mornings or afternoons a week. A day or even two without classes is even better.

Otherwise, you'll find yourself, crazed and distracted, trying to prepare for an interview in the ten-minute period between classes. Not the best way to make a first impression and certainly not the way you want to approach an important meeting.

The Self-Evaluation Process

Learning about who you are, what you want to be, what you can be, are critical first steps in the job search process and, unfortunately, the ones most often ignored by job seekers everywhere, especially students eager to leave the ivy behind and plunge into the "real world." But avoiding this crucial self-evaluation can hinder your progress and even damage some decent prospects.

Why? Because in order to land a job with a company at which you'll actually be happy, you need to be able to identify those firms and/or job descriptions that best match your own skills, likes, and strengths. The more you know about yourself, the more you'll bring to this process and the more accurate the "match-ups." You'll be able to structure your presentation (resume, cover letter, interviews, follow up) to stress your most marketable skills and talents (and, dare we say it, conveniently avoid your weaknesses?). Later, you'll be able to evaluate potential employers and job offers on the basis of your own needs and desires. This spells the difference between waking up in the morning ready to enthusiastically tackle a new day of challenges and shutting off the alarm in the hopes the day (and your job) will just disappear.

Creating Your Self-Evaluation Form

If your self-evaluation is to have any meaning, you must first be honest with yourself. This self-evaluation form should help you achieve that goal by providing a structured environment to answer these tough questions.

Take a sheet of lined notebook paper. Set up eight columns across the top—Strengths, Weaknesses, Skills, Hobbies, Courses, Experience, Likes, Dislikes.

Now, fill in each of these columns according to these guidelines:

Strengths: Describe personality traits you consider your strengths (and try to look at them as an employer would)—e.g., persistence, organization, ambition, intelligence, logic, assertiveness, aggression, leadership, etc.

Weaknesses: The traits you consider glaring weaknesses—e.g., impatience, conceit, etc. Remember: Look at these as a potential employer would. Don't assume that the personal traits you consider weaknesses will necessarily be considered negatives in the business world. You may be "easily bored," a trait that led to lousy grades early on because teachers couldn't keep you interested in the subjects they were teaching. Well, many entrepreneurs need ever-changing challenges. Strength or weakness?

Skills: Any skill you have, whether you think it's marketable or not. Everything from basic business skills—like typing, word processing, and stenography—to computer or teaching experience and foreign language literacy. Don't forget possibly obscure but marketable skills like "good telephone voice."

Hobbies: The things you enjoy doing that, more than likely, have no overt connection to career objectives. These should be distinct from the skills listed above, and may include activities such as reading, games, travel, sports, and the like. While these may not be marketable in any general sense, they may well be useful in specific circumstances.

Courses: All the general subject areas (history, literature, etc.) and/or specific courses you've taken which may be marketable, you really enjoyed, or both.

Experience: Just the specific functions you performed at any part-time (school year) or full-time (summer) jobs. Entries may include "General Office" (typing, filing, answering phones, etc.), "Basic Nursing Care," etc.

Likes: List all your "likes," those important considerations that you haven't listed anywhere else yet. These might include the types of people you like to be with, the kind of environment you prefer (city, country, large places, small places, quiet, loud, fast-paced, slow-paced) and anything else which hasn't shown up somewhere on this form. Try to think of "likes" that you have that are related to the job you are applying for. For example, if you're applying for a job at a major corporation, mention that you enjoy reading the Wall St. Journal. However, try not to include entries which refer to specific jobs or companies. We'll list those on another form.

Dislikes: All the people, places and things you can easily live without.

Now assess the "marketability" of each item you've listed. (In other words, are some of your likes, skills or courses easier to match to a marketing job description, or do they have little to do with a specific job or company?) Mark highly marketable skills with an "H." Use "M" to characterize those skills which may be marketable in a particular set of circumstances, "L" for those with minimal potential application to any job.

Referring back to the same list, decide if you'd enjoy using your marketable skills or talents as part of your everyday job—"Y" for yes, "N" for no. You may type 80 words a minute but truly despise typing or worry that stressing it too much will land you on the permanent clerical staff. If so, mark typing with an "N." (Keep one thing in mind— just because you dislike typing shouldn't mean you absolutely won't accept a job that requires it. Almost every professional job today requires computer-based work that makes typing a plus.)

Now, go over the entire form carefully and look for inconsistencies.

To help you with your own form, we've included a sample one on the following page.

The Value of a Second Opinion

There is a familiar misconception about the self-evaluation process that gets in the way of many new job applicants—the belief that it is a process which must be accomplished in isolation. Nothing could be further from the truth. Just because the family doctor tells you you need an operation doesn't mean you run right off to the hospital. Prudence dictates that you check out the opinion with another physician. Getting such a "second opinion"—someone else's, not just your own—is a valuable practice throughout the job search process, as well.

So after you've completed the various exercises in this chapter, review them with a friend, relative, or parent—just be sure it's someone who knows you well and cares about you. These second opinions may reveal some aspects of your self-description on which you and the rest of the world differ. If so, discuss them, learn from them and, if necessary, change some conclusions. Should everyone concur with your self-evaluation, you will be reassured that your choices are on target.

Establishing Your Career Objective(s)

For better or worse, you now know something more of who and what you are. But we've yet to establish and evaluate another important area—your overall needs, desires, and goals. Where are you going? What do you want to accomplish?

If you're getting ready to graduate from college or graduate school, the next five years are the most critical period of your whole career. You need to make the initial transition from college to the workplace, establish yourself in a new and completely unfamiliar company environment, and begin to build the professional credentials necessary to achieve your career goals.

If that strikes you as a pretty tall order, well, it is. Unless you've narrowly prepared yourself for a specific profession, you're probably most ill-prepared for any

	Strength	Weakness	Skill	Hobby	Course	Experience	Like	Dislike
Marketable?								
Enjoy?								
Marketable?								
Enjoy?								
Marketable?								
Enjoy?								

real job. Instead, you've (hopefully) learned some basic principles—research and analytical skills that are necessary for success at almost any level—and, more or less, how to think.

It's tough to face, but face it you must: No matter what your college, major, or degree, all you represent right now is potential. How you package that potential and what you eventually make of it is completely up to you. It's an unfortunate fact that many companies will take a professional with barely a year or two experience over any newcomer, no matter how promising. Smaller firms, especially, can rarely afford to hire someone who can't begin contributing immediately.

So you have to be prepared to take your comparatively modest skills and experience and package them in a way that will get you interviewed and hired. Quite a challenge.

There are a number of different ways to approach such a task. If you find yourself confused or unable to list such goals, you might want to check a few books in your local library that have more time to spend on the topic of "goal-oriented planning."

But Is Healthcare Right for You?

Presuming you now have a much better idea of yourself and where you'd like to be, let's make sure some of your basic assumptions are right. We presume you purchased this *Career Directory* because you're considering a career in some area of healthcare. Are you sure? Do you know enough about the industry as a whole and the particular part you're heading for to decide whether it's right for you? Probably not. So start your research now—learn as much about your potential career field as you now know about yourself.

Start with the essays in the Advice from the Pro's section—these will give you an excellent overview of healthcare, some very specialized (and growing) areas, and some things to keep in mind as you start on your career search. They will also give you a relatively simplified, though very necessary, understanding of just what people who work in all these areas of healthcare actually do.

Other sources you should consider consulting to learn more about this business are listed in the Career Resources section of this book.

In that section, we've listed trade associations and publications associated with healthcare, together with many other resources that will help your job search. (Consult the "How to Locate Career Resources" section in the front of this directory for a complete description of the Career Resource section.) Where possible in the association entries, we've included details on educational information they make available, but you should certainly consider writing each of the pertinent associations, letting them know you're interested in a career in their area of specialization and would appreciate whatever help and advice they're willing to impart. You'll find many sponsor seminars and conferences throughout the country, some of which you may be able to attend.

The trade publications are dedicated to the highly specific interests of healthcare professionals. These magazines are generally not available at newsstands, but you may be able to obtain back issues at your local library (most major libraries have extensive collections of such journals) or by writing to the magazines' circulation/subscription departments. We've also included regional and local magazines.

You may also try writing to the publishers and/or editors of these publications. State in your cover letter what area of healthcare you're considering and ask them for whatever help and advice they can offer. But be specific. These are busy professionals and they do not have the time or the inclination to simply "tell me everything you can about working as a registered nurse."

If you can afford it now, we strongly suggest subscribing to whichever trade magazines are applicable to the specialty you're considering. If you can't subscribe to all of them, make it a point to regularly read the copies that arrive at your local public or college library.

These publications may well provide the most imaginative and far-reaching information for your job search. Even a quick perusal of an issue or two will give you an excellent "feel" for the industry. After reading only a few articles, you'll already get a handle on what's happening in the field and some of the industry's peculiar and particular jargon. Later, more detailed study will aid you in your search for a specific job.

Authors of the articles themselves may well turn out to be important resources. If an article is directly related to your chosen specialty, why not call the author and ask some questions? You'd be amazed how willing many of these professionals will be to talk to you and answer your questions, and the worst they can do is say no. (But *do* use common sense—authors will not *always* respond graciously to your invitation to "chat about the business." And don't be *too* aggressive here.)

You'll find such research to be a double-edged sword. In addition to helping you get a handle on whether the area you've chosen is really right for you, you'll slowly learn enough about particular specialties, companies, the industry, etc., to actually sound like you know what you're talking about when you hit the pavement looking for your first job. And nothing is better than sounding like a pro—except being one.

Healthcare Is It. Now What?

After all this research, we're going to assume you've reached that final decision—you really do want a career in some aspect of healthcare. It is with this vague certainty that all too many of you will race off, hunting for any company or hospital willing to give you a job.

It is simply not enough to narrow your job search to a specific industry. And so far, that's all you've done. You must now establish a specific career objective—the job you want to start, the career you want to pursue. Just knowing that you "want to get into healthcare" doesn't mean anything to anybody. If that's all you can tell an interviewer, it demonstrates a lack of research into the industry itself and your failure to think ahead.

Interviewers will *not* welcome you with open arms if you're still vague about your career goals. If you've managed to get an "informational interview" with an executive whose hospital currently has no job openings, what is he or she supposed to do with your resume after you leave? Who should he or she send it to for future consideration? Since *you* don't seem to know exactly what you want to do, how's he or she going to figure it out? Worse, that person will probably resent your asking him or her to function as your personal career counselor.

Remember, the more specific your career objective, the better your chances of finding a job. It's that simple and that important. Naturally, before you declare your objective to the world, check once again to make sure your specific job target matches the skills and interests you defined in your self-evaluation. Eventually, you may want to state such an objective on your resume, and "To obtain an entry-level position as a nursing assistant at a large hospital," is quite a bit better than "I want a career in healthcare." Do not consider this step final until you can summarize your job/career objective in a single, short, accurate sentence.

CHAPTER SIXTEEN

Targeting Prospective Employers and Networking for Success

As you move along the job search path, one fact will quickly become crystal clear—it is primarily a process of **elimination**: your task is to consider and research as many options as possible, then—for good reasons—**eliminate** as many as possible, attempting to continually narrow your focus.

Your Ideal Company Profile

Let's establish some criteria to evaluate potential employers. This will enable you to identify your target companies, the places you'd really like to work. (This process, as we've pointed out, is not specific to any industry or field; the same steps, with perhaps some research resource variations, are applicable to any job, any company, any industry.)

Take a sheet of blank paper and divide it into three vertical columns. Title it "Target Company—Ideal Profile." Call the left-hand column "Musts," the middle column "Preferences," and the right-hand column "Nevers."

We've listed a series of questions below. After considering each question, decide whether a particular criteria *must* be met, whether you would simply *prefer* it or *never* would consider it at all. If there are other criteria you consider important, feel free to add them to the list below and mark them accordingly on your Profile.

1. What are your geographical preferences? (Possible answers: U.S., Canada, International, Anywhere). If you only want to work in the U.S., then "Work in United States" would be the entry in the "Must" column. "Work in Canada or Foreign Country" might be the first entry in your "Never" column. There would be no applicable entry for this question in the "Preference" column. If, however, you will consider working in two of the three, then your "Must" column entry might read "Work in U.S. or

Canada," your "Preference" entry—if you preferred one over the other—could read "Work in U.S.," and the "Never" column, "Work Overseas."

2. If you prefer to work in the U.S. or Canada, what area, state(s) or province(s)? If overseas, what area or countries?

3. Do you prefer a large city, small city, town, or somewhere as far away from civilization as possible?

4. In regard to question three, any specific preferences?

5. Do you prefer a warm or cold climate?

6. Do you prefer a large or small company? Define your terms (by sales, income, employees, offices, etc.).

7. Do you mind relocating right now? Do you want to work for a firm with a reputation for *frequently* relocating top people?

8. Do you mind travelling frequently? What percent do you consider reasonable? (Make sure this matches the normal requirements of the job specialization you're considering.)

9. What salary would you *like* to receive (put in the "Preference" column)? What's the *lowest* salary you'll accept (in the "Must" column)?

10. Are there any benefits (such as an expense account, medical and/or dental insurance, company car, etc.) you must or would like to have?

11. Are you planning to attend graduate school at some point in the future and, if so, is a tuition reimbursement plan important to you?

12. Do you feel that a formal training program is necessary?

It's important to keep revising this new form, just as you should continue to update your Self-Evaluation Form. After all, it contains the criteria by which you will judge every potential employer. Armed with a complete list of such criteria, you're now ready to find all the companies that match them.

Targeting Individual Companies

To begin creating your initial list of targeted companies, start with the **Job Opportunities Databank** in this directory. We've listed many major hospitals and healthcare service companies, most of which were contacted by telephone for this edition. These listings provide a plethora of data concerning the companies' overall operations, hiring practices, and other important information on entry-level job opportunities. This latter information includes key contacts (names), the average number of entry-level people they hire each year, along with complete job descriptions and requirements.

One word of advice. You'll notice that some of the companies list "0" under average entry-level hiring. This is more a reflection of the current economic times than a long-range projection. In past editions of this book, these companies did list an average number of new hires, and they will again in the future. We have listed these companies for three reasons: 1) to present you with the overall view of prospective employers; 2) because even companies that don't plan to do any hiring will experience unexpected job openings; and 3) things change, so as soon as the economy begins to pick up, expect entry-level hiring to increase again.

We have attempted to include information on those major firms that represent most of the entry-level jobs out there. But there are, of course, many other companies of all sizes and shapes that you may also wish to research. In the Career Resources section, we have listed other reference tools you can use to obtain more information on the companies we've listed, as well as those we haven't.

The Other Side of the Iceberg

You are now better prepared to choose those companies that meet your own list of criteria. But a word of caution about these now- "obvious" requirements—they are not the only ones you need to take into consideration. And you probably won't be able to find all or many of the answers to this second set of questions in any reference book—they are known, however, by those persons already at work in the industry. Here is the list you will want to follow:

Promotion

If you are aggressive about your career plans, you'll want to know if you have a shot at the top. Look for companies that traditionally promote from within.

Training

Look for companies in which your early tenure will actually be a period of on-the-job training, hopefully ones in which training remains part of the long-term process. As new techniques and technologies enter the workplace, you must make sure you are updated on these skills. Most importantly, look for training that is craft- or function-oriented—these are the so-called **transferable skills**, ones you can easily bring along with you from job-to- job, company-to-company, sometimes industry-to-industry.

▼

Ask the Person Who Owns One

Some years ago, this advice was used as the theme for a highly successful automobile advertising campaign. The prospective car buyer was encouraged to find out about the product by asking the (supposedly) most trustworthy judge of all—someone who was already an owner.

You can use the same approach in your job search. You all have relatives or friends already out in the workplace—these are your best sources of information about those industries. Cast your net in as wide a circle as possible. Contact these valuable resources. You'll be amazed at how readily they will answer your questions. I suggest you check the criteria list at the beginning of this chapter to formulate your own list of pertinent questions. Ideally and minimally you will want to learn: how the industry is doing, what its long-term prospects are, the kinds of personalities they favor (aggressive, low key), rate of employee turnover, and the availability of training.

Salary

Some industries are generally high paying, some not. But even an industry with a tradition of paying abnormally low salaries may have particular companies or job functions (like sales) within companies that command high remuneration. But it's important you know what the industry standard is.

Benefits

Look for companies in which health insurance, vacation pay, retirement plans, 401K accounts, stock purchase opportunities, and other important employee benefits are extensive—and company paid. If you have to pay for basic benefits like medical coverage yourself, you'll be surprised at how expensive they are. An exceptional benefit package may even lead you to accept a lower-than-usual salary.

Unions

Make sure you know about the union situation in each industry you research. Periodic, union-mandated salary increases are one benefit nonunion workers may find hard to match.

Making Friends and Influencing People

Networking is a term you have probably heard; it is definitely a key aspect of any successful job search and a process you must master.

Informational interviews and **job interviews** are the two primary outgrowths of successful networking.

Referrals, an aspect of the networking process, entail using someone else's name, credentials and recommendation to set up a receptive environment when seeking a job interview.

All of these terms have one thing in common: Each depends on the actions of other people to put them in motion. Don't let this idea of "dependency" slow you down, however. A job search *must* be a very pro-active process—*you* have to initiate the action. When networking, this means contacting as many people as you can. The more you contact, the better the chances of getting one of those people you are "depending" on to take action and help you out.

So what *is* networking? How do you build your own network? And why do you need one in the first place? The balance of this chapter answers all of those questions and more.

Get your telephone ready. It's time to make some friends.

Not the World's Oldest Profession, But...

Networking is the process of creating your own group of relatives, friends, and acquaintances who can feed you the information you need to find a job—identifying where the jobs are and giving you the personal introductions and background data necessary to pursue them.

If the job market were so well-organized that details on all employment opportunities were immediately available to all applicants, there would be no need for such a process. Rest assured the job market is *not* such a smooth-running machine— most applicants are left very much to their own devices. Build and use your own network wisely and you'll be amazed at the amount of useful job intelligence you will turn up.

While the term networking didn't gain prominence until the 1970s, it is by no means a new phenomenon. A selection process that connects people of similar skills, backgrounds, and/or attitudes—in other words, networking—has been in existence in a variety of forms for centuries. Attend any Ivy League school and you're automatically part of its very special centuries-old network.

And it works. Remember your own reaction when you were asked to recommend someone for a job, club or school office? You certainly didn't want to look foolish, so you gave it some thought and tried to recommend the best-qualified person that you thought would "fit in" with the rest of the group. It's a built-in screening process.

Creating the Ideal Network

As in most endeavors, there's a wrong way and a right way to network. The following tips will help you construct your own wide-ranging, information-gathering, interview- generating group—*your* network.

Diversify

Unlike the Harvard or Princeton network—confined to former graduates of each school—your network should be as diversified and wide-ranging as possible. You never know who might be in a position to help, so don't limit your group of friends. The more diverse they are, the greater the variety of information they may supply you with.

Don't Forget...

...to include everyone you know in your initial networking list: friends, relatives, social acquaintances, classmates, college alumni, professors, teachers, your dentist, doctor, family lawyer, insurance agent, banker, travel agent, elected officials in your community, ministers, fellow church members, local tradesmen, and local business or social club officers. And everybody they know!

Be Specific

Make a list of the kinds of assistance you will require from those in your network, then make specific requests of each. Do they know of jobs at their company? Can they introduce you to the proper executives? Have they heard something about or know someone at the company you're planning to interview with next week?

The more organized you are, the easier it will be to target the information you need and figure out who might have it. Begin to keep a business card file or case so you can keep track of all your contacts. A small plastic case for file cards that is available at any discount store will do nicely. One system you can use is to staple the card to a 3 x 5 index card. On the card, write down any information about that contact that you might need later—when you talked to them, job leads they provided, specific job search advice, etc. You will then have all the information you need about each company or contact in one easily accessible location.

Learn the Difference...

...between an **informational** interview and a **job** interview. The former requires you to cast yourself in the role of information gatherer; *you* are the interviewer and knowledge is your goal—about an industry, company, job function, key executive, etc. Such a meeting with someone already doing what you soon hope to be doing is by far the best way to find out everything you need to know—before you walk through the door and sit down for a formal job interview, at which time your purpose is more sharply defined: to get the job you're interviewing for.

If you learn of a specific job opening during an informational interview, you are in a position to find out details about the job, identify the interviewer and, possibly, even learn some things about him or her. In addition, presuming you get your contact's permission, you may be able to use his or her name as a referral. Calling up the interviewer and saying, "Joan Smith in your human resources department suggested I contact you regarding openings for nursing assistants," is far superior to "Hello. Do you have any job openings in your hospital?"

(In such a case, be careful about referring to a specific job opening, even if your contact told you about it. It may not be something you're supposed to know about. By presenting your query as an open-ended question, you give your prospective employer the option of exploring your background without further commitment. If there is a job there and you're qualified for it, you'll find out soon enough.)

Don't Waste a Contact

Not everyone you call on your highly-diversified networking list will know about a job opening. It would be surprising if each one did. But what about *their* friends and colleagues? It's amazing how everyone knows someone who knows someone. Ask—you'll find that someone.

Value Your Contacts

If someone has provided you with helpful information or an introduction to a friend or colleague, keep him or her informed about how it all turns out. A referral that's panned out should be reported to the person who opened the door for you in the first place. Such courtesy will be appreciated—and may lead to more contacts. If someone has nothing to offer today, a call back in the future is still appropriate and may pay off.

The lesson is clear: Keep your options open, your contact list alive. Detailed records of your network—whom you spoke with, when, what transpired, etc.—will help you keep track of your overall progress and organize what can be a complicated and involved process.

Informational Interviews

So now you've done your homework, built your network, and begun using your contacts. It's time to go on your first informational interview.

A Typical Interview

You were, of course, smart enough to include John Fredericks, the bank officer who handled your dad's mortgage, on your original contact list. He knew you as a bright and conscientious college senior; in fact, your perfect three-year repayment record on the loan you took out to buy that '67 Plymouth impressed him. When you called him, he was happy to refer you to his friend, Jane Jones, a top healthcare administrator at Metropolitan Hospital. Armed with permission to use Fredericks' name and recommendation, you wrote a letter to Jane Jones, the gist of which went something like this:

> *I am writing at the suggestion of Mr. John Fredericks at Fidelity National Bank. He knows of my interest in healthcare and, given your position at Metropolitan, thought you might be able to help me gain a better understanding of this specialized field and the career opportunities it presents.*
>
> *While I am working towards a degree in nursing, I know I need to speak with professionals such as yourself to learn how to apply my studies to a work environment.*
>
> *If you could spare a half hour to meet with me, I'm certain I would be able to get enough information about this specialty to give me the direction I need.*
>
> *I'll call your office next week in the hope that we can schedule a meeting.*

Send a copy of this letter to Mr. Fredericks at the bank—it will refresh his memory should Ms. Jones call to inquire about you. Next step: the follow-up phone call. After you get Ms. Jones' secretary on the line, it will, with luck, go something like this:

> *"Hello, I'm Pauline Smith. I'm calling in reference to a letter I wrote to Ms. Jones requesting an appointment."*
>
> *"Oh, yes. You're the young woman interested in nursing. Ms. Jones can see you on June 23rd. Will 10 A.M. be satisfactory?"*
>
> *"That's fine. I'll be there."*

Well, the appointed day arrives. Well-scrubbed and dressed in your best (and most conservative) suit, you are ushered into Ms. Jones' office. She offers you coffee (you decline) and says that it is okay to light up if you wish to smoke (you decline). The conversation might go something like this:

You: "Thank you for seeing me, Ms. Jones. I know you are busy and appreciate your taking the time to talk with me."

Jones: "Well it's my pleasure since you come so highly recommended. I'm always pleased to meet someone interested in my field."

You: "As I stated in my letter, my interest in nursing is very real, but I'm having trouble seeing how all of my studies will adapt to the work environment. I think I'll be much better prepared to evaluate future job offers if I can learn more about your experiences in healthcare. May I ask you a few questions about working at Metropolitan Hospital?"

Jones: "Fire away, Pauline".

Ms. Jones relaxes. She realizes this is a knowledge hunt you are on, not a thinly-veiled job interview. Your approach has kept her off the spot—she doesn't have to be concerned with making a hiring decision. You've already gotten high marks for not putting her on the defensive.

You: "I have a few specific questions I'd like to ask. First, at a hospital such as yours, where does an entry-level person start?"

Jones: "In this hospital, we rotate new people through all the areas we work in— intensive care, obstetrics, etc. You'd spend about two months in each area, then specialize in the one you're most interested in or the area where we need you most."

You: "Where and how fast does someone progress after that?"

Jones: "Obviously, that depends on the person, but given the proper aptitude and ability, that person would simply get more responsibility to handle. How well you do all along the way will determine how far and how fast you progress."

You: "What is the work environment like—is it pretty hectic?"

Jones: "We try to keep the work load at an even keel. The comfort of our workers is of prime importance to us. Excessive turnover is costly, you know. But healthcare is an exciting career, and things change sometimes minute-to-minute. It's not a profession for the faint-hearted!"

You: "If I may shift to another area, I'd be interested in your opinion about healthcare in general and what you see as the most likely areas of opportunity in the foreseeable future. Do you think this is a growth career area, despite the many changes that have occurred in the last 18 months?"

Jones: "Well, judging by the hiring record of our hospital, I think you'll find it's an area worth making a commitment to. At the entry level, we've hired a number of new people in the past three or four years. There always seems to be opportunities, though it's gotten far more competitive."

You: "Do you think someone with my qualifications and background could get started in nursing at a major hospital? Perhaps a look at my resume would be helpful to you." *(Give it to Ms. Jones.)*

Jones: "Your course work looks appropriate. I especially like the volunteer work you've done at your local hospital. I think you have a real chance to break into this field. I don't think we're hiring right now, but I know a couple of hospitals that are looking for bright young people with qualifications like yours. Let me give you a couple of phone numbers." *(Write down names and phone numbers.)*

You: "You have been very generous with your time, but I can see from those flashing buttons on your phone that you have other things to do. Thank you again for taking the time to talk with me."

Jones: "You're welcome."

After the Interview

The next step should be obvious: **Two** thank-you letters are required, one to Ms. Jones, the second to Mr. Fredericks. Get them both out immediately. (And see the chapter on writing letters if you need help writing them.)

Keeping Track of the Interview Trail

Let's talk about record keeping again. If your networking works the way it's supposed to, this was only the first of many such interviews. Experts have estimated that the average person could develop a contact list of 250 people. Even if we limit your initial list to only 100, if each of them gave you one referral, your list would suddenly have 200 names. Presuming that it will not be necessary or helpful to see all of them, it's certainly possible that such a list could lead to 100 informational and/or job interviews! Unless you keep accurate records, by the time you're on No. 50, you won't even remember the first dozen!

So get the results of each interview down on paper. Use whatever format with which you're comfortable. You should create some kind of file, folder, or note card that is an "Interview Recap Record." If you have access to a personal computer, take advantage of it. It will be much easier to keep you information stored in one place and well-organized. Your record should be set up and contain something like the following:

Name: Metropolitan Hospital

Address: 333 44th St., NY, NY 10000

Phone: (212) 555-4000

Contact: Jane L. Jones

Type of Business: Healthcare

Referral Contact: Mr. Fredericks, Fidelity National Bank

Date: January 30, 1993

At this point, you should add a one- or two-paragraph summary of what you found out at the meeting. Since these comments are for your eyes only, you should be both objective and subjective. State the facts—what you found out in response to your specific questions—but include your impressions—your estimate of the opportunities for further discussions, your chances for future consideration for employment.

"I Was Just Calling To..."

Find any logical opportunity to stay in touch with Ms. Jones. You may, for example, let her know when you graduate and tell her your grade point average, carbon her in on any letters you write to Mr. Fredericks, even send a congratulatory note if you read something in the local paper about her department. This type of follow up has the all-important effect of keeping you and your name in the forefront of others' minds. Out of sight *is* out of mind. No matter how talented you may be or how good an impression you made, you'll have to work hard to "stay visible."

There Are Rules, Just Like Any Game

It should already be obvious that the networking process is not only effective, but also quite deliberate in its objectives. There are two specific groups of people you must attempt to target: those who can give you information about an industry or career area and those who are potential employers. The line between these groups may often blur. Don't be concerned—you'll soon learn when (and how) to shift the focus from interviewer to interviewee.

To simplify this process, follow a single rule: Show interest in the field or job area under discussion, but wait to be asked about actually working for that company. During your informational interviews, you will be surprised at the number of times the person you're interviewing turns to you and asks, "Would you be interested in...?" Consider carefully what's being asked and, if you *would* be interested in the position under discussion, make your feelings known.

Why Should You Network?

- To unearth current information about the industry, company and pertinent job functions. Remember: Your knowledge and understanding of broad industry trends, financial health, hiring opportunities, and the competitive picture are key.
- To investigate each company's hiring policies—who makes the decisions, who the key players are (personnel, staff managers), whether there's a hiring season, whether they prefer applicants going direct or through recruiters, etc.
- To sell yourself—discuss your interests and research activities—and leave your calling card, your resume.
- To seek out advice on refining your job search process.
- To obtain the names of other persons (referrals) who can give you additional information on where the jobs are and what the market conditions are like.
- To develop a list of follow-up activities that will keep you visible to key contacts.

If the Process Scares You

Some of you will undoubtedly be hesitant about, even fear, the networking process. It is not an unusual response—it is very human to want to accomplish things "on your own," without anyone's help. Understandable and commendable as such independence might seem, it is, in reality, an impediment if it limits your involvement in this important process. Networking has such universal application because **there is no other effective way to bridge the gap between job applicant and job.** Employers are grateful for its existence. You should be, too.

Whether you are a first-time applicant or reentering the work force now that the children are grown, the networking process will more than likely be your point of entry. Sending out mass mailings of your resume and answering the help-wanted ads may well be less personal (and, therefore, "easier") approaches, but they will also be far less effective. The natural selection process of the networking phenomenon is your assurance that water does indeed seek its own level—you will be matched up with companies and job opportunities in which there is a mutual fit.

Six Good Reasons to Network

Many people fear the networking process because they think they are "bothering" others with their own selfish demands. Nonsense! There are good reasons—six of them, at least—why the people on your networking list will be happy to help you:

1. **Some day you will get to return the favor.** An ace insurance salesman built a successful business by offering low-cost coverage to first-year medical students. Ten years later, these now-successful practitioners remembered the company (and person) that helped them when they were just getting started. He gets new referrals every day.

2. **They, too, are seeking information.** An employer who has been out of school for several years might be interested in what the latest developments in the classroom are. He or she may be hoping to learn as much from you as you are from them, so be forthcoming in offering information. This desire for new information may be the reason he or she agreed to see you in the first place.

3. **Internal politics.** Some people will see you simply to make themselves appear powerful, implying to others in their organization that they have the authority to hire (they may or may not), an envied prerogative.

4. **They're "saving for a rainy day".** Executives know that it never hurts to look and that maintaining a backlog of qualified candidates is a big asset when the floodgates open and supervisors are forced to hire quickly.

5. **They're just plain nice.** Some people will see you simply because they feel it's the decent thing to do or because they just can't say "no."

6. **They are looking themselves.** Some people will see you because they are anxious to do a friend (whoever referred you) a favor. Or because they have another friend seeking new talent, in which case you represent a referral they can make (part of their own continuing network process). You see, networking never does stop—it helps them and it helps you.

Before you proceed to the next chapter, begin making your contact list. You may wish to keep a separate sheet of paper or note card on each person (especially the dozen or so you think are most important), even a separate telephone list to make your communications easier and more efficient. However you set up your list, be sure to keep it up to date—it won't be long before you'll be calling each and every name on the list.

CHAPTER SEVENTEEN

Preparing Your Resume

Your resume is a one-page summary of you—your education, skills, employment experience and career objective(s). It is not a biography, but a "quick and dirty" way to identify and describe you to potential employers. Most importantly, its real purpose is to sell you to the company you want to work for. It must set you apart from all the other applicants (those competitors) out there.

So, as you sit down to formulate your resume, remember you're trying to present the pertinent information in a format and manner that will convince an executive to grant you an interview, the prelude to any job offer. All resumes must follow two basic rules—excellent visual presentation and honesty—but it's important to realize that different career markets require different resumes. The resume you are compiling for your career in healthcare is different than one you would prepare for a finance career. As more and more resume " training" services become available, employers are becoming increasingly choosy about the resumes they receive. They expect to view a professional presentation, one that sets a candidate apart from the crowd. Your resume has to be perfect and it has to be specialized—clearly demonstrating the relationship between your qualifications and the job you are applying for.

An Overview of Resume Preparation

- **Know what you're doing**—your resume is a personal billboard of accomplishments. It must communicate your worth to a prospective employer in specific terms.

- **Your language should be action-oriented,** full of "doing"-type words. And less is better than more—be concise and direct. Don't worry about using complete sentences.

- **Be persuasive.** In those sections that allow you the freedom to do so, don't hesitate to communicate your worth in the strongest language. This does not mean a numbing list of self-congratulatory superlatives; it does mean truthful claims about your abilities and the evidence (educational, experiential) that supports them.

- **Don't be cheap or gaudy.** Don't hesitate to spend the few extra dollars necessary to present a professional-looking resume. Do avoid outlandish (and generally ineffective) gimmicks like oversized or brightly-colored paper.

- **Find an editor.** Every good writer needs one, and you are writing your resume. At the very least, it will offer you a second set of eyes proofreading for embarrassing typos. But if you are fortunate enough to have a professional in the field—a recruiter or personnel executive—critique a draft, grab the opportunity and be immensely grateful.

- **If you're the next Michelangelo,** so multitalented that you can easily qualify for jobs in different career areas, don't hesitate to prepare two or more completely different resumes. This will enable you to change the emphasis on your education and skills according to the specific career objective on each resume, a necessary alteration that will correctly target each one.

- **Choose the proper format.** There are only three we recommend—chronological, functional, and targeted format—and it's important you use the one that's right for you.

Considerations in the Electronic Age

Like most other areas of everyday life, computers have left their mark in the resume business. There are the obvious changes—the increased number of personal computers has made it easier to produce a professional-looking resume at home—and the not so obvious changes, such as the development of resume databases.

There are two kinds of resume databases: 1) An internal file maintained by a large corporation to keep track of the flood of resumes it gets each day (U.S. News and World Report stated that Fortune 50 companies receive more than 1,000 unsolicited resumes a day and that four out of every five are thrown away after a quick review). 2) Commercial databases that solicit resumes from job-seekers around the United States and make them available to corporations, who pay a fee to search the database.

Internal Databases Mean the Old Rules Don't Apply

The internal databases maintained by large companies are changing some of the time-honored traditions of resume preparation. In the past, it was acceptable, even desirable, to use italic type and other eye-catching formats to make a resume more visually appealing. Not so today. Most of the companies that have a database enter resumes into it by using an optical scanner that reads the resume character by character and automatically enters it into the database. While these scanners are becoming more and more sophisticated, there are still significant limits as to what they can recognize and interpret.

What does this mean to you? It means that in addition to the normal screening process that all resumes go through, there is now one more screening step that determines if the scanner will be able to read your resume. If it can't, chances are your resume is going to be one of the four that is thrown away, instead of the one that is kept. To enhance the chances of your resume making it past this scanner test, here are some simple guidelines you can follow:

- Use larger typefaces (nothing smaller than 12 point), and avoid all but the most basic typefaces. Among the most common are Times Roman and Universal.

- No italics or underlining, and definitely no graphic images or boxes.

- Do not send copies. Either print a fresh copy out on your own printer, or take the resume to a print shop and have it professionally copied onto high-quality paper. Avoid dot-matrix printers.

- Use 8 1/2 x 11 paper, unfolded. Any words that end up in a crease will not be scannable.

- Use only white or beige paper. Any other color will lessen the contrast between the paper and the letters and make it harder for the scanner to read.

- Use only a single column format. Scanners read from right to left on a page, so two- or three-column formats lead to nonsensical information when the document is scanned.

- While it is still appropriate to use action words to detail your accomplishments (initiated, planned, implemented, etc.), it is also important to include precise technical terms whenever possible as well. That's because databases are searched by key words, and only resumes that match those key words will be looked at. For example, if a publishing company was seeking someone who was experienced in desktop publishing, they might search the database for all occurrences of "PageMaker" or "Ventura," two common desktop publishing software packages. If your resume only said "Successfully implemented and oversaw in-house desktop publishing program," it would be overlooked, and you wouldn't get the job!

National Databases: Spreading Your Good Name Around

Commercial resume databases are also having an impact on the job search process in the 1990s, so much so that anyone about to enter the job market should seriously consider utilizing one of these services.

Most of these new services work this way: Job-seekers send the database company a copy of their resume, or they fill out a lengthy application provided by the company. The information is then loaded into the company's mainframe computer, along with hundreds of other resumes from other job-seekers. The cost of this listing is usually nominal—$20 to $50 for a six- to 12-month listing. Some colleges operate systems for their graduates that are free of charge, so check with your placement office before utilizing a commercial service.

Once in the system, the resumes are available for viewing by corporate clients who have openings to fill. This is where the database companies really make their money—depending on the skill-level of the listees and the professions covered, companies can pay thousands of dollars for annual subscriptions to the service or for custom searches of the database.

Worried that your current employer might just pull up *your* resume when it goes searching for new employees? No need to be—most services allow listees to designate companies that their resume should not be released to, thus allowing you to conduct a job search with the peace of mind that your boss won't find out!

One warning about these services—most of them are new, so do as much research as you can before paying to have your resume listed. If you hear about a database you think you might want to be listed in, call the company and ask some questions:

- How long have they been in business?
- What has their placement rate been?
- What fields do they specialize in? (In other words, will the right people even *see* your resume?)
- Can you block certain companies from seeing your resume?
- How many other resumes are listed in the database? How many in your specialty?
- Is your experience level similar to that of other listees in the database?

The right answers to these questions should let you know if you have found the right database for you.

To help you locate these resume databases, we have listed many of them in the **Career Resources** chapter of this book.

The Records You Need

The resume-writing process begins with the assembly and organization of all the personal, educational, and employment data from which you will choose the pieces that actually end up on paper. If this information is properly organized, writing your resume will be a relatively easy task, essentially a simple process of just shifting data from a set of the worksheets to another, to your actual resume. At the end of this chapter, you'll find all the forms you need to prepare your resume, including worksheets, fill-in-the-blanks resume forms, and sample resumes.

As you will soon see, there is a great deal of information you'll need to keep track of. In order to avoid a fevered search for important information, take the time right now to designate a single location in which to store all your records. My recommendation is either a filing cabinet or an expandable pocket portfolio. The latter is less expensive, yet it will still enable you to sort your records into an unlimited number of more-manageable categories.

Losing important report cards, citations, letters, etc., is easy to do if your life's history is scattered throughout your room or, even worse, your house! While copies of many of these items may be obtainable, why put yourself through all that extra work? Making good organization a habit will ensure that all the records you need to prepare your resume will be right where you need them when you need them.

For each of the categories summarized below, designate a separate file folder in which pertinent records can be kept. Your own notes are important, but keeping actual report cards, award citations, letters, etc. is even more so. Here's what your record-keeping system should include:

Transcripts (Including GPA and Class Rank Information)

Transcripts are your school's official record of your academic history, usually available, on request, from your high school's guidance office or college registrar's office. Your college may charge you for copies and "on request" doesn't mean "whenever you want"—you may have to wait some time for your request to be processed (so **don't** wait until the last minute!).

Your school-calculated GPA (Grade Point Average) is on the transcript. Most schools calculate this by multiplying the credit hours assigned to each course times a numerical grade equivalent (e.g., "A" = 4.0, "B" = 3.0, etc.), then dividing by total credits/courses taken. Class rank is simply a listing of GPAs, from highest to lowest.

Employment Records

Details on every part-time or full-time job you've held, including:

- Each employer's name, address and telephone number
- Name of supervisor
- Exact dates worked
- Approximate numbers of hours per week
- Specific duties and responsibilities
- Specific skills utilized and developed
- Accomplishments, honors
- Copies of awards, letters of recommendation

Volunteer Activities

Just because you weren't paid for a specific job—stuffing envelopes for the local Democratic candidate, running a car wash to raise money for the homeless, manning a drug hotline—doesn't mean that it wasn't significant or that you shouldn't include it on your resume.

So keep the same detailed notes on these volunteer activities as you have on the jobs you've held:

- Each organization's name, address and telephone number
- Name of supervisor
- Exact dates worked
- Approximate numbers of hours per week
- Specific duties and responsibilities

- Specific skills utilized
- Accomplishments, honors
- Copies of awards, letters of recommendation

Extracurricular Activities

List all sports, clubs, or other activities in which you've participated, either inside or outside school. For each, you should include:

- Name of activity/club/group
- Office(s) held
- Purpose of club/activity
- Specific duties/responsibilities
- Achievements, accomplishments, awards

If you were a long-standing member of a group or club, also include the dates that you were a member. This could demonstrate a high-level of commitment that could be used as a selling point.

Honors and Awards

Even if some of these honors are previously listed, specific data on every honor or award you receive should be kept, including, of course, the award itself! Keep the following information in your awards folder:

- Award name
- Date and from whom received
- What it was for
- Any pertinent details

Military Records

Complete military history, if pertinent, including:

- Dates of service
- Final rank awarded
- Duties and responsibilities
- All citations and awards
- Details on specific training and/or special schooling
- Skills developed
- Specific accomplishments

At the end of this chapter are seven **Data Input Sheets**. The first five cover employment, volunteer work, education, activities, and awards and are essential to any resume. The last two—covering military service and language skills—are important if, of course, they apply to you. I've only included one copy of each but, if you need to, you can copy the forms you need or simply write up your own using these as models.

Here are some pointers on how to fill out these all-important Data Sheets:

Employment Data Input Sheet: You will need to record the basic information—employer's name, address, and phone number; dates of employment; and supervisor's name—for your own files anyway. It may be an important addition to your networking list and will be necessary should you be asked to supply a reference list.

Duties should be a series of brief action statements describing what you did on this job. For example, if you worked as a hostess in a restaurant, this section might read: "Responsible for the delivery of 250 meals at dinner time and the supervision of 20 waiters and busboys. Coordinated reservations. Responsible for check and payment verification."

Skills should enumerate specific capabilities either necessary for the job or developed through it.

If you achieved *specific results*—e.g., "developed new filing system," "collected over $5,000 in previously-assumed bad debt," "instituted award-winning art program," etc.—or *received any award, citation or other honor*—"named Employee of the Month three times," "received Mayor's Citation for Innovation," etc.—make sure you list these.

Prepare one employment data sheet for each of the last three positions you have held; this is a basic guideline, but you can include more if relevant. Do not include sheets for short-term jobs (i.e., those that lasted one month or less).

Volunteer Work Data Input Sheet: Treat any volunteer work, no matter how basic or short (one day counts!), as if it were a job and record the same information. In both cases, it is especially important to note specific duties and responsibilities, skills required or developed and any accomplishments or achievements you can point to as evidence of your success.

Educational Data Input Sheet: If you're in college, omit details on high school. If you're a graduate student, list details on both graduate and undergraduate coursework. If you have not yet graduated, list your anticipated date of graduation. If more than a year away, indicate the numbers of credits earned through the most recent semester to be completed.

Activities Data Input Sheet: List your participation in the Student Government, Winter Carnival Press Committee, Math Club, Ski Patrol, etc., plus sports teams and/or any participation in community or church groups. Make sure you indicate if you were elected to any positions in clubs, groups, or on teams.

Awards and Honors Data Input Sheet: List awards and honors from your school (prestigious high school awards can still be included here, even if you're in graduate school), community groups, church groups, clubs, etc.

Military Service Data Input Sheet: Many useful skills are learned in the armed forces. A military stint often hastens the maturation process, making you a more attractive candidate. So if you have served in the military, make sure you include details in your resume. Again, include any computer skills you gained while in the service.

Language Data Input Sheet: An extremely important section for those of you with a real proficiency in a second language. And do make sure you have at least conversational fluency in the language(s) you list. One year of college French doesn't count, but if you've studied abroad, you probably are fluent or proficient. Such a talent could be invaluable, especially in today's increasingly international business climate.

While you should use the Data Input Sheets to summarize all of the data you have collected, do not throw away any of the specific information—report cards, transcripts, citations, etc.—just because it is recorded on these sheets. Keep all records in your files; you'll never know when you'll need them again!

Creating Your First Resume

There are many options that you can include or leave out. In general, we suggest you always include the following data:

1. Your name, address and telephone number
2. Pertinent educational history (grades, class rank, activities, etc.) Follow the grade point "rule of thumb"—mention it only if it is above 3.0.
3. Pertinent work history
4. Academic honors
5. Memberships in organizations
6. Military service history (if applicable)

You have the option of including the following:

1. Your career objective
2. Personal data
3. Hobbies
4. Summary of qualifications
5. Feelings about travel and relocation (Include this if you know in advance that the job you are applying for requires it. Often times, for future promotion, job seekers **must** be willing to relocate.

And you should never include the following:

1. Photographs or illustrations (of yourself or anything else) unless they are required by your profession—e.g., actors' composites
2. Why you left past jobs
3. References
4. Salary history or present salary objectives/requirements (if salary history is specifically requested in an ad, it may be included in your cover letter)

Special note: There is definitely a school of thought that discourages any mention of personal data—marital status, health, etc.—on a resume. While I am not vehemently opposed to including such information, I am not convinced it is particularly necessary, either.

As far as hobbies go, I would only include such information if it were in some way pertinent to the job/career you're targeting, or if it shows how well-rounded you are. Your love of reading is pertinent if, for example, you are applying for a part-time job at a library. But including details on the joys of "hiking, long walks with my dog and Isaac Asimov short stories" is nothing but filler and should be left out.

Maximizing Form and Substance

Your resume should be limited to a single page if possible. A two-page resume should be used **only** if you have an extensive work background related to a future goal. When you're laying out the resume, try to leave a reasonable amount of "white space"—generous margins all around and spacing between entries. It should be typed or printed (not Xeroxed) on 8 1/2" x 11" white, cream, or ivory stock. The ink should be black. Don't scrimp on the paper quality—use the best bond you can afford. And since printing 100 or even 200 copies will cost only a little more than 50, if you do decide to print your resume, *over*estimate your needs and opt for the highest quantity you think you may need. Prices at various "quick print" shops are not exorbitant and the quality look printing affords will leave the impression you want.

Use Power Words for Impact

Be brief. Use phrases rather than complete sentences. Your resume is a summary of your talents, not a term paper. Choose your words carefully and use "power words" whenever possible. "Organized" is more powerful than "put together;" "supervised" better than "oversaw;" "formulated" better than "thought up." Strong words like these can make the most mundane clerical work sound like a series of responsible, professional positions. And, of course, they will tend to make your resume stand out. Here's a starter list of words that you may want to use in your resume:

Choose the Right Format

There is not much mystery here—your background will generally lead you to the right format. For an entry-level job applicant with limited work experience, the chronological format, which organizes your educational and employment history by date (most recent first) is the obvious choice. For older or more experienced

accomplished	built	delegated	formulated
achieved	calculated	delivered	gathered
acted	chaired	demonstrated	gave
adapted	changed	designed	generated
addressed	classified	determined	guided
administered	collected	developed	implemented
advised	communicated	devised	improved
allocated	compiled	directed	initiated
analyzed	completed	discovered	installed
applied	composed	drafted	instituted
approved	computed	edited	instructed
arranged	conceptualized	established	introduced
assembled	conducted	estimated	invented
assessed	consolidated	evaluated	issued
assigned	contributed	executed	launched
assisted	coordinated	expanded	learned
attained	critiqued	fixed	lectured
budgeted	defined	forecast	led

litigated	presented	restored	systematized
lobbied	presided	reviewed	taught
made	produced	revised	tested
managed	programmed	rewrote	trained
marketed	promoted	saved	updated
mediated	proposed	scheduled	upgraded
moderated	publicized	selected	utilized
negotiated	ran	served	won
obtained	recommended	sold	wrote
operated	recruited	solved	
organized	regulated	started	
overhauled	remodeled	streamlined	
participated	renovated	studied	
planned	reorganized	suggested	
prepared	researched	supervised	

applicants, the functional—which emphasizes the duties and responsibilities of all your jobs over the course of your career, may be more suitable. If you are applying for a specific position in one field, the targeted format is for you. While I have tended to emphasize the chronological format in this chapter, one of the other two may well be the right one for you

A List of Do's and Don't's

In case we didn't stress them enough, here are some rules to follow:

- **Do** be brief and to the point—Two pages if absolutely necessary, one page if at all possible. Never longer!

- **Don't** be fancy. Multicolored paper and all-italic type won't impress employers, just make your resume harder to read (and easier to discard). Use plain white or ivory paper, black ink and an easy-to-read standard typeface.

- **Do** forget rules about sentences. Say what you need to say in the fewest words possible; use phrases, not drawn-out sentences.

- **Do** stick to the facts. Don't talk about your dog, vacation, etc.

- **Don't** ever send a resume blind. A cover letter should always accompany a resume and that letter should always be directed to a specific person.

- **Don't** have any typos. Your resume must be perfect—proofread everything as many times as necessary to catch any misspellings, grammatical errors, strange hyphenations, or typos.

- **Do** use the spell check feature on your personal computer to find errors, and also try reading the resume backwards—you'll be surprised at how errors jump out at you when you do this. Finally, have a friend proof your resume.

- **Do** use your resume as your sales tool. It is, in many cases, as close to you as an employer will ever get. Make sure it includes the information necessary to sell yourself the way you want to be sold!

- **Do** spend the money for good printing. Soiled, tattered or poorly reproduced copies speak poorly of your own self-image. Spend the money and take the time to make sure your resume is the best presentation you've ever made.

- **Do** help the reader, by organizing your resume in a clear-cut manner so key points are easily gleaned.

- **Don't** have a cluttered resume. Leave plenty of white space, especially around headings and all four margins.

- **Do** use bullets, asterisks, or other symbols as "stop signs" that the reader's eye will be naturally drawn to.

On the following pages, I've included a "fill-in-the-blanks" resume form so you can construct your own resume right away, plus one example each of a chronological, functional, and targeted resume.

EMPLOYMENT DATA INPUT SHEET

Employer name: _____

Address: _____

Phone: _____ Dates of employment: _____

Hours per week: _____ Salary/Pay: _____

Supervisor's name and title: _____

Duties: _____

_____

_____

Skills utilized: _____

_____

_____

_____

Accomplishments/Honors/Awards: _____

_____

_____

_____

Other important information: _____

_____

_____

_____

VOLUNTEER WORK DATA INPUT SHEET

Organization name: _____

Address: _____

Phone: _____ Dates of activity: _____

Hours per week: _____

Supervisor's name and title: _____

Duties: _____

_____

_____

Skills utilized: _____

_____

_____

_____

Accomplishments/Honors/Awards: _____

_____

_____

_____

Other important information: _____

_____

_____

_____

HIGH SCHOOL DATA INPUT SHEET

School name: _____

Address: _____

Phone: _____ Years attended: _____

Major studies: _____

GPA/Class rank: _____

Honors: _____

Important courses: _____

_____

_____

_____

OTHER SCHOOL DATA INPUT SHEET

School name: _____

Address: _____

Phone: _____ Years attended: _____

Major studies: _____

GPA/Class rank: _____

Honors: _____

Important courses: _____

_____

_____

_____

COLLEGE DATA INPUT SHEET

College:_____

Address:_____

Phone:_____Years attended:_____

Degrees earned:_____Major:_____Minor:_____

Honors:_____

Important courses:_____

_____

_____

_____

_____

GRADUATE SCHOOL DATA INPUT SHEET

College: _____

Address: _____

Phone: _____Years attended: _____

Degrees earned:_____ Major:_____Minor:_____

Honors: _____

Important courses: _____

_____

_____

_____

_____

MILITARY SERVICE DATA INPUT SHEET

Branch: _____

Rank (at discharge): _____

Dates of service: _____

Duties and responsibilities: _____

_____

_____

_____

Special training and/or school attended: _____

_____

_____

_____

Citations or awards: _____

_____

_____

_____

Specific accomplishments: _____

_____

_____

_____

_____

ACTIVITIES DATA INPUT SHEET

Club/Activity:_____ Office(s) Held:_____

Description of participation:_____

_____

_____

Duties/Responsibilities: _____

_____

Club/Activity:_____ Office(s) Held:_____

Description of participation:_____

_____

_____

Duties/responsibilities: _____

_____

Club/activity: _____ Office(s) Held:_____

Description of participation:_____

_____

_____

Duties/Responsibilities:_____

_____

AWARDS AND HONORS DATA INPUT SHEET

Name of Award or Citation: _____

From Whom Received: _____ Date: _____

Significance: _____

_____

Other pertinent information: _____

_____

Name of Award or Citation: _____

From Whom Received: _____ Date: _____

Significance: _____

_____

Other pertinent information: _____

_____

Name of Award or Citation: _____

From Whom Received: _____ Date: _____

Significance: _____

_____

Other pertinent information: _____

_____

LANGUAGE DATA INPUT SHEET

Language:_____

___Read   ___Write   ___Converse

Background (number of years studied, travel, etc.) _____

_____

_____

_____

Language:_____

___Read   ___Write   ___Converse

Background (number of years studied, travel, etc.) _____

_____

_____

_____

Language:

___Read   ___Write   ___Converse

Background (number of years studied, travel, etc.) _____

_____

_____

_____

FILL-IN-THE-BLANKS RESUME OUTLINE

Name: _____

Address: _____

City, state, ZIP Code: _____

Telephone number: _____

OBJECTIVE: _____

_____

_____

_____

_____

SUMMARY OF QUALIFICATIONS: _____

_____

_____

_____

EDUCATION

GRADUATE SCHOOL: _____

Address: _____

City, state, ZIP Code: _____

Expected graduation date: _____ Grade Point Average: _____

Degree earned (expected): _____ Class Rank: _____

Important classes, especially those related to your career: —————————

————————————————————————————

————————————————————————————

————————————————————————————

————————————————————————————

————————————————————————————

COLLEGE: ——————————————————————

Address: ———————————————————————

City, state, ZIP Code: ————————————————————

Expected graduation date:——————Grade Point Average: —————————

Class rank: ————— Major: ————— Minor:———————————

Important classes, especially those related to your career: —————————

————————————————————————————

————————————————————————————

————————————————————————————

————————————————————————————

————————————————————————————

————————————————————————————

HIGH SCHOOL:_____

Address:_____

City, state, ZIP Code:_____

Expected graduation date:_____Grade Point Average:_____

Class rank:_____

Important classes, especially those related to your career:_____

_____

_____

_____

_____

_____

_____

_____

HOBBIES AND OTHER INTERESTS (OPTIONAL) _____

_____

_____

_____

_____

_____

_____

_____

EXTRACURRICULAR ACTIVITIES (Activity name, dates participated, duties and responsibilities, offices held, accomplishments): _____

_____

_____

_____

_____

_____

_____

_____

_____

AWARDS AND HONORS (Award name, from whom and date received, significance of the award and any other pertinent details): _____

_____

_____

_____

_____

_____

_____

_____

_____

WORK EXPERIENCE. Include job title, name of business, address and telephone number, dates of employment, supervisor's name and title, your major responsibilities, accomplishments, and any awards won. Include volunteer experience in this category. List your experiences with the most recent dates first, even if you later decide not to use a chronological format.

_____

_____

_____

_____

_____

_____

_____

_____

_____

_____

_____

_____

_____

_____

_____

_____

_____

REFERENCES. Though you should *not* include references in your resume, you do need to prepare a separate list of at least three people who know you fairly well and will recommend you highly to prospective employers. For each, include job title, company name, address, and telephone number. Before you include anyone on this list, make sure you have their permission to use their name as a reference and confirm what they intend to say about you to a potential employer.

1. _____

_____

_____

2. _____

_____

_____

3. _____

_____

_____

4. _____

_____

_____

5. _____

_____

_____

ELEANOR D. FRANK

Current Address
East Quad #456
Detroit, MI 48221
(313) 555-8964

Permanent Address
509 Spruce Trail
Detroit, MI 48226
(313) 555-3468

EDUCATION

University of Detroit Mercy
Detroit, MI
Bachelor of Science in Nursing
December, 1993
GPA: 3.8

Harper Hospital School of Nursing
Detroit, MI
Diploma with Honors, 1989
GPA: 3.9

PROFESSIONAL EXPERIENCE
1989 - Present

Staff Nurse, Children's Hospital   Detroit, MI
● Provide care to pre- and post-operative care patients.
● Developed methods to assess quality of care on unit.
● Instruct patients and families in at-home care.

1988 - 89

Nurse Assistant, Detroit Medical Center   Detroit, MI
● Emergency room and surgical care rotation.

HONORS

Nursing "Student of the Year," 1992
Founders Scholarship Recipient

AFFILIATIONS

American Nurses Association
Michigan Nurses Association, Detroit District
Special Olympics Organizer
Red Cross Volunteer

LICENSES

Registered Nurse in the State of Michigan

REFERENCES

Available Upon Request

DANIELLE B. SMITH
123 North Street
Englewood, NJ 09876
(201) 555-5867

CAREER GOAL   To continue personal and professional growth in a challenging management position in the Nursing Field.

EDUCATION   New Jersey State   Englewood, NJ
School of Nursing
Bachelor of Science, December, 1992
Honors: Graduated Magna Cum Laude

Scotsdale Community College   Scotsdale, AR
Associate Degree in Nursing, 1979

ADMINISTRATION
- Instituted system for new employee orientation, included writing handbook.
- Continued service on hospital committees.
- Responsible for planning, directing, and evaluating patient care for 200 bed facility.

INTERPERSONAL
- Commended by supervisor for outstanding patient care.
- Direct patient care and supervision of auxiliary personnel in caring for patients in their homes.
- Re-instituted Student Chapter of National Student Nurses Association; 30 members.

**PROFESSIONAL
EXPERIENCE**
June, 1990 -   Riverside Hospital   Englewood, NJ
Present   Head Nurse on CC Unit

March, 1988 -   Visiting Nurse Association   Englewood, NJ
May, 1990   Staff Nurse

June, 1980 -   Memorial Hospital   Scotsdale, AR
February, 1988   Staff Nurse, OR

LICENSES/   Registered Nurse, 1979
CERTIFICATION Certification as a C.C.R.N. through American Nurses Association

AFFILIATIONS   National Nurses Association
Sigma Theta Tau, Nursing Honor Society, Rho Chapter
Association of Critical Care Nursing

NANCY P. FERNANDEZ
420 Abbott Street
Bakersfield, CA 90410
(213) 555-0100

CAREER OBJECTIVE   Critical Care Nursing Position.

EDUCATION   California State University, Bakersfield, CA
Bachelor of Science in Nursing, May, 1993
Grade Point Average: 3.8

**PROFESSIONAL
EXPERIENCE**   Grace Hospital
Bakersfield, CA
9/88 - Present
Began as a student nursing assistant; advanced/promoted to
Registered Nurse after successful completion of Boards.
● Total patient care of high risk infant/mother unit.
● Participation on the Educational Committee.
● Student Liaison to Administration.

**VOLUNTEER
EXPERIENCE**   New Life Missions
Guatemala City
Summer, 1991
● Acute care treatment and preventive health teaching to
  villagers.
● Team member, under supervision of physician and with an
  interpreter, assessed and treated acute medical conditions of
  children and adults.
● Taught hygiene and nutrition.

LICENSES   Registered Nurse in the State of California

ACTIVITIES   National Student Nurses Association, 1988-Present
Dean's Council
Soup Kitchen, Volunteer
Fluent in Spanish

Professional/Personal References Will Be Furnished Upon Request

CHAPTER EIGHTEEN

Writing Better Letters

Stop for a moment and review your resume draft. It is undoubtedly (by now) a near-perfect document that instantly tells the reader the kind of job you want and why you are qualified. But does it say anything personal about you? Any amplification of your talents? Any words that are ideally "you?" Any hint of the kind of person who stands behind that resume?

If you've prepared it properly, the answers should be a series of ringing "no's"—your resume should be a mere sketch of your life, a bare-bones summary of your skills, education, and experience.

To the general we must add the specific. That's what your letters must accomplish—adding the lines, colors, and shading that will help fill out your self-portrait. This chapter will cover the kinds of letters you will most often be called upon to prepare in your job search. There are essentially nine different types you will utilize again and again, based primarily on what each is trying to accomplish. One well-written example of each is included at the end of this chapter.

Answer these Questions

Before you put pencil to paper to compose any letter, there are five key questions you must ask yourself:

- **Why** are you writing it?
- To **Whom**?
- **What** are you trying to accomplish?
- **Which** lead will get the reader's attention?
- **How** do you organize the letter to best accomplish your objectives?

Why?

There should be a single, easily definable reason you are writing any letter. This reason will often dictate what and how you write—the tone and flavor of the letter—as well as what you include or leave out.

Have you been asked in an ad to amplify your qualifications for a job and provide a salary history and college transcripts? Then that (minimally) is your objective in writing. Limit yourself to following instructions and do a little personal selling—but very little. Including everything asked for and a simple, adequate cover letter is better than writing a "knock 'em, sock 'em" letter and omitting the one piece of information the ad specifically asked for.

If, however, you are on a networking search, the objective of your letter is to seek out contacts who will refer you for possible informational or job interviews. In this case, getting a name and address—a referral—is your stated purpose for writing. You have to be specific and ask for this action.

You will no doubt follow up with a phone call, but be certain the letter conveys what you are after. Being vague or oblique won't help you. You are after a definite yes or no when it comes to contact assistance. The recipient of your letter should know this. As they say in the world of selling, at some point you have to ask for the order.

Who?

Using the proper "tone" in a letter is as important as the content—you wouldn't write to the owner of the local meat market using the same words and style as you would employ in a letter to the director of personnel of a major company. Properly addressing the person or persons you are writing to is as important as what you say to them.

Always utilize the recipient's job title and level (correct title, and spelling are a **must**). If you know what kind of person they are (based on your knowledge of their area of involvement), use that knowledge as well. It also helps if you know his or her hiring clout, but even if you know the letter is going through a screening stage instead of to the actual person you need to contact, don't take the easy way out. You have to sell the person doing the screening just as convincingly as you would the actual contact, or else you might get passed over instead of passed along! Don't underestimate the power of the person doing the screening.

For example, it pays to sound technical with technical people—in other words, use the kinds of words and language which they use on the job. If you have had the opportunity to speak with them, it will be easy for you. If not, and you have formed some opinions as to their types then use these as the basis of the language you employ. The cardinal rule is to say it in words you think the recipient will be comfortable hearing, not in the words you might otherwise personally choose.

What?

What do you have to offer that company? What do you have to contribute to the job, process or work situation that is unique and/or of particular benefit to the recipient of your letter.

For example, if you were applying for a sales position and recently ranked number one in a summer sales job, then conveying this benefit is logical and desirable. It is a factor you may have left off your resume. Even if it was listed in the skills/accomplishment section of the resume, you can underscore and call attention to it in your letter. Repetition, when it is properly focused, can be a good thing.

Which?

Of all the opening sentences you can compose, which will immediately get the reader's attention? If your opening sentence is dynamic, you are already 50 percent of the way to your end objective—having your entire letter read. Don't slide into it. Know the point you are trying to make and come right to it. One word of caution: your first sentence **must** make mention of what led you to write—was it an ad, someone at the company, a story you saw on television? Be sure to give this point of reference.

How?

While a good opening is essential, how do you organize your letter so that it is easy for the recipient to read in its entirety. This is a question of *flow*—the way the words and sentences naturally lead one to another, holding the reader's interest until he or she reaches your signature.

If you have your objective clearly in mind, this task is easier than it sounds: Simply convey your message(s) in a logical sequence. End your letter by stating what the next steps are—yours and/or the reader's.

One More Time

Pay attention to the small things. Neatness still counts. Have your letters typed. Spend a few extra dollars and have some personal stationery printed.

And most important, make certain that your correspondence goes out quickly. The general rule is to get a letter in the mail during the week in which the project comes to your attention or in which you have had some contact with the organization. I personally attempt to mail follow-up letters the same day as the contact; at worst, within 24 hours.

When to Write

- To answer an ad
- To prospect (many companies)
- To inquire about specific openings (single company)
- To obtain a referral
- To obtain an informational interview
- To obtain a job interview
- To say "thank you"
- To accept or reject a job offer
- To withdraw from consideration for a job

In some cases, the letter will accompany your resume; in others, it will need to stand alone. Each of the above circumstances is described in the pages that follow. I have included at least one sample of each type of letter at the end of this chapter.

Answering an Ad

Your eye catches an ad in the Positions Available Section of the Sunday paper for a registered nurse. It tells you that the position is in a large hospital and that, though some experience would be desirable, it is not required. Well, you possess *those* skills. The ad asks that you send a letter and resume to a Post Office Box. No salary is indicated, no phone number given. You decide to reply.

Your purpose in writing—the objective (why?)—is to secure a job interview. Since no person is singled out for receipt of the ad, and since it is a large company, you assume it will be screened by Human Resources.

Adopt a professional, formal tone. You are answering a "blind" ad, so you have to play it safe. In your first sentence, refer to the ad, including the place and date of publication and the position outlined. (There is a chance that the company is running more than one ad on the same date and in the same paper, so you need to identify the one to which you are replying.) Tell the reader what (specifically) you have to offer that company. Include your resume, phone number, and the times it is easiest to reach you. Ask for the order—tell them you'd like to have an appointment.

Blanket Prospecting Letter

In June of this year you will graduate from a four-year college with a degree in nursing. You seek a position (internship or full-time employment) in a major hospital. You have decided to write to 50 top hospitals, sending each a copy of your resume. You don't know which, if any, have job openings.

Such blanket mailings are effective given two circumstances: 1) You must have an exemplary record and a resume which reflects it; and 2) You must send out a goodly number of packages, since the response rate to such mailings is very low.

A blanket mailing doesn't mean an impersonal one—you should always be writing to a specific executive. If you have a referral, send a personalized letter to that person. If not, do not simply mail a package to the Human Resources department; identify the department head and *then* send a personalized letter. And make sure you get on the phone and follow up each letter within about ten days. Don't just sit back and wait for everyone to call you. They won't.

Just Inquiring

The inquiry letter is a step above the blanket prospecting letter; it's a "cold-calling" device with a twist. You have earmarked a company (and a person) as a possibility in your job search based on something you have read about them. Your general research tells you that it is a good place to work. Although you are not aware of any specific openings, you know that they employ entry-level personnel with your credentials.

While ostensibly inquiring about any openings, you are really just "referring yourself" to them in order to place your resume in front of the right person. This is what I would call a "why not?" attempt at securing a job interview. Its effectiveness depends on their actually having been in the news. This, after all, is your "excuse" for writing.

Networking

It's time to get out that folder marked "Contacts" and prepare a draft networking letter. The lead sentence should be very specific, referring immediately to the friend, colleague, etc. "who suggested I write you about..." Remember: Your objective is to secure an informational interview, pave the way for a job interview, and/or get referred to still other contacts.

This type of letter should not place the recipient in a position where a decision is necessary; rather, the request should be couched in terms of "career advice." The second paragraph can then inform the reader of your level of experience. Finally, be specific about seeking an appointment.

Unless you have been specifically asked by the referring person to do so, you will probably not be including a resume with such letters. So the letter itself must highlight your credentials, enabling the reader to gauge your relative level of experience. For entry-level personnel, education, of course, will be most important.

For an Informational Interview

Though the objectives of this letter are similar to those of the networking letter, they are not as personal. These are "knowledge quests" on your part and the recipient will most likely not be someone you have been referred to. The idea is to convince the reader of the sincerity of your research effort. Whatever selling you do, if you do any at all, will arise as a consequence of the meeting, not beforehand. A positive response to this type of request is in itself a good step forward. It is, after all, exposure, and amazing things can develop when people in authority agree to see you.

Thank-You Letters

Although it may not always seem so, manners do count in the job world. But what counts even more are the simple gestures that show you actually care—like writing a thank-you letter. A well-executed, timely thank-you note tells more about your personality than anything else you may have sent, and it also demonstrates excellent follow-through skills. It says something about the way you were brought up—whatever else your resume tells them, you are, at least, polite, courteous and thoughtful.

Thank-you letters may well become the beginning of an all-important dialogue that leads directly to a job. So be extra careful in composing them, and make certain that they are custom made for each occasion and person.

The following are the primary situations in which you will be called upon to write some variation of thank-you letter:

1. After a job interview
2. After an informational interview
3. Accepting a job offer

4. Responding to rejection: While optional, such a letter is appropriate if you have been among the finalists in a job search or were rejected due to limited experience. Remember: Some day you'll *have* enough experience; make the interviewer want to stay in touch.

5. Withdrawing from consideration: Used when you decide you are no longer interested in a particular position. (A variation is usable for declining an actual job offer.) Whatever the reason for writing such a letter, it's wise to do so and thus keep future lines of communication open.

10 E. 89th Street
New York, NY 10028
February 22, 1993

The New York Times
PO Box 7520
New York, NY 10128

Dear Sir or Madam:

This letter is in response to your advertisement for a nursing assistant which appeared in the February 20th issue of the *New York Times*.

I have the qualifications you are seeking. I graduated magna cum laude from Emerson College with a Bachelor's degree in nursing and a minor in biology.

I worked for the past three summers as a nurses aide in a local nursing home, have participated in several seminars conducted by the American Nurses' Association, and have worked as a volunteer for a community service organization that provides basic healthcare services to the disabled.

My resume is enclosed. I would like to have the opportunity to meet with you personally to discuss your requirements for the position. I can be reached at (212) 785-1225 between 8:00 a.m. and 5:00 p.m. and at (212) 785-4221 after 5:00 p.m. I look forward to hearing from you.

Sincerely,

Karen Weber

Enclosure: Resume

PROSPECTING LETTER

Kim Kerr
8 Robutuck Hwy.
Hammond, IN 54054
555-875-2392

February 22, 1993

Mr. Fred Jones
Personnel Director
National Medical Corp.
One Lakeshore Drive
Chicago, Illinois 60606

Dear Mr. Jones:

The name of NMC continually pops up in our classroom discussions of outstanding healthcare companies. Given my interest in healthcare as a career, I've taken the liberty of enclosing my resume.

As you can see, I have just completed my B.S.N. at Brownstown University. Though my resume does not indicate it, I will be graduating in the top 10% of my class, with honors.

I have worked as a nurses aide for the past two summers at a local nursing home, have participated in several seminars conducted by the National League of Nursing and am particularly interested in geriatric care in a large metropolitan hospital.

I will be in the Chicago area on March 22 and will call your office to see when it is convenient to arrange an appointment.

Sincerely yours,

Kim Kerr

Enclosure: Resume

42 7th Street
Ski City, Vermont 85722
February 22, 1993

Mr. Michael Maniaci
Director of Recruiting
Western Medical Center
521 West Elm Street
Indianapolis, IN 83230

Dear Mr. Maniaci:

I just completed reading the article in the February issue of *Fortune* on your facility's record-breaking quarter. Congratulations!

Your innovative approach to recruiting minorities is of particular interest to me because of my background in healthcare and minority recruitment.

I am interested in learning more about your work as well as the possibilities of joining your firm. My qualifications include:

- B.S. in Nursing
- Research on minority recruitment
- Healthcare Seminar participation (Univ. of Virginia)
- Reports preparation on critical care nursing, occupational therapy and minorities

I will be in Connecticut during the week of March 23 and hope your schedule will permit us to meet briefly to discuss our mutual interests. I will call your office next week to see if such a meeting can be arranged.

I appreciate your consideration.

Sincerely yours,

Ronald W. Sommerville

Richard A. Starky
42 Bach St., Musical City, IN 20202   317-555-1515

February 22, 1993

Ms. Michelle Fleming
Vice President —Recruiting
Johnson Hospital
42 Jenkins Avenue
Fulton, Mississippi 23232

Dear Ms. Fleming:

Sam Kinney suggested I write you. I am interested in an entry-level dietician position in a large
metropolitan hospital. Sam felt it would be mutually beneficial for us to meet and talk.

I completed my Bachelor's and Plan IV/V requirements at Fulton University in 1990. For the
past two years, I have been working full-time toward my Master's degree and in an Approved
Preprofessional Practice Program (AP4) part-time. I expect to complete my studies this spring
and take the Registration Examination for Dieticians.

I know from Sam how similar our backgrounds are—the same training, the same interest in
healthcare. And, of course, I am aware of how successful you have been—four healthcare
excellence awards in five years!

As I begin my job search during the next few months, I am certain your advice would help me.
Would it be possible for us to meet briefly? My resume is enclosed.

I will call your office next week to see when your schedule would permit such a meeting.

Sincerely,

Richard A. Starky

Enclosure: Resume

16 NW 128th Street
Raleigh, NC 757755
February 22, 1993

Mr. Johnson B. McClure
Vice President —Recruiting
Bassett Pharmeutical Corporation
484 Smithers Road
Awkmont, North Carolina 76857

Dear Mr. McClure:

I'm sure a good deal of the credit for the recent award your company received from the National Pharmacology Council was due to your aggressive hiring of entry-level pharmaceutical salespeople. I hope to obtain a position for a company just as committed to growth.

I have four years of sterling sales results to boast of, experience acquired while working part-time as an assistant at a small pharmaceutical company in Raleigh. I believe my familiarity with the healthcare and insurance industries, and Bachelor's degree in pharmacy with a minor in marketing from American University have properly prepared me for a career in pharmaceutical sales.

As I begin my job search, I am trying to gather as much information and advice as possible before applying for positions. Could I take a few minutes of your time next week to discuss my career plans? I will call your office on Monday, March 22 to see if such a meeting can be arranged.

I appreciate your consideration and look forward to meeting you.

Sincerely,

Karen R. Burns

Lazelle Wright
921 West Fourth Street
Steamboat, Colorado 72105
303-310-3303

February 22, 1993

Mr. James R. Payne
Recruitment Manager
Bradley Finch Corp.
241 Snowridge
Ogden, Utah 72108

Dear Mr. Payne:

Jinny Bastienelli was right when she said you would be most helpful in advising me on a career in sports medicine.

I appreciated your taking the time from your busy schedule to meet with me. Your advice was most helpful and I have incorporated your suggestions into my resume. I will send you a copy next week.

Again, thanks so much for your assistance. As you suggested, I will contact Joe Simmons at Sherry County Hospital next week in regard to a possible opening with his company.

Sincerely,

Lazelle Wright

1497 Lilac Street
Old Adams, MA 01281
February 22, 1993

Mr. Rudy Delacort
Director of Personnel
Ann Grace Hospital
175 Boylston Avenue
Ribbit, Massachusetts 02857

Dear Mr. Delacort:

Thank you for the opportunity to interview yesterday for the nursing assistant position. I enjoyed meeting with you and Claire Stoudt and learning more about Ann Grace.

Your organization appears to be growing in a direction which parallels my interests and goals. The interview with you and your staff confirmed my initial positive impressions of Ann Grace, and I want to reiterate my strong interest in working for you.

I am convinced my prior experience as a nurses aide at the Fellowes Nursing Home in Old Adams, participation in several healthcare seminars conducted by the National Nurses Organization, and my college training in nursing would enable me to progress steadily through your training program and become a productive member of your staff.

Again, thank you for your consideration. If you need any additional information from me, please feel free to call.

Yours truly,

Harold Beaumont

cc: Ms. Claire Stoudt
    Pediatrics

1497 Lilac Street
Old Adams, MA 01281
February 22, 1993

Mr. Rudy Delacort
Director of Personnel
Ann Grace Hospital
175 Boylston Avenue
Ribbit, Massachusetts 01281

Dear Mr. Delacort:

I want to thank you and Ms. Stoudt for giving me the opportunity to work for Ann Grace. I am very pleased to accept the position as a nursing assistant with your geriatrics ward. The position entails exactly the kind of work I want to do, and I know that I will do a good job for you.

As we discussed, I shall begin work on April 5, 1993. In the interim, I shall complete all the necessary employment forms, obtain the required physical examination and locate housing.

I plan to be in Ribbit within the next two weeks and would like to deliver the paperwork to you personally. At that time, we could handle any remaining items pertaining to my employment. I'll call next week to schedule an appointment with you.

Sincerely yours,

Harold Beaumont

cc: Ms. Claire Stoudt
    Geriatrics

1497 Lilac Street
Old Adams, MA 01281
February 22, 1993

Mr. Rudy Delacort
Director of Personnel
Ann Grace Hospital
175 Boylston Avenue
Ribbit, Massachusetts 01281

Dear Mr. Delacort:

It was indeed a pleasure meeting with you and Ms. Stoudt last week to discuss your needs for a nursing assistant in your obstetrics ward. Our time together was most enjoyable and informative.

As I discussed with you during our meetings, I believe one purpose of preliminary interviews is to explore areas of mutual interest and to assess the fit between the individual and the position. After careful consideration, I have decided to withdraw from consideration for the position.

My decision is based primarily upon the one factor we discussed in some detail —the position would simply require more overtime than I am able to accept, given my other responsibilities.

I want to thank you for interviewing me and giving me the opportunity to learn about your needs. You have a fine staff and I would have enjoyed working with them.

Yours truly,

Harold Beaumont

cc: Ms. Claire Stoudt
Obstetrics

IN RESPONSE TO REJECTION

1497 Lilac Street
Old Adams, MA 01281
February 22, 1993

Mr. Rudy Delacort
Director of Personnel
Ann Grace Hospital
175 Boylston Avenue
Ribbit, Massachusetts 01281

Dear Mr. Delacort:

Thank you for giving me the opportunity to interview for the nursing assistant position. I appreciate your consideration and interest in me.

Although I am disappointed in not being selected for your current vacancy, I want you to know that I appreciated the courtesy and professionalism shown to me during the entire selection process. I enjoyed meeting you, Claire Stoudt, and the other members of your staff. My meetings confirmed that Ann Grace would be an exciting place to work and build a career.

I want to reiterate my strong interest in working for you. Please keep me in mind if a similar position becomes available in the near future.

Again, thank you for the opportunity to interview and best wishes to you and your staff.

Sincerely yours,

Harold Beaumont

cc: Ms. Claire Stoudt
    Outpatient Care

CHAPTER NINETEEN

Questions for You, Questions for Them

You've finished your exhaustive research, contacted everyone you've known since kindergarten, compiled a professional-looking and sounding resume, and written brilliant letters to the dozens of companies your research has revealed are perfect matches for your own strengths, interests, and abilities. Unfortunately, all of this preparatory work will be meaningless if you are unable to successfully convince one of those firms to hire you.

If you were able to set up an initial meeting at one of these companies, your resume and cover letter obviously piqued someone's interest. Now you have to traverse the last minefield—the job interview itself. It's time to make all that preparation pay off.

This chapter will attempt to put the interview process in perspective, giving you the "inside story" on what to expect and how to handle the questions and circumstances that arise during the course of a normal interview—and even many of those that surface in the bizarre interview situations we have all experienced at some point.

Why Interviews Shouldn't Scare You

Interviews shouldn't scare you. The concept of two (or more) persons meeting to determine if they are right for each other is a relatively logical idea. As important as research, resumes, letters, and phone calls are, they are inherently impersonal. The interview is your chance to really see and feel the company firsthand, so think of it as a positive opportunity, your chance to succeed.

That said, many of you will still be put off by the inherently inquisitive nature of the process. Though many questions *will* be asked, interviews are essentially experiments in chemistry. Are you right for the company? Is the company right for you? Not just on paper—*in the flesh.*

If you decide the company is right for you, your purpose is simple and clear-cut—to convince the interviewer that you are the right person for the job, that you will fit in, and that you will be an asset to the company now and in the future. The interviewer's purpose is equally simple—to decide whether he or she should buy what you're selling.

This chapter will focus on the kinds of questions you are likely to be asked, how to answer them, and the questions you should be ready to ask of the interviewer. By removing the workings of the interview process from the "unknown" category, you will reduce the fear it engenders.

But all the preparation in the world won't completely eliminate your sweaty palms, unless you can convince yourself that the interview is an important, positive life experience from which you will benefit—even if you don't get the job. Approach it with enthusiasm, calm yourself, and let your personality do the rest. You will undoubtedly spend an interesting hour, one that will teach you more about yourself. It's just another step in the learning process you've undertaken.

What to Do First

Start by setting up a calendar on which you can enter and track all your scheduled appointments. When you schedule an interview with a company, ask them how much time you should allow for the appointment. Some require all new applicants to fill out numerous forms and/or complete a battery of intelligence or psychological tests—all before the first interview. If you've only allowed an hour for the interview—and scheduled another at a nearby firm 10 minutes later—the first time you confront a three-hour test series will effectively destroy any schedule.

Some companies, especially if the first interview is very positive, like to keep applicants around to talk to other executives. This process may be planned or, in a lot of cases, a spontaneous decision by an interviewer who likes you and wants you to meet some other key decision makers. Other companies will tend to schedule such a series of second interviews on a separate day. Find out, if you can, how the company you're planning to visit generally operates. Otherwise, a schedule that's too tight will fall apart in no time at all, especially if you've traveled to another city to interview with an number of firms in a short period of time.

If you need to travel out-of-state to interview with a company, be sure to ask if they will be paying some or all of your travel expenses. (It's generally expected that you'll be paying your own way to firms within your home state.) If they don't offer—and you don't ask—presume you're paying the freight.

Even if the company agrees to reimburse you, make sure you have enough money to pay all the expenses yourself. While some may reimburse you immediately, the majority of firms may take from a week to a month to send you an expense check.

Research, Research, and More Research

The research you did to find these companies is nothing compared to the research you need to do now that you're beginning to narrow your search. If you followed our detailed suggestions when you started targeting these firms in the first place, you've already amassed a great deal of information about them. If you didn't do the research *then,* you sure better decide to do it *now.* Study each company as if you were going to be tested on your detailed knowledge of their organization and operations. Here's a complete checklist of the facts you should try to know about each company you plan to visit for a job interview:

The Basics

1. The address of (and directions to) the office or hospital you're visiting
2. Headquarters location (if different)
3. Relative size (compared to other similar companies)
4. Annual billings, sales, and/or income (last two years)
5. Subsidiary companies and/or specialized divisions
6. Departments (overall structure)

The Subtleties

1. History of the company or hospital (specialties, honors, awards, famous names)
2. Names, titles, and backgrounds of top management
3. Existence (and type) of training program
4. Relative salaries (compared to other companies in field or by size)
5. Recent developments concerning the company or hospital (from your trade magazine and newspaper reading)
6. Everything you can learn about the career, likes, and dislikes of the person(s) interviewing you

The amount of time and work necessary to be this well prepared for an interview is considerable. It will not be accomplished the day before the interview. You may even find some of the information you need is unavailable on short notice.

Is it really so important to do all this? Well, somebody out there is going to. And if you happen to be interviewing for the same job as that other, well-prepared, knowledgeable candidate, who do you think will impress the interviewer more?

As we've already discussed, if you give yourself enough time, most of this information is surprisingly easy to obtain. In addition to the reference sources covered in the Career Resources chapter, the company or hospital itself can probably supply you with a great deal of data. A firm's annual report—which all publicly-owned companies must publish yearly for their stockholders—is a virtual treasure trove of information. Write each company and request copies of their last two annual reports. A comparison of sales, income, and other data over this period may enable you to discover some interesting things about their overall financial health and growth potential. Many libraries also have collections of annual reports from major corporations.

Attempting to learn about your interviewer is hard work, the importance of which is underestimated by most applicants (who then, of course, don't bother to do it). Being one of the exceptions may get you a job. Find out if he or she has written any articles that have appeared in the trade press or, even better, books on his or her area(s) of expertise. Referring to these writings during the course of an interview, without making it too obvious a compliment, can be very effective. We all have egos and we all like people to talk about us. The interviewer is no different from the rest of us. You might also check to see if any of your networking contacts worked with him or her at his current (or a previous) company and can help "fill you in."

Selection vs. Screening Interviews

The process to which the majority of this chapter is devoted is the actual **selection interview,** usually conducted by the person to whom the new hire will be reporting. But there is another process—the **screening interview**—which many of you may have to survive first.

Screening interviews are usually conducted by a member of the personnel department. Though they may not be empowered to hire, they are in a position to screen out or eliminate those candidates they feel (based on the facts) are not qualified to handle the job. These decisions are not usually made on the basis of personality, appearance, eloquence, persuasiveness, or any other subjective criteria, but rather by clicking off yes or no answers against a checklist of skills. If you don't have the requisite number, you will be eliminated from further consideration. This may seem arbitrary, but it is a realistic and often necessary way for corporations to minimize the time and dollars involved in filling even the lowest jobs on the corporate ladder.

Remember, screening personnel are not looking for reasons to *hire* you; they're trying to find ways to *eliminate* you from the job search pack. Resumes sent blindly to the personnel department will usually be subjected to such screening; you will be eliminated without any personal contact (an excellent reason to construct a superior resume and not send out blind mailings).

If you are contacted, it will most likely be by telephone. When you are responding to such a call, keep these three things in mind: 1) It is an interview, be on your guard; 2) Answer all questions honestly; 3) Be enthusiastic; and 4) Don't offer any more information than you are asked for. Remember, this is another screening step, so don't say anything that will get you screened out before you even get in. You will get the standard questions from the interviewer—his or her attempts to "flesh out" the information included on your resume and/or cover letter. Strictly speaking, they are seeking out any negatives which may exist. If your resume is honest and factual (and it should be), you have no reason to be anxious, because you have nothing to hide.

Don't be nervous—be glad you were called and remember your objective: to get past this screening phase so you can get on to the real interview.

The Day of the Interview

On the day of the interview, wear a conservative (not funereal) business suit—

not a sports coat, *not* a "nice" blouse and skirt. Shoes should be shined, nails cleaned, hair cut and in place. And no low-cut or tight-fitting clothes.

It's not unusual for resumes and cover letters to head in different directions when a company starts passing them around to a number of executives. If you sent them, both may even be long gone. So bring along extra copies of your resume and your own copy of the cover letter that originally accompanied it.

Whether or not you make them available, we suggest you prepare a neatly-typed list of references (including the name, title, company, address, and phone number of each person). You may want to bring along a copy of your high school or college transcript, especially if it's something to brag about. (Once you get your first job, you'll probably never use it—or be asked for it—again, so enjoy it while you can!)

On Time Means Fifteen Minutes Early

Plan to arrive fifteen minutes before your scheduled appointment. If you're in an unfamiliar city or have a long drive to their offices, allow extra time for the unexpected delays that seem to occur with mind-numbing regularity on important days.

Arriving early will give you some time to check your appearance, catch your breath, check in with the receptionist, learn how to correctly pronounce the interviewer's name, and get yourself organized and battle ready.

Arriving late does not make a sterling first impression. If you are only a few minutes late, it's probably best not to mention it or even excuse yourself. With a little luck, everybody else is behind schedule and no one will notice. However, if you're more than fifteen minutes late, have an honest (or at least serviceable) explanation ready and offer it at your first opportunity. Then drop the subject as quickly as possible and move on to the interview.

You Don't Have to Say a Word

"Eighty percent of the initial impression you make is nonverbal," asserts Jennifer Maxwell Morris, a New York-based image consultant, quoting a University of Minnesota study. Some tips: walk tall, enter the room briskly while making eye contact with the person you're going to speak to, keep your head up, square your shoulders and keep your hand ready for a firm handshake that involves the whole hand but does not pump.

Source: *Working Woman*

The Eyes Have It

When you meet the interviewer, shake hands firmly. People notice handshakes and often form a first impression based solely on them.

Try to maintain eye contact with the interviewer as you talk. This will indicate you're interested in what he or she has to say. Eye contact is important for another reason—it demonstrates to the interviewer that you are confident about yourself and your job skills. That's an important message to send.

Sit straight. Body language is also another important means of conveying confidence.

Should coffee or a soft drink be offered, you may accept (but should do so only if the interviewer is joining you).

Keep your voice at a comfortable level, and try to sound enthusiastic (without imitating Charleen Cheerleader). Be confident and poised and provide direct, accurate, and honest answers to the trickiest questions.

And, as you try to remember all this, just be yourself, and try to act like you're comfortable and almost enjoying this whole process!

Don't Name Drop. . .Conspicuously

A friendly relationship with other company employees may have provided you with valuable information prior to the interview, but don't flaunt such relationships. The interviewer is interested only in how you will relate to him or her and how well he or she surmises you will fit in with the rest of the staff. Name dropping may smack of favoritism. And you are in no position to know who the interviewer's favorite (or least favorite) people are.

On the other hand, if you have established a complex network of professionals through informational interviews, attending trade shows, reading trade magazines, etc., it is perfectly permissible to refer to these people, their companies, conversations you've had, whatever. It may even impress the interviewer with the extensiveness of your preparation.

Fork on the Left, Knife on the Right

Interviews are sometimes conducted over lunch, though this is not usually the case with entry-level people. If it does happen to you, though, try to order something in the middle price range, neither filet mignon nor a cheeseburger.

Do not order alcohol—ever! If your interviewer orders a carafe of wine, politely decline. You may meet another interviewer later who smells the alcohol on your breath, or your interviewer may have a drinking problem. It's just too big a risk to take after you've come so far. Just do your best to maintain your poise, and you'll do fine.

The Importance of Last Impressions

There are some things interviewers will always view with displeasure: street language, complete lack of eye contact, insufficient or vague explanations or answers, a noticeable lack of energy, poor interpersonal skills (i.e., not listening or the basic inability to carry on an intelligent conversation), and a demonstrable lack of motivation.

Every impression may count. And the very *last* impression an interviewer has may outweigh everything else. So, before you allow an interview to end, summarize why you want the job, why you are qualified, and what, in particular, you can offer their company.

Then, take some action. If the interviewer hasn't told you about the rest of the interview process and/or where you stand, ask him or her. Will you be seeing other people that day? If so, ask for some background on anyone else with whom you'll be interviewing. If there are no other meetings that day, what's the next step? When can you expect to hear from them about coming back?

Ask for a business card. This will make sure you get the person's name and title right when you write your follow-up letter. You can staple it to the company file for easy reference as you continue networking. When you return home, file all the business cards, copies of correspondence, and notes from the interview(s) with each company in the appropriate files. Finally, but most importantly, ask yourself which firms you really want to work for and which you are no longer interested in. This will quickly determine how far you want the process at each to develop before you politely tell them to stop considering you for the job.

Immediately send a thank-you letter to each executive you met. These should, of course, be neatly typed business letters, not handwritten notes (unless you are most friendly, indeed, with the interviewer and want to stress the "informal" nature of your note). If you are still interested in pursuing a position at their company, tell them in no uncertain terms. Reiterate why you feel you're the best candidate and tell each of the executives when you hope (expect?) to hear from them.

On the Eighth Day God Created Interviewers

Though most interviews will follow a relatively standard format, there will undoubtedly be a wide disparity in the skills of the interviewers you meet. Many of these executives (with the exception of the Personnel staff) will most likely not have extensive interviewing experience, have limited knowledge of interviewing techniques, use them infrequently, be hurried by the other duties, or not even view your interview as critically important.

Rather than studying standardized test results or utilizing professional evaluation skills developed over many years of practice, these nonprofessionals react intuitively—their initial (first five minutes) impressions are often the lasting and over-riding factors they remember. So you must sell yourself—fast.

The best way to do this is to try to achieve a comfort level with your interviewer. Isn't establishing rapport—through words, gestures, appearance common interests, etc.—what you try to do in *any* social situation? It's just trying to know one another better. Against this backdrop, the questions and answers will flow in a more natural way.

A new style of interview called the "situational interview," or low-fidelity simulation, asks prospective employees what they would do in hypothetical situations, presenting illustrations that are important in the job opening. Recent research is encouraging employers to use this type of interview approach, because studies show that what people say they would do is pretty much what they will do when the real-life situation arises.

Source: *Working Woman*

The Set Sequence

Irrespective of the competence levels of the interviewer, you can anticipate an interview sequence roughly as follows:

- Greetings
- Social niceties (small talk)
- Purpose of meeting (let's get down to business)
- Broad questions/answers
- Specific questions/ answers
- In-depth discussion of company, job, and opportunity
- Summarizing information given & received
- Possible salary probe (this should only be brought up at a second interview)

• Summary/indication as to next steps

When you look at this sequence closely, it is obvious that once you have gotten past the greeting, social niceties and some explanation of the job (in the "getting down to business" section), the bulk of the interview will be questions—yours and the interviewer's. In this question and answer session, there are not necessarily any right or wrong answers, only good and bad ones.

Be forewarned, however. This sequence is not written in stone, and some interviewers will deliberately **not** follow it. Some interviewers will try to fluster you by asking off-the-wall questions, while others are just eccentric by nature. Be prepared for anything once the interview has started.

It's Time to Play Q & A

You can't control the "chemistry" between you and the interviewer—do you seem to "hit it off" right from the start or never connect at all? Since you can't control such a subjective problem, it pays to focus on what you *can* control—the questions you will be asked, your answers and the questions you had better be prepared to ask.

Not surprisingly, many of the same questions pop up in interview after interview, regardless of company size, type, or location. I have chosen the 14 most common— along with appropriate hints and answers for each—for inclusion in this chapter. Remember: There are no right or wrong answers to these questions, only good and bad ones.

Substance counts more than speed when answering questions. Take your time and make sure that you listen to each question—there is nothing quite as disquieting as a lengthy, intelligent answer that is completely irrelevant to the question asked. You wind up looking like a programmed clone with stock answers to dozens of questions who has, unfortunately, pulled the wrong one out of the grab bag.

Once you have adequately answered a specific question, it is permissible to go beyond it and add more information if doing so adds something to the discussion and/or highlights a particular strength, skill, course, etc. But avoid making lengthy speeches just for the sake of sounding off. Even if the interviewer asks a question that is right up your "power alley", one you could talk about for weeks, keep your answers short. Under two minutes for any answer is a good rule of thumb.

Study the list of questions (and hints) that follow, and prepare at least one solid, concise answer for each. Practice with a friend until your answers to these most-asked questions sound intelligent, professional and, most important, unmemorized and unrehearsed.

"Why do you want to be in this field?"

Using your knowledge and understanding of the particular field, explain why you find the business exciting and where and what role you see yourself playing in it.

"Why do you think you will be successful in this business?"

Using the information from your self-evaluation and the research you did on that particular company, formulate an answer which marries your strengths to their's and to the characteristics of the position for which you're applying.

"Why did you choose our hospital?"

This is an excellent opportunity to explain the extensive process of education and research you've undertaken. Tell them about your strengths and how you match up with their hospital. Emphasize specific things about their hospital that led you to seek an interview. Be a salesperson—be convincing.

"What can you do for us?"

Construct an answer that essentially lists your strengths, the experience you have which will contribute to your job performance, and any other unique qualifications that will place you at the head of the applicant pack. Use action-oriented words to tell exactly what you think you can do for the company—all your skills mean nothing if you can't use them to benefit the company you are interviewing with. Be careful: This is a question specifically designed to *eliminate* some of that pack. Sell yourself. Be one of the few called back for a second interview.

"What position here interests you?"

If you're interviewing for a specific position, answer accordingly. If you want to make sure you don't close the door on other opportunities of which you might be unaware, you can follow up with your own question: "I'm here to apply for your Nursing Assistant opening. Is there another position open for which you feel I'm qualified?"

If you've arranged an interview with a company without knowing of any specific openings, use the answer to this question to describe the kind of work you'd like to do and why you're qualified to do it. Avoid a specific job title, since they will tend to vary from firm to firm.

If you're on a first interview with the personnel department, just answer the question. They only want to figure out where to send you.

"What jobs have you held and why did you leave them?"

Or the direct approach: "Have you ever been fired?" Take this opportunity to expand on your resume, rather than precisely answering the question by merely recapping your job experiences. In discussing each job, point out what you liked about it, what factors led to your leaving, and how the next job added to your continuing professional education. If you have been fired, say so. It's very easy to check.

"What are your strengths and weaknesses?"

Or **"What are your hobbies (or outside interests)?"** Both questions can be easily answered using the data you gathered to complete the self-evaluation process. Be wary of being too forthcoming about your glaring faults (nobody expects you to volunteer every weakness and mistake), but do not reply, "I don't have any." They won't believe you and, what's worse, you won't believe you. After all, you did the evaluation—you know it's a lie!

Good answers to these questions are those in which the interviewer can identify benefits for him or herself. For example: "I consider myself to be an excellent planner. I am seldom caught by surprise and I pride myself on being able to anticipate problems and schedule my time to be ahead of the game. I devote a prescribed number of hours each week to this activity. I've noticed that many people just react. If you plan ahead, you should be able to cut off most problems before they arise."

You may consider disarming the interviewer by admitting a weakness, but doing it in such a way as to make it relatively unimportant to the job function. For example: "Higher mathematics has never been my strong suit. Though I am competent enough, I've always envied my friends with a more mathematical bent. In nursing, though, I haven't found this a liability. I'm certainly quick enough in figuring out how close I am to the end of my shift and, of course, I keep track of my remaining responsibilities."

"Do you think your extracurricular activities were worth the time you devoted to them?"

This is a question often asked of entry-level candidates. One possible answer: "Very definitely. As you see from my resume, I have been quite active in the Student Government and French Club. My language fluency allowed me to spend my junior year abroad as an exchange student, and working in a functioning government gave me firsthand knowledge of what can be accomplished with people in the real world. I suspect my marks would have been somewhat higher had I not taken on so many activities outside of school, but I feel the balance they gave me contributed significantly to my overall growth as a person."

"What are your career goals?"

Interviewers are always seeking to probe the motivations of prospective employees. Nowhere is this more apparent than when the area of ambition is discussed. The key answer to this question might be; "Given hard work, company growth, and personal initiative, I'd look forward to being in a top executive position by the time I'm 35. I believe in effort and the risk/reward system—my research on this company has shown me that it operates on the same principles. I would hope it would select its future leaders from those people who display such characteristics."

"At some future date would you be willing to relocate?"

Pulling up one's roots is not the easiest thing in the world to do, but it is often a fact of life in the corporate world. If you're serious about your career (and such a move often represents a step up the career ladder), you will probably not mind such a move. Tell the interviewer. If you really *don't* want to move, you may want to say so, too—though I would find out how probable or frequent such relocations would be before closing the door while still in the interview stage.

Keep in mind that as you get older, establish ties in a particular community, marry, have children, etc., you will inevitably feel less jubilation at the thought of moving once a year or even "being out on the road." So take the opportunity to experience new places and experiences while you're young. If you don't, you may never get the chance.

"How did you get along with your last supervisor?"

This question is designed to understand your relationship with (and reaction to) authority. Remember: Companies look for team players, people who will fit in with their hierarchy, their rules, their ways of doing things. An answer might be: "I prefer to work with smart, strong people who know what they want and can express themselves. I learned in the military that in order to accomplish the mission, someone has to be the leader and that person has to be given the authority to lead. Someday I aim to be that leader. I hope then my subordinates will follow me as much and as competently as I'm ready to follow now."

"What are your salary requirements?"

If they are at all interested in you, this question will probably come up, though it is more likely at a second interview. The danger, of course, is that you may price yourself too low or, even worse, right out of a job you want. Since you will have a general idea of industry figures for that position (and may even have an idea of what that company tends to pay new people for the position), why not refer to a range of salaries, such as $25,000 - $30,000?

If the interviewer doesn't bring up salary at all, it's doubtful you're being seriously considered, so you probably don't need to even bring the subject up. (If you know you aren't getting the job or aren't interested in it if offered, you may try to nail down a salary figure in order to be better prepared for the next interview.)

"Tell me about yourself"

Watch out for this one! It's often one of the first questions asked. If you falter here, the rest of the interview could quickly become a downward slide to nowhere. Be prepared, and consider it an opportunity to combine your answers to many of the previous questions into one concise description of who you are, what you want to be, and why that company should take a chance on you. Summarize your resume—briefly—and expand on particular courses or experiences relevant to the firm or position. Do not go on about your hobbies or personal life, where you spent your summer vacation, or anything that is not relevant to securing that job. You may explain how that particular job fits in with your long-range career goals and talk specifically about what attracted you to their company in the first place.

"Do you have any questions?"

It's the last fatal question on our list, often the last one an interviewer throws at you after an hour or two of grilling. Even if the interview has been very long and unusually thorough, you *should* have questions—about the job, the company, even the industry. Unfortunately, by the time this question off-handedly hits the floor, you are already looking forward to leaving and may have absolutely nothing to say.

Preparing yourself for an interview means more than having answers for some of the questions an interviewer may ask. It means having your own set of questions—at least five or six—for the interviewer. The interviewer is trying to find the right person for the job. You're trying to find the right job. So you should be just as curious about him or her and the company as he or she is about you. Be careful with any list of questions prepared ahead of time. Some of them were probably answered during the course of the interview, so to ask that same question at this stage would demonstrate poor listening skills. Listening well is becoming a lost art, and its importance cannot be stressed enough. (See the box on this page for a short list of questions you may consider asking on any interview).

The Not-So-Obvious Questions

Every interviewer is different and, unfortunately, there are no rules saying he or she has to use all or any of the "basic" questions covered above. But we think the odds are against his or her avoiding all of them. Whichever of these he or she includes, be assured most interviewers do like to come up with questions that are "uniquely theirs." It may be just one or a whole series—questions developed over the years that he or she feels help separate the wheat from the chaff.

You can't exactly prepare yourself for questions like, "What would you do if...(fill in the blank with some obscure occurrence)?," "What do you remember about kindergarten?," or "What's your favorite ice cream flavor?" Every interviewer we know has his or her favorites and all of these questions seem to come out of left field. Just stay relaxed, grit your teeth (quietly), and take a few seconds to frame a reasonably intelligent reply.

Your Turn to Ask the Questions

1. What will my typical day be like?
2. What happened to the last person who had this job?
3. Given my attitude and qualifications, how would you estimate my chances for career advancement at your hospital?
4. Why did you come to work here? What keeps you here?
5. If you were I, would you start here again?
6. How would you characterize the management philosophy of your hospital?
7. What characteristics do the successful employees at your hospital have in common?
8. What's the best (and worst) thing about working here?

The Downright Illegal Questions

Some questions are more than inappropriate—they are illegal. The Civil Rights Act of 1964 makes it illegal for a company to discriminate in its hiring on the basis of race, color, religion, sex, or national origin. It also means that any interview questions covering these topics are strictly off-limits. In addition to questions about race and color, what other types of questions can't be asked? Some might surprise you:

- Any questions about marital status, number and ages of dependents, or marriage or child-bearing plans.

- Any questions about your relatives, their addresses, or their place of origin.

- Any questions about your arrest record. If security clearance is required, it can be done after hiring but before you start the job.

A Quick Quiz to Test Your Instincts

After reading the above paragraphs, read through the 10 questions below. Which ones do you think would be legal to ask at a job interview? Answers provided below.

1. Confidentially, what is your race?
2. What kind of work does your spouse do?
3. Are you single, married, or divorced?
4. What is your native language?
5. Who should we notify in case of an emergency?
6. What clubs, societies, or organizations do you belong to?
7. Do you plan to have a family?
8. Do you have any disability?
9. Do you have a good credit record?
10. What is your height and weight?

The answers? Not a single question out of the 10 is legal at a job interview, because all could lead to a discrimination suit. Some of the questions would become legal once you were hired (obviously a company would need to know who to notify in an emergency), but none belong at an interview.

Now that you know what an interviewer can't ask you, what if he or she does? Well, don't lose your cool, and don't point out that the question may be outside the law—the nonprofessional interviewer may not realize such questions are illegal, and such a response might confuse, even anger, him or her.

Instead, whenever any questions are raised that you feel are outside legal boundaries, politely state that you don't understand how the question has bearing on the job opening and ask the interviewer to clarify his or herself. If the interviewer persists, you may be forced to state that you do not feel comfortable answering questions of that nature. Bring up the legal issue as a last resort, but if things reach that stage, you probably don't want to work for that company after all.

Testing and Applications

Though not part of the selection interview itself, job applications, skill tests, and psychological testing are often part of the pre-interview process. You should know something about them.

The job application is essentially a record-keeping exercise—simply the transfer of work experience and educational data from your resume to a printed application form. Though taking the time to recopy data may seem like a waste of time, some companies simply want the information in a particular order on a standard form. One difference: Applications often require the listing of references and salary levels achieved. Be sure to bring your list of references with you to any interview (so you can transfer the pertinent information), and don't lie about salary history; it's easily checked.

Many companies now use a variety of psychological tests as additional mechanisms to screen out undesirable candidates. Although their accuracy is subject to question, the companies that use them obviously believe they are effective at identifying applicants whose personality makeups would preclude their participating positively in a given work situation, especially those at the extreme ends of the behavior spectrum.

Their usefulness in predicting job accomplishment is considered limited. If you are normal (like the rest of us), you'll have no trouble with these tests and may even find them amusing. Just don't try to outsmart them—you'll just wind up outsmarting yourself.

Stand Up and Be Counted

Your interview is over. Breathe a sigh of relief. Make your notes—you'll want to keep a file on the important things covered for use in your next interview. Some people consider one out of 10 (one job offer for every 10 interviews) a good score—if you're keeping score. We suggest you don't. It's virtually impossible to judge how others are judging you. Just go on to the next interview. Sooner than you think, you'll be hired. For the right job.

JOB
OPPORTUNITIES
DATABANK

CHAPTER TWENTY

Job Opportunities Databank

The Job Opportunities Databank contains listings for more than 200 hospitals, health services companies, and pharmaceutical firms that offer entry-level hiring and/or internships in the United States. It is divided into two sections: Entry-Level Job and Internship Listings, which provides full descriptive entries for hospitals and companies in the United States and Canada; and Additional Companies, which includes name, address, and telephone information only for companies that did not respond to our inquiries. For complete details on the information provided in this chapter, please consult "How to Use the Job Opportunities Databank" in the front of this directory.

Entry-Level Job and Internship Listings

Abbott Laboratories

1 Abbott Park Rd.
Abbott Park, IL 60064-3500
Phone: (708)937-6100

Business Description: Manufacturer of healthcare products, including pharmaceuticals, hospital and laboratory products, and nutritional products. Also produces chemicals and nutritional products for the livestock and aquaculture market.

Officers: Duane L. Burnham, CEO; James A. Hanley, VP & Treasurer; Robert L. Parkinson, Jr., VP of Mktg.

Employees: 40,929.

Application Procedures: Places newspaper advertisements for certain openings. Accepts unsolicited resumes. Applications can be filled out on site, or applications will be mailed upon request. Send resume and cover letter to the attention of Corporate Placement.

Allergan Inc.

2525 Dupont Dr.
PO Box 19534
Irvine, CA 92713-9534
Phone: (714)752-4500
Toll-free: 800-347-4500

Business Description: Produces prescription and non-prescription eye and skin care products, including contact lenses and lens care products, ophthalmic surgical products, and pharmaceuticals.

Officers: Edgar J. Cummins, Sr. VP & CFO; Gavin S. Herbert, CEO & Chairman of the Board.

Employees: 6,344.

Benefits: Benefits include medical insurance, dental insurance, vision insurance, life insurance, long-term disability, short-term disability, a savings plan, profit sharing, tuition assistance, bonuses/incentives, 10-11 paid holidays and two personal/sick days per year, 10 vacation days after one year, maternity leave, company-sponsored sports teams, a cafeteria, flex time, a smoke-free environment, and training programs.

Human Resources: Randy Starling, Human Resources Asst.

Application Procedures: Send resume and cover letter to the attention of Human Resources.

Alta Bates-Herrick Hospital

2855 Telegraph, Ste. 614
Berkeley, CA 94131
Phone: (510)540-1584
Fax: (510)204-4852

Business Description: Services provided are for acute care, rehabilitation, and mental health, both psychiatric and rehabilitative. There are also two Sportcare outpatient facilities.

Employees: 2,600. The entry level hiring number indicates 40 nursing positions, and 50 non-nursing positions.

Average Entry-Level Hiring: 90.

Opportunities: Physical therapy, speech therapy, occupational therapy, nursing, medical social workers—B.S. degree and California license registration. Radiology technicians, respiratory therapist, radiation oncology—certification required. Clerical and support positions available in business services, accounting, admitting, administration, engineering, medical records, and other specialized areas such as the AIDS clinic.

Human Resources: Mary Martha Beaton, Placement Specialist; Linda Camezon, Recruiter.

Alza Corp.

950 Page Mill Rd.
PO Box 10950
Palo Alto, CA 94303-0802
Phone: (415)494-5000
Fax: (415)494-5151

Business Description: Develops, manufactures, and markets therapeutic systems for both humans and animals. The company's two subsidiaries, ALZA Development Corp. and ALZA Ltd., are also involved in the development of therapeutic systems. The goal of ALZA products is to administer a consistent level of medication for a specified length of time. Specific medications incorporate ALZA technology for delivery systems, with a drug developed or marketed by another company. Joint ventures in the past have involved companies such as Pfizer, Ciba Consumer Pharmaceuticals, Glaxo Holdings, and others. The company also provides contract manufacturing and packing services for other pharmaceutical companies.

Officers: Dr. Harriet Benson, VP of Regulatory Affairs; Dr. Pieter P. Bonsen, Sr. VP of Product Development; Dr. Terry L. Burkoth, VP of Production; Dr. Gary V. Fulscher, VP of Admin.; Martin S. Gerstel, Co-Chairman & CEO; David R. Hoffmann, VP & Treasurer; Arnold Kaufman, VP of Quality Assurance; Gary S. Lyman, VP of Operations; Edward L. Mandeu, VP & Legal Counsel; Dr. Jane E. Shaw, Pres. & Chairman of the Board; Julian N. Stern, Secretary; Dr. Felix Theeuwes, Sr. VP of Research.

Employees: 750.

Benefits: Benefits include medical insurance, dental insurance, life insurance, short-term disability, long-term disability, an employee pension plan, tuition assistance, an employee counseling program, company-sponsored sports teams, a cafeteria, flex time, a smoke-free environment, training programs, an employee stock purchase plan, the Commute Alternatives Program, award plans, a 401(K) plan, the Hatching Charitable Contribution, personal/sick days, sabbaticals, eight paid holidays per year, two flexible holidays per year, maternity leave, and bereavement leave of three to five days. Vacations are awarded as follows: 12 days in the first year of service; 16 days in years two through four; 20 days after four years of service.

Human Resources: Fran Charlson; Darlene Markovich, Human Resources Dir.; Laura Mills.

Application Procedures: Send resume and cover letter to the attention of Darlene Markovich, Human Resources Dir.

American Health Partners

28 W. 23rd St.
New York, NY 10011
Phone: (212)366-8900
Fax: (212)366-8648

Employees: 98.

Average Entry-Level Hiring: 2-3.

Opportunities: Positions as editorial assistants and research assistants require a college degree, typing and computer skills, knowledge of grammar, good writing skills, and an independent attitude.

Human Resources: Mary Witherall, Editor.

▶ **Internships**

Type: The company does not offer an internship program.

American Healthcare Management Inc.

660 American Ave., Ste. 200
King of Prussia, PA 19406
Phone: (215)768-5900

Business Description: Owns and operates hospitals, with emphasis on acute care.

Officers: Bruce J. Colburn, Controller; Brian G. Costello, Vice Pres.; Robert M. Dubbs, VP, Counsel & Sec.; Robert W. Fleming, Jr., Sr. VP; William A. Johnsen, Sr. VP & Finance Officer; Marvin Rushkoff, Chairman of the Board; Thomas M. Sposito, Vice Pres.; Steven Volla, Pres., CEO, CFO & Treasurer.

Employees: 3,500.

Human Resources: Brian G. Costello, Vice Pres.

Application Procedures: Send resume and cover letter to the attention of Brian G. Costello, Vice Pres. PO Box 1509, King of Prussia, PA 19406.

American Home Products Corp.

685 3rd Ave.
New York, NY 10017-4085
Phone: (212)878-5000

Business Description: American Home Products, through its subsidiaries, manufactures and markets health care products, consumer health care products, medical supplies and hospital products, and food products. The company has operations throughout the United States, other Americas, Europe, Africa, Asia, and Australia.

Officers: Robert G. Blount, Exec. VP & CFO; Bernard Canavan, MD, President; John R. Considine, VP & Treasurer; John R. Stafford, CEO & Chairman of the Board.

Employees: 24,265.

Average Entry-Level Hiring: The company hires entry-level college graduates.

Benefits: Benefits include a stock option plan, an employee pension plan, post-retirement benefits, and a management incentive plan.

Application Procedures: Send resume and cover letter to the attention of Personnel Recruiter.

> ▌ all cases, the people with an edge will be those who
> ▌ know how to use a computer to do their jobs more efficiently, who can present ideas cogently and who work well in teams.
>
> Source: *U.S. News & World Report*

American Medical International Inc.

414 N. Camden Dr.
Beverly Hills, CA 90210
Phone: (213)278-6200

Business Description: American Medical International and its affiliates operate about 50 hospitals in the United States. The company is the nation's 3rd largest hospital chain and employs nearly 37,000 at its hospitals.

Officers: Harry J. Gray, CEO & Chairman of the Board; W. Randolph Smith, Sr. VP & CFO.

Employees: 50,000.

Application Procedures: Accepts unsolicited resumes. Applications will be mailed to those requesting them by mail and by phone. Apply in person or send resume and cover letter to the attention of Human Resources.

Amgen Inc.
1840 DeHavilland Dr.
Thousand Oaks, CA 91320-1789
Phone: (805)499-5725

Business Description: A biotechnology company that produces and markets erythropoietin (EPO), a protein that is essential to the production of red blood cells. Fu-Kuen Lin, a scientist working for Amgen, isolated the genetic combination of erythropoietin so that it could be reproduced. The product, sold under the trademark Epogen, is used by kidney dialysis patients and though it may be used for anemia not caused by kidney failure, another company holds the patent on its sale for that purpose. It also produces and markets versions of granulocyte colony-stimulating factor (G-CSF), which stimulates the body to make white blood cells. The product, sold under the trademark Neupogen, is used by cancer patients whose ability to produce white blood cells has been decreased by chemotherapy. Amgen has been embroiled in legal battles concerning its patents. Amgen is currently building a distribution facility in Louisville, Kentucky, that will open in 1992 and employ 25-50 people.

Officers: Gordon M. Binder, CEO; Paul R. Dawson, VP of Mktg. & Sales; Lowell E. Sears, VP & CFO.

Human Resources: Bill Puchlevic, VP of Human Resources.

Application Procedures: Send resume and cover letter.

ARA Group Inc.
ARA Tower
1 Reading Center
Philadelphia, PA 19107
Phone: (215)238-3000

Business Description: Engaged in providing or managing services, including food and leisure services; textile rental and maintenance services; health and education services; distribution services. It also conducts operations, primarily management of food services, in Belgium, Canada, Germany, Japan, and the United Kingdom. Customers include business, government, education, health care, and others.

Officers: Alan J. Callander, Vice Chairman of the Board; Joseph Neubauer, Pres. & Chairman of the Board; Anthony J. Tanzola, VP, Controller & CFO.

Employees: 134,000.

Benefits: Benefits include employee pension plan and a retirement savings plan.

Human Resources: Kim Myerson, Human Resources Coordinator.

Application Procedures: Send resume and cover letter to the attention of Kim Myerson, Human Resources Coordinator.

ARA Services Inc.
1101 Market St.
Philadelphia, PA 19107
Phone: (215)238-3000
Fax: (215)238-3333

Business Description: Provides food service, including vending machines, cafeterias, dining rooms, concession stands, and coffee service, to businesses, correctional facilities, hospitals, universities, schools, parks, resorts, stadiums, and convention centers. The company also has food service operations in Canada, Europe, and Japan.

Officers: James E. Ksansnak, Sr. VP & CFO; William Leonard, President; Joseph Neubauer, CEO & Chairman of the Board; Martin Spector, Exec. VP of Mktg. & Sales.

Employees: 135,000.

Opportunities: Opportunities include associate programmers, accounting tax asset management, accounts receivable management, credit representatives, and auditors.

Human Resources: Kim Meyerson, Human Resources Specialist; Lisa Staley, Human Resources Specialist; Diane Weltman, Human Resources.

Application Procedures: Places newspaper advertisements for certain openings. Some hiring is done through an employment agency. Send resume and cover letter to the attention of Human Resource Department.

Arizona State Hospital
2500 E. Van Buren St.
Phoenix, AZ 85008
Phone: (602)244-1331
Fax: (602)220-6234

Employees: 900.

Average Entry-Level Hiring: 5-6 per week.

Opportunities: Social worker—M.S.W. required. Registered nurse—associate or bachelor's degree. Physical therapist—bachelor's degree in physical therapy. Pharmacist—five years of study.

Human Resources: Gloria Gonzales, Employment Contact.

Application Procedures: Call for more information.

Barnert Memorial Hospital Center
680 Broadway
Paterson, NJ 07514
Phone: (201)977-6655
Fax: (201)279-2924

Employees: 900.

Average Entry-Level Hiring: 10.

Opportunities: RNs, LPNs, laboratory technicians, physical therapists, social workers, pharmacy technicians, respiratory and radiology technicians, clerical staff, and speech therapists.

Human Resources: Liz Giannisis, Asst. Dir. of Human Resources.

Application Procedures: Call for more information.

Barnes Hospital
1 Barnes Hospital Plz.
St. Louis, MO 63110
Phone: (314)362-0701
Fax: (314)362-0708

Employees: 6,000.

Average Entry-Level Hiring: Unknown.

Opportunities: Nurse—two-, three-, or four-year degree. Occupational and physical therapists—bachelor's degree.

Human Resources: Carol Esrock, Personnel Mgr.; Wally Kline, Personnel Dept.

Application Procedures: Call for more information.

Baxter Healthcare Corp.
1 Baxter Pkwy.
Deerfield, IL 60015
Phone: (708)948-2000

Business Description: Manufacturer and marketer of health care products and supplies. The company recently introduced a delivery service for hospitals that delivers supplies at the time they are needed, thus eliminating the need for hospitals to warehouse large inventories.

Officers: Wilbert H. Gantz, President; Michael Heschel, VP of Info. Systems; Robert Lambrix, Sr. VP & CFO; Robert Simons, Exec. VP.

Employees: 42,800.

Average Entry-Level Hiring: Unknown.

Human Resources: Anthony Rucci, Sr. VP of Human Resources.

Application Procedures: Send resume and cover letter to the attention of Professional Staffing.

Baxter International Inc.
1 Baxter Pkwy.
Deerfield, IL 60015
Phone: (708)948-2000

Business Description: Manufactures and distributes a broad range of products for hospitals and clinical laboratories; develops and markets a variety of specialized medical products used for patient care, blood therapy, diagnostic testing, and cardiac care; provides management consulting services used by home patients and alternate-site providers; and manufactures and markets products for educational and government laboratories, industrial research and development facilities, and manufacturing facilities. With sales to health-care providers in 100 countries, Baxter offers more than 120,000 products.

Officers: G. Marshall Abbey, Sr. VP & General Counsel; John F. Gaither, Jr., General Counsel & Sec.; William B. Graham, Sr. Chairman of the Board; Melvyn R. Kalas, Controller; Robert J. Lambrix, Sr. VP & CFO; Vernon R. Loucks, Jr., CEO & Chairman of the Board; James R. Tobin, COO & Pres.

Employees: 64,300.

Benefits: Benefits include an employee pension plan and employee stock purchase plan.

Application Procedures: Contact the company for more information.

Baystate Medical Center
759 Chestnut St.
Springfield, MA 01199
Phone: (413)784-3666
Fax: (413)784-3325

Employees: 4,500.

Opportunities: RN—associate or bachelor's degree required. PT, OT, and RT—no requirements specified.

Application Procedures: Contact the human resources department for more information.

Beecham Inc.
1 Franklin Plz.
Philadelphia, PA 19102
Phone: (215)751-4000

Business Description: Engaged in manufacturing, fabricating and/or processing drugs in pharmaceutical preparations.

Application Procedures: Send resume and cover letter to the Employment Administrator.

▶ Internships

Type: Nonpaid internships are available.

> ne way to improve your chances in the job hunt is to define "you" as broadly as possible . . . . Defining yourself in terms of your skills rather than your job history is the key.
>
> Source: *Business Monday/Detroit Free Press*

Bergan Mercy Hospital
7500 Mercy Rd.
Omaha, NE 68124
Phone: (402)398-6168
Fax: (402)398-6920

Employees: 2,600.

Average Entry-Level Hiring: 500+ per year.

Opportunities: All positions require Nebraska state licensure or eligibility for licensure. RN/LPN home care—two years of acute care experience. Physical therapist—B.S. in physical therapy from an accredited PT school. Occupational therapist—B.S. in OT, AOTA licensure. Medical technologist—B.S. ASCP registry. Radiology technologist—Completion of 24 month program in radiology from an accredited program, ARRT registered. Radiation therapy technologist—same as RT, including completion of 12 month program in radiation therapy. Pharmacist—B.S. or Doctorate in pharmacy.

Human Resources: Katie Staebell, Recruiter; Gail Hafer, Employment Coordinator.

Beth Abraham Hospital
612 Allerton Ave.
Bronx, NY 10467
Phone: (212)920-6021
Fax: (212)920-2632

Employees: 950.

Average Entry-Level Hiring: Unknown.

Opportunities: Physician assistants—New York State registration required. Physical therapist, registered nurses, LPNs, occupational therapist—New York State license required. Nursing attendant—New York State certification and completion of 102 hour course for nursing home aide. Registered pharmacist—New York State registration required. Secretary—typing and word processing skills required, Lotus 1-2-3.

Human Resources: Matt Stollper, Human Resources Dir.

Beth Israel Hospital
70 Parker Ave.
Passaic, NJ 07055
Phone: (201)365-5008
Fax: (201)471-5531

Employees: 900.

Average Entry-Level Hiring: Unknown.

Opportunities: RN—two-, three-, or four-year degrees. Many other entry-level positions available.

Human Resources: Patricia Wilson, Human Resources Dir.

Application Procedures: Call for more information.

Beverly Enterprises Inc.
PO Box 3324
Fort Smith, AR 72913
Phone: (501)452-6712

Business Description: Operates nursing homes, institutional pharmacies, retirement living centers, and home health centers across the country.

Officers: David R. Banks, CEO & Chairman of the Board; Andre C. Dimitriadis, Exec. VP & CFO; Boyd W. Hendrickson, Exec. VP of Mktg.

Employees: 96,000.

Average Entry-Level Hiring: Unknown.

Opportunities: Opportunities available in the areas of clerical, finance, accounting, tax, legal administration, and acquisitions.

Benefits: Benefits include medical insurance, dental insurance, life insurance, an employee pension plan, profit sharing, tuition assistance, paid holidays, flexible holidays, personal/sick days, vacation days, a smoke-free environment, child-care programs, and training programs.

Human Resources: Carol A. Johnson, VP of Human Resources.

Application Procedures: Send resume and cover letter to the attention of Human Resources Department.

▶ **Internships**

Number Available Annually: None.

Block Drug Company Inc.

257 Cornelison Ave.
Jersey City, NJ 07302-9988
Phone: (201)434-3000
Fax: (201)333-3585

Business Description: Develops, manufactures and sells products, classified into the following 3 categories: dental products, including consumer oral hygiene and professional dental products; consumer products, including proprietary over-the-counter and household products; and ethical pharmaceuticals.

Officers: Michael C. Alfano, D.M.D., Ph.D., Sr. VP of Research & Development; James A. Block, Chairman of the Board; Leonard Block, Sr. Chairman of the Board; Thomas R. Block, Pres. & Treasurer; Melvin Kopp, VP & Controller; Donald H. LeSieur, Exec. VP of Mktg.; Peter C. Mann, Sr. VP; John E. Peters, VP, General Counsel & Sec.; Gilbert M. Seymann, VP of Operations.

Employees: 3,000.

Benefits: Benefits include retirement plans, defined contribution profit-sharing plan, and an employee pension plan.

Human Resources: Thomas J. McNamara, Human Resources Dir.

Application Procedures: Send resume and cover letter to the attention of Thomas J. McNamara, Human Resources Dir.

W.R. Bonsal Co.

8201 Arrowridge Blvd.
Charlotte, NC 28217
Phone: (704)525-1621
Fax: (704)529-5261

Business Description: Engaged in collecting and preparing sand and/or gravel for use in construction. Manufacturer of concrete products other than block and brick.

Officers: Johnsie Beck, Dir. of Mktg.; W.R. Bonsal III, President; Debra Ferry, Dir. of Data Processing; J. Tietsma, Finance Officer.

Employees: 450.

Human Resources: Don Johnson, Human Resources Dir.

Bridgeport Hospital

267 Grant St.
Bridgeport, CT 06610
Phone: (203)384-3384
Fax: (203)384-3966

Employees: 2,500.

Average Entry-Level Hiring: Unknown.

Opportunities: Medical technicians, PTs, OTs, nuclear medicine technicians—experience preferred.

Human Resources: Jedd Santos, Employment Contact.

Application Procedures: Call for more information.

Bristol Hospital, Inc.

Brewster Rd.
Bristol, CT 06010
Phone: (203)585-3211
Fax: (203)585-3028

Employees: 1,500.

Average Entry-Level Hiring: Unknown.

Human Resources: Mark Rouleau, Employment Specialist; Sharon Osenkonski, Personnel Asst.

Application Procedures: Call for current vacancies and requirements.

Bristol-Myers Squibb Co.

345 Park Ave.
New York, NY 10154
Phone: (212)546-4341
Fax: (212)546-9707

Business Description: Formed by the 1989 merger of Bristol Myers and Squibb Corp., the company is engaged in the scientific research, development, and manufacturing of a wide variety of pharmaceuticals, medical devices, and consumer and nutritional products worldwide.

Officers: Michael E. Autera, Exec. VP; Harrison M. Bains, Jr., Treasurer; Richard M. Furlaud, President; Richard L. Gelb, CEO & Chairman of the Board; Pamela D. Kasa, Secretary; William R. Miller, Vice Chairman of the Board; Anthony W. Ruggiero, Sr. VP & Controller; Barry W. Wilson, President Pharmaceutical Group-Europe.

Employees: 40,000.

Average Entry-Level Hiring: Unknown.

Benefits: Benefits include retirement income plans and pension plans.

Application Procedures: Contact Human Resources.

▶ **Internships**

Type: The company does not offer an internship program.

Employment is expected to grow faster than average for physicians due to a growing and aging population and technological improvements that encourage expansion of the health industry. Job prospects should be better in internal medicine, family practice, geriatrics, and preventive medicine than in other specialties.

Source: *Occupational Outlook Quarterly*

Bronx-Lebanon Hospital Center
1650 Grand Concourse
Bronx, NY 10457
Phone: (212)590-1800
Fax: (212)409-7718

Employees: 3,200.

Average Entry-Level Hiring: 500.

Opportunities: Social worker for psychiatry and medical surgery—M.S.W. required. Entry-level salary starts at $35,000/year. Openings for the following positions as well; pharmacy interns, X-ray technicians, physician assistants, GRNs, RNs and LPNs. Recent graduates encouraged to apply for all positions.

Human Resources: Steve Carter, Recruiter PAs AIDS Program; Denise Corvino, Recruiter Technical; Sheila Haynes, Recruiter Nursing; Robert Martinez, Employment Mgr.

Brookwood Medical Center
2010 Brookwood Medical Center Dr.
Birmingham, AL 35209
Phone: (205)877-1000

Employees: 2,300.

Average Entry-Level Hiring: 100 per month.

Human Resources: John Loya, Director.

Application Procedures: Call the Job-Line at (205)877-1910, for more information.

Butterworth Hospital
100 Michigan NE
Grand Rapids, MI 49503
Phone: (617)774-1760
Toll-free: 800-347-5455

Employees: 3,750.

Average Entry-Level Hiring: 300.

Opportunities: A program is available for nursing students with clinical experience.

Human Resources: Mary Smania, Recruiter Nursing; Sandy Groot, Recruiter Nursing; Bobbie Neal, Recruiter; Sheri Peacock, Recruiter; Marcel Adams, Recruiter Secretarial/Clerical; Camille VaDyk Loss Prevention/Distribution.

Care Enterprises
2742 Dow Ave.
Tustin, CA 92680
Phone: (714)544-4443

Business Description: Operator of skilled nursing care facilities other than hospitals.

Employees: 6,000.

Average Entry-Level Hiring: Unknown.

Opportunities: Opportunities exist in accounting, the mail room, and in clerical areas. One year experience required.

▶ **Internships**

Type: Internships are available for administrators in training at nursing home locations; available year-round. **Number Available Annually:** 4-5.

Qualifications: Applicant must have a degree in the field he or she is applying in.

Care Tenders Inc.
9200 Shelbyville Rd., Ste. 220
Louisville, KY 40222
Phone: (502)425-4701

Business Description: Operator of nursing or personal care facilities that require a lesser degree of care than skilled or intermediate care facilities.

Officers: Jeffrey Hutter, VP of Mktg. & Sales; Frank Ward, Finance Officer; Mary Yarmuth, President.

Employees: 200.

Human Resources: Mike DeWitt, Personnel Dir.

Carolina Medicorp, Inc.
3333 Sials Creek Pkwy.
Winston-Salem, NC 27103
Phone: (919)718-5420
Toll-free: 800-777-1876
Fax: (919)718-9253

Business Description: Forsyth Memorial Hospital is the second largest hospital in North Carolina with 911 beds.

Employees: 3,800. 2800 at Forsyth Memorial Hospital.

Average Entry-Level Hiring: 500.

Opportunities: Registered nurses—B.S.N. or associate degree, all clinical areas. Allied health—B.S. degree or two-year technical degree. Areas include respiratory, medical technology, physical and occupational therapy, pharmacology, radiology, radiation oncology, and cytotechnology.

Human Resources: Ann Nusser, Employment Contact; Diane Poindexter, Employment Contact; Manika Stanley, Employment Contact; Sophie Pawlak, Employment Contact.

Cedars Medical Center
1400 NW 12th Ave.
Miami, FL 33136
Phone: (305)325-4991

Employees: 1,845.

Average Entry-Level Hiring: 200.

Opportunities: Nurse's aide—state certification and one year of hospital experience. RN, LPN, medical technologists—Florida state license. Respiratory therapy, physical and occupational therapists—graduate of an accredited program and Florida license. Secretary—must be able to type 40-45 WPM and have one to two years experience. Related experience in all areas preferred.

Human Resources: Elly Howard, Vice Pres.

Central State Hospital
3000 W. Washington St.
Indianapolis, IN 46222
Phone: (317)639-3600
Fax: (317)639-3864

Employees: 625.

Average Entry-Level Hiring: Unknown.

Opportunities: Social workers—M.S.W. required. Other positions available.

Human Resources: Dalen Shank, Employment Contact.

Application Procedures: Call for more information.

Charter Medical Corp.
577 Mulberry St.
PO Box 209
Macon, GA 31298
Phone: (912)742-1161
Fax: (912)746-5123

Business Description: An international hospital management company.

Officers: C. Michael Ford, VP of Finance; William McAfee, Jr., President; Don Serfass, Dir. of Info. Systems.

Employees: 17,000.

Human Resources: Al Joyner, Personnel Dir.

Application Procedures: Places newspaper advertisements for certain openings. Accepts unsolicited resumes; send resume and cover letter to the attention of Al Joyner, Personnel Dir.

Children's Hospital
8301 Dodge St.
Omaha, NE 68114
Phone: (402)390-8834
Fax: (402)390-8755

Employees: 570. The number of entry level people reflects 50 people in medical positions and 25 people in non-medical positions.

Average Entry-Level Hiring: 75.

Opportunities: RN, pharmacist—Nebraska license, accredited graduate. Radiology technician—ART registered. Medical technologists—bachelor's degree, ASCP registered. Respiratory therapist—registered or registry eligible.

Human Resources: Sarah Minarick, Personnel Recruiter.

Children's Medical Center of Dallas

1935 Motor St.
Dallas, TX 75235
Phone: (214)640-2345
Fax: (214)640-2860

Employees: 2,100.

Average Entry-Level Hiring: Unknown.

Opportunities: RN—two-, three-, or four-year degree. Pediatrics experience or internship program experience also required.

Human Resources: Janet Theaker, Employment Contact.

Thirty seconds. 1001, 1002, 1003 . . . That's all the time your cover letter will have to generate interest and create an impression. If the employer isn't grabbed, the letter won't be finished. The hours you spent on your resume will mean nothing. Provide the reader with steak and sizzle.

Source: *Business Monday/Detroit Free Press*

Children's Specialized Hospital

150 New Providence Rd.
Mountainside, NJ 07092
Phone: (908)233-3720
Fax: (908)233-4176

Employees: 550.

Average Entry-Level Hiring: 1-100.

Opportunities: RN—New Jersey license and associate diploma or bachelor's degree required. LPN—New Jersey license and diploma required. Pharmacist—New Jersey license and bachelor's degree from pharmacy school. Social worker—M.S.W. required. Speech-language pathologist, audiologist—MA/CCC and New Jersey license required. Physical therapist—New Jersey license, bachelor's degree, and pediatrics affiliation. Occupational therapist—AOTA-certified, bachelor's degree, and pediatrics affiliation.

Recreational therapist—bachelor's degree and pediatrics affiliation. PT assistant—associate degree and New Jersey license required. OT assistant—AOTA-certified and associate degree.

Application Procedures: Contact the human resources department for more information.

Clarke Institute of Psychiatry

250 College St.
Toronto, ON, Canada M5T 1R8
Phone: (416)979-2221
Fax: (416)979-0170

Employees: 850.

Average Entry-Level Hiring: 25.

Human Resources: Joan Snapp, Human Resources Dir.

Application Procedures: A variety of opportunities are available; call for more information.

Colmery-O'Neil Department of Veterans Affairs Medical Center

2200 Gage Blvd.
Topeka, KS 66622
Phone: (913)272-3111
Fax: (913)271-4309

Employees: 1,120.

Average Entry-Level Hiring: 20.

Opportunities: The following positions require a college degree: medical technologist, vocational rehabilitation specialist, pharmacist, physical therapist, occupational therapist, dietician, physician assistant, and social work associate. Psychologist—Ph.D. required. Social worker—M.S.W. required. Registered nurse—must be a graduate of a professional nursing program or have a bachelor's degree. Nurse anesthetist—must be a graduate of a school of professional nursing and anesthesia. LPN, PTA, OTA—specialized education required.

Human Resources: Christine Myers, Personnel Mgt. Specialist; Wanda Lyon, Personnel Mgt. Specialist.

Colorado State Hospital

1600 W. 24th St.
Pueblo, CO 81003
Phone: (719)546-4000
Fax: (719)546-4484

Employees: 0.

Average Entry-Level Hiring: Unknown.

Opportunities: Nurses, M.S.W.s, physical and occupational therapists—requirements not specified.

Human Resources: Jack Ford, Director.

Application Procedures: Contact Personnel for more information.

Community Hospitals Indianapolis

1500 N. Ritter Ave.
Indianapolis, IN 46219
Phone: (317)355-5483
Fax: (317)351-7726

Business Description: Operates a network of three hospitals.

Employees: 6,000. Employee figure represents a total from all three hospitals.

Average Entry-Level Hiring: Unknown.

Opportunities: RN—at least an associate degree. Physical or occupational therapist, medical technician—bachelor's degree. Laboratory technician—associate degree. PT assistant, speech pathologist, nurse anesthetist, nuclear medical technician, respiratory therapist, pharmacist—no requirements specified.

Human Resources: Jim Bennett East; Erin Farrell North; Kay Vohs South; Sarah Cole Nurse Recruiter.

Application Procedures: Call for more information; North—(317)841-5326; South—(317)887-7280.

Community Lifecare Enterprises

PO Box 20130
Springfield, IL 62708-0130
Phone: (217)523-9368

Business Description: Operator of skilled nursing care facilities other than hospitals. Operator of nursing or personal care facilities that require a lesser degree of care than skilled or intermediate care facilities.

Employees: 1,880.

Human Resources: Gary Engelmann, Controller.

Application Procedures: Send resume and cover letter to the attention of Gary Engelmann, Controller.

Community Psychiatric Centers

24502 Pacific Park Dr.
Laguna Hills, CA 92656
Phone: (714)831-1166

Business Description: Community Psychiatric Centers' principal line of business is the ownership and operation of acute psychiatric hospitals. The company operated 45 acute psychiatric hospitals and one 32 bed alcohol treatment facility. Each hospital in the United States is accredited by the Joint Commission on Accreditation of Healthcare Organizations (JCAHO).

Officers: James W. Conte, Pres. & Chairman of the Board; Richard L. Conte, Exec. VP, Chief Admin. Officer, General Counsel & Sec.; Barry Dyches, Sr. VP; Theodore Johson, Vice Pres.; Patrick Kelly, Vice Pres.; Sharon Kurz, Vice Pres.; Kay E. Seim, Vice Pres.; Loren B. Shook, Exec. VP; James P. Smith, Sr. VP, Sec. & Treasurer; David Wakefield, Sr. VP; Ronald Yates, Vice Pres.

Employees: 5,329.

Benefits: Benefits include employee pension plan and profit sharing.

Application Procedures: Hiring is done through individual divisions. Contact the company for more information.

Concord Hospital

250 Pleasant St.
Concord, NH 03301
Phone: (603)225-2711

Employees: 1,200.

Average Entry-Level Hiring: Unknown.

Opportunities: RNs and physical and occupational therapists.

Human Resources: Jacqui McGettigan, Employment Coordinator.

Application Procedures: Call for more information.

Connecticut Valley Hospital

Silver St., Box 351
Middletown, CT 06457
Phone: (203)344-2648
Fax: (203)344-2587

Employees: 950.

Average Entry-Level Hiring: Unknown.

Opportunities: Nurses, respiratory therapists, physical and occupational therapists, radiology and nuclear medicine technologists—requirements not specified.

Human Resources: Ray Cioffi, Employment Contact.

Application Procedures: Call for more information.

Cook County Hospital
749 S. Winchester
Chicago, IL 60612
Phone: (312)633-7571

Employees: 6,000.

Average Entry-Level Hiring: 50 per year.

Opportunities: RN—associate, diploma, or bachelor's degree required. Many other entry-level positions are typically available.

Application Procedures: Contact the human resources department for more information.

S ome people will find the training they need right at the office. American companies desperate to produce more with fewer, better-skilled workers now are pumping $30 billion annually into employee-training programs that run the gamut from basic computer courses to company-sponsored M.B.A. degrees.

Source: *U.S. News & World Report*

Cornell University Medical College
1300 York Ave., Olin 211
New York, NY 10021
Phone: (212)746-1036
Fax: (212)746-8766

Business Description: Cornell University is a medical school employing 2,500 people in research, education, and patient care. Benefit package and tuition reimbursement programs are offered. Upward mobility within the institution is encouraged.

Employees: 2,500.

Average Entry-Level Hiring: 500.

Opportunities: Research technicians, senior research technicians—a B.S. and M.S. required, respectively in biology, chemistry, or other sciences. Entry-level clerical positions require a

B.A. in liberal arts. Secretarial skills are necessary to advance to higher level health care management positions.

Human Resources: Janet Garber, Employment Mgr.

Dana-Farber Cancer Institute
44 Binney St.
Boston, MA 02115
Phone: (617)732-3052
Fax: (617)735-8975

Employees: 1,700.

Average Entry-Level Hiring: Unknown.

Opportunities: RN—four-year B.S. degree. Lab technician—high school education. Other requirements not specified.

Application Procedures: Contact the nurse recruiter for information.

Deer Lodge Centre
2109 Portage Ave.
Winnipeg, MB, Canada R3J 0L3
Phone: (204)831-2105
Fax: (204)888-5574

Business Description: Deer Lodge Centre is strictly a geriatric care facility, long-term and chronic care, not acute care.

Employees: 858.

Average Entry-Level Hiring: Minimal.

Opportunities: RNs, RPNs, LPNs, nurses aides, occupational therapy, speech language, diagnostic services—requirements not specified. Dietary, housekeeping, messengers—on-the-job training.

Department of Veterans Affairs
3350 La Jolla Village Dr.
San Diego, CA 92161
Phone: (619)552-8585
Fax: (619)552-7452

Employees: 2,500.

Average Entry-Level Hiring: Unknown.

Opportunities: RN—U.S. citizen, current, full and unrestricted license in any state; proficient in written and spoken English; graduate of school of professional nursing approved by appropriate state accrediting agency; salary commensurate with experience. Nurse anesthetist—U.S. citizen, current, full and unrestricted license in any state; proficient in written and spoken English; graduate of school of professional nursing approved by state accrediting agency; and graduate of school of anesthesia approved by the American Association of Nurse Anesthetists; salary commensurate with experience. Medical clerk—U.S. citizen; one year experience or two years education above the high school level. File clerk—six months experience or high school graduation or equivalent. Clerk-typist—one year experience or two years education above the high school level, and must type at least 40 wpm.

Application Procedures: Contact the Personnel Service for information.

Department of Veterans Affairs Medical Center

Shreveport Hwy.
Alexandria, LA 71301
Phone: (318)473-0010

Employees: 978. The number of entry level positions reflects the number of RNs hired.

Average Entry-Level Hiring: 15-20.

Opportunities: Nurses—bachelor's degree in nursing, graduation from a three-year diploma program in nursing, or graduation from associate degree program in a school of professional nursing or comparable education. Pharmacist—bachelor's degree in pharmacy, one-year of internship, and licensed to practice pharmacy. Physical therapist—bachelor's degree in physical therapy and one-year of professional physical therapy experience or graduate education in appropriate field.

Human Resources: Hilda S. McBride, Recruiter; Cora C. Chauppette, Personnel Mgt. Specialist Pharmacist, physical therapy.

District of Columbia General Hospital

19th & Massachusetts Ave., SE
Washington, DC 20003
Phone: (202)675-7351
Fax: (202)675-7819

Employees: 2,300.

Average Entry-Level Hiring: Varies.

Opportunities: RN—two-, three-, or four-year degree. No other requirements specified.

Human Resources: Anthony Jacks, Personnel Dir.

Application Procedures: Call for more information.

E.I. du Pont de Nemours & Company Inc.

1007 Market St.
Wilmington, DE 19898
Phone: (302)774-1000

Business Description: Engaged in manufacturing, fabricating and/or processing drugs in pharmaceutical preparations. Manufacturer of medical, surgical, ophthalmic and/or veterinary instruments and apparatus. Manufacturer of X-ray or other irradiation apparatus.

Officers: Thomas E. Minnich, Manager; M. Suwyn, Group VP.

Application Procedures: Contact the company for more information.

Duke University Medical Center

Box 40001
Durham, NC 27706
Phone: (919)684-2015
Fax: (919)681-7926

Opportunities: RN—associate or bachelor's degree. Various other allied health positions available.

Application Procedures: Call the employment office for more information.

Eastern Idaho Regional Medical Center

PO Box 2077
Idaho Falls, ID 83403
Phone: (208)529-6080
Fax: (208)529-6081

Employees: 1,200.

Average Entry-Level Hiring: Unknown.

Opportunities: RN—associate degree required. Laboratory technician—ASCP certified. Physical therapist—master's degree required.

Human Resources: Cheryl O'Connell, Employment Specialist.

Application Procedures: Call for more information.

Englewood Hospital

350 Engle St.
Englewood, NJ 07631
Phone: (201)894-3490
Fax: (201)894-4791

Employees: 2,500.

Average Entry-Level Hiring: Unknown.

Opportunities: No information on specific opportunities available.

E mployment for licensed practical nurses is expected to grow much faster than average in response to the long-term care needs of a rapidly growing aged population and growth in health care in general. The job outlook should remain good unless the number of people completing L.P.N. training increases substantially.

Source: *Occupational Outlook Quarterly*

Fairfax Hospital

3300 Gallows Rd.
Falls Church, VA 22046
Phone: (703)698-3298
Toll-free: 800-234-4405
Fax: (703)698-3448

Employees: 3,500.

Average Entry-Level Hiring: Varies.

Opportunities: RNs, physical therapists, medical technicians, and pharmacists.

Application Procedures: Call for more information.

FHP International Corp.

9900 Talbert Ave.
Fountain Valley, CA 92708
Phone: (714)963-7233

Business Description: Family Health Program, (FHP) is the operating subsidiary of FHP International Corporation. FHP provides medical and dental care to more than half a million members in California, Utah, Arizona, New Mexico and Guam. Through its commercial plan, FHP offers a full range of medical benefits to employees and their families. FHP now operates 45 medical and dental centers in four states and Guam, with two hospitals and one skilled nursing facility in Southern California.

Officers: William R. Benz, CFO; Robert Gumbiner, CEO & Chairman of the Board.

Employees: 7,500.

Application Procedures: Contact the company for more information.

Flambeau Medical Center

98 Sherry Ave., Box 310
Park Falls, WI 54552
Phone: (715)762-2484
Fax: (715)762-4257

Employees: 70.

Average Entry-Level Hiring: 10.

Opportunities: RN—three-, or four-year degree. Physical therapist—four-year degree. Anesthetist CRNE—two-year degree after nursing.

Human Resources: Judy Reese, Secretary.

Foothills Provincial General Hospital

1403 29th St. NW
Calgary, AB, Canada T2N 2T9
Phone: (403)670-1005
Fax: (403)670-1041

Employees: 5,000.

Average Entry-Level Hiring: Unknown.

Opportunities: All professional positions require Alberta licensure.

Application Procedures: Contact the human resources department for information.

Forbes Health System

500 Finley St.
Pittsburgh, PA 15206
Phone: (412)665-3841
Fax: (412)665-3852

Employees: 2,700.

Average Entry-Level Hiring: Unknown.

Opportunities: Registered nurses (all specialties), physical therapist, occupational therapist, radiology technicians—no requirements specified.

Human Resources: Davida Brown, Personnel Mgr.; Anne Marie Grzybek, Personnel Mgr.; Mary Jane Krosoff, Personnel Dir.

Foundation Health Corp.

3400 Data Dr.
Rancho Cordova, CA 95670
Phone: (916)631-5381
Fax: (916)631-5335

Business Description: Offers managed health care services through its health maintenance organization (HMO) and government contracting subsidiaries.

Officers: Owen Brant, VP of Info. Systems; Dan Crowley, Pres. & CEO; Jeffrey L. Elder, VP & CFO; Steven D. Tough, COO; Annette Wimmer, VP of Sales.

Employees: 1,100.

Benefits: Benefits include an employee pension plan and an employee stock purchase plan.

Human Resources: Dan Smithson, Human Resources.

Application Procedures: Send resume and cover letter to the attention of Dan Smithson, Human Resources.

Fulton State Hospital

600 E. 5th St.
Fulton, MO 65251-1798
Phone: (314)592-4100
Fax: (314)592-3000

Employees: 1,200.

Average Entry-Level Hiring: Unknown.

Opportunities: RN—associate or bachelor's degree in nursing. Physical therapist, occupational therapist—bachelor's degree preferred.

Application Procedures: Contact personnel for more information.

Genentech Inc.

460 Point San Bruno Blvd.
South San Francisco, CA 94080
Phone: (415)266-1000

Business Description: A biotechnology company focusing on the development, manufacture, and marketing of human pharmaceutical products produced by recombinant DNA technology.

Officers: Richard B. Brewer, VP of Mktg.; James M. Gower, Sr. VP; Louis J. Lavigne, Jr., VP & CFO; John P. McLaughlin, VP, General Counsel & Sec.; G. Kirk Raab, CEO & Pres.; Robert A. Swanson, Chairman of the Board; William D. Young, Sr. VP.

Employees: 1,790.

Benefits: Benefits include an employee pension plan, an employee stock ownership plan, and a child development and day care center.

Human Resources: Larry Setren, VP of Human Resources; Lloyd Sidney, Human Resources Dir.

Application Procedures: Send resume and cover letter to the attention of one of the following individuals: Larry Setren, VP of Human Resources.; Lloyd Sidney, Human Resources Dir.

What makes one job better than another? High pay? Prestige? Pleasant working conditions? Or, these days, might the clincher be job security? The answer is that there is no single deciding factor. Truly great jobs offer all of the above and more minuses.

Source: *Money*

Glaxo Inc.

5 Moore Dr.
Research Triangle Park, NC 27709
Phone: (919)248-2100

Business Description: A research based company whose corporate purpose is the discovery, development, manufacturing and marketing of safe, effective medicines of the highest quality, including anti-ulcerants, commodity antibiotics, and fine chemicals. The company is Glaxo Holdings' largest subsidiary.

Officers: Dr. E. Mario, CEO; Dr. C.A. Sanders.

Human Resources: Steve Sons, Human Resources Dir.

Application Procedures: Places newspaper advertisements for certain openings. Send resume and cover letter.

Grady Memorial Hospital

PO Box 26208
Atlanta, GA 30035-3801
Phone: (404)616-1900
Fax: (404)616-6033

Human Resources: Carolyn Hughes, Employment Contact.

Greenville Hospital System

701 Grove Rd.
Greenville, SC 29605
Phone: (803)455-8976
Fax: (803)455-5959

Employees: 5,600. The entry-level hiring numbers indicate positions in different areas; administration, nursing, laboratory, and other allied health areas.

Average Entry-Level Hiring: 331-395.

Opportunities: Registered nurses in all clinical areas, medical technologists, occupational and physical therapists. Administrative—master's degree.

Human Resources: Robin Stelling, Recruiter Nurse; Cheryl Dyer, Recruiter Professional/Allied Health.

Halifax Medical Center

PO Box 2830
Daytona Beach, FL 32115-2830
Phone: (904)254-4035
Fax: (904)254-4285

Employees: 2,000.

Average Entry-Level Hiring: Unknown.

Opportunities: RN—two-, three-, or four-year degree.

Human Resources: Robert Diano, Employment Contact.

Hartford Hospital

80 Seymour St.
Hartford, CT 06115
Toll-free: 800-356-7288
Fax: (203)524-7066

Employees: 6,000.

Average Entry-Level Hiring: Unknown.

Opportunities: No information on specific opportunities is available.

Application Procedures: Call for more information.

Health Care & Retirement Corp.

1 Seagate
Toledo, OH 43666
Phone: (419)247-5000

Business Description: Operator of skilled nursing care facilities other than hospitals.

Employees: 16,000.

Average Entry-Level Hiring: Unknown.

Opportunities: Openings exist in many areas, both in the corporate office and in field positions. A one-year "administrator in training" program is available.

Human Resources: Patt Morr, Secretary.

HealthTrust Inc.

4525 Harding Rd.
Nashville, TN 37205
Phone: (615)383-4444

Business Description: HealthTrust is one of the largest hospital management companies in the U.S. It owns and operates more than 80 acute-care hospitals. Healthtrust's facilities are located in 21 southern and western states; 40 are the only providers of acute-care services in their communities. The hospitals generally provide a full range of inpatient and outpatient health care services, including medical/surgical, obstetrics and pediatric care, pharmacies, laboratories, and other support facilities and emergency care. Some of the company's facilities include Selma Medical Center, Selma, Alabama; Encino Hospital, Encino, California; Palm Beach Regional Hospital, Lake Worth, Florida; Edward White Hospital, St. Petersburg, Florida; Medical Center of Baton Rouge, Baton Rouge, Louisiana; Brownwood Regional Hospital, Brownwood, Texas; Diagnostic Center Hospital and Sun Belt Regional Medical Center, Houston, Texas; Bayshore Medical Center, Pasadena, Texas; Northern Virginia Doctors Hospital, Arlington, Virginia. The company also operates facilities in joint venture with other corporations.

Officers: Michael A. Koban, Jr., VP & Treasurer; R. Clayton McWhorter, CEO & Chairman of the Board.

Employees: 30,000.

Benefits: Benefits include an employee pension plan, an employee stock ownership plan, and bonuses/incentives.

Human Resources: Tom Neill, Personnel Dept.

Application Procedures: Send resume and cover letter to the attention of Tom Neill, Personnel Dept.

Hennepin County Medical Center
701 Park Ave.
Minneapolis, MN 55415
Phone: (612)347-2277
Fax: (612)347-3377

Employees: 2,000.

Average Entry-Level Hiring: Nurses—109; physical therapists—50.

Opportunities: RNs and physical therapists.

Human Resources: Annette Stech, Recruiter.

Application Procedures: Call for more information.

Henrietta Egleston Hospital for Children
1405 Clifton Rd., NE
Atlanta, GA 30322
Phone: (404)325-6000
Fax: (404)315-2059

Employees: 1,400.

Average Entry-Level Hiring: 409.

Opportunities: Nurses—bachelor's degree required.

Human Resources: Paul Owen, Employment Mgr.

Application Procedures: Call for more information.

Hillcrest Medical Center
1120 S. Utica Ave.
Tulsa, OK 74104
Phone: (918)584-1351
Fax: (918)584-6636

Opportunities: Nurses—bachelor's degree required.

Application Procedures: Contact the personnel department for more information.

Hillhaven Corp.
1148 Broadway Plaza
Tacoma, WA 98402
Phone: (206)572-4901

Business Description: Engaged in the operation of retail drug stores. Operator of skilled nursing care facilities other than hospitals.

Officers: Richard K. Eamer, CEO & Chairman of the Board; Robert F. Pacquer, Sr. VP & CFO.

Employees: 34,000.

Application Procedures: Contact the company for more information.

Hoechst-Roussel Pharmaceuticals Inc.
Rte. 202-206 N.
Somerville, NJ 08876
Phone: (201)231-2000

Business Description: Engaged in manufacturing, fabricating and/or processing drugs in pharmaceutical preparations.

Officers: Hubert E. Huckle, Chairman of the Board; Gerald McMurtry, Exec. VP of Mktg. & Sales; Anthony Tursi, VP of Finance.

Employees: 1,900.

Human Resources: Rob Slone, Human Resources Dir.

To economize on headhunters' fees and classified advertising, a growing number of companies are now filing the resumes that snow in each year where they might actually do job seekers some good: in an electronic database.

Source: *U.S. News & World Report*

Hoffman-La Roche Inc.
340 Kingsland St.
Nutley, NJ 07110
Phone: (201)235-5000

Business Description: Manufacturer of pharmaceuticals. The company's products are marketed worldwide.

Officers: I. Lerner, CEO & Pres.

Employees: 10,000.

Average Entry-Level Hiring: Unknown.

Human Resources: A. Vinson, Human Resources Dir.

Application Procedures: Recruits at the Michigan Collegiate Job Fair for pharmaceutical sales positions. Qualifying majors include biology, chemistry, and business.

Holy Cross Hospital

4725 N. Federal Hwy.
Ft. Lauderdale, FL 33351
Phone: (305)771-8000
Fax: (305)776-3129

Employees: 1,700.

Opportunities: Laboratory technician, laboratory technologist—four year degree in the sciences, preferably chemistry or hematology, and a Florida Medical One Laboratory Technician's license. Pharmacist—college pharmacy degree and Florida license. Radiologic technologist—must have graduated from an accredited program for radiologic technologists and have a Florida license. Radiation therapy technologist, nuclear medicine technologist—must have graduated from an accredited program in their speciality. Physical therapist—B.S. degree in physical therapy and Florida license. Physical therapy assistant—must be a graduate of a two-year accredited PT assistant program and licensed or eligible in Florida.

Human Resources: Maria Ferrante, Employment Coordinator; Helaiwe Nelles, Employment Contact.

Hospital Corporation of America

1 Park Plaza
Nashville, TN 37202
Phone: (615)327-9551

Business Description: A Nashville-based health care company. Which either owns or manages hospitals, psychiatric units, and other medical facilities in the United States. In 1989, the company and Doheny Development Corp. embarked on a joint venture to produce a 200,000 square-foot medical mart facility in Dallas, Texas.

Officers: Thomas F. Frist, Jr., CEO, Pres. & Chairman of the Board; Roger E. Mick, Exec. VP & CFO.

Employees: 49,640.

Application Procedures: Send resume and cover letter to the Employee Relations Department.

Howard University Hospital

400 Byrant St.
Washington, DC 20059
Phone: (202)806-7714
Fax: (202)483-6693

Employees: 2,000.

Average Entry-Level Hiring: Unknown.

Opportunities: Nurses, M.S.W.s, respiratory therapists, physical and occupational therapists—requirements not specified.

Application Procedures: Contact Employment Services for information.

Humana Inc.

The Humana Bldg.
500 W. Main St.
PO Box 1438
Louisville, KY 40201-1438
Phone: (502)580-1000

Business Description: Providers of an integrated system of health care services. Operates acute-care hospitals and a variety of health benefit plans for employee groups and Medicare beneficiaries. Owns and operates 83 hospitals in 19 states, England, and Switzerland and has 1.7 million members enrolled in its health plans.

Officers: William C. Ballard, Jr., Exec. VP of Finance; Brenda C. Bryant, VP of Mktg.; Carl F. Pollard, CEO & Pres.

Employees: 55,100.

Human Resources: Steven L. Durbin, VP of Employee Relations; Michael R. Smith, VP of Human Resources.

Application Procedures: Send resume and cover letter to the attention of Human Resources Department.

IMCERA Group Inc.

2315 Sanders Rd.
Northbrook, IL 60062
Phone: (708)564-8600

Business Description: IMCERA Group Inc. consists of three businesses: Mallinckrodt Medical, Mallinckrodt Specialty Chemicals and Pitman-Moore. IMCERA also owns approximately 38 percent of the common stock of IMC Fertilizer Group Inc. Mallinckrodt Medical's products are used primarily in diagnosis. Major products include Hexabrix and Optiray. Mallickrodt Specialty Chemicals are used in the production of drugs and cosmetics. It also produces catalyst and performance chemicals and science products. Pitman-Moore produces feed for cattle and poultry as well as vaccines and diagnostics for animals. It also produces antibacterial and antifungal products for cattle, sheep, swine, and poultry.

Officers: James C. Bryan, Vice Pres.; John A. Edwardson, Exec. VP & CFO; M. Blakeman Ingle, CEO.

Employees: 9,600.

Benefits: Benefits include an employee pension plan.

Human Resources: Peggy Baumrock, Human Resources Dir.

Application Procedures: Send resume and cover letter to the attention of Peggy Baumrock, Human Resources Dir.

Ingalls Memorial Hospital and Health System

1 Ingalls Dr.
Harvey, IL 60426
Phone: (708)333-0737
Fax: (708)333-2300

Employees: 2,500.

Average Entry-Level Hiring: Unknown.

Opportunities: Nurse—associate or bachelor's degree or state work permit. Physical therapists—bachelor's degree required.

Application Procedures: All applicants must have a resume. Contact the personnel office for more information.

Jersey Shore Medical Center

1945 Rte. 33
Neptune, NJ 07754
Phone: (908)775-5500
Toll-free: 800-426-4714
Fax: (908)776-4239

Human Resources: Margaret Frucci, Employment Contact.

Johns Hopkins Hospital

600 Wolfe St.
Baltimore, MD 21205
Phone: (301)955-6749

Employees: 6,000.

Average Entry-Level Hiring: Unknown.

Opportunities: RN—associate or bachelor's degree required.

Application Procedures: Contact Personnel for information.

Lifetime Corp.

99 Summer St., Ste. 1600
Boston, MA 02110
Phone: (617)330-5080

Business Description: Engaged in the operation of establishments providing home health care services.

Officers: Barry P. Coombes, Exec. VP & CFO; Anthony H. Reeves, CEO, Pres. & Treasurer.

Employees: 26,000.

Application Procedures: Contact the company for more information.

> Job-seekers long have looked to health care as one of their most dependable sources of openings. That's not going to change any time soon, especially as the number of people age 75 and over climbs sharply in the 1990s.
>
> Source: *Business Week*

Eli Lilly & Co.

Lilly Corporate Center
Indianapolis, IN 46285
Phone: (317)276-3219
Toll-free: 800-833-8699

Business Description: A research-based corporation that develops, manufactures, and markets pharmaceuticals, medical instruments, diagnostic products, and agricultural products.

Officers: Vaughn D. Bryson, Exec. VP; James M. Cornelius, VP of Finance & CFO; Earl B. Herr, Ph.D., Exec. VP; J.B. King, VP & General Counsel; Mel Perelman, Ph.D., Exec. VP; Eugene L. Step, Exec. VP; Richard D. Wood, CEO, Pres. & Chairman of the Board.

Employees: 29,900.

Average Entry-Level Hiring: 5-15.

Opportunities: Opportunities include financial analyst positions.

Benefits: Benefits include medical, dental, life, and short- and long-term disability insurances; an employee pension plan; a savings plan; profit sharing; tuition assistance; bonuses/incentives; maternity leave; paternity leave; vacation days; paid holidays; flexible holidays; employee parking; recreational programs; an employee counseling program; an employee cafeteria; flex time;

a smoke-free environment; and training programs.

Human Resources: Karen Friss, Human Resources Representative; Ida Simmons, Benefits; Stephen A. Stitle, VP of Human Resources.

Application Procedures: Recruits primarily at college campuses nationwide. Send resume and cover letter to the attention of Stephen A. Stitle, VP of Human Resources.

Lincoln Health Resources

250 E. Dunlap
Phoenix, AZ 85020
Phone: 800-727-4767
Fax: (602)870-6066

Business Description: Lincoln Health Resources is a 235 bed acute care facility with a designated trauma unit.

Employees: 1,800. The number of entry level employees reflects 25 people hired for nursing positions and 500 people hired for other positions.

Average Entry-Level Hiring: 525.

Opportunities: Nurse—B.S.N. or A.D.N. medical technician, occupational therapist—bachelor's degree required. Physical therapy—five years of education. Lab, radiology, and respiratory technicians—associate degree.

Human Resources: Michelle Stillinger Nurse Recruiter; Ann Sponebraker, Employment Coordinator.

Loma Linda University Medical Center

24887 Taylor St., Box 2000
Loma Linda, CA 92354
Phone: (714)824-4330
Toll-free: 800-722-2770
Fax: (714)824-4058

Employees: 5,000.

Average Entry-Level Hiring: 200-300.

Opportunities: Pharmacists—requires California State Board of Pharmacy license; both full-time and part-time, day and evening positions available. Respiratory therapist—California license required and graduate of two-year AMA approved school. Medical technologist—California license required. Occupational therapist—B.S. degree in OT, member of AOTA.

Physical therapist—B.S. degree in physical therapy and California license. Registered nurse radiologic technologist—valid certificate in General Diagnostic Radiological Technology issued by the State of California Department of Health.

Human Resources: Elmerissa, Personnel Officer; Tom Hudson, Employment Specialist.

Application Procedures: Send resume and cover letter. For information regarding other available positions, call the job line at (714)824-4330.

Lutheran Hospital—La Crosse

1910 South Ave.
La Crosse, WI 54601
Phone: (608)785-0530
Fax: (608)785-2181

Employees: 2,300.

Average Entry-Level Hiring: 200.

Opportunities: Physical and occupational therapists, medical lab technicians, and medical records staff.

Human Resources: Judy Eddy, Recruiting Specialist.

Application Procedures: Call for more information.

Maine Medical Center

22 Bramhall St.
Portland, ME 04102
Phone: (207)871-2974
Fax: (207)871-4999

Employees: 3,800.

Average Entry-Level Hiring: Unknown.

Opportunities: RNs—two- or four-year degree required.

Human Resources: Holly MacEvan, Recruitment Mgr.

Application Procedures: Call for more information.

Manatee Memorial Hospital

206 2nd St., E.
Bradenton, FL 34208
Phone: (813)746-5111
Fax: (813)745-7405

Employees: 1,434.

Average Entry-Level Hiring: Unknown.

Opportunities: RN—two; three-, or four-year degree required. No other requirements specified.

Human Resources: Carol Pennock, Human Resources.

Manor Care Inc.

10750 Columbia Pike
Silver Spring, MD 20901
Phone: (301)681-9400

Business Description: Holding company with interests in the healthcare and hospitality industries.

Officers: Stewart Bainnum, Jr., CEO, Pres. & Chairman of the Board; Joseph Buckley, Sr. VP Information Resources and Development; James A. MacCutcheon, Sr. VP of Finance & Treasurer.

Employees: 20,800.

Human Resources: Roberta McCall, Employment Specialist; Charles A. Shields, VP of Human Resources.

Application Procedures: Send resume and cover letter to the attention of Roberta McCall, Employment Specialist.

Medical Center Hospital of Vermont

University of Vermont
111 Colchester Ave.
Burlington, VT 05401
Phone: (802)656-2825
Fax: (802)656-2792

Business Description: MCHV is a teaching hospital with 500 beds.

Employees: 3,000.

Average Entry-Level Hiring: Unknown.

Opportunities: Registered nurses, medical-surgical/maternal-child; medical, radiology, and nuclear medicine technologists; physical, radiation, occupational, and respiratory therapists; respiratory technicians; pharmacists; dieticians; health record analysts—no requirements specified.

Application Procedures: Contact Human Resources for information.

Medical College of Georgia

Personnel Div./Employment Section
1120 15th St.
Augusta, GA 30912-8100
Phone: (706)721-3081
Fax: (706)721-7192

Employees: 6,000.

Average Entry-Level Hiring: 200.

Opportunities: Registered nurses, LPNs (all areas), physical therapists, occupational therapists, respiratory therapists, medical technologists, medical secretaries/transcriptionists—no requirements specified.

Human Resources: Mary Haygan, Personnel Dept.

Application Procedures: Call for more information.

A career path should not be restrictive—there should be forks in the path, allowing you to adapt as changes occur within professional and personal lifestyles. The best intentions can go astray, leading to discouragement and disillusionment if alternative paths have not been prepared.

Source: *The Canadian Nurse*

Medical University of South Carolina

State Institution
171 Ashley Ave.
Charleston, SC 29425-1035
Phone: (803)792-2071
Fax: (816)792-9533

Business Description: The MUSC Medical Center is made up of the Medical University Hospital, the Children's Hospital, the Storm Eye Institute, the Institute of Psychiatry, all outpatient clinics, and the Charleston Memorial Hospital. The mission of the MUSC Medical Center includes teaching students and physicians, the provision of tertiary care, and human research. Research programs are ongoing and staff is needed to support the research projects. There are 572 beds in the teaching hospital, which will soon have 600 beds. All patients will soon be in single bedrooms and there will be 50 intensive care beds.

Employees: 7,700.

Average Entry-Level Hiring: 800-1000.

Opportunities: There is a job vacancy listing published annually which identifies hard-to-fill vacancies; these are always available. Another listing, published weekly, includes clerical openings, some patient care aide, and administrative and managerial openings. Call for listing(s).

Human Resources: Jean W. Turner, Employment Mgr.; Kathy Leitch, Recruiting Specialist; Nancy Adams, Recruiter Nursing.

Memorial Hospital of South Bend and Memorial Health System

615 N. Michigan St.
South Bend, IN 46601
Phone: (219)284-7407
Fax: (219)284-7445

Employees: 240.

Average Entry-Level Hiring: Unknown.

Opportunities: RN—license and two-, three- or four-year degree required. Physical and occupational therapists—bachelor's degree.

Human Resources: Sue Long, Secretary.

Application Procedures: Call for more information.

Merck & Company Inc.

PO Box 2000
Rahway, NJ 07065
Phone: (908)594-4000

Business Description: Discovers, develops, and markets medicines and human and animal health products. Operates numerous plant facilities and research laboratories.

Officers: Judy C. Lewent, VP & Treasurer; John E. Lyons, Vice Chairman of the Board; P. Roy Vagelos, M.D., CEO, Pres. & Chairman of the Board.

Employees: 34,400.

Average Entry-Level Hiring: 5.

Human Resources: Steven M. Darien, VP of Human Resources Worldwide Personnel; Anthony Rizzello Mgr. of College Relations.

Application Procedures: Send resume and cover letter to the attention of Anthony Rizzello, Mgr. of College Relations.

Mercy Hospital

2215 Truxton Ave.
Box 119
Bakersfield, CA 93302
Phone: (805)632-5580
Fax: (805)861-9727

Employees: 1,500.

Average Entry-Level Hiring: 200.

Opportunities: Nurses—two-, three-, or four-year degrees. Physical therapist—master's degree. Technicians require an academic education.

Human Resources: Smoki Francisco, Recruiter Nursing.

Mercy Hospital Medical Center

6th & University
Des Moines, IA 50314
Phone: (515)247-3100
Fax: (515)298-8831

Employees: 4,200.

Average Entry-Level Hiring: Unknown.

Opportunities: RN—associate or bachelor's degree. Social workers—M.S.W. required. Occupational therapists—bachelor's degree required. Physician assistants—state licensure required.

Application Procedures: Contact personnel for more information.

Methodist Hospital

8303 Dodge St.
Omaha, NE 68114
Phone: (402)390-8827
Fax: (402)390-8722

Employees: 2,333. The number of entry level employees hired reflects 70 people hired for medical positions and 25 people hired for non-medical positions.

Average Entry-Level Hiring: 95.

Opportunities: RN (all areas), physical therapy, pharmacy, radiologic technologist, nuclear medicine technicians, radiation therapy, respiratory therapy technicians—Nebraska licensure and accredited graduate.

Human Resources: Jeannie Fields Medical recruiter; Tracy Stabbe Clerical; Joan Hilts Entry-level; Kelli Green Business.

MetroHealth Medical Center

2500 MetroHealth Dr.
Cleveland, OH 44109
Phone: (216)459-4134
Fax: (216)459-5234

Employees: 6,000.

Average Entry-Level Hiring: Unknown.

Opportunities: Registered nurse—associate degree or diploma required; B.S.N. preferred. Physical therapist, occupational therapist, clinical dietitian, and pharmacist—bachelor's degree and state licensure. Medical technologist—B.S. in chemistry or biology, or NRCC or ASCP certification. Respiratory therapist—associate degree. X-ray technician—associate degree or certification.

Human Resources: Shelley Thompson, Employment Coordinator.

Miles Inc.

1127 Myrtle St.
Elkhart, IN 46514
Phone: (219)264-8111

Business Description: Engaged in manufacturing, fabricating and/or processing drugs in pharmaceutical preparations.

Officers: Klaus Risse, CEO & Pres.; John Tremse, VP of Systems; Jon Wyne, Treasurer.

Employees: 14,000.

Human Resources: John W. Schulz, VP of Human Resources.

Mills-Peninsula Hospitals

1783 El Camino Real
Burlingame, CA 94010
Phone: (415)696-7885
Fax: (415)696-5890

Human Resources: Shirley Wheeler, Recruiter Nursing.

Mississippi Baptist Medical Center

1225 N. State St.
Jackson, MS 39202-2002
Phone: (601)968-1296
Toll-free: 800-844-1084
Fax: (601)968-4137

Employees: 3,000.

Average Entry-Level Hiring: Unknown.

Opportunities: Radiologic technologists, physi-

cal therapists, and other allied health professionals.

Application Procedures: Contact the human resources department for more information.

Mount Auburn Hospital

330 Mt. Auburn St.
Cambridge, MA 02238
Phone: (617)499-5066
Fax: (617)499-5584

Employees: 1,800.

Opportunities: RN—certified, two- or four-year degree; must pass Massachusetts board. Laboratory technician, respiratory therapy—four year degree. No other requirements specified.

Application Procedures: Contact the company for more information.

> Last year 1991, 36 million Americans were jobless, earned poverty-level wages or were part-timers who wanted a fulltime job.
>
> Source: *U.S. News & World Report*

Mount Sinai Hospital

600 University Ave.
Toronto, ON, Canada M5G 1X5
Phone: (416)586-5044
Fax: (416)586-5045

Human Resources: Marilyn Gall, Mgr. of Recruitment Services.

Mount Sinai Hospital

500 Blue Hills Ave.
Hartford, CT 06112
Phone: (203)242-4431
Toll-free: 800-882-6602
Fax: (203)286-4629

Human Resources: Colette Austin, Employment Mgr.

Muscatatuck State Developmental Center

PO Box 77
Butlerville, IN 47223
Phone: (812)346-4401
Fax: (812)346-6308

Employees: 1,350.

Average Entry-Level Hiring: Unknown.

Opportunities: Nurse IV—possession of a valid license to practice nursing in the state of Indiana as an RN. Charge nurse—one year of full-time paid professional experience in psychiatric, developmental disability, or geriatric nursing; possession of a valid license to practice nursing in the state of Indiana as an RN; an accredited bachelor's degree in nursing may substitute for the required experience. Behavior clinician III— one year of full-time paid professional experience in the performance of psychological services, which includes diagnostic interviewing, report preparation, interpretation of test results, and/or treatment of emotional disorders; a master's degree in psychology, educational psychology, guidance and counseling, tests and measurements, or psychometry required; internship training at the doctoral level or doctoral coursework in any of the above areas may substitute for the required experience with a maximum substitution of one year. Mental Health Administrator III— two years of full-time paid professional work experience in the provision of therapeutic patient services for the mentally ill or mentally retarded; a bachelor's degree in business administration, nursing, mental health technology, psychology, social work, education, vocational rehabilitation, speech pathology and audiology, or one of the adjunctive therapies (music, recreation, physical, occupational, or industrial) required; accredited graduate training in any of the above areas may substitute for the required experience with a maximum substitution of two years. Audiologist III—licensure as an audiologist by the Indiana Board of Examiners on Speech Pathology and Audiology required. Dietitian IV—registration as a dietitian or proof of eligibility for admission to the Dietitian Registration Examination; must successfully pass the Dietitian's Registration Examination of the Commission on Dietetic Registration prior to the granting of permanent status. Psychologist I—current certification as a psychologist by the Indiana State Psychology Board, proof must accompany application. Psychiatric Attendant V—two years of full-time paid work experience; a high school diploma may substitute for the required experience.

Human Resources: Julie Broome, Employment Contact Nursing; Patricia Spanagel, Employment Contact Dietitians.

Application Procedures: All applicants must be certified to an eligible list by filing a State Application PD/100 with Indiana State Personnel Department, Indianapolis, IN; and be available for Jennings County, No. 40.

National Health Laboratories Inc.

7590 Fay Ave.
La Jolla, CA 92037
Phone: (619)454-3314

Business Description: Operator of medical laboratories.

Officers: R.E. Draper, CEO & Pres.

Employees: 4,700.

Application Procedures: Accepts unsolicited resumes, or applications can be filled out on site.

National Healthcare Inc.

2727 Paces Ferry Rd., Ste. 1000
Atlanta, GA 30339
Phone: (404)431-1500

Business Description: Operator of specialty hospitals.

Officers: J.T. McAfee, CEO & Pres.

Employees: 3,500.

Application Procedures: Contact the company for more information.

National HealthCorp L.P.

PO Box 1398
Murfreesboro, TN 37133
Phone: (615)890-2020

Business Description: Engaged in the operation of apartment buildings. Operator of skilled nursing care facilities other than hospitals. Operator of nursing or personal care facilities that require a lesser degree of care than skilled or intermediate care facilities.

Officers: W. Andrew Adams, President; Charlotte A. Swafford, Treasurer.

Employees: 8,616.

Application Procedures: Contact the company for more information.

National Industries Inc.

9200 Shelbyville Rd.
Suite 810
Louisville, KY 40222
Phone: (502)425-4701
Fax: (502)425-4708

Business Description: Engaged in the operation of eating establishments. Holding company engaged in holding or owning the securities of companies in order to exercise some degree of control over the companies' activities. Operator of nursing or personal care facilities that require a lesser degree of care than skilled or intermediate care facilities.

Officers: Timothy O. Coffey, Sr. VP of Mktg.; Jack Tonini, Dir. of Data Processing; Frank Ward, Chairman of the Board & Finance Officer; W.B. Yarmuth, President.

Employees: 500.

Human Resources: Timothy Luckett, Human Resources Dir.

National Medical Care Inc.

1601 Trapelo Rd.
Waltham, MA 02154
Phone: (617)466-9850

Business Description: Operator of nursing or personal care facilities that require a lesser degree of care than skilled or intermediate care facilities. Engaged in the operation of establishments providing home health care services.

Officers: Robert Armstrong, VP & Controller; Constantine L. Hampers, CEO & Chairman of the Board.

Employees: 300.

Application Procedures: Contact the company for more information.

National Medical Enterprises Inc.

2700 Colorado Ave.
Santa Monica, CA 90404
Phone: (213)315-8000

Business Description: One of the largest health care service companies in the United States, owning and operating over 500 acute-care, psychiatric, and rehabilitation hospitals, and long-term care and substance abuse treatment facilities. Also operates internationally.

Officers: Richard K. Eamer, CEO & Chairman

of the Board; Taylor R. Jenson, Exec. VP & CFO.

Employees: 77,000.

Human Resources: Alan R. Ewalt, Sr. VP of Human Resources.

Application Procedures: Send resume and cover letter to the attention of Human Resources Department.

New England Baptist Hospital

125 Parker Hill Ave.
Boston, MA 02120
Phone: (617)739-5233
Fax: (617)731-5742

Employees: 1,200.

Average Entry-Level Hiring: Unknown.

Opportunities: RN—associate or bachelor's degree required.

Human Resources: Laura Adam, Human Resources Asst.

Application Procedures: Call for more information.

The rule of thumb, says Dale Breaden of the Federation of State Medical Boards, is that a physician who is five to seven years out of medical school is a year behind the current state of knowledge in her specialty, unless she's made an effort to keep up.

Source: *Glamour*

New England Journal of Medicine

1440 Main St.
Waltham, MA 02154
Phone: (617)893-3800

Business Description: Engaged in publishing, or in publishing and printing periodicals.

Officers: Lawrence Altrich, Dir. of Info. Systems; Robie Nickerson, Controller; A.S. Relman, Publisher; Arthur Wilschek, Dir. of Mktg. & Sales.

Employees: 250.

Human Resources: Jack King, Head of Personnel.

New Medico Associates Inc.
100 Federal St., 29th Fl.
Boston, MA 02110
Phone: (617)426-4100
Fax: (617)426-3030

Business Description: Operator of nursing or personal care facilities that require a lesser degree of care than skilled or intermediate care facilities. Operator of general medical and surgical hospitals. Operator of specialized outpatient facilities.

Officers: Jeffery Goldshine, President.

Employees: 8,200.

Application Procedures: Contact the company for more information.

Newark Beth-Israel Medical Center
201 Lyons Ave.
Newark, NJ 07112
Phone: (201)926-7521
Fax: (201)926-3457

Employees: 2,900.

Average Entry-Level Hiring: Unknown.

Opportunities: Clinical nurse specialist— B.S.N. and Master's in nursing, certification, labor and delivery unit experience.

Human Resources: Sondra Helfand Nursing.

Application Procedures: Contact the Human Resources Department for more information.

North Broward Hospital District
303 SE 17th St.
Fort Lauderdale, FL 33316
Phone: 800-222-4337

Employees: 5,500.

Average Entry-Level Hiring: Unknown.

Opportunities: Positions for all allied health professionals, pharmacists, and medical technologists are available; no requirements specified.

Application Procedures: Contact Human Resources for information.

Northwest Community Hospital
800 W. Central Rd.
Arlington Heights, IL 60005
Phone: (708)259-1000
Fax: (708)506-4395

Employees: 2,500.

Average Entry-Level Hiring: Unknown.

Opportunities: RN—two-, three-, or four-year degree. Many other entry-level positions are available.

Human Resources: Karolynn Kuecher, Recruiter Nursing.

Application Procedures: Call for more information.

Northwest Connecticut Healthcare Systems, Inc.
540 Litchfield St.
Torrington, CT 06790
Phone: (203)496-6540
Fax: (203)496-6631

Employees: 900.

Average Entry-Level Hiring: Unknown.

Opportunities: Nurses—state licensure or two years of B.S. degree. Lab technician—no requirements specified.

Human Resources: Sandra Cocco, Recruiter Nursing.

Nu-Med Inc.
PO Box 1800
Encino, CA 91436
Phone: (818)990-2000

Business Description: Operator of psychiatric hospitals. Operator of specialty hospitals.

Officers: Stuart Bruck, VP of Mktg.; Yoram Dor, Exec. VP & CFO; Maurice Lewitt, CEO & Chairman of the Board.

Employees: 2,700.

Application Procedures: Contact the company for more information.

Orlando Regional Healthcare System
1414 S. Kuhl Ave.
Orlando, FL 32806
Phone: (407)841-5186
Fax: (407)237-6374

Employees: 5,000.

Average Entry-Level Hiring: Unknown.

Opportunities: RN—two-, three-, or four-year degree required. Other positions are also available.

Application Procedures: Call Personnel for more information.

Ortho Pharmaceutical Corp.

Rte. 202
PO Box 300
Raritan, NJ 08869
Phone: (908)524-0400

Business Description: Engaged in manufacturing, fabricating and/or processing drugs in pharmaceutical preparations.

Application Procedures: Send resume and cover letter to the attention of Personnel.

PacifiCare Health Systems Inc.

5995 Plaza Dr.
Cypress, CA 90630-5028
Phone: (714)952-1121

Business Description: Owns and operates health maintenance organizations (HMOs) with more than 673,000 members in California, Oklahoma, Oregon, and Texas. Patient care is provided by physicians under contract with the company. The company also owns a life insurance company and is considering opening its own pharmacies (1990 annual report).

Officers: Lucy M. Cunningham, Vice Pres. Senior Services; Terry Hartshorn, CEO & Pres.; Alan Hoops, Evec. VP, COO & Sec.; Hal C. Hylton, VP of Mktg. & Development; Richard Kislowski, VP of Info. Systems; Joseph S. Konowiecki, General Counsel & Asst. Sec.; Richard Lipeles, Sr. VP; Wayne Lowell; Carmen Ness, HSD., VP Government Relations; John Ninomiya, Vice Pres. Health Data Analysis; Fred Ryder, VP & Controller; John Siefker, Sr. VP; Len Whyte, Vice Pres. HMO Services.

Employees: 1,393.

Benefits: Benefits include profit sharing; stock option plan for officers and key employees; and bonuses/incentives for officers, managers, and key employees.

Human Resources: C. William Wood, VP of Human Resources.

Application Procedures: Send resume and cover letter to the attention of Human Resources Dept.

Palo Alto Veterans Administration Medical Center

3801 Miranda Ave.
Palo Alto, CA 94304
Phone: (415)858-3951
Fax: (415)852-3318

Employees: 2,500.

Average Entry-Level Hiring: Unknown.

Opportunities: Many opportunities are available, including positions in nursing, physical therapy, rehabilitation, and as clerks.

Human Resources: Amy Lee, Staffing Specialist Nursing.

Application Procedures: Call for more information.

Most of us have at least one thing at work that really bugs us. If you have been chronically repeating your pet complaint for more than a couple of months, it's fair to assume that nobody else is going to come and fix it for you. So take some action on your own. What can *you* do to make it better for yourself? *With whom* can you team up to solve this problem? If you're not willing to commit yourself to solving a problem that bugs you, you can conclude only that you actually prefer complaining.

Source: *Business Monday/Detroit Free Press*

Pfizer Inc.

235 E. 42nd St.
New York, NY 10017
Phone: (212)573-2323

Business Description: A diversified, worldwide health care company. Although eighty percent of its sales are in health-related categories, Pfizer also produces intermediates, such as food ingredients, minerals for paper production, and refractory products for the production of glass and steel.

Officers: William E. Mullin, VP of Info. Systems; Edmund T. Pratt, Jr., CEO & Chairman of the Board; Jean-Paul Valles, VP of Finance.

Employees: 42,500.

Human Resources: Bruce R. Ellig, VP of Personnel.

Application Procedures: Places newspaper

advertisements for certain openings. Send resume and cover letter to the attention of Personnel.

The Presbyterian Hospital

Columbia Presbyterian Medical Center
New York, NY 10032-3784
Phone: (212)305-1956
Fax: (212)305-2012

Employees: 8,000.

Average Entry-Level Hiring: 450.

Opportunities: Registered nurse—associate degree or B.S.N. eligible for New York State license. Physician assistant—B.S. degree, minimum New York State license. Laboratory technologist, pharmacist—B.S. degree, eligible for New York State license. Physical therapist, occupational therapist—B.A. or B.S. degree, eligible for New York State license. Radiation therapy technician, radiology technician, respiratory technician—associate degree, eligible for New York State license. Social worker—M.S.W. required, and CSW eligible.

Human Resources: Letty Mintz, Recruiter Nursing; Jo Ann Olson, Employment Mgr.

Prince County Hospital

259 Beattie Ave.
Summerside, PE, Canada C1N 2A9
Phone: (902)436-9131
Fax: (902)436-1501

Employees: 450.

Average Entry-Level Hiring: 12-15.

Opportunities: Registered nurses, licensed nursing assistants, laboratory technologists, respiratory therapists, pharmacists, ultrasound technologists, physiotherapists—requirements not specified.

Human Resources: Nancy Darling, Personnel Mgr.

Application Procedures: Send resume to the Personnel Department or call for more information.

Providence Hospital

1550 Varnum St. NE
Washington, DC 20017
Phone: (202)269-7925
Fax: (202)269-7492

Employees: 1,800.

Average Entry-Level Hiring: Nurses—20.

Opportunities: RNs—associate or bachelor's degree. Other titles contracted out.

Human Resources: Carol Lieberman, Personnel Coordinator Nursing.

Application Procedures: Send a letter of recommendation with applications. Call for more information.

Ramsay Health Care, Inc.

3425 Melrose Rd.
Fayetteville, NC 28304
Phone: (919)485-7181
Fax: (919)485-8465

Business Description: Cumberland Hospital is a private, 175-bed psychiatric/chemical dependency treatment hospital offering inpatient and outpatient services to all age groups.

Employees: 300. The number of entry level people reflects 25 RNs and 5 M.S.W.s hired.

Average Entry-Level Hiring: 30.

Opportunities: RNs—psychiatric background preferred but not required. Social workers—M.S.W. required. Chemical dependency counselors—state certification required. Occupational therapists, COTAs, and recreation therapists—state registration required. Physician assistant—state licensure required.

Human Resources: Robert Reylea, Human Resources Dir.

Ranchos Los Amigos Medical Center

7601 E. Imperial Hwy.
Downey, CA 90242
Phone: (310)940-7111
Fax: (310)803-3486

Employees: 2,500.

Average Entry-Level Hiring: Unknown.

Opportunities: RN, physical therapist, occupational therapist—bachelor's degree.

Application Procedures: Contact Human Resources for more information.

Republic Health Corp.

15303 Dallas Pkwy., Ste. 1400
Dallas, TX 75248-4634
Phone: (214)851-3100
Fax: (214)851-3121

Business Description: Operator of general

medical and surgical hospitals. Provider of management consulting services.

Officers: Patrick G. Mackey, VP & CFO; Brian P. Marsal, CEO & Pres.

Employees: 6,500.

Human Resources: James Johnston, VP of Human Resources.

Application Procedures: Contact the company for more information.

Richardson-Vicks USA Inc.

1 Far Mill Crossing
Shelton, CT 06484
Phone: (203)925-6000

Business Description: Engaged in manufacturing, fabricating and/or processing drugs in pharmaceutical preparations. Manufacturer of cosmetics, perfumes or other toilet preparations.

Officers: William I. Bergman, President; Wayne Matthai, Dir. of Systems.

Employees: 16,000.

Human Resources: Charles D. Wright, Head of Personnel.

Roger Williams Medical Center

825 Chalkstone Ave.
Providence, RI 02908
Phone: (401)456-2288
Fax: (401)456-2029

Employees: 1,500.

Average Entry-Level Hiring: Unknown.

Opportunities: RN—two-, three- or four-year degree required. No other requirements specified.

Human Resources: Rosemary G. Barber, Employment Contact.

Royal Alexandra Hospitals

10240 Kingsway
Edmonton, AB, Canada T5H 3V9
Phone: (403)477-4111
Fax: (403)477-4960

Employees: 3,000.

Average Entry-Level Hiring: Unknown.

Opportunities: Nursing—diploma or degree. LPN—diploma.

Application Procedures: Contact the Human Resources Department for information.

St. Anthony Medical Center

1313 St. Anthony Pl.
Louisville, KY 40204-1749
Phone: (502)627-1000
Fax: (502)627-1040

Employees: 900.

Average Entry-Level Hiring: Unknown.

Opportunities: RN—bachelor's degree required.

Human Resources: Sarah McKenny, Personnel Specialist.

Application Procedures: Call for more information.

> In today's competitive marketplace, people who have not thought about their future may not have one, or at least not a very bright one. Job seekers must be able to match their skills to the jobs available. You'll stand a better chance of having the right skills if you know which ones will be in demand.
>
> Source: *Occupational Outlook Quarterly*

St. Elizabeth's Hospital of Boston

736 Cambridge St.
Boston, MA 02135
Phone: (617)789-2647

Employees: 2,400.

Average Entry-Level Hiring: Unknown.

Opportunities: Nurses—medical, surgical, critical care, emergency room; no requirements specified.

Human Resources: Karen Nenter, Human Resources.

Application Procedures: Call for more information.

St. John's Hospital

800 E. Carpenter St.
Springfield, IL 62769
Phone: (217)544-6464
Fax: (217)525-5601

Employees: 3,600.

Average Entry-Level Hiring: Unknown.

Opportunities: Registered nurse—bachelor's degree or state permit required. Physical therapist, occupational therapist—bachelor's degree required.

Human Resources: Joan Stennard, Employment Contact; Tracie Sayre, Employment Contact.

Application Procedures: Call for more information.

St. John's Mercy Medical Center
615 S. New Ballas Rd.
St. Louis, MO 63141
Phone: (314)569-6110
Fax: (314)569-6218

Employees: 4,006.

Average Entry-Level Hiring: 500.

Opportunities: Registered nurses, professionals, management, technicians, clerical, service—educational and skill requirements will vary depending on individual positions.

Human Resources: Mary Jo Lehmann, Recruiter RN, Nursing; Sandi Pingleton, Personnel Coordinator; Karen Lucash, Recruiter; Donna Aumiller, Recruiter.

A shortage of doctors in some areas and pressures on hospitals and health maintenance organizations to contain costs have thrown open the doors to nurse practitioners, who are able to treat many patients without a doctor's supervision. According to the American Academy of Nurse Practitioners, for every graduate of a nurse practitioner program an estimated four jobs beckon.

Source: *U.S. News & World Report*

St. John's Regional Medical Center
2727 McClelland Blvd.
Joplin, MO 64804
Phone: (417)625-2003
Fax: (417)625-2896

Employees: 506.

Average Entry-Level Hiring: 300.

Opportunities: Nurses—license certified and at least two years of education. Pharmacy, med-

ical technicians, occupational and respiratory therapists—bachelor's degree required.

Human Resources: Howard Smith, Employment Mgr.

▶ **Internships**

Type: Offers an internship program. Internship(s) are offered on a case by case program.

St. Joseph Medical Center
3600 E. Harry St.
Wichita, KS 67218
Phone: (316)689-4839
Fax: (316)689-6338

Employees: 2,400.

Average Entry-Level Hiring: 20—Health. 20—Non-Health.

Opportunities: RN—two-, three-, or four-year degrees. Physical and occupational therapists—bachelor's degree required.

Human Resources: Dan Urenda, Personnel Asst.

St. Joseph Mercy Hospitals of Macomb
17001 19 Mile Rd.
Mt. Clemens, MI 48044
Phone: (313)263-2801
Fax: (313)263-2803

Employees: 2,000.

Average Entry-Level Hiring: 20-30.

Opportunities: Registered nurse, LPN, nurse assistant, nurse technician in critical care (ER, ICU, CCU, Telemetry), neurology/family practice, oncology, psychiatric services, physical medicine and rehabilitation, orthopedics, pediatrics, surgical services, and women's health; nursery, labor and delivery, and gynecology. Nurse assistant—six months experience in acute care. Nurse technician—completion of medical/surgical rotation in accredited nursing school. Surgical technician—LPN or completion of accredited surgical tech program. Medical technologist—bachelor's degree and ASCP certification. Histology technologist—accredited program in histology. Occupational and physical therapists—bachelor's degree. Physical therapy assistant—associate degree. Radiology technologist—approved school of radiologic technology, American Registry of Radiologic Technologists.

Nuclear medicine technologist—accredited Nuclear Medicine Technology program, ARRT or NMTCB. Ultrasound technologist—registered diagnostic medical sonographer and ARRT. Computer tomography technologist—approved school of Radiologic Technology. Respiratory therapist—two-year respiratory therapist program, RRT preferred. Respiratory technician—six months training in approved respiratory therapy program, CRTT preferred.

Human Resources: Diana Palmeri, Employment Representative; Virginia Kastner, Employment Representative.

▶ **Internships**

Type: Internship(s) are available in some areas.

St. Joseph's Care Group

801 E. LaSalle Ave.
South Bend, IN 46634
Phone: (219)237-7368
Fax: (219)282-8920

Business Description: A member of the Holy Cross Health System, which includes St. Joseph's Medical Center in South Bend, Indiana, and Holy Cross Parkview Hospital in Plymouth, Indiana.

Opportunities: Numerous positions are typically available, including entry-level technical, nursing, professional, and management positions.

Human Resources: Mary Coursey, Employment Contact.

Application Procedures: Call for information.

St. Luke's Metrohealth Medical Center

11311 Shaker Blvd.
Cleveland, OH 44104-9989
Phone: (216)368-7445
Fax: (216)368-7457

Employees: 2,000.

Average Entry-Level Hiring: Unknown.

Opportunities: RN—associate or bachelor's degree. Occupational therapist—bachelor's degree.

Human Resources: Charlotte Stein, Employment Specialist.

Application Procedures: Call for more information.

St. Michael's Hospital

30 Bond St.
Toronto, ON, Canada M5B 1W8
Phone: (416)360-4000
Fax: (416)867-7488

Employees: 2,400.

Average Entry-Level Hiring: Unknown.

Opportunities: RN—a two-, three-, or four-year degree is required. Other positions available.

Application Procedures: Call the employment coordinator in human resources at (416)867-7401 for more information.

St. Vincent Carmel Hospital

13500 N. Meridian St.
Carmel, IN 46032
Phone: (317)573-7170
Fax: (317)573-7492

Business Description: St. Vincent Carmel Hospital is a 100-bed medical-surgical acute care hospital located twelve miles north of Indianapolis, with full service emergency, surgical, and ambulatory services. It is one of four Daughters of Charity National Health Care Systems' inpatient facilities in central Indiana. The medical-surgical floors and ambulatory surgery areas are designed to facilitate the delivery of nursing care, with decentralization of supplies, medications, and information systems. The philosophy of the nursing division focuses on patient/family-centered care, provided through a professional nursing practice model emphasizing autonomous, independent decision-making and collaboration. The hospital continues to grow in size and services since opening in 1985, along with the growing community.

Employees: 500.

Average Entry-Level Hiring: 100-300.

Opportunities: RNs: Surgery—one year recent OR experience. Medical, surgical and oncology—graduate or an accredited school of nursing, also hire G.N.s. Emergency, ICU/CCU, PACU/Ambulatory surgery—one year recent critical care experience. Medical technologist—graduate of a medical technology school and ASCP certified, or eligible. Radiological technologist—graduate of a radiological technical school and ARRT registered, or registry eligible.

Human Resources: Marianne Riggins, Human Resources Specialist.

Sandoz Pharmaceuticals Corp.
59 Rte. 10
East Hanover, NJ 07936
Phone: (201)503-7500

Business Description: Engaged in manufacturing, fabricating and/or processing drugs in pharmaceutical preparations.

Officers: Ed Heimers, VP of Mktg. & Sales; E. Iveson, Sr. VP of Operations; Jacques Rejeange, CEO & Pres.; S. Rendel, Sr. VP & CFO.

Employees: 3,595.

Human Resources: William V. Alexander, VP of Human Resources.

Schering-Plough Corp.
1 Giralda Farms
PO Box 1000
Madison, NJ 07940-1000
Phone: (201)822-7000

Business Description: Develops, manufactures, and markets prescription and over-the-counter medicines and drugs, veterinary medicines and products, cosmetics, and other personal care products.

Officers: Harold R. Hiser Jr., Exec. VP of Finance; Robert P. Luciano, CEO & Chairman of the Board.

Employees: 21,300.

Benefits: Benefits include a management recognition plan. training programs include personal development courses as a part of the management training program. Schering-Plough identifies employees with management potential and provides them with such courses as assertiveness training, problem solving, decision making, and communications.

Application Procedures: Send resume and cover letter.

G.D. Searle & Co.
5200 Old Orchard Rd.
Skokie, IL 60077
Phone: (708)982-7000
Fax: (708)982-1480

Business Description: Develops, manufactures, and markets pharmaceuticals for the cardiovascular system, the central nervous system, and the gastrointestinal tract, as well as oral contraceptives, low-calorie sweeteners, anti-inflammatory drugs, and anti-infective drugs. Research and development laboratories are located in Skokie, Illinois; Chesterfield, Missouri; Belgium; India; Japan; and England. Manufacturing facilities are located in Augusta, Georgia; Mt. Prospect, Illinois; Caguas, Puerto Rico; Australia; Belgium; Canada; France; Germany; India; Japan; Korea; Mexico; Pakistan; South Africa; Spain; England; and Venezuela.

Officers: Richard U. Deschutter, Exec. VP; Sheldon Gilgore, M.D., CEO, Pres. & Chairman of the Board.

Employees: 8,500.

Application Procedures: Places newspaper advertisements for certain openings. Send resume and cover letter to the attention of Human Resources Department, 4901 Searle Park Rd., Skokie, IL 60077.

SmithKline Beecham Corp.
PO Box 7929
Philadelphia, PA 19101
Phone: (215)751-4000
Fax: (215)751-3400

Business Description: Pharmaceutical operations are headquartered in Philadelphia, Pennsylvania. The company also operates a research center in Upper Merion, Pennsylvania; a Consumer Brands operation, which develops and produces over-the-counter health products, is headquartered in Pittsburgh, Pennsylvania; Animal Health operations, located in West Chester, Pennsylvania; clinical laboratories operations, headquartered in King of Prussia, Pennsylvania; and 26 other laboratories in the U.S.

Officers: Robert Bauman, CEO & Chairman of the Board; K.N. Kermes, Exec. VP of Finance.

Employees: 21,300.

Benefits: Benefits include an employee pension plan, cost-sharing benefit programs, performance-related rewards for certain jobs, and health and life insurance for retired employees.

Application Procedures: Send resume and cover letter to the attention of Personnel.

Southbury Training School
PO Box 872
Southbury, CT 06488
Phone: (203)262-9609
Fax: (203)264-2117

Business Description: State-operated residential facility for the developmentally disabled.

Employees: 2,200.

Average Entry-Level Hiring: 200.

Opportunities: Certified occupational therapist assistant—associate degree from an approved COTA program, including affiliation experience. Occupational therapist—bachelor's degree in OT and Connecticut license or temporary permit. Physical therapist—bachelor's degree in PT and Connecticut license or temporary permit. Physician assistant—graduation from a training program approved by the AMA. Speech/language pathologist—master's degree in speech/language pathology and Connecticut license. Staff nurse—graduation from an accredited nursing program and Connecticut license or temporary permit.

Human Resources: Janet C. Papini, Personnel Officer; Linda Larson, Personnel Asst.

Southern Baptist Hospital
2700 Napoleon Ave.
New Orleans, LA 70115
Phone: (504)897-5841
Toll-free: 800-627-4724
Fax: (504)897-4449

Employees: 1,400.

Average Entry-Level Hiring: Unknown.

Opportunities: RNs, physical therapists, and allied health professionals.

Application Procedures: Contact the Human Resources Department for more information.

Sparks Regional Medical Center
1311 S. I St.
Fort Smith, AR 72901
Phone: (501)441-4000
Fax: (501)441-5397

Employees: 1,700.

Average Entry-Level Hiring: Unknown.

Opportunities: Registered nurse—associate or bachelor's degree required. Experience preferred but not required. Also hires pharmacists, dieticians, and other allied health professionals.

Application Procedures: Contact the Human Resources Department for more information.

Staten Island University Hospital
475 Seaview Ave.
Staten Island, NY 10305
Phone: (718)226-9305
Fax: (718)226-8255

Employees: 3,500.

Average Entry-Level Hiring: 150.

Opportunities: Physical therapists, occupational therapists, respiratory therapists, radiation therapy technologists—completion of appropriate training and licensing.

Human Resources: Ann M. Conneli, Recruiting Mgr.

Some companies use creative gimmicks to motivate workers. Each year, John Brady Design Consultants, Pittsburgh, gives a jar of 12 marbles to its 18 employees, a different color for each person. Over the year, employees give the marbles as rewards to co-workers who help them out or achieve great feats. At year's end, the firm can see who recognizes others and who doesn't.

Source: *The Wall Street Journal*

Sterling Drug Inc.
90 Park Ave.
New York, NY 10016
Phone: (212)907-2000

Business Description: Engaged in manufacturing, fabricating and/or processing drugs in pharmaceutical preparations.

Officers: George S. Benjamin, VP & CFO; Louis P. Mattis, Pres. & Chairman of the Board.

Employees: 1,500 employees at the corporate headquarters.

Average Entry-Level Hiring: Varies.

Human Resources: R. Kyle Greer, VP of Human Resources.

Stockton Developmental Center
510 E. Magnolia St.
Stockton, CA 95202
Phone: (209)948-7335
Fax: (209)948-7646

Business Description: All clients served are developmentally disabled. The majority are adults. The youngest age served is fourteen.

Employees: 900.

Average Entry-Level Hiring: Approximately 10 percent turnover annually.

Opportunities: Physician, surgeon, clinical, educational, and counseling psychologists, psychiatric social workers (M.S.W.), physical therapists, occupational therapists, recreation therapists, music therapists, registered nurses, psychiatric technicians, and pharmacists.

Human Resources: Thomas P. Thompson, Personnel Officer.

Stormont-Vail Regional Medical Center

1500 W. 10th
Topeka, KS 66604
Phone: (913)354-6153
Fax: (913)354-5889

Employees: 1,850.

Average Entry-Level Hiring: 40.

Opportunities: Typically hires 40 entry-level nurses per year, two physical therapists, two occupational therapists, ten respiratory therapists, one social service worker, three radiologists, three medical technicians, and three pharmacists.

Human Resources: Laurie Florence, Personnel Recruiter; Betty Hadison, Personnel Recruiter.

Summit Health Ltd.

2600 W. Magnolia Blvd.
PO Box 2100
Burbank, CA 91507-2100
Phone: (818)841-8750

Business Description: An integrated health care company operating hospitals, nursing centers, and other health-related facilities in Arizona, California, Iowa, and Texas.

Officers: Donald J. Amaral, Pres. & COO; Don Freeberg, CEO, Pres. & Chairman of the Board; Frank S. Osen, Sr. VP & General Counsel; William C. Scott, Sr. VP; Randolph H. Speer, Sr. VP & CFO.

Employees: 4,600.

Human Resources: David Rubardt, Human Resources Dir.

Application Procedures: Send resume and cover letter to the attention of David Rubardt, Human Resources Dir.

Syntex Corp.

3401 Hillview Ave.
Palo Alto, CA 94304
Phone: (415)855-5050

Business Description: Involved in the research, development, manufacturing and marketing of human and animal pharmaceutical products and medical diagnostic systems.

Officers: Paul E. Freiman, CEO, Pres. & Chairman of the Board; Thomas L. Gutshall, Exec. VP; Richard P. Powers, Sr. VP & CFO.

Employees: 10,300.

Benefits: Benefits include employee pension plan, and employees restricted stock plan.

Human Resources: Andrew Oravets, Sr. VP of Human Resources; Paulette Stepp, Recruiting Mgr.

Application Procedures: Send resume and cover letter.

Toledo Mental Health Center

930 S. Detroit/Caller No. 10002
Toledo, OH 43699-0002
Phone: (419)381-1881
Fax: (419)389-1967

Employees: 460. Total employee count includes 59 registered nurses and ten psychiatrists.

Average Entry-Level Hiring: Psychiatrists—1-3.

Opportunities: Psychiatrist—certificate to practice medicine per section 4731.13 of Revised Code, and satisfactory completion of residency training program in psychiatry.

Human Resources: Steve Hansen, Human Resources Admin.; Janet Conkey, Personnel Mgr.

United Health Inc.

105 W. Michigan St.
Milwaukee, WI 53203
Phone: (414)271-9696
Fax: (414)274-2709

Business Description: Operator of skilled nursing care facilities other than hospitals. Operator of intermediate care facilities.

Officers: Robert Abramowski, CFO; Richard Herman, Dir. of Mktg.; Guy W. Smith, President.

Employees: 15,000.

Human Resources: William Wagner.

Application Procedures: Contact the company for more information.

U.S. Healthcare Inc.
PO Box 1109
Blue Bell, PA 19422
Phone: (215)628-4800

Business Description: Engaged in the operation of establishments that provide general or specialized medicine or surgery by medical doctors.

Officers: Leonard Abramson, President; Costas C. Nicolaides, Exec. VP & CFO; Melvin H. Stein, Sr. VP of Sales.

Employees: 1,655.

Application Procedures: Contact the company for more information.

Universal Health Services Inc.
367 S. Gulph Rd.
King of Prussia, PA 19406
Phone: (215)768-3300

Business Description: A hospital management company for acute care and psychiatric hospitals. Operates 20 acute care hospitals and 13 psychiatric hospitals. Three hospitals are located in the United Kingdom.

Officers: Alan B. Miller, CEO & Pres.; Sidney Miller, Exec. VP.

Human Resources: Ilene Bove, Human Resources Dir.

Application Procedures: Send resume and cover letter to the attention of Ilene Bove, Human Resources Dir.

University of Alabama Hospital
620 20th St.
Birmingham, AL 35233
Phone: (205)934-4745
Fax: (205)934-6321

Employees: 4,000.

Average Entry-Level Hiring: 200-300.

Opportunities: RN—associate or bachelor's degree required.

Human Resources: Bill Baker, Recruiter.

Application Procedures: Call for more information.

University of Connecticut Health Center
263 Farmington Ave.
Farmington, CT 06030
Phone: (203)679-4375
Fax: (203)679-4115

Employees: 3,579.

Average Entry-Level Hiring: Unknown.

Human Resources: Sharon Powell, Employment Contact Nurse Recruiter; Marianne Caine, Director Nursing Recruitment.

Application Procedures: Call for more information.

University of Virginia Health Sciences Center
Nursing Resource Office
Box 405
Charlottesville, VA 22908
Phone: 800-237-9230
Fax: (804)924-2451

Employees: 1,200.

Average Entry-Level Hiring: Nurses—100.

Opportunities: Nurses have multiple opportunities in a vast medical center consisting of 44 inpatient nursing units. U.V.A. Health Sciences Center is a tertiary care facility with a Level 1 trauma center. Extensive services exist within the fields of pediatrics, obstetrics and gynecology, medicine, surgery, neurology, neurosurgery, urology, plastics, burn medicine, critical care ICUs, oncology, neonatology, transplantation, orthopedics, psychiatry, and rehabilitation. Nurses are encouraged to challenge a career ladder which rewards those who stay at bedside. Clinician 1's are new graduate and re-entry level nurses, Clinician 2's are intermediate practitioners, Clinician 3's are proficient practitioners, and level 4's are expert clinicians.

Application Procedures: Call fore a brochure and information.

Upjohn Co.

7000 Portage Rd.
Kalamazoo, MI 49001
Phone: (616)323-4000

Business Description: Develops, manufactures, and markets pharmaceuticals and other health care products for humans and animals. Also develops and markets agronomic seeds. Provides health care services.

Officers: Theodore Cooper, CEO & Chairman of the Board; Jack J. Jackson, VP of Sales; Robert C. Salisbury, VP & CFO.

Employees: 18,500.

Application Procedures: Send resume and cover letter.

VA Medical Center

Leestown Rd.
Lexington, KY 40511
Phone: (606)233-4511
Fax: (606)281-3994

Employees: 2,000.

Average Entry-Level Hiring: Unknown.

Opportunities: RN—two-, three-, or four-year degree required. No other information available.

Human Resources: D.C. Schmonsky, Personnel Dept.

Application Procedures: Call for information.

VA Medical Center

5500 Armstrong Rd.
Battle Creek, MI 49016
Phone: (616)966-5600
Fax: (616)966-5433

Employees: 1,600.

Average Entry-Level Hiring: 200.

Opportunities: Registered nurses, physicians, and physical therapists are needed in the areas of acute psychiatry, intermediate medicine, general medicine, and gerontology. Registered nurses—license required. Physicians—requires license and either Board eligible or certified. Physical therapist—requires appropriate degree and certification.

Human Resources: Mary Lightbody, Recruiter; Cynthis Sipp, Personnel Mgt. Specialist; Ronald Kelly, Employment Contact.

VA Medical Center

113 Holland Ave.
Albany, NY 12208
Phone: (518)462-3311
Fax: (518)462-2519

Opportunities: Not hiring at this time.

Human Resources: Carol Ann Bedford, Recruiter RN, Nursing; Lawrence H. Flesh, Recruiter MD, Chief of Staff; Alice A. Flynn, Personnel Mgt. Specialist.

VA Medical Center

Fort Meade, SD 57741
Phone: (605)347-2511

Employees: 529.

Average Entry-Level Hiring: Unknown.

Opportunities: Registered nurse—associate or bachelor's degree in nursing. LPN/LVN—completed vocational training. Physical therapist—bachelor's degree in physical therapy.

Human Resources: Sylvia Desjarlais, Employment Contact Registered Nurse; Ron Jacobs, Personnel Dept. Management Specialist; Mike Larson, Personnel Dept.

Application Procedures: Those dedicated to, and interested in helping veterans in a quality work environment are encouraged to apply.

Vanderbilt University Medical Center

Medical Center North
Nashville, TN 37232-2410
Phone: (615)322-2116
Fax: (615)322-3490

Employees: 10,000.

Average Entry-Level Hiring: Unknown.

Opportunities: RN—bachelor's degree. Laboratory technician—associate degree and licensure.

Application Procedures: Contact Human Resources for more information.

Villa Feliciana Chronic Disease Hospital & Rehabilitation Center

PO Box 438
Jackson, LA 70748
Phone: (504)634-4000
Fax: (504)634-4191

Business Description: Villa Feliciana is a long-term care hospital located in a rural setting 30 miles north of Baton Rouge.

Employees: 90. There is currently a shortage of applicants for permanent positions.

Average Entry-Level Hiring: 25.

Opportunities: Registered nurse—valid Louisiana State license or temporary permit to practice professional nursing. Licensed practical nurse—license to practice practical nursing in Louisiana. Respiratory care technician—license or temporary permit to practice as a respiratory therapy technician.

Human Resources: Mary W. Bankston, Human Resources Dir.

Application Procedures: Quick thinking and a calm manner are necessary in handling patients with the possibility of disruptive behavior.

Warner-Lambert Co.

201 Tabor Rd.
Morris Plains, NJ 07950
Phone: (201)540-2000

Business Description: Develops, markets, and manufactures health care and consumer products, including ethical and non-prescription pharmaceuticals, chewing gum, breath mints, shaving products, and empty hard gelatin capsules. The company has focused its research on cognitive disorders, central nervous system conditions such as Alzheimer's disease, schizophrenia, and cardiovascular diseases such as congestive heart failure.

Officers: Robert J. Dircks, Exec. VP & CFO; Melvin R. Goodes, Pres. & COO; Joseph D. Williams, CEO & Chairman of the Board.

Employees: 33,000.

Benefits: Benefits include paternity leave, vacation days, personal/sick days, overtime pay, child-care referrals, elder-care referrals, telecommuting, extended leave, part-time employment, job sharing, employee parking, flex time, and summer hours.

Human Resources: Raymond M. Fino, VP of Human Resources.

Application Procedures: Send resume and cover letter to the attention of Raymond M. Fino, VP of Human Resources.

Washington Hospital Center

.110 Irving St., NW
Washington, DC 20010
Phone: (202)877-6048
Toll-free: 800-432-3993
Fax: (202)877-7315

Business Description: Washington Hospital Center is an acute care, level one trauma center with 907 beds.

Employees: 5,100.

Average Entry-Level Hiring: 50-75.

Opportunities: Positions available in the following areas: nursing, PT, OT, medical technology, radiology, nuclear medicine, medical social work, respiratory therapy, pharmacy, surgical technology, cardiovascular technology, and as physician assistants. For the respective occupations, graduation from an accredited program, college, or university, and licensure is required.

Human Resources: Cynthia Wolfe, RN, Employment Specialist Nursing; Terra Cox, RN, Employment Specialist; Denise Stribling, RN, Employment Specialist.

Application Procedures: Contact Terra Cox for the following positions; PT, OT, medical technology, radiology, medical social work, nuclear medicine, and respiratory therapy. Contact Denise Stribling for the following positions; pharmacy, surgical technology, physician's assistant, and cardiovascular technology.

The average new RN in 1990 was five years older than the typical nursing graduate of 1988, reports the National League for Nursing in a study of over 28,000 recently licensed RNs. League surveys have found the age level of new graduates increasing steadily, from 24.8 in 1982 to 31 last year.

Source: *American Journal of Nursing*

Wausau Hospital

333 Pine Ridge Blvd.
Wausau, WI 54401
Phone: (715)847-2800
Fax: (715)847-2017

Employees: 1,700.

Average Entry-Level Hiring: Varies with occupation.

Opportunities: RN—associate or bachelor's

degree required. Also fills positions in PT, OT, medical technology, radiology, nuclear medicine, medical social work, respiratory therapy, pharmacy, surgical technology, and cardiovascular technology.

Human Resources: Cecilia R. Rudolph, Employment Mgr., RN.

Application Procedures: Call for more information.

Wesley Medical Center

550 N. Hillside Ave.
Wichita, KS 67214
Phone: (316)688-2603
Fax: (316)688-7931

Employees: 3,500.

Average Entry-Level Hiring: Unknown.

Opportunities: Pharmacy, physical therapy, speech therapy, occupational therapy, nursing, medical social workers—B.S. degree required.

Application Procedures: Contact the Human Resources Department for more information.

Whitehall Laboratories Division

Business Description: Engaged in manufacturing, fabricating and/or processing drugs in pharmaceutical preparations.

Employees: 1,000.

Average Entry-Level Hiring: Unknown.

Application Procedures: Send resume and cover letter to the Personnel Department.

▶ Internships

Type: The company does not offer an internship program.

Woodhull Medical & Mental Health Center

760 Broadway
Brooklyn, NY 11206
Phone: (718)963-8000
Fax: (718)963-8169

Employees: 3,000.

Average Entry-Level Hiring: Unknown.

Opportunities: RN—associate or bachelor's degree required. Social workers—M.S.W. required. Occupational and physical therapist—bachelor's degree.

Application Procedures: Contact the Human Resources Department for more information.

Wyoming Medical Center

1233 E. 2nd St.
Casper, WY 82601
Phone: 800-526-5190

Business Description: As a teaching hospital for the University of Wyoming and Casper College, WMC is committed to education. In addition to 100% tuition reimbursement, WMC offers on-site, satellite, and national conferences and seminars; staff development and management programs; multiple certification classes; and OR and Critical Care Residency Programs. Orientation is unit-based and individualized and includes an extended program for new graduates.

Employees: 1,025.

Average Entry-Level Hiring: 15-30.

Opportunities: A wide variety of nursing specialities are available; pediatrics, cardiac surgery, rehabilitation, neurology, oncology, plastic surgery, emergency services, orthopedics, obstetrics and gynecology, and intensive and coronary care.

Human Resources: Mark Smith, Recruitment Mgr.; Marilyn Thomas, Recruiting Asst.

Additional Companies

A. H. Robins Co., Inc.

1407 Cummings Dr.
Richmond, VA 23220
Phone: (804)257-2000

Burroughs Wellcome Co.

3030 Cornwallis Rd.
Research Triangle Park, NC 27709
Phone: (919)248-3000

Cleveland Clinic Hospital
9500 Euclid Ave.
Cleveland, OH 44195
Phone: (216)444-2200

HCA Lawnwood Regional Medical Center
1700 S. 23rd St.
Fort Pierce, FL 34950
Phone: (407)468-4411
Fax: (407)468-4499

Huntington Memorial Hospital
100 Congress
Pasadena, CA 91105
Phone: (213)440-5400
Fax: (818)397-5000

Massachusetts General Hospital
55 Fruit St.
Boston, MA 02114
Phone: (617)726-2000

Mayo Clinic—Saint Marys Hospital
1216 2nd St., SW
Rochester, MN 55902
Phone: (507)255-5123

Memorial Medical Center
800 N. Rutledge
Springfield, IL 62781
Phone: (217)788-3583
Fax: (217)788-5539

Memorial Sloan-Kettering Cancer Center
1275 York Ave.
New York, NY 10021
Phone: (212)639-2000

Stanford University Hospital
300 Pasteur Dr.
Stanford, CA 94305
Phone: (415)723-1245

University of California-Los Angeles Medical Center
10833 LeConte Ave.
Los Angeles, CA 90024
Phone: (310)825-0644

University of California-San Francisco Medical Center
Box 0208
San Francisco, CA 94143
Phone: (415)476-1000

University of Texas M.D. Anderson Cancer Center
1515 Holcombe Blvd.
Houston, TX 77030
Phone: (713)792-2121

CAREER
RESOURCES

CHAPTER TWENTY-ONE

Career Resources

The Career Resources chapter covers additional sources of job-related information that will aid you in your job search. It includes full, descriptive listings for sources of help wanted ads, professional associations, employment agencies and search firms, career guides, professional and trade periodicals, and basic reference guides and handbooks. Each of these sections is arranged alphabetically by organization, publication, or service name. For complete details on the information provided in this chapter, please consult "How to Use Career Resources" in the front of this directory.

Sources of Help Wanted Ads

20/20
Jobson Publishing Corp.
352 Park Ave. S.
New York, NY 10010
Phone: (212)685-4848
Fax: (212)696-5318

Twelve times/year. $65.00/year; $7.50/single issue.

AACP News
American Association of Colleges of Pharmacy (AACP)
1426 Prince St.
Alexandria, VA 22314
Phone: (703)739-2330

Monthly. Free to members; $10.00/year for non-members. Newsletter; includes information on employment opportunities, association activities, and new members.

AAMD — Academy Digest
American Academy of Medical Directors (AAMD)
1 Urban Center
Ste. 648
Tampa, FL 33609
Phone: (813)287-2000

Bimonthly. Free to members. Includes employment opportunities and calendar of events and lists new members and member promotions.

AANA Journal
216 Higgins Rd.
Park Ridge, IL 60068
Phone: (708)692-7050
Fax: (708)692-6968
Six times/year. $24.00/year; $5.00/single issue.

AAO-HNS Bulletin

American Academy of Otolaryngology -
Head and Neck Surgery (AAO-HNS)
1 Prince St.
Alexandria, VA 22314
Phone: (703)836-4444
Fax: (703)683-5100

Monthly. Free to members; $40.00/year for non-members. Newsletter including employment opportunity listings, academy news, calendar of events, legislative news, and research updates.

AAOHN Journal

6900 Grove Rd.
Thorofare, NJ 08086
Phone: (609)848-1000
Fax: (609)853-5991

Monthly. $40.00/year; $53.00/year for institutions; $8.00/single issue.

AAPA Newsletter

American Association of Pathologists'
Assistants (AAPA)
c/o Leo J. Kelly
Dept. of Pathology
VA Medical Center
West Haven, CT 06516
Phone: (203)932-5711

Quarterly. Free to members. Includes employment and educational opportunity listings.

ABNF Newsletter

Association of Black Nursing Faculty in
Higher Education (ABNF)
5823 Queens Cove
Lisle, IL 60532
Phone: (708)969-3809
Fax: (708)810-0128

Quarterly. Free to members; $25.00/year for nonmembers. Includes job opportunities, member profiles and activities, research abstracts, conference information, and fellowship information.

ACHA Action

American College Health Association
(ACHA)
1300 Piccard Dr.
Ste. 200
Rockville, MD 20850
Phone: (301)963-1100
Fax: (301)330-6781

Bimonthly. Free to members. Newsletter including employment opportunity listings, calendar of events, college health resources listings, leadership directory, and annual report to the board of directors.

ACOS News

American College of Osteopathic Surgeons
(ACOS)
123 N. Henry St.
Alexandria, VA 22314
Phone: (703)684-0416

Monthly. Free to members. Lists employment opportunities and includes calendar of events. Covers association activities and legislative and regulatory issues affecting osteopathic surgeons.

ACSM Career Services Bulletin

American College of Sports Medicine
(ACSM)
PO Box 1440
Indianapolis, IN 46206-1440
Phone: (317)637-9200
Fax: (317)634-7817

Monthly. $5.00/year for members; $20.00/year for nonmembers. Newsletter listing career and fellowship opportunities in sports medicine in the United States and abroad.

Adnet Online

Employment Advertising Network
5987 E. 71st St., Ste. 206
Indianapolis, IN 46220
Phone: (317)579-6922

Online database that provides descriptions of job openings listed by subscribing organizations. Enables job candidates to identify positions for which they qualify. Available online through CompuServe Information Service, GE Information Services, Prodigy, America Online, and other services.

Advance Job Listings

PO Box 900
New York, NY 10020

Advances in Nursing Science

200 Orchard Ridge Dr.
Gaithersburg, MD 20878
Phone: (301)417-7617
Fax: (301)417-7550

Quarterly. $53.00/year.

Affirmative Action Register for Effective Equal Opportunity Recruitment

AAR, Inc.
8356 Olive Blvd.
St. Louis, MO 63132
Phone: (314)991-1335

Green, Warren H., editor. Published monthly. $15.00/year. Provides listing of state, university, and other publicly-funded positions directed to women, minorities, veterans, and handicapped job seekers.

American Association for Geriatric Psychiatry—Newsletter

American Association for Geriatric Psychiatry (AAGP)
PO Box 376-A
Greenbelt, MD 20768
Phone: (301)220-0952
Fax: (301)220-0941

Bimonthly. Contains employment listings. Provides brief articles on psychiatric topics and case reports pertaining to elderly patients; includes association news, geriatric psychiatry bibliography, and meetings calendar.

American College of Physicians Observer

American College of Physicians
Independence Mall W.
6th St. at Race
Philadelphia, PA 19106-1572
Phone: (215)351-2400

Eleven times/year. $12.00/year; $1.50/single issue.

American Druggist

Hearst Business Publishing Group
60 E. 42nd St.
New York, NY 10165
Phone: (212)297-9680

Monthly. $36.00/year; $3.00/single issue.

American Family Physician

8880 Ward Pkwy.
Kansas City, MO 64114
Phone: (816)333-9700

Monthly. $60.00/year; $6.00/issue.

The American Journal of Cardiology

Yorke Medical Group
Cahners Publishing Co.
249 W. 17th St.
New York, NY 10011
Phone: (212)463-6463

Twice monthly. $66.00/year; $12.00/single issue.

American Journal of Diseases of Children

American Medical Association (AMA)
515 N. State St.
Chicago, IL 60610
Phone: (312)464-4818
Fax: (312)464-4184

Monthly. $40.50/year for members; $58.00/year for nonmembers; $29.00/year for residents and medical students. Oriented toward the pediatric clinician. Includes employment opportunity listings, book reviews, annual index, and index of advertisers.

American Journal of Epidemiology

2007 E. Monument St.
Baltimore, MD 21205
Phone: (301)955-3441

Semimonthly. $190.00/year; $12.00/issue.

American Journal of Hospital Pharmacy

American Society of Hospital Pharmacists
4630 Montgomery Ave.
Bethesda, MD 20814
Phone: (301)657-3000

Monthly. $105.00/year. Journal for directors and staffs of pharmaceutical departments in hospitals and health-care institutions.

American Journal of Medical Genetics

605 3rd Ave.
New York, NY 10158
Phone: (212)850-8800

Monthly.

The American Journal of Medicine

Yorke Medical Group
Cahners Publishing Co.
249 W. 17th St.
New York, NY 10011
Phone: (212)463-6463

Monthly. $66.00/year; $10.00/single issue.

American Journal of Nursing

American Nurses' Association (ANA)
2420 Pershing Rd.
Kansas City, MO 64108
Phone: (816)474-5720
Fax: (816)471-4903

Monthly. $24.00/year for individuals; $30.00/year for institutions. Contains employment listings, advertisers' index, calendar of events, continuing education course listings, and information on new equipment.

American Journal of Obstetrics and Gynecology

11830 Westline Industrial Dr.
St. Louis, MO 63146
Phone: (314)872-8370

Monthly. $71.50/year; $130.00/year for institutions; $38.00/year for students; $7.00/issue.

American Journal of Ophthalmology

435 N. Michigan Ave.
Ste.1415
Chicago, IL 60611
Phone: (312)787-3853

Monthly. $52.00/year.

American Journal of Optometry and Physiological Optics

428 E. Preston St.
Baltimore, MD 21202
Phone: (301)528-4068

Monthly. $75.00/year; $105.00/year for foreign subscribers; $12.00/single issue.

American Journal of Pathology

J.B. Lippincott Company
E. Washington Sq.
Philadelphia, PA 19105
Phone: (215)238-4283

Monthly. $145.00/year; $90.00/year for interns and residents; $210.00/year for institutions; $24.00/single issue.

American Journal of Pediatric Hematology and Oncology

Raven Press, Ltd.
1185 Avenue of the Americas
New York, NY 10036

American Journal of Psychiatry

American Psychiatric Association
1400 K St. NW
Washington, DC 20005
Phone: (202)682-6250

Monthly. $56.00/year; $7.00/single issue.

American Journal of Public Health

American Public Health Association (APHA)
1015 15th St., NW
Washington, DC 20005
Phone: (202)789-5600
Fax: (202)789-5681

Monthly. Free to members; $80.00/year for non-members. Includes annual membership directory and news briefs.

The American Journal of Sports Medicine

Williams and Wilkins
428 E. Preston St.
Baltimore, MD 21202
Phone: (301)528-4000

Bimonthly. $50.00/year.

American Journal of Surgery

249 W. 17th St.
New York, NY 10011
Phone: (212)463-6465

Monthly. $69.00/year.

American Journal of Surgical Pathology

Raven Press, Ltd.
1185 Avenue of the Americas
New York, NY 10036
Phone: (212)930-9500

Monthly. $110.00/year; $29.00/single issue.

The American Nurse

American Nurses' Association (ANA)
2420 Pershing Rd.
Kansas City, MO 64108
Phone: (816)474-5720
Fax: (816)471-4903

Ten times/year. Free to members; $15.00/year

for nonmembers; $10.00/year for full-time nursing students. Includes employment listings.

American Optometric Association News

American Optometric Association (AOA)
243 N. Lindbergh Blvd.
St. Louis, MO 63141
Phone: (314)991-4100
Fax: (314)991-4101

Semimonthly. $16.00/year for members; $35.00/year for nonmembers. Includes employment listings, promotional news, and obituaries.

American Pharmacy: The Journal of the American Pharmaceutical Association

American Pharmaceutical Association
2215 Constitution Ave., NW
Washington, DC 20037
Phone: (202)628-4410

Monthly. $50.00/year.

American Surgeon

J.B. Lippincott Co.
227 E. Washington Sq.
Philadelphia, PA 19106
Phone: (215)238-4273
Fax: (215)238-4227

Monthly. $70.00/year; $13.00/single issue.

Anesthesia and Analgesia: Journal of the International Anesthesia Research Society

655 Avenue of the Americas
New York, NY 10010
Phone: (212)989-5800

Monthly. $100.00/year; $140.00/year for institutions.

Anesthesiology

J.B. Lippincott Co.
E. Washington Sq.
Philadelphia, PA 19105
Phone: (215)238-4274

Monthly. $100.00/year; $120.00/year for institutions; $150.00/year for foreign subscribers; $15.00/single issue.

Annals of Behavioral Medicine

103 S. Adams St.
Rockville, MD 20850
Phone: (301)251-2790

Quarterly. $57.00/year.

Annals of Emergency Medicine

American College of Emergency Physicians
PO Box 619911
Dallas, TX 75261-9911
Phone: (214)550-0911

Monthly. $55.00/year.

Annals of Internal Medicine

American College of Physicians
Independence Mall W.
6th St. at Race
Philadelphia, PA 19106-1572
Phone: (215)351-2400

Semimonthly. $65.00/year.

Annals of Neurology: Journal of the American Neurological Association and the Child Neurology Society

34 Beacon St.
Boston, MA 02108
Phone: (617)859-5609

Monthly. $102.00/year.

Annals of Plastic Surgery

34 Beacon St.
Boston, MA 02108
Phone: (617)859-5612

Monthly. $115.00/year.

Annals of Surgery

J.B. Lippincott Co.
E. Washington Sq.
Philadelphia, PA 19105
Phone: (215)238-4200

Monthly. $65.00/year; $75.00/year for residents; $100.00/year for institutions; $13.00/single issue.

The Annals of Thoracic Surgery

Elsevier Science Publishing Co., Inc.
655 Avenue of the Americas
New York, NY 10010
Phone: (212)989-5800

Monthly. $80.00/year; $128.00/year for institutions.

AORN Journal
Association of Operating Nurses, Inc.
10170 E. Mississippi Ave.
Denver, CO 80231
Phone: (303)755-6300

Monthly. $32.00/year.

**AOSA Foresight: Optometry
Looking Forward**
American Optometric Student Association
(AOSA)
243 N. Lindbergh
St. Louis, MO 63141
Phone: (314)991-4100

Quarterly. Free to members. Reports information concerning internships, scholarships, grants, and other educational issues related to the study of optometry. Includes calendar of events and research reports.

APAP Update
Association of Physician Assistant Programs
(APAP)
950 N. Washington St.
Alexandria, VA 22314
Phone: (703)836-2272

Monthly. Free to members. Includes employment listings and meeting announcements. Newsletter for physician assistant program faculty and others concerned with curricula and government/legislative developments affecting the profession.

Archives of Dermatology
American Medical Association (AMA)
515 N. State St.
Chicago, IL 60610
Phone: (312)464-4818
Fax: (312)464-4184

Monthly. $51.00/year for members; $73.00/year for nonmembers; $36.50/year for residents and medical students. Journal oriented to the dermatologic clinician. Includes employment opportunity listings, book reviews, annual index, and index of advertisers.

Archives of General Psychiatry
American Medical Association (AMA)
515 N. State St.
Chicago, IL 60610
Phone: (312)464-4818
Fax: (312)464-4184

Monthly. $40.50/year for members; $58.00/year

for nonmembers; $29.00/year for residents and medical students. Journal oriented toward the psychiatric clinician. Includes employment opportunity listings, book reviews, annual index, and index of advertisers.

Archives of Internal Medicine
American Medical Association (AMA)
515 N. State St.
Chicago, IL 60610
Phone: (312)464-4818
Fax: (312)464-4184

Monthly. $45.50/year for members; $65.00/year for nonmembers; $32.50/year for residents and medical students. Journal; includes employment opportunity listings, annual index, and index of advertisers.

Archives of Neurology
American Medical Association (AMA)
515 N. State St.
Chicago, IL 60610
Phone: (312)464-4818
Fax: (312)464-4184

Periodic. $52.00/year for members; $74.00/year for nonmembers; $37.00/year for residents and medical students. Journal oriented toward the neurologic clinician. Includes employment opportunity listings, annual index, and index of advertisers.

Archives of Ophthalmology
American Medical Association (AMA)
515 N. State St.
Chicago, IL 60610
Phone: (312)464-4818
Fax: (312)464-4184

Monthly. $45.50/year for members; $65.00/year for nonmembers; $32.50/year for residents and medical students. Journal; includes employment opportunity listings, case reports, book reviews, annual index, and index of advertisers.

Archives of Surgery
American Medical Association (AMA)
515 N. State St.
Chicago, IL 60610
Phone: (312)464-4818
Fax: (312)464-4184

Monthly. $43.50/year for members; $62.00/year for nonmembers; $31.00/year for medical students and residents. Journal; includes employment opportunity listings, calendar of events, book reviews, index of advertisers, and annual index.

Biomedical Instrumentation & Technology

Association for the Advancement of Medical Instrumentation (AAMI)
3330 Washington Blvd.
Ste. 400
Arlington, VA 22201-4598
Phone: (703)525-4890
Fax: (703)276-0793

Bimonthly. Free to members; $60.00 for non-members. Peer-reviewed journal which lists employment opportunities and includes association news, book reviews, advertisers and annual subject indexes, and statistics.

The Black Collegian

1240 S. Broad St.
New Orleans, LA 70125
Phone: (504)821-5694

Quarterly. $10.00/year; $5.00/year for students; $2.50/issue. Career and job-oriented publication for black college students.

Cancer

Lippincott Company
E. Washington Sq.
Philadelphia, PA 19105
Phone: (215)238-4200

Biweekly. $95.00/year; $150.00/year for institutions; $13.00/ single issue.

CAP Job Placement Bulletin

College of American Pathologists (CAP)
325 Waukegan Rd.
Northfield, IL 60093-2750
Phone: (708)446-8800
Fax: (708)446-8807

Bimonthly. Free to members. Updating service providing job listings.

Cardio

Miller Freeman, Inc.
600 Harrison St.
San Francisco, CA 94107
Phone: (415)905-2200
Fax: (415)905-2232

Monthly.

Career Opportunities News

Garrett Park Press
PO Box 190 C
Garrett Park, MD 20986-0190
Phone: (301)946-2553

Calvert, Robert, Jr., and French, Mary Blake, editors. Bimonthly. $30.00/year; $4.00 sample issue. Each issue covers such things as resources to job seekers, special opportunities for minorities, women's career notes, and the current outlook in various occupations. Cites free and inexpensive job-hunting materials and new reports and books.

Career Woman

Equal Opportunity Publications, Inc.
44 Broadway
Greenlawn, NY 11740

Three times/year. $13.00/year. Recruitment magazine for women. Provides free resume service and assists women in identifying employers and applying for positions.

Clinical Cardiology

PO Box 832
Mahwah, NJ 07430
Phone: (201)818-1010
Fax: (201)818-0086

Monthly. $60.00/year; $15.50/single issue.

Clinical Nurse Specialist

428 E. Preston St.
Baltimore, MD 21202
Phone: (301)528-4068
Fax: (301)528-8596

Quarterly. $42.00/year; $55.00/year for institutions; $57.00/year for foreign subscribers; $70.00/year for foreign institutions; $14.00/single issue; $16.00/single issue for foreign subscribers.

Clinical Pediatrics

International Publishing Group
4959 Commerce Pkwy.
Cleveland, OH 44128
Phone: (216)464-1210
Fax: (216)464-1835

Monthly. $50.00/year; $11.00/single issue.

Clinical Pharmacology & Therapeutics

Mosby-Year Book Inc.
11830 Westline Ind. Dr.
St. Louis, MO 63146
Phone: (314)872-8370
Fax: (314)432-1380

Monthly. $85.00/year; $7.50/single issue.

Clinical Pharmacy

American Society of Hospital Pharmacists
4630 Montgomery Ave.
Bethesda, MD 20814
Phone: (301)657-3000
Fax: (301)652-8278

Monthly. $45.00/year; $6.00/single issue.

Clinical Psychiatry News

International Medical News Group
770 Lexington Ave.
New York, NY 10021
Phone: (212)421-0707

Monthly. $54.00/year; $4.00/single issue.

College Digest

American College of Physician Executives
(ACPE)
4890 W. Kennedy Blvd.
Ste. 200
Tampa, FL 33609
Phone: (813)287-2000
Fax: (813)287-8993

Bimonthly. Free to members. Newsletter; includes employment opportunity and new member listings.

College Recruitment Database (CRD)

Executive Telecom System, Inc.
College Park North
9585 Valparaiso Ct.
Indianapolis, IN 46268
Phone: (317)872-2045

Contains resume information for graduating undergraduate and graduate students in all disciplines at all colleges and universities for recruitment purposes. Enables the employer to create and maintain a private 'skill' file meeting selection criteria. Typical entries include student identification number, home and campus addresses and telephone numbers, schools, degrees, dates of attendance, majors, grade point averages, date available, job objective, curricular statement, activities/honors, and employment history. Available online through the Human Resource Information Network.

Community Jobs

ACCESS: Networking in the Public Interest
1601 Connecticut Ave., NW
6th Fl.
Washington, DC 20009
Phone: (202)667-0661
Fax: (202)387-7915

Monthly. $45.00/year to institutions; $25.00/year to nonprofit organizations; $20.00/year to individuals; $3.95/issue. Covers: Jobs and internships available with nonprofit organizations active in issues such as the environment, foreign policy, consumer advocacy, housing, education, etc. Entries include: Position title, name, address, and phone of contact; description, responsibilities, requirements, salary. Arrangement: Geographical.

Contemporary OB/GYN

Medical Economics Publishing
5 Paragon Dr.
Montvale, NJ 07645-1742
Phone: (201)358-7200
Fax: (201)573-8979

Fifteen times/year. $69.00/year.

Contemporary Pediatrics

Medical Economics Publishing
5 Paragon Dr.
Montvale, NJ 07645-1742
Phone: (201)358-7200
Fax: (201)573-8979

Monthly.

Contemporary Urology

Medical Economics Publishing
5 Paragon Dr.
Montvale, NJ 07645-1742
Phone: (201)358-7200
Fax: (201)573-8979

Monthly.

Critical Care Medicine

Williams & Wilkins Co.
428 E. Preston St.
Baltimore, MD 21202-3993
Phone: (301)528-4000
Fax: (301)528-4452

Monthly. $70.00/year.

Critical Care Nurse

Cahners Publishing Co.
Health Care Group
249 West 17th St.
New York, NY 10011
Phone: (212)645-0067

Ten times/year. $27.00/year.

Cutis

Yorke Medical Group
Cahners Publishing Co.
249 W. 17th St.
New York, NY 10011
Phone: (212)463-6463
Fax: (212)463-6560

Monthly. $62.00/year; $12.00/single issue.

Diabetes

American Diabetes Association, Inc.
1660 Duke St.
Alexandria, VA 22314
Phone: 800-232-3472

Monthly. $90.00/year; $10.00/single issue.

Diabetes Care

American Diabetes Association, Inc.
1660 Duke St.
Alexandria, VA 22314
Phone: (703)549-1500

Monthly. $65.00/year; $8.00/single issue.

Diagnostic Imaging

Miller Freeman, Inc.
600 Harrison St.
San Francisco, CA 94107
Phone: (415)905-2200
Fax: (415)905-2232

Monthly. $85.00/year; $8.00/single issue.

Dialysis & Transplantation

Creative Age Publications, Inc.
7628 Densmore Ave.
Van Nuys, CA 91406-2088
Phone: (818)782-7328
Fax: (818)782-7450

Monthly. $35.00/year; $4.00/single issue.

Diseases of the Colon & Rectum

Williams & Wilkins Co.
428 E. Preston St.
Baltimore, MD 21202-3993
Phone: (301)528-4000
Fax: (301)528-4312

Monthly. $85.00/year; $13.00/single issue.

The DO

American Osteopathic Association
142 E. Ontario
Chicago, IL 60611
Phone: (312)280-5800

Monthly. $10.00/year; $1.00/single issue.

Drug Topics

Medical Economics Publishing
5 Paragon Dr.
Montvale, NJ 07645-1742
Phone: (201)356-7200
Fax: (201)573-8979

23 times/year. $55.00/year; $5.00/single issue.

Ear, Nose and Throat Journal

International Publishing Group
4959 Commerce Pkwy.
Cleveland, OH 44128
Phone: (216)464-1210
Fax: (216)464-1835

Twelve times/year.

EEO Bi-monthly

CRS Recruitment Publications
1800 Sherman Pl.
Ste. 200
Evanston, IL 60201-3777
Phone: (708)475-8800

Monthly, except December. $72.00/year; $24.00/three issues; $9.00/issue. Covers about 100 employers nationwide who anticipate having technical, professional or management employment opportunities in the coming six months. Consists of five regional editions for Pacific, Western, Midwestern, Southern, and Eastern states. Entries include: Company name, address, phone, name of contact, date established, number of employees, description of the company and its products, and general description of openings expected. Arranged alphabetically and geographically.

Emergency Medical Services

Creative Age Publications, Inc.
7628 Densmore Ave.
Van Nuys, CA 91406-2088
Phone: (818)782-7328
Fax: (818)782-7450

Twelve times/year. $18.95/year; $2.50/single issue.

Emergency Medicine News

Lippincott Healthcare Publications
130 Madison Ave.
3rd Fl.
New York, NY 10016
Phone: (212)679-9710

Monthly. $60.00/year; $11.00/single issue.

Equal Opportunity Magazine

Equal Opportunity Publications
44 Broadway
Greenlawn, NY 11740

Three times/year. $13.00/year. Minority recruitment magazine. Includes a resume service.

Family Practice News

International Medical News Group
770 Lexington Ave.
New York, NY 10021
Phone: (212)421-0707

Semimonthly. $84.00/year; $3.00/single issue.

Federal Career Opportunities

Federal Research Service, Inc.
243 Church St. NW
Vienna, VA 22183
Phone: (703)281-0200

Biweekly. $160.00/year; $75.00/six months; $38.00/three months; $7.50/copy. Provides information on more than 4,200 current federal job vacancies in the United States and overseas; includes permanent, part-time, and temporary positions. Entries include: Position title, location, series and grade, job requirements, special forms, announcement number, closing date, application address. Arrangement: Classified by federal agency and occupation.

Federal Jobs Digest

Federal Jobs Digest
325 Pennsylvania Ave., SE
Washington, DC 20003
Phone: (914)762-5111

Biweekly. $110.00/year; $29.00/three months; $4.50/issue. Covers over 20,000 specific job openings in the federal government in each issue. Entries include: Position name, title, General Schedule grade and Wage Grade, closing date for applications, announcement number, application address, phone, and name of contact. Arrangement: By federal department or agency, then geographical.

Feedback

Health Sciences Communications Association (HESCA)
6105 Lindell Blvd.
St. Louis, MO 63112
Phone: (314)725-4722
Fax: (314)721-6675

Bimonthly. Free to members; $25.00/year for nonmembers. Includes employment listings, association news, information in the field of biocommunications, and regional news.

Fertility and Sterility

American Fertility Society (AFS)
2140 11th Ave., S.
Ste. 200
Birmingham, AL 35205
Phone: (205)933-8494

Monthly. Free to members; $150.00/year for nonmembers. Journal; includes employment opportunities, book reviews and announcements of meetings, courses, and services.

Focus on Critical Care

Mosby-Year Book Inc.
11830 Westline Ind. Dr.
St. Louis, MO 63146
Phone: (314)872-8370
Fax: (314)432-1380

Bimonthly. $25.00/year; $5.50/single issue.

Geriatric Nursing

American Journal of Nursing Co.
555 W. 57th St.
New York, NY 10019-2961
Phone: (212)582-8820
Fax: (212)315-3187

Bimonthly. $23.00/year; $5.00/single issue.

Group Practice Journal

American Group Practice Association (AGPA)
1422 Duke St.
Alexandria, VA 22314
Phone: (703)838-0033

Bimonthly. Free to members; $48.00/year for nonmembers. Includes employment opportunity listings, advertiser index, book reviews, and member profiles. Covers market trends, health care policy and legislation, and management topics affecting the medical profession.

Health Progress

Catholic Health Association of the U.S.
4455 Woodson Rd.
St. Louis, MO 63134
Phone: (314)427-2500

Ten times/ year. $35.00/year; $40.00/year for foreign subscribers; $4.00/issue. Magazine for administrative-level and other managerial personnel in Catholic health care and other related organizations.

Heart and Lung—Journal of Critical Care

11830 Westline Industrial Dr.
St. Louis, MO 63146
Phone: (314)872-8370

Bimonthly. $24.50/year; $85.00/year for institutions; $16.00/year for students; $6.00/issue.

HispanData

Hispanic Business
360 S. Hope Ave., Ste. 300C
Santa Barbara, CA 93105
Phone: (805)682-5843

Database that contains resumes of Hispanic professionals and recent college graduates who are seeking employment with Fortune 500 corporations. Includes job listings from 20 corporations.

HMO Practice

Lippincott Healthcare Publications
130 Madison Ave.
3rd Fl.
New York, NY 10016
Phone: (212)679-9710
Fax: (212)679-9716

Bimonthly. $50.00/year; $13.00/single issue.

Homecare

6133 Bristol Pkwy.
PO Box 3640
Culver City, CA 90231-3640
Phone: (213)337-9717

Monthly. $40.00/year.

Hospital & Community Psychiatry

American Psychiatric Association
1400 K St., NW
Washington, DC 20005
Phone: (202)682-6070

Monthly. $37.00/year; $55.00/year for institutions; $6.00/single issue.

Hospital Pharmacist Report

Medical Economics Publishing
5 Paragon Dr.
Montvale, NJ 07645-1742
Phone: (201)356-7200
Fax: (201)573-8979

Monthly. $35.00/year; $3.00/single issue.

Hospital Pharmacy

Lippincott Healthcare Publications
130 Madison Ave.
3rd Fl.
New York, NY 10016
Phone: (212)679-9710

Monthly. $60.00/year; $11.00/single issue.

Hospital Physician

Turner White Communications, Inc.
353 W. Lancaster Ave.
Ste. 200
Wayne, PA 19087
Phone: (215)975-4541

Monthly. $55.00/year; $7.00/single issue.

Hospital Tribune

257 Park Ave., S.
New York, NY 10010

Hospitals
American Hospital Publishing, Inc.
211 E. Chicago Ave.
Chicago, IL 60611
Phone: (312)440-6800

Semimonthly. $50.00/year.

Infectious Disease News
Slack, Inc.
6900 Grove Rd.
Thorofare, NJ 08086-9447
Phone: (609)848-1000

Monthly. $50.00/year.

Infectious Diseases in Children
Slack, Inc.
6900 Grove Rd.
Thorofare, NJ 08086-9447
Phone: (609)848-1000

Monthly.

Internal Medicine News & Cardiology News
International Medical News Group
770 Lexington Ave.
New York, NY 10021
Phone: (212)421-0707

Semimonthly. $84.00/year.

International Employment Hotline
International Employment Hotline
PO Box 3030
Oakton, VA 22124
Phone: (703)620-1972
Fax: (703)620-1973

Monthly. $36.00/year. Covers temporary and career job openings overseas and advice for international job hunters. Entries include: Company name, job title, description of job, requirements, geographic location of job. Arranged geographically.

International Journal of Dermatology
J.B. Lippincott Co.
227 E. Washington Sq.
Philadelphia, PA 19106
Phone: (215)238-4206

Monthly. $70.00/year; $13.00/single issue.

JEN—Journal of Emergency Nursing
The C.V. Mosby Company
11830 Westline Industrial Dr.
St. Louis, MO 63146
Phone: (314)872-8370

Bimonthly. $26.25/year; $85.00/year for institutions; $16.00/year for students; $5.50/issue.

JOB ADS USA
Militran, Inc.
Box 490
Southeastern, PA 19399-0490

Monthly. Comprehensive source of help-wanted ads, cumulated from employment listings in 100 top newspapers nationwide. Also lists job postings at federal agencies. Organized in job sections which correspond to definitions in the Standard Occupational Classification manual. Entries provide description of position, requirements, whom to contact, newspaper source, and salary ranges, when available.

The Job HUNTER
University of Missouri-Columbia
Career Planning and Placement Center
100 Noyes Bldg.
Columbia, MO 65211

Biweekly. $75.00/year; $50.00/six months. Lists opportunities for college graduates with 0-3 years experience in many fields. Includes information on internships and summer jobs.

The Journal of Allergy and Clinical Immunology
Mosby-Year Book Inc.
11830 Westline Ind. Dr.
St. Louis, MO 63146
Phone: (314)872-8370
Fax: (314)432-1380

Monthly. $70.00/year; $8.00/single issue.

Journal of Allied Health
1101 Connecticut Ave., NW, Ste. 700
Washington, DC 20036

Journal of the American Academy of Nurse Practitioners

E. Washington
Philadelphia, PA 19105
Phone: (215)238-4450
Fax: (215)238-4227

Quarterly. $20.00/year for residents in the U.S.; $40.00/year for foreign subscribers; $45.00/year for institutions; $55.00/year for foreign institutions; $15.00/single issue.

Journal of the American Academy of Tropical Medicine

American Academy of Tropical Medicine (AATM)
16126 E. Warren
Detroit, MI 48224
Phone: (313)882-0641

Semiannual. $125.00/year. Includes employment opportunity listings, book reviews, and information on new diagnostic equipment.

Journal of the American Association of Occupational Health Nurses

50 Lenox Pointe
Atlanta, GA 30324

Journal of American Association of Osteopathic Specialists

American Association of Osteopathic Specialists (AAOS)
804 Main St., Ste. D
Forest Park, GA 30050
Phone: (404)363-8263
Fax: (404)361-2285

Periodic. Free to members. Includes employment opportunities, new member biographies, upcoming meeting highlights, certification and scholarship information, and obituaries.

Journal of the American Medical Association

American Medical Association (AMA)
515 N. State St.
Chicago, IL 60610
Phone: (312)464-4818
Fax: (312)464-4184

Weekly. Free to members; $79.00/year for non-members; $39.50/year for medical students and residents. Covers topics in general medicine; includes employment opportunity listings, book reviews, calendar of events, case reports, and obituaries. Also contains annual index and index of advertisers.

Journal of the American Medical Women's Association

801 N. Fairfax St.
Alexandria, VA 22314
Phone: (703)838-0500

Bimonthly. $35.00/year; $40.00/year for foreign subscribers; $5.00/issue.

Journal of American Osteopathic Association

142 E. Ontario St.
Chicago, IL 60611-2864
Phone: (312)280-5800

Monthly. Free to qualified subscribers. $20.00/year.

Journal of the American Podiatry Association

Box 5037
Station A
Champaign, IL 61820-9037

Journal of Career Planning and Employment

College Placement Council, Inc.
62 Highland Ave.
Bethlehem, PA 18017
Phone: (215)868-1421

Four issues/year. Free to members. Can be used to provide assistance to students in planning and implementing a job search.

The Journal of Clinical Psychiatry

Physicians Postgraduate Press, Inc.
PO Box 240008
Memphis, TN 38124
Phone: (901)682-1001
Fax: (901)682-6992

Monthly. $60.00/year; $8.00/single issue.

The Journal of Continuing Education in Nursing

6900 Grove Rd.
Thorofare, NJ 08086
Phone: (609)848-1000

Bimonthly. $42.00/year.

Journal of Emergency Nursing

Mosby-Year Book Inc.
11830 Westline Ind. Dr.
St. Louis, MO 63146
Phone: (314)872-8370
Fax: (314)432-1380

Bimonthly. $29.00/year; $5.50/single issue.

The Journal of Family Practice

Appleton and Lange
25 Van Zant St.
East Norwalk, CT 06856
Phone: (203)838-4400

Monthly. Free to qualified subscribers.
$66.00/year; $87.00/year for institutions.

Journal of General Internal Medicine

Hanley & Belfus, Inc.
210 S. 13th St.
Philadelphia, PA 19107
Phone: (215)546-0313
Fax: (215)790-9330

Bimonthly. $70.00/year; $16.00/single issue.

Journal of Gerontological Nursing

6900 Grove Rd.
Thorofare, NJ 08086
Phone: (609)848-1000

Monthly. $34.00/year.

Journal of Immunology

American Association of Immunologists (AAI)
9650 Rockville Pike
Bethesda, MD 20014
Phone: (301)530-7178

Semimonthly. Free to members. Includes list of
employment opportunities, abstract index, calendar of events, and obituaries. Reports on original
research efforts in: cellular immunology; clinical
immunology and immunopathology; cytokines,
mediators, and regulatory molecules; immuno-
chemistry; immunopharmacology; microbial
immunology; molecular biology and molecular
genetics; tumor immunology.

Journal of Intensive Care Medicine

Blackwell Scientific Publications, Inc.
3 Cambridge Ctr.
Ste. 208
Cambridge, MA 02142
Phone: (617)225-0401
Fax: (617)225-0412

Bimonthly. $56.00/year; $17.00/single issue.

Journal of Intravenous Nursing

J.B. Lippincott Co.
227 E. Washington Sq.
Philadelphia, PA 19106
Phone: (215)238-4206
Fax: (215)238-4227

Bimonthly. $50.00/year; $17.00/single issue.

The Journal of Invasive Cardiology

Health Management Publications, Inc.
Allendale Square 2
550 American Ave.
King of Prussia, PA 19406
Phone: (215)337-4466
Fax: (215)337-0890

Bimonthly.

Journal of the National Medical Association

Slack, Inc.
6900 Grove Rd.
Thorofare, NJ 08086-9447
Phone: (609)848-1000
Fax: (609)853-5991

Monthly. $65.00/year; $7.00/single issue.

Journal of Nurse-Midwifery

655 Avenue of the Americas
New York, NY 10010
Phone: (212)989-5800
Fax: (212)633-3990

Six times/year. $86.00/year for institutions;
$112.00/year for foreign subscribers.

The Journal of Nursing Administration

J.B. Lippincott Company
E. Washington Sq.
Philadelphia, PA 19105
Phone: (215)238-4200

Monthly. $45.00/year; $13.00/single issue.

Journal of Nursing Education

6900 Grove Rd.
Thorofare, NJ 08086-9447
Phone: (609)848-1000

Journal of Obstetric, Gynecologic, and Neonatal Nursing

J.B. Lippincott Company
E. Washington Sq.
Philadelphia, PA 19105
Phone: (215)238-4283

Bimonthly. $35.00/year; $13.00/single issue.

Journal of Occupational Medicine

Williams and Wilkins
428 E. Preston St.
Baltimore, MD 21202
Phone: (301)528-4000

Monthly. $77.00/year; $10.00/single issue.

Journal of Pediatric Health Care

Mosby-Year Book Inc.
11830 Westline Ind. Dr.
St. Louis, MO 63146
Phone: (314)872-8370
Fax: (314)432-1380

Bimonthly. $25.00/year; $6.00/single issue.

The Journal of Pediatrics

11830 Westline Industrial Dr.
St. Louis, MO 63146
Phone: (314)872-8370

Monthly. $59.00/year; $120.50/year for institutions; $30.00/year for students; $6.50/issue.

Journal of Psychosocial Nursing and Mental Health Services

6900 Grove Rd.
Thorofare, NJ 08086
Phone: (609)848-1000

Monthly. $35.00/year; $7.00/issue.

Journal of the Student National Medical Association

Spectrum Unlimited
3330 N. Causeway Blvd.
Ste. 428
Metairie, LA 70001
Phone: (504)830-4785

Quarterly. $8.00/year; $2.50/single issue.

The Journal of Trauma

Williams and Wilkins
428 E. Preston St.
Baltimore, MD 21202
Phone: (301)528-4000

Monthly. $89.00/year; $12.00/single issue.

The Journal of Urology

Williams & Wilkins Co.
428 E. Preston St.
Baltimore, MD 21202
Phone: (301)528-4000
Fax: (301)528-4452

Monthly. $120.00/year.

Journal of Visual Impairment and Blindness

American Foundation for the Blind
15 W. 16th St.
New York, NY 10011
Phone: (212)620-2000

Ten times/year. $30.00/year; $45.00/year for institutions; $4.00/issue.

Kennedy's Career Strategist

Marilyn Moats Kennedy Career Strategies
1153 Wilmette Ave.
Wilmette, IL 60091

12/year. $89.00/year. Offers job search guidance.

kiNexus

kiNexus, Inc.
640 N. LaSalle St., Ste. 560
Chicago, IL 60610
Phone: (312)335-0787

CD-ROM (Compact Disc-Read Only Memory) database that contains the complete text of more than 155,000 resumes of new and recent college and university graduates representing 1850 academic institutions, as well as some experienced college graduates wishing to find new employment. Job-seekers may fill out a questionnaire to have their resume listed in the database.

The Lancet

Williams & Wilkins Co.
428 E. Preston St.
Baltimore, MD 21202-3993
Phone: (301)528-4000
Fax: (301)528-4312

Weekly. $85.00/year; $7.00/single issue.

Managing Your Career

Dow Jones and Co.
420 Lexington Ave.
New York, NY 10170

College version of the *National Business Employment Weekly*. Excludes job openings, but provides job-hunting advice.

McKnight's Long-Term Care News

McKnight Medical Communications, Inc.
1419 Lake Cook Rd.
Ste. 110
Deerfield, IL 60015
Phone: (708)945-0345
Fax: (708)945-0532

Monthly. $41.00/year; $5.00/single issue.

MCN: The American Journal of Maternal Child Nursing

555 W. 57th St.
New York, NY 10019-2961
Phone: (212)582-8820

Six times/year. $23.00/year.

Medical Economics

5 Paragon Dr.
Montvale, NJ 07645-1742
Phone: (201)358-7200

Biweekly. $75.00/year. Magazine covering practice management, professional relations, and financial affairs for physicians.

Medical Electronic Products

Measurements & Data Corp.
2994 W. Liberty Ave.
Pittsburgh, PA 15216
Phone: (412)343-9666

Six times/year. $22.00/year; $5.00/single issue.

Medical Tribune

275 Park Ave.
New York, NY 10010
Phone: (212)674-8500

Thirty-six times/year. $65.00/year. Tabloid reporting on health and medical sciences for office-based physicians.

Medical World News

500 Howard St.
San Francisco, CA 94105-3002
Phone: (415)397-1881

Monthly. $50.00/year in the U.S. and Canada; $85.00/year for foreign subscribers.

Military Medicine

9320 Old Georgetown Rd.
Bethesda, MD 20814

Monthly. $35.00/year; $40.00/year for foreign subscribers; $4.50/issue.

Minority Graduate Database

McLure-Lundberg Associates, Inc.
13260 U St., NW
Washington, DC 20009
Phone: (202)483-4107

Online database that provides information on recent minority college graduates and alumni as well as undergraduates nearing graduation from some 350 colleges and universities. Available online through Executive Telecom System International.

Modern Healthcare

Crain Communications, Inc.
740 N. Rush St.
Chicago, IL 60611
Phone: (312)649-5200

Weekly. $110.00/year.

MPA

Physicians Postgraduate Press
785 Crossover Ln.
Bldg. B
Ste. 209
Memphis, TN 38117
Phone: (901)682-1001
Fax: (901)682-6992

Bimonthly. $24.00/year; $4.00/single issue.

The National Ad Search

National Ad Search, Inc.
PO Box 2083
Milwaukee, WI 53201

50/year. $235.00/year; $145.00/six months; $75.00/three months. Contains listings of 'over 2,000 current career opportunities from over 72 employment markets.'

National Business Employment Weekly

Dow Jones and Company, Inc.
PO Box 300
Princeton, NJ 08543
Phone: (609)520-4000

Weekly. $199.00/year; $112.00/six months. Newspaper containing help-wanted advertising from four regional editions of the *Wall Street Journal*. Includes statistics and articles about employment opportunities and career advancements.

National Employment Listing Service Bulletin
Sam Houston State University
College of Criminal Justice
Huntsville, TX 77341

Monthly. $30.00/year for individuals; $65.00/year for institutions/agencies.

The Nation's Health
American Public Health Association (APHA)
1015 15th St., NW
Washington, DC 20005
Phone: (202)789-5600
Fax: (202)789-5681

Ten times/year. Free to members; $8.00/year for nonmembers. Includes employment opportunity listings and reports on current health issues, association actions, and legislative, regulatory, and policy issues affecting public health.

Neonatal Intensive Care
Goldstein & Assoc., Inc.
1150 Yale St.
No. 12
Santa Monica, CA 90403
Phone: (213)828-1309
Fax: (213)829-1169

Six times/year.

Neonatal Network
191 Lynch Creek Way
Ste. 101
Petaluma, CA 94954-2313
Phone: (707)762-2646

Eight times/year. $28.00/year; $5.00/single issue.

New England Employment Week
PO Box 806
Rockport, ME 04856

The New England Journal of Medicine
1440 Main St.
Waltham, MA 02154-1649
Phone: (617)893-3800

Weekly. $89.00/year.

The New Physician
1890 Preston White Dr.
3rd Fl.
Reston, VA 22091
Phone: (703)620-6600

Nine times/year. $18.00/year included in membership; $30.00/year for foreign subscribers. Magazine covering ethical, social, and economic issues relating to medical students.

Nova
American Osteopathic College of Pathologists (AOCP)
c/o Joan Gross
12368 NW 13th Ct.
Pembroke Pines, FL 33026
Phone: (305)432-9640

Monthly. Free to members. Newsletter including reports on employment opportunities and topics of interest.

NRA Newsletter: Committed to Enhancing the Lives of Persons with Disabilities
National Rehabilitation Association (NRA)
633 S. Washington St.
Alexandria, VA 22314
Phone: (703)836-0850
Fax: (703)836-2209

Eight times/year. Free to members. Includes listing of employment opportunities, calendar of events, and chapter news.

Nurse Educator
J.B.Lippincott Company
E. Washington Sq.
Philadelphia, PA 19105
Phone: (215)238-4200

Bimonthly. $35.00/year; $40.00/year for foreign subscribers; $60.00/year for institutions; $70.00/year for institutions in other countries; $15.00/single issue.

Nurse Practitioner Forum
PO Box 6467
Duluth, MN 55806-9854
Phone: 800-654-2452

Quarterly. $39.00/year; $29.00/year for students; $49.00/year for institutions; $18.00/single issue.

Nursing '92

Springhouse Corp.
1111 Bethlehem Pike
Springhouse, PA 19477
Phone: (215)646-8700
Fax: (215)646-4399

Monthly. $28.00/year.

Nursing Economics

Anthony J. Janetti, Inc.
Box 56
N. Woodbury Rd.
Pitman, NJ 08071
Phone: (609)589-2319
Fax: (609)589-7463

Bimonthly.

Nursing & Health Care

National League for Nursing, Inc.
350 Hudson St.
New York, NY 10014
Phone: (212)989-9393

Monthly, September through June. $50.00/year;
$5.00/single issue.

Nursing Management

103 N. 2nd St.
Ste. 200
West Dundee, IL 60118
Phone: (708)426-6100
Fax: (708)426-6416

Monthly. $25.00/year.

Nursing Outlook

555 W. 57th St.
New York, NY 10019-2961
Phone: (212)582-8820

Bimonthly. $25.00/year; $35.00/year for institutions; $5.00/issue.

Nursing Research

555 W. 57th St.
New York, NY 10019-2961
Phone: (212)582-8820

Bimonthly. $23.00/year.

Nursing World Journal

Prime National Publishing Corporation
470 Boston Post Rd.
Weston, MA 02193
Phone: (617)899-2702

Monthly. $22.00.

Ob. Gyn. News

International Medical News Group
770 Lexington Ave.
New York, NY 10021
Phone: (212)421-0707

Semimonthly. $54.00/year; $3.00/single issue.

OBG Management

Dowden Publishing Co., Inc.
110 Summit Ave.
Montvale, NJ 07645
Phone: (201)391-9100
Fax: (201)391-2778

Monthly.

Obstetrics and Gynecology

Elsevier Science Publishing Co., Inc.
655 Avenue of the Americas
New York, NY 10010
Phone: (212)989-5800

Monthly. $98.00/year; $156.00/year for institutions.

Occupational Outlook Quarterly

U.S. Government Printing Office
Superintendent of Documents
Washington, DC 20402
Phone: (202)783-3238

Quarterly. $6.50/year; $2.50/single issue.
Contains articles and information about career
choices and job opportunities in a wide range of
occupations.

Ocular Surgery News

Slack, Inc.
6900 Grove Rd.
Thorofare, NJ 08086-9447
Phone: (609)848-1000

Twice/month. $50.00/year; $7.00/single issue.

OE Reports

PO Box 10
Bellingham, WA 98227-0010
Phone: (206)676-3290

Monthly. Free to qualified subscribers. Includes
an employment opportunity section.

Oncology Nursing Forum

The Oncology Nursing Press, Inc.
N. Woodbury Rd.
Box 56
Pitman, NJ 08071
Phone: (609)589-2319
Fax: (609)589-7463

Eight times/year. $24.00/year; $6.00/single issue.

Oncology Times

Lippincott Healthcare Publications
130 Madison Ave.
3rd Fl.
New York, NY 10016
Phone: (212)679-9710

Monthly. $60.00/year; $11.00/single issue.

Ophthalmic Surgery

Slack, Inc.
6900 Grove Rd.
Thorofare, NJ 08086-9447
Phone: (609)848-1000
Fax: (609)853-5991

Monthly. $40.00/year; $7.00/single issue.

Ophthalmology Management

Gralla Publications
1515 Broadway
New York, NY 10036
Phone: (212)869-1300

Ten times/year.

Opportunities in Non-Profit Organizations

ACCESS/Networking in the Public Interest
96 Mt. Auburn St.
Cambridge, MA 02138

Monthly. Lists opportunities in many fields, including public interest law.

Opportunity Placement Register

American Medical Association (AMA)
Physicians Career Resource
515 N. State St.
Chicago, IL 60610
Phone: (312)645-4712

Monthly. Available free to AMA member physicians seeking positions; $50.00 to others.

Covers: Employment or practice opportunities for physicians. Also has lists of practices for sale, state medical societies, executive and professional recruiting firms, hospital or clinic management companies, medical schools, national medical specialty societies, health maintenance organizations, etc. Entries include: Medical specialty, location and type of practice, beginning financial arrangements, income range, size of community, physician population, date available. For entries in other lists—Name, address, phone. Arrangement: Opportunities listed geographically, then by medical specialty. Indexes: Medical specialty. Other information: A companion volume, *Physician Placement Register* lists key data from registered physicians seeking positions.

Opportunity Report

Job Bank, Inc.
PO Box 6028
Lafayette, IN 47903
Phone: (317)447-0549

Biweekly. $252.00/year. Lists 3,000-4,000 positions across the United States, from entry-level to upper management, in a variety of occupational fields. Ads are derived from newspapers, primarily in growth markets. Ads contain position description, employment requirements, and contact information.

Optical Index

Professional Press Group
825 7th Ave.
New York, NY 10019
Phone: (212)887-1832

Monthly. $40.00/year.

Optical Management

5 N. Greenwich Rd.
Armonk, NY 10504

Options

Project Concern
PO Box 85323
San Diego, CA 92186

Bimonthly. $10.00/year. Aimed at health services professionals. Lists international openings.

Orthopaedic Nursing

N. Woodburg Rd.
PO Box 56
Pitman, NJ 08071
Phone: (609)589-2319
Fax: (609)589-7463

Six times/year. $21.00/year; $28.00/year for institutions; $5.00/single issue.

Orthopaedic Review

301 Gibraltar Rd.
Box 528
Morris Plains, NJ 07950
Phone: (201)644-0802

Monthly. $55.00/year; $65.00/year for institutions; $82.00/year for foreign subscribers; $7.50/single issue.

Orthopedics Today

6900 Grove Rd.
Thorofare, NJ 08086-9447
Phone: (609)848-1000

Monthly. $110.00/year.

Osteopathic Medical News

Compendium Publishing Co., Inc.
9 Pheasant Run
Newtown, PA 18940
Phone: (215)860-9560
Fax: (215)860-9558

Monthly.

Ostomy/Wound Management: The Journal for Extended Patient Care Management

Health Management Publications, Inc.
Allendale Square 2
550 American Ave.
King of Prussia, PA 19406
Phone: (215)337-4466
Fax: (215)337-0890

Bimonthly. $24.00/year; $4.00/single issue.

Pain Management

Core Publishing Division
Excerpta Medica, Inc.
3131 Princeton Pike
Bldg. 2A
Lawrenceville, NJ 08648
Phone: (609)896-9450
Fax: (609)896-8089

Bimonthly. $55.00/year; $10.00/single issue.

PAJF Employment Magazine

American Academy of Physician Assistants
(AAPA)
950 N. Washington St.
Alexandria, VA 22314
Phone: (703)836-2272
Fax: (703)684-1924

Biweekly. $20.00/year for members; $50.00/year for nonmembers. Provides nationwide listing of employment opportunities for physician assistants.

Part-Time Professional

Association of Part-Time Professionals (APTP)
Crescent Plaza
7700 Leesburg Pike
No. 216
Falls Church, VA 22043
Phone: (703)734-7975

Monthly. Newsletter for part-time professional workers, managers involved in the flexible workforce, and public policy officials; includes articles about trends in part-time and temporary employment.

Patient Care

Medical Economics Publishing
5 Paragon Dr.
Montvale, NJ 07645-1742
Phone: (201)358-7200
Fax: (201)573-8979

Twenty times/year. $59.00/year.

Pediatric Annals

Slack, Inc.
6900 Grove Rd.
Thorofare, NJ 08086-9447
Phone: (609)848-1000
Fax: (609)853-5991

Monthly. $27.50/year; $2.50/single issue.

Pediatric Management

Dowden Publishing Co., Inc.
110 Summit Ave.
Montvale, NJ 07645
Phone: (201)391-9100
Fax: (201)391-2778

Monthly.

Pediatric News

International Medical News Group
770 Lexington Ave.
New York, NY 10021
Phone: (212)421-0707

Monthly. $60.00/year.

Pediatric Nursing

N. Woodbury Rd.
Box 56
Pitman, NJ 08071
Phone: (609)589-2319

Bimonthly. $18.00/year; $24.00/year for institutions.

Pediatrics

American Academy of Pediatrics
PO Box 927
Elk Grove Village, IL 60009-0927
Phone: (708)228-5005

Monthly. $50.00/year; $60.00/year for foreign subscribers.

Perinatal Press

Perinatal Center
Sutter Memorial Hospital
52nd and F Sts.
Sacramento, CA 95819
Phone: (916)733-1750

Bimonthly. $17.50/year.

Perinatology—Neonatology

11742 Wilshire Blvd.
Los Angeles, CA 90025
Phone: (213)473-1354

Bimonthly. $40.00/year.

Perspectives in Psychiatric Care

1211 Locust St.
Philadelphia, PA 19107
Phone: (215)545-7222
Fax: (215)545-8107

Quarterly.

Physicians Assistant

Academy of Physician Assistants
117 N. Nineteenth St.
Arlington, VA 22209

Podiatry Management

Kane Communications, Inc.
7000 Terminal Sq.
Ste. 210
Upper Darby, PA 19082
Phone: (215)734-2420

Nine times/year. $29.00/year; $5.00/single issue.

Provider

American Health Care Association
1201 L St., NW
Washington, DC 20005
Phone: (202)842-4444

Monthly. $36.00/year. Magazine covering health care issues.

Psychiatric Annals

6900 Grove St.
Thorofare, NJ 08086
Phone: (609)848-1000

Monthly. $85.00/year; $95.00/year for institutions. Journal analyzing concepts and practices in every area of psychiatry.

Psychiatric News

American Psychiatric Association
1400 K St., NW
Washington, DC 20005
Phone: (202)682-6133

Semimonthly. $40.00/year.

The Psychiatric Times

1924 E. Deere Ave.
Santa Ana, CA 92705
Phone: (714)250-1008
Fax: (714)250-0445

Monthly.

Rehabilitation Nursing Journal

Association of Rehabilitation Nurses
5700 Old Orchard Rd.
Skokie, IL 60077-1024
Phone: (708)966-3433

Bimonthly. $35.00/year; $45.00/year for institutions; $7.00/issue.

Rescue-EMS Magazine
Lifesaving Communications, Inc.
PO Box 165
Milford, DE 19963
Phone: (302)422-2772

Bimonthly. $15.00/year; $2.50/single issue.

Research in Nursing & Health
605 3rd Ave.
New York, NY 10158-0012
Phone: (212)850-6289

Six times/year. $60.00/year.

Resident & Staff Physician
Romaine Pierson Publishers, Inc.
80 Shore Rd.
PO Box 911
Port Washington, NY 11050
Phone: (516)883-6350
Fax: (516)883-6609

Monthly. $55.00/year; $9.00/single issue.

Resumes on Computer
Curtis Development Company
1000 Waterway Blvd.
Indianapolis, IN 46202
Phone: (317)633-2045

Online database that contains more than 3300 professionally produced resumes of people actively seeking employment. Resumes are held for 24 weeks. Available online through Executive Telecom System International.

Retina
J.B. Lippincott Co.
227 E. Washington Sq.
Philadelphia, PA 19106
Phone: (215)238-4206
Fax: (215)238-4227

Quarterly. $75.00/year; $35.00/single issue.

RN
Medical Economics Publishing
5 Paragon Dr.
Montvale, NJ 07645-1742
Phone: (201)358-7200

Monthly. $35.00/year; $40.00/year for subscribers in Canada; $17.50/year for students.

Rocky Mountain Employment Newsletter
Intermountain Referral Service
3565 Pitch Pl.
Colorado Springs, CO 80908
Phone: (719)488-0320

Biweekly. $7.00/month for one edition. Employment newsletter covering jobs in all occupational areas. Specializes in summer/winter seasonal openings and in ranch, horse, livestock, and farm opportunities. Published in a Colorado-Wyoming edition, an Idaho-Montana edition, and an Arizona-New Mexico edition.

Rural Health Care
National Rural Health Association (NRHA)
301 E. Armour Blvd.
Ste. 420
Kansas City, MO 64111
Phone: (816)756-3140
Fax: (816)756-3144

Bimonthly. Free to members. Association newsletter; includes listing of employment opportunties, listing of publications, book reviews, information on new members, and legislative and state news.

The Search Bulletin
8300 Boone Blvd.
Ste. 500
Vienna, VA 22182
Phone: (703)848-9220
Fax: (703)848-4586

22 issues/year. Provides listings of employment opportunities available across the country for senior executives.

Seminars in Oncology Nursing
Independence Sq. W.
Philadelphia, PA 19106-3399
Phone: (215)238-7800
Fax: (215)238-7883

Six times/year. $91.00/year; $120.00/year for institutions; $53.00/year for residents and interns in the U.S.; $135.00/year for foreign subscribers; $30.00/single issue.

Skin & Allergy News
International Medical News Group
770 Lexington Ave.
New York, NY 10021
Phone: (212)421-0707

Monthly. $54.00/year; $3.00/single issue.

Southern Medical Journal

35 Lakeshore Dr.
PO Box 190088
Birmingham, AL 35219-0088
Phone: (205)945-1840

Monthly. $45.00/year.

Southwest Medical Opportunities

6750 West Loop S.
Ste. 500
Bellaire, TX 77401
Phone: (713)666-8976

Bimonthly. Healthcare recruitment journal.

Spare Time

Kipen Publishing Corp.
5810 W. Oklahoma Ave.
Milwaukee, WI 53219
Phone: (414)543-8110

Surgery, Gynecology and Obstetrics

The Franklin H. Martin Memorial Foundation
54 E. Erie St.
Chicago, IL 60611
Phone: (312)787-9282

Monthly. $60.00/year; $10.00/single issue.

Surgical Rounds

80 Shore Rd.
Port Washington, NY 11050
Phone: (516)883-6350

Monthly. $50.00/year; $92.00/two years.

TeamRehab Report

Miramar Publishing
6133 Bristol Pkwy.
PO Box 3640
Culver City, CA 90231-3640
Phone: (213)337-9717

Bimonthly. $24.00/year.

Today's OR Nurse

6900 Grove Rd.
Thorofare, NJ 08086
Phone: (609)848-1000

Monthly. $30.00/year.

Transplantation Proceedings

Appleton & Lange
25 Van Zant St.
PO Box 5630
Norwalk, CT 06856
Phone: (203)838-4400

Bimonthly. $156.00/year; $42.00/single issue.

Urology

500 Plaza Dr.
PO Box 643
Secaucus, NJ 07094
Phone: (201)864-4000

Monthly. $75.00/year.

Vision Monday

Jobson Publishing Corp.
352 Park Ave. S.
New York, NY 10010
Phone: (212)685-4848
Fax: (212)696-5318

26 times/year. $39.95/year; $3.00/single issue.

Western Journal of Medicine

California Medical Association
PO Box 7602
221 Main St.
San Francisco, CA 94120
Phone: (415)541-0900

Monthly. $40.00/year; $7.50/single issue.

Work Times

New Ways to Work (NWW)
149 9th St.
San Francisco, CA 94103
Phone: (415)552-1000

Quarterly. $35.00/year for individuals; $75.00/year for organizations. Newsletter focusing on alternative work options.

Professional Associations

Academy for Health Services Marketing (AHSM)

c/o American Marketing Association
250 S. Wacker Dr.
Ste. 200
Chicago, IL 60606
Phone: (312)648-0536

Membership: Marketing professionals in the health care field; vice presidents and directors of hospitals, health maintenance organizations, nursing homes, and other health care institutions. Activities: Offers placement service. Promotes the marketing of health services; sponsors continuing education for and professional development of members to this end. Conducts seminars; bestows Philip Kotler and Academy Achievement and Contribution awards. A subsidiary of the American Marketing Association.

Accreditation Review Committee on Education for Physicians Assistants (ARC-PA)

American Medical Association
515 N. State St.
Chicago, IL 60610
Phone: (312)464-4623
Fax: (312)464-5830

Purpose: Serves as an accrediting review body for physician assistant education nationwide. Makes recommendations to Committee on Allied Health Education and Accreditation.

American Academy of Clinical Toxicology (AACT)

Kansas State University
Comparative Toxicology Laboratories
Manhattan, KS 66506-5606
Phone: (913)532-4334
Fax: (913)532-4481

Membership: Physicians, veterinarians, pharmacists, research scientists, and analytical chemists. Activities: Maintains placement services. Objectives are to: unite medical scientists and facilitate the exchange of information; encourage the development of therapeutic methods and technology; establish a mechanism for the certification of medical scientists in clinical toxicology. Conducts workshops and professional training in poison information and emergency service personnel. Maintains speakers' bureau. Bestows awards.

American Academy of Dermatology (AAD)

1567 Maple Ave.
PO Box 3116
Evanston, IL 60201-3116
Phone: (708)869-3954
Fax: (708)869-4382

Membership: Professional society of medical doctors specializing in skin diseases. Activities:

Provides placement service. Conducts educational programs. Bestows awards; compiles statistics. Maintains DERM/INFONET, an online service containing 14 data bases.

American Academy of Family Physicians (AAFP)

8880 Ward Pkwy.
Kansas City, MO 64114
Phone: (816)333-9700

Membership: Professional society of family physicians who provide continuing comprehensive care to patients. Activities: Maintains placement service. Bestows awards including the Mead Johnson awards for graduate training in family practice, 20 awards of $1500 each for residents in family practice, 12 annual Parke-Davis Teacher Development awards of $1400 each, and research in family practice and student research assistantship awards.

American Academy of Medical Administrators (AAMA)

30555 Southfield Rd., Ste. 150
Southfield, MI 48076
Phone: (313)540-4310

Membership: Individuals involved in medical administration at the executive- or middle-management levels. **Purpose:** Promotes educational courses for the training of persons in medical administration, conducts research, and offers placement service. **Publication(s):** *American Academy of Medical Administrators-Executive,* bimonthly.

American Academy of Medical Directors (AAMD)

1 Urban Center
Ste. 648
Tampa, FL 33609
Phone: (813)287-2000

Membership: Physicians with full- or part-time administrative, management, or leadership responsibilities. Activities: Serves as placement service for members seeking new locations or career opportunities. Provides career placement and counseling service through the Physician Executive Management Center. Acts as an educational forum exclusively for physicians to aid them in preparing for positions of organizational leadership. Sponsors continuing education programs including Physician in Management seminars. Offers scholarship program for physicians practicing management in minority fields. Compiles statistics. Affiliated With: American College of Physician Executives.

American Academy of Neurology (AAN)

2221 University Ave., SE
Ste. 335
Minneapolis, MN 55414
Phone: (612)623-8115

Membership: Professional society of medical doctors specializing in nerve and nervous system diseases. Activities: Maintains placement service. Presents annual research awards; sponsors research and educational programs.

American Academy of Nursing (AAN)

2420 Pershing Rd.
Kansas City, MO 64108
Phone: (816)474-5720
Fax: (816)471-4903

Purpose: Advance new concepts in nursing and health care; identify and explore issues in health, the professions, and society that concern nursing; examine interrelationships among segments within nursing and the interaction among nurses as these affect the development of the nursing profession; identify and propose resolutions to issues and problems confronting nursing and health, including alternative plans for implementation. **Publication(s):** *American Academy of Nursing Directory,* biennial. • *Nursing Outlook,* bimonthly.

American Academy of Otolaryngology - Head and Neck Surgery (AAO-HNS)

1 Prince St.
Alexandria, VA 22314
Phone: (703)836-4444
Fax: (703)683-5100

Membership: Professional society of medical doctors specializing in otolaryngology (diseases of the ear, nose, and throat) and head and neck surgery. Activities: Maintains job information exchange service. Represents otolaryngology in governmental and socioeconomic areas, and provides high-quality medical education for otolaryngologists. Coordinates Combined Otolaryngological Spring Meetings for six national otolaryngological societies. Bestows awards; sponsors competitions.

American Academy of Pediatrics (AAP)

141 Northwest Point Blvd.
PO Box 927
Elk Grove Village, IL 60009-0927
Phone: (708)228-5005
Fax: (708)228-5097

Membership: Professional medical society of pediatricians and pediatric subspecialists. **Purpose:** Operates small member library of books and journals on pediatric medicine, office practice, and child health care policy. Maintains 42 committees, councils and task forces including: Accident and Poison Prevention; Early Childhood, Adoption and Dependent Care; Infectious Diseases. **Publication(s):** *AAP News,* monthly. • *Fellowship List,* annual. • *Pediatrics,* monthly.

Arecent study by Northwestern National Life Insurance Co. found that 46 percent of American workers worry about their jobs and feel more pressured to prove their value because of the recession . . . . Unfortunately, the more you worry about whether you are doing a good enough job, the more likely you are to erode your efficiency, creativity and morale—and damage your health.

Source: *Business Monday/Detroit Free Press*

American Academy of Physician Assistants (AAPA)

950 N. Washington St.
Alexandria, VA 22314-1552
Phone: (703)836-2272
Fax: (703)684-1924

Membership: Physician assistants who have graduated from an American Medical Association accredited program and/or are certified by the National Commission on Certification of Physician Assistants; individuals who are enrolled in an accredited PA educational program. **Purpose:** To educate the public about the physician assistant profession; represent physician assistants' interests before Congress, government agencies, and health-related organizations; assure the competence of physician assistants through development of educational curricula and accreditation programs; provide services for members. Organizes annual National PA Day. Develops research and education programs; maintains library. Awards scholarships; compiles statistics. **Publication(s):** *AAPA Bulletin*, monthly. • *AAPA News*, monthly. • *Journal of the American Academy of Physician Assistants*, bimonthly. • *Legislative Watch*, monthly. • *Membership Directory*, annual. • *PAJF Employment Magazine*, biweekly.

Works to help eliminate prejudice in nursing; interest men in the nursing profession; provide opportunites for the discussion of common problems; encourage education and promote further professional growth; advise and assist in areas of professional inequity; help develop sensitivities to various social needs; promote the principles and practices of positive health care. Acts as a clearinghouse for information on men in nursing. **Publication(s):** *Interaction*, quarterly.

American Academy of Psychiatrists in Alcoholism and Addictions (AAPAA)
PO Box 376
Greenbelt, MD 20768
Phone: (301)220-0951

Membership: Psychiatrists and residents in training. Activities: Conducts placement service. Purposes are: to provide a forum for discussion of issues related to substance abuse; to further education, research, and clinical work in the field; to assist in the development of appropriate standards of care for alcoholics and other drug-dependent persons. Facilitates worldwide communication among psychiatrists and others on issues and practices related to substance abuse and addiction. Bestows awards; maintains speakers' bureau; compiles statistics.

American Academy of Tropical Medicine (AATM)
16126 E. Warren
Detroit, MI 48224
Phone: (313)882-0641

Membership: Physicians and allied health professionals interested in tropical medicine. Activities: Provides placement service. Provides postgraduate continuing medical education; confers certificates and diplomas. Sponsors competitions; maintains speakers' bureau and library. Conducts research and compiles statistics. Bestows fellowship awards; offers children's services.

American Assembly for Men in Nursing (AAMN)
PO Box 31753
Independence, OH 44131
Membership: Registered nurses. **Purpose:**

American Association of Certified Orthoptists (AACO)
Hermann Eye Center
6411 Fannin
Houston, TX 77030-1697
Phone: (713)797-1777

Membership: Orthoptists certified by the American Orthoptic Council after completing a minimum of 24 months of special training in order to treat defects in binocular function. Activities: Maintains placement listing service. Assists in postgraduate instruction courses; conducts programs and courses at international, national, and regional meetings; helps individual orthoptists with special or unusual problem cases; trains new orthoptists. Offers awards; maintains Jean Robinson Memorial Library in Atlanta, GA.

American Association of Colleges of Osteopathic Medicine (AACOM)
6110 Executive Blvd., No. 405
Rockville, MD 20852
Phone: (301)468-0990

Membership: Osteopathic medical colleges. **Purpose:** Operates centralized application service; monitors and works with Congress and other government agencies in the planning of health care programs. Gathers statistics on osteopathic medical students, faculty, and diplomates. **Publication(s):** *AACOM Organizational Guide*, annual. • *American Association of Colleges of Osteopathic Medicine—Annual Statistical Report*. • *Debts and Career Plans of Osteopathic Medical Students*, annual. • Also publishes *Osteopathic Medical Education*, *Education of Osteopathic Physicians*, *Osteopathic*

Medical Education: A Handbook for Minority Applicants, and brochure.

American Association of Colleges of Podiatric Medicine (AACPM)

1350 Piccard Dr., Ste. 322
Rockville, MD 20852
Phone: (301)990-7400
Toll-free: 800-922-9266

Membership: Professional organization of administrators, faculty, practitioners, students, and other individuals associated with podiatric medical education. **Purpose:** Provides vocational guidance material for secondary schools and colleges. Conducts public affairs activities and legislative advocacy. Compiles statistics. **Publication(s):** *Newsletter*, 3/year.

American Association for Geriatric Psychiatry (AAGP)

PO Box 376-A
Greenbelt, MD 20768
Phone: (301)220-0952
Fax: (301)220-0941

Membership: Psychiatrists interested in promoting better mental health care for the elderly. Activities: Maintains placement service. Operates speakers' bureau.

American Association of Immunologists (AAI)

9650 Rockville Pike
Bethesda, MD 20014
Phone: (301)530-7178
Fax: (301)571-1816

Membership: Scientists engaged in immunological research including aspects of virology, bacteriology, biochemistry, genetics, and related disciplines. Activities: Maintains placement service. Goals are to advance knowledge of immunology and related disciplines and to facilitate the interchange of information among investigators in various fields. Promotes interaction between laboratory investigators and clinicians. Conducts training courses, symposia, workshops, and lectures. Maintains library; bestows awards; compiles statistics.

American Association of Neuropathologists (AANP)

c/o Reid R. Heffner, Jr., M.D.
Buffalo Medical School/ SUNY
Department of Pathology
204 Farber Hall
Buffalo, NY 14214
Phone: (716)898-3114

Membership: Professional society of physicians specializing in neuropathology. Activities: Offers placement service. Seeks to advance research and training in neuropathology. Presents awards for best basic and clinical papers presented at annual meeting.

> **A**verage starting salary for an M.B.A. with a liberal arts bachelor's degree: $35,734. A technical bachelor's degree adds $5,579.
>
> Source: *U.S. News & World Report*

American Association of Occupational Health Nurses (AAOHN)

50 Lenox Pointe
Atlanta, GA 30324
Phone: (404)262-1162
Fax: (404)262-1165

Membership: Registered professional nurses employed by business and industrial firms; nurse educators, nurse editors, nurse writers, and others interested in occupational health nursing. Activities: Offers placement service. Maintains library of 1200 volumes on occupational health and general nursing.

American Association of Osteopathic Specialists (AAOS)

804 Main St.
Ste. D
Forest Park, GA 30050
Phone: (404)363-8263
Fax: (404)361-2285

Membership: Osteopathic surgeons and anesthesiologists. Activities: Offers placement services. Formed for the benevolent, scientific, and educational purposes of improving the practice of the specialty disciplines. Promotes the study and education of specialty disciplines and high intellectual, moral, and ethical standards in specialty practice. Encourages improved quality of osteopathic medical and surgical patient care. Maintains continuing education programs: American Academy of Osteopathic Anesthesiologists; American Academy of Osteopathic Family Practitioners; American Academy of Osteopathic Internists; American Academy of Osteopathic Neurologists and Psychiatrists; American Academy of Osteopathic Obstetricians and Gynecologists; American Academy of Osteopathic Radiologists; American Academy o f Osteopathic Orthopedic Surgeons. Provides certification programs in the areas of general surgery, neurosurgery, plastic and reconstructive surgery, cardiovascular and thoracic surgery, gynecological surgery, urological surgery, and anesthesiology. Bestows degree of Fellow and an annual nursing scholarship. Maintains 1000 volume library, biographical archives, hall of fame, and speakers' bureau.

American Association of Pathologists' Assistants (AAPA)

c/o Leo J. Kelly
Dept. of Pathology
VA Medical Center
West Haven, CT 06516
Phone: (203)932-5711

Membership: Pathologists' assistants and individuals qualified by academic and practical training to provide service in anatomic pathology under the direction of a qualified pathologist who is responsible for the performance of the assistant. Activities: Offers placement services. Purposes of AAPA are to promote the mutual association of trained pathologists' assistants and to inform the public and the medical profession concerning the goals of this profession. Presents Newsletter Contributor Award. Compiles statistics on salaries, geographic distribution, and duties of pathologists' assistants. Sponsors a continuing medical education program.

American Association of Pharmaceutical Scientists (AAPS)

1650 King St.
Alexandria, VA 22314-2747
Phone: (703)548-3000
Fax: (703)684-7349

Membership: Pharmaceutical scientists.

Activities: Offers placement service. Provides a forum for exchange of scientific information; serves as a resource in forming public policies to regulate pharmaceutical sciences and related issues of public concern. Promotes pharmaceutical sciences and provides for recognition of individual achievement; works to foster career growth and the development of members. Bestows awards.

American Association of Podiatric Physicians and Surgeons (AAPPS)

603 Griswold St.
Port Huron, MI 48060
Phone: (313)987-3150

Membership: Podiatrists. Activities: Provides placement service. Seeks to represent members' interests and educate podiatrists and the public. Provides training and certification for podiatry and podiatric surgery. Offers accreditation to agencies providing podiatric services, education, or training; also provides podiatric peer review. Operates Council on Podiatry Education and speakers' bureau; compiles statistics; bestows awards.

American Association of Surgeon Assistants (AASA)

1600 Wilson Blvd., Ste. 905
Arlington, VA 22209
Phone: (703)525-1191
Fax: (703)276-8196

Membership: Surgeon assistants, surgical physician assistants, students, physicians, surgeons, and allied health professionals. **Purpose:** Promotes academic and clinical excellence among members, responds to the needs of surgical physician assistants and surgeon assistants, and educates the medical community and the public about the role of surgical physician assistants and surgeon assistants in health care. **Publication(s):** *The Sutureline,* quarterly.

American Board of Internal Medicine (ABIM)

3624 Market St.
Philadelphia, PA 19104
Phone: (215)243-1500

Purpose: Determine the qualifications of, administer examinations to, and certify as specialists in internal medicine those doctors meeting its standards of clinical competence. **Publication(s):** *Policies and Procedures,* annual.

American Board of Medical Specialties (ABMS)

1 Rotary Center, Ste. 805
Evanston, IL 60201
Phone: (708)491-9091
Fax: (708)328-3596

Membership: Primary medical specialty boards and conjoint boards and organizations with related interests. **Purpose:** Acts as spokesman for approved medical specialty boards as a group; is actively concerned with the establishment, maintenance, and elevation of standards for the education and qualification of physicians recognized as specialists through the certification procedures of its members; cooperates with other groups concerned in establishing standards, policies, and procedures for ensuring the maintenance of continued competence of such physicans. **Publication(s):** *ABMS Compendium of Certified Medical Specialists,* biennial. • *ABMS Record,* periodic. • *American Board of Medical Specialties-Annual Report and Reference Handbook,* annual.

American Board of Neurological and Orthopaedic Medicine and Surgery (ABNOMS)

2320 Rancho Dr.
Ste. 108
Las Vegas, NV 89102-4592
Phone: (702)385-6886

Membership: Individuals proficient in neurological and orthopaedic medicine and surgery who have previous board certification and proper preceptorship and have made significant contributions to the field. **Activities:** Operates placement service. Objective is to demonstrate expertise and capability in the field of neurological and orthopaedic medicine and surgery through written and oral certification examinations. Conducts research and educational programs on neuromusculoskeletal disorders of the limbs and spine. Maintains library, biographical archives, and hall of fame. Operates charitable program; bestows awards. Affiliated with American Academy of Neurological and Orthopaedic Surgeons.

American Board of Surgery (ABS)

1617 John F. Kennedy Blvd., Ste. 860
Philadelphia, PA 19103
Phone: (215)568-4000

Membership: Drawn from 18 national and regional surgical and specialty societies and organizations. **Purpose:** Examining and certifying board in general surgery; also certifies Special Qualifications in Pediatric Surgery, General Vascular Surgery and Added Qualifications in General Vascular Surgery, Surgical Critical Care, and Hand Surgery. **Publication(s):** *Service Booklets of Information,* annual.

American Cancer Society (ACS)

1599 Clifton Rd., NE
Atlanta, GA 30329
Phone: (404)320-3333
Toll-free: 800-ACS-2345
Fax: (404)325-0230

Purpose: Supports education and research in cancer prevention, diagnosis, detection, and treatment. Provides special services to cancer patients. Conducts medical and eductional programs. **Publication(s):** *American Cancer Society-Annual Report.* • *CA-A Cancer Journal for Clinicians,* bimonthly. • *Cancer,* semimonthly. • *Cancer Facts and Figures,* annual. • *Cancer News,* 3/year. • *Cancer Nursing News,* quarterly. • *World Smoking and Health,* 3/year.

American College of Clinical Pharmacy (ACCP)

3101 Broadway
Ste. 380
Kansas City, MO 64111
Phone: (816)531-2177

Membership: Clinical pharmacists dedicated to: promoting rational use of drugs in society; advancing the practice of clinical pharmacy and interdisciplinary health care; assuring high quality clinical pharmacy by establishing and maintaining standards in education and training at advanced levels. Activities: Maintains placement service. Encourages research and recognizes excellence in clinical pharmacy. Offers educational programs, symposia, research forums, fellowship training, and college-funded grants through competitions; bestows Therapeutic Frontiers Lecture Award.

American College Health Association (ACHA)

1300 Piccard Dr.
Ste. 200
Rockville, MD 20850
Phone: (301)963-1100
Fax: (301)330-6781

Activities: Maintains placement listings for physicians and other personnel seeking positions in college health. Promotes health in its broadest aspects for students and all other members of the college community. Offers continuing education programs for health professionals; conducts seminars and training programs. Bestows awards; compiles statistics.

The size of an institution continues to be a key factor in the size of a paycheck. By Cole's calculation, med-surg nurses at the largest hospitals averaged $34,100 compared to the $29,500 typical at those with under 100 beds.

Source: *American Journal of Nursing*

American College of Health Care Administrators (ACHCA)

325 S. Patrick St.
Alexandria, VA 22314
Phone: (703)549-5822
Fax: (703)739-7901

Membership: Persons actively engaged in the administration of long-term care institutions, in medical administration, or in activities designed to improve the quality of nursing home administration. **Purpose:** Certifies members' ability to meet and maintain a standard of competence in nursing home and long-term care administration. Works to elevate the standards in the field and to develop and promote a code of ethics and standards of education and training. Seeks to inform allied professions and the public that good administration of nursing homes calls for special formal academic training and experience. Encourages research in all aspects of geriatrics, the chronically ill, and adminstration. **Publication(s):** *Journal of Long-Term Care Adminstration*, quarterly. • *Long-Term Care Administrator*, monthly.

American College of Healthcare Executives (ACHE)

840 N. Lake Shore Dr., Ste. 1103W
Chicago, IL 60611
Phone: (312)943-0544
Fax: (312)943-3791

Membership: Professional society for hospital and health service administrators. **Purpose:** Keeps members abreast of current and future trends, issues, and developments; shapes productive and effective organizational strategies and professional performance; increases the visibility and recognition of the health care management profession; acts as advocate for health care management in legislative activities and with government agencies; develops cooperation among professional societies and other health care associations in dealing with current issues; strengthens and encourages the profession's code of ethics; maintains professional standards. Maintains data base of personal and career data on its membership, holds educational seminars and training programs on health care management, and offers student loans and scholarships and personal loan program. Also operates health administration career library, maintains committees and task forces, conducts research, and compiles statistics. **Publication(s):** *Directory*, biennial. • *Frontiers of Health Services Management*, quarterly. • *Health Services Research*, bimonthly. • *Healthcare Executive*, bimonthly. • *Hospital and Health Services Administration*, quarterly. • *Medical Care Review*, quarterly. • *Career Mart.*

American College of Medical Quality

1531 S. Tamiami Trail
Ste. 703
Venice, FL 34292
Phone: (813)497-3340
Fax: (813)497-5573

Membership: Physicians, affiliates, and institutions seeking to set standards of competence in the field of quality assurance and utilization review. Activities: Offers placement services. Conducts educational seminars and workshops. Compiles statistics on numbers of physicians and allied health personnel working in quality assurance and utilization review. Sponsors competitions; bestows awards; maintains speakers' bureau. Holds regional seminars.

American College of Nurse-Midwives (ACNM)

1522 K St., NW, Ste. 1000
Washington, DC 20005
Phone: (202)289-0171
Fax: (202)289-4395

Membership: Registered nurses certified to extend their practice into providing gynecological services and care of mothers and babies throughout the maternity cycle; members have completed an ACNM accredited program of study and clinical experience in midwifery and passed a national certification exam. **Purpose:** Cooperates with allied groups to enable nurse-midwives to concentrate their efforts in the improvement of services for mothers and newborn babies. Seeks to identify areas of nurse-midwifery practices as they relate to the total service and educational aspects of maternal and newborn care. Studies and evaluates activities of nurse-midwives in order to establish qualifications; cooperates in planning and developing educational programs. Conducts research and continuing education workshops, sponsors research, compiles statistics, bestows awards offers placement service. **Publication(s):** *American College of Nurse-Midwives Membership Directory Supplement*, annual. • *Directory of Nurse-Midwifery Practices*, annual. • *Journal of Nurse-Midwifery*, bimonthly. • *Quickening*, bimonthly.

American College of Osteopathic Internists (ACOI)

300 5th St.
Washington, DC 20002
Phone: (202)546-0095
Fax: (202)543-5584

Membership: Osteopathic doctors who limit their practice to internal medicine and various subspecialties and who intend, through postdoctoral education, to qualify as certified specialists in the field. Activities: Offers placement service. Aims to provide educational programs and to improve educational standards in the field of osteopathic internal medicine. Sponsors competitions and presents awards. Compiles statistics.

American College of Osteopathic Surgeons (ACOS)

123 N. Henry St.
Alexandria, VA 22314
Phone: (703)684-0416

Membership: Professional society of osteopathic physicians specializing in surgery and surgical specialties. Activities: Maintains placement service. Conducts postgraduate courses and seminars in continuing surgical education. Presents awards; provides research and fellowship grants.

American College of Physician Executives (ACPE)

4890 W. Kennedy Blvd.
Ste. 200
Tampa, FL 33609
Phone: (813)287-2000
Fax: (813)287-8993

Membership: Physicians whose primary professional responsibility is the management of health care organizations. Activities: Offers specialized career planning, counseling, recruitment and placement services. Provides for continuing education and certification of the physician executive and the advancement and recognition of the physician executive and the profession. Conducts research and maintains information data on physician managers.

American College of Physicians (ACP)

Independence Mall West
6th St. at Race
Philadelphia, PA 19106
Phone: (215)351-2400
Fax: (215)351-2448

Membership: Professional society of medical doctors specializing in internal medicine and closely related specialties. **Purpose:** Sponsors annual postgraduate courses for practicing physicians, and sponsors teaching and research scholarship competition. **Publication(s):** *Annals of Internal Medicine*, bimonthly. • *Directory*, periodic. • *Medical Knowledge Self-Assessment*, triennial. • *Observer*, monthly.

American College of Radiology (ACR)

1891 Preston White Dr.
Reston, VA 22091
Phone: (703)648-8900

Membership: Professional society of physicians and radiologic physicists who specialize in the use of X-ray, ultrasound, nuclear medicine magnetic resonance, and other imaging modalities for the diagnosis of disease and treatment and management of cancer. Activities: Operates placement service. Conducts research programs and offers specialized education service. Provides insurance program. Sponsors competitions; bestows awards. Maintains 2000 volume library, speakers' bureau, biographical archives, and museum; compiles statistics. Affiliated With: International Society of Radiology.

At the same time that whale-size firms are whacking away the blubber, a net of 1.9 million new jobs will be created this year 1992, estimates Dun & Bradstreet, and 80 percent of them will be at companies with fewer than 100 employees.

Source: *U.S. News & World Report*

American College of Sports Medicine (ACSM)

PO Box 1440
Indianapolis, IN 46206-1440
Phone: (317)637-9200
Fax: (317)634-7817

Activities: Offers placement service. Advances and disseminates information dealing with the benefits and effects of exercise and the treatment and prevention of injuries incurred in sports, exercise, and fitness activities. Bestows Honor Award for outstanding contribution to the field of sports medicine. Certifies fitness instructors, exercise test technologists, exercise specialists, and exercise program directors. Grants continuing medical education and continuing education credits. Sponsors regional workshops, seminars, and lecture tours. Maintains biographic archives and operates 16 committees. Affiliated With: American Alliance for Health, Physical Education, Recreation and Dance; International Federation of Sports Medicine; United States Olympic Committee.

American College of Surgeons (ACS)

55 E. Erie St.
Chicago, IL 60611
Phone: (312)664-4050
Fax: (312)440-7014

Membership: Professional association of surgeons. **Purpose:** Seeks to improve the quality

of care for surgical patients by elevating the standards of surgical education and practice. Conducts nationwide programs to improve emergency medical services and hospital cancer programs. Sponsors continuing education and self-assessment courses for surgeons in practice. **Publication(s):** *American College of Surgeons Yearbook*, triennial. • *Bulletin of the American College of Surgeons*, monthly. • *Factbook*, annual. • *Surgery, Gynecology and Obstetrics*, monthly. • *Surgical Forum*, annual.

American College of Utilization Review Physicians (ACURP)

1531 S. Tamiami Tr.
Ste. 703
Venice, FL 34292
Phone: (813)497-3340
Fax: (813)497-5573

Membership: Physicians, affiliates, and institutions seeking to set standards of competence in the field of quality assurance and utilization review. Activities: Offers placement services. Conducts educational seminars and workshops in quality assurance and utilization review. Compiles statistics on numbers of physicians and allied health personnel working in quality assurance and utilization review. Sponsors competitions; bestows awards; maintains speakers' bureau. Holds regional seminars.

American Federation of Medical Accreditation (AFMA)

522 Rossmore Dr.
Las Vegas, NV 89110
Phone: (702)385-6886

Membership: Medical associations that have primary certifying boards; scientific organizations. **Purpose:** Accredits medical and scientific organizations and continuing medical education for member organizations. Also credits those organizations having primary certifying board examinations and nonprofit, charitable schools, colleges, and medical schools.

American Fertility Society (AFS)

2140 11th Ave., S.
Ste. 200
Birmingham, AL 35205-2800
Phone: (205)933-8494
Fax: (205)930-9904

Membership: Gynecologists, obstetricians,

urologists, reproductive endocrinologists, veterinarians, research workers, and others interested in reproductive health in man and animals. Activities: Sponsors placement service. Seeks to extend knowledge of all aspects of fertility and problems of infertility and mammalian reproduction; provides a rostrum for the presentation of scientific studies dealing with these subjects. Offers patient resource information; maintains film library. Conducts six to eight workshops and six regional postgraduate courses per year.

American Foundation for AIDS Research (AmFAR)

5900 Wilshire Blvd., 2nd Fl.
E. Satellite
Los Angeles, CA 90036
Phone: (213)857-5900

Purpose: Raises funds to support research on AIDS. Research is currently focused on discovering the causes of the syndrome, developing early diagnosis, and determining successful treatment. Is currently organizing state and local fundraising and developing educational programs as a preventative to the spread of the disease. **Publication(s):** *AIDS/HIV Treatment Directory,* quarterly. • *Facts About AIDS.*

American Gastroenterological Association (AGA)

6900 Grove Rd.
Thorofare, NJ 08086
Phone: (609)848-9218
Fax: (609)853-5991

Membership: Physicians of internal medicine certified in gastroenterology; radiologists, pathologists, surgeons, and physiologists with special interest and competency in gastroenterology. Activities: Offers placement service. Formed to study normal and abnormal conditions of the digestive organs and problems connected with their metabolism and to conduct scientific research.

American Group Practice Association (AGPA)

1422 Duke St.
Alexandria, VA 22314
Phone: (703)838-0033
Fax: (703)548-1890

Membership: Private group practice medical and dental clinics representing more than 23,000

physicians. Activities: Offers placement service. Fosters accreditation of medical clinics; compiles statistics on group practice; sponsors research and patient education programs. Conducts symposia. Operates speakers' bureau; bestows awards. Maintains data base and biographical archives.

American Health Care Association (AHCA)

1201 L St. NW
Washington, DC 20005
Phone: (202)842-4444
Fax: (202)842-3860

Membership: Federation of state associations of long-term health care facilities. **Purpose:** Promotes standards for professionals in long-term health care delivery and quality care for patients and residents in a safe environment. Focuses on issues of availability, quality, affordability, and fair payment. Conducts seminars that provide continuing education for nursing home personnel. Maintains liaison with governmental agencies, Congress, and professional associations. Presents awards; compiles statistics. **Publication(s):** *AHCA Notes,* biweekly. • *Provider: For Long Term Care Professionals,* monthly. • Also publishes *A Consumer's Guide to Long Term Care, Thinking About a Nursing Home?, Welcome to Our Nursing Home,* and career information and training manuals; produces audiovisual aids.

Women are nearly as likely as men to have many types of postsecondary degrees, but men hold professional degrees and doctorates at more than double the rate of women.

Source: *The Wall Street Journal*

American Heart Association (AHA)

7320 Greenville Ave.
Dallas, TX 75231
Phone: (214)373-6300
Fax: (214)706-1341

Membership: Physicians, scientists, and laypersons. **Purpose:** Supports research, education, and community service programs with the objective of reducing premature death and disability from cardiovascular diseases and stroke; coordinates the efforts of physicians, nurses, health professionals, and others engaged in the fight against heart and circulatory disease. **Publication(s):** *Arteriosclerosis and Thrombosis: A Journal of Vascular Biology*, bimonthly. • *Cardiovascular Nursing*, bimonthly. • *Circulation*, monthly. • *Circulation Research*, monthly. • *Hypertension*, monthly. • *Stroke-A Journal of Cerebral Circulation*, monthly.

American Hospital Association (AHA)

840 N. Lake Shore Dr.
Chicago, IL 60611
Phone: (312)280-6000
Fax: (312)280-5979

Membership: Individuals and health care institutions including hospitals, health care systems, and pre- and postacute health care delivery organizations. **Purpose:** Is dedicated to promoting the welfare of the public through its leadership and assistance to its members in the provision of better health services for all people. Carries out research and education projects in such areas as health care administration, hospital economics, and community relations; represents hospitals in national legislation; offers programs for institutional effectiveness review, technology assessment, and hospital administrative services to hospitals; conducts educational programs furthering the in-service education of hospital personnel; collects and analyzes data; furnishes multimedia educational materials; maintains 44,000 volume health care administration library, and biographical archive. Bestows awards. **Publication(s):** *AHANews*, weekly. • *Guide to the Health Care Field*, annual. • *Hospital Statistics*, annual. • *Hospitals*, biweekly.

American Institute of Biological Sciences (AIBS)

730 11th St., NW
Washington, DC 20001-4521
Phone: (202)628-1500
Toll-free: 800-992-AIBS
Fax: (202)628-1509

Membership: Professional biological associations and laboratories whose members have an interest in the life sciences. **Purpose:** Promotes unity and effectiveness of effort among persons engaged in biological research, education, and application of biological sciences, including agri-

culture, environment, and medicine. Seeks to further the relationships of biological sciences to other sciences, the arts, and industries. Operates placement service and maintains educational consultant panel. **Publication(s):** *American Institute of Biological Sciences-Forum: Public Issues, the Life Sciences and You*, bimonthly. • *Annual Meeting Program*. • *BioScience*, 11/year. • *Membership Directory*, biennial.

American Licensed Practical Nurses Association (ALPNA)

1090 Vermont Ave., NW, Ste. 1200
Washington, DC 20005
Phone: (202)682-5800
Fax: (202)682-0168

Membership: Licensed practical nurses. **Purpose:** Promotes the practical nursing profession; lobbies and maintains relations with the government on issues and legislation that may have an impact on LPNs. Conducts continuing education classes.

American Managed Care and Review Association (AMCRA)

1227 25th St., NW
No. 610
Washington, DC 20037
Phone: (202)728-0506
Fax: (202)728-0609

Membership: Medical organizations of alternative health care delivery representing over 200,000 practicing physicians. Activities: Maintains placement service. Seeks to provide better medical care and to render the most appropriate and economical setting for its delivery. Conducts clinical sessions and seminars. Sponsors educational programs and offers speakers' bureau. Operates Aileen Johnson Memorial Library.

American Medical Association (AMA)

515 N. State St.
Chicago, IL 60610
Phone: (312)464-5000
Fax: (312)645-4184

Membership: County medical societies and physicians. **Purpose:** Disseminates scientific information to members and the public. Informs members on significant medical and health legislation on state and national levels and represents the profession before Congress and governmental agencies. Cooperates in setting standards for medical schools, hospitals, residency programs, and continuing medical education courses. Offers physician placement service and counseling on practice management problems. Operates library which lends material and provides specific medical information to physicians. Ad-hoc committees are formed for such topics as health care planning and principles of medical ethics. **Publication(s):** *American Journal of Diseases of Children*, monthly. • *American Medical News*, weekly. • *Archives of Dermatology*, monthly. • *Archives of General Psychiatry*, monthly. • *Archives of Internal Medicine*, monthly. • *Archives of Neurology*, periodic. • *Archives of Ophthalmology*, monthly. • *Archives of Otolaryngology—Head and Neck Surgery*, monthly. • *Archives of Pathology and Laboratory Medicine*, monthly. • *Archives of Surgery*, monthly. • *Journal of the American Medical Association*, weekly.

American Medical Directors Association (AMDA)

10480 Little Patuxent Pkwy., Ste. 760
Columbia, MD 21044
Toll-free: 800-321-AMDA
Fax: (301)740-4572

Membership: Physicians providing care in long-term facilities such as nursing homes and other geriatric facilities. **Purpose:** Sponsors continuing medical education in geriatrics. Promotes improved geriatric care. **Publication(s):** *AMDA Reports,* quarterly.

American Medical Peer Review Association (AMPRA)

810 1st St., NE
Ste. 410
Washington, DC 20002
Phone: (202)371-5610

Membership: Institutions and individuals. Activities: Sponsors placement service. Purpose is to develop communications programs for physicians, institutions, and others interested in peer review organizations (PROs). Provides a national forum for the interchange of ideas, techniques, and information relating to medical quality assessment. Conducts courses and on-site assistance programs on increasing physicians' involvement and leadership in PROs, improving

practice patterns through review, understanding and using PRO data to improve service delivery, preadmission review, profile analysis, retrospective review, and organizational development. Maintains 1000 volume library.

American Medical Record Association (AMRA)

919 N. Michigan Ave.
Chicago, IL 60611
Phone: (312)787-2672

Membership: Registered record administrators; accredited record technicians with expertise in health information management, biostatistics, classification systems, and systems analysis. **Purpose:** Sponsors Independent Study Program in Medical Record Technology. Conducts annual qualification examinations to credential medical record personnel. **Publication(s):** *American Medical Record Association-Membership Roster*, semiannual. • *From the Couch: Official Newsletter of the Mental Health Record Section of the American Medical Record Association*, quarterly. • *The Gavel: AMRA State Presidents' Newsletter*, quarterly. • *Journal of AMRA: America's Health Information Leaders*, monthly. • *Medical Record Educator*, quarterly. • *QA Section Connection*, bimonthly. • *Spectrum*, quarterly.

American Medical Technologists (AMT)

710 Higgins Rd.
Park Ridge, IL 60068
Phone: (708)823-5169
Fax: (708)823-0458

Membership: National professional registry of medical laboratory technologists, technicians, medical assistants, and dental assistants. **Purpose:** Bestows awards, and maintains placement service. **Publication(s):** *AMT Events and Continuing Education Supplement*, 8/year. • *Manual of the Accrediting Bureau of Health Education Schools*.

American Nurses' Association (ANA)

600 Maryland Ave., SW, Ste. 100 W.
Washington, DC 20024-2571
Phone: (202)554-4444
Fax: (202)554-2262

Membership: Member associations representing registered nurses. **Purpose:** Sponsors American Nurses' Foundation (for research), American Academy of Nursing, Center for Ethics and Human Rights, International Nursing Center, and American Nurses Credential Center. Presents awards; maintains hall of fame. **Publication(s):** *American Journal of Nursing*, monthly. • *The American Nurse*, 10/year. • *Annual Report*. • *Facts About Nursing*, semiannual. • *Proceedings of the House of Delegates*, annual. • Also publishes nursing standards, publications catalog, and professional literature.

> **M**ore than any other profession, medicine is constantly evolving, changing quickly with every new piece of hightech equipment or the latest published research.
>
> Source: *Glamour*

American Nurses' Foundation (ANF)

1101 14th St., NW, Ste. 200
Washington, DC 20005
Phone: (202)789-1800
Fax: (202)842-4375

Membership: Board of trustees elected by the board of directors of the American Nurses' Association. **Purpose:** Conducts research, offers grants, and bestows awards.

American Nursing Assistant's Association (ANAA)

PO Box 103
Ottawa, KS 66067-0103

Membership: Professional organization of certified nursing assistants and nurses' aides. **Purpose:** Represents the interests of members, sponsors seminars, offers scholarships, and bestows awards. **Publication(s):** *Nursing Notes*, 2/year.

American Osteopathic Association (AOA)

142 E. Ontario St.
Chicago, IL 60611
Phone: (312)280-5800
Toll-free: 800-621-1773
Fax: (312)280-5893

Membership: Osteopathic physicians, surgeons, and graduates of approved colleges of osteopathic medicine. Associate members include teaching, research, administrative, and executive employees of approved colleges, hospitals, divisional societies, and affiliated organizations. Forms (with its affiliates) an officially recognized structure of the osteopathic profession. **Purpose:** To promote the public health, to encourage scientific research, and to maintain and improve high standards of medical education in osteopathic colleges. Inspects and accredits colleges and hospitals; conducts a specialty certification program; sponsors a national examining board satisfactory to state licensing agencies; maintains mandatory program of continuing medical education for members. Compiles statistics on location and type of practice of osteopathic physicians. Sponsors research activities through Bureau of Research in osteopathic colleges and hospitals. Maintains Physician Placement Service. Awards student scholarships and loans annually. Produces public service radio and television programs; maintains 2000 item library and biographical archives on osteopathic medicine and history. Offers speakers' bureau. **Publication(s):** *American Osteopathic Association Yearbook and Directory.* • *The D.O.*, monthly. • *Journal of AOA*, monthly. • Also publishes brochures.

American Osteopathic College of Pathologists (AOCP)

c/o Joan Gross
12368 NW 13th Ct.
Pembroke Pines, FL 33026
Phone: (305)432-9640

Membership: Osteopathic physicians who have completed residency training programs in pathology and clinical pathology; candidate members are in residency training in pathology. Activities: Offers placement service. Establishes guidelines for training programs in pathology and clinical pathology for osteopathic physicians; maintains standards in residency training programs. Provides mid-year tutorial program. Maintains collection of slide study sets. Bestows awards.

American Podiatric Medical Association (APMA)

9312 Old Georgetown Rd.
Bethesda, MD 20814
Phone: (301)571-9200
Fax: (301)530-2752

Membership: Professional society of podiatrists. **Purpose:** Bestows awards. **Publication(s):** *APMA News,* monthly. • *Catalogue of Audiovisual, Informational and Educational Materials,* periodic. • *Desk Reference of the APMA,* annual. • *Journal,* monthly. • Also publishes foot health literature.

American Podiatric Medical Students Association (APMSA)

9312 Old Georgetown Rd.
Bethesda, MD 20814
Phone: (301)493-9667

Membership: Podiatric medical students enrolled at seven podiatric schools in the U.S. **Purpose:** Represents the interests of podiatric medical students in legislative, professional, and educational programs. **Publication(s):** *First Step,* biennial.

American Psychiatric Association (APA)

1400 K St. NW
Washington, DC 20005
Phone: (202)682-6000
Fax: (202)682-6114

Purpose: Psychiatrists united to further the study of the nature, treatment, and prevention of mental disorders. Assists in formulating programs to meet mental health needs; compiles and disseminates facts and figures about psychiatry; furthers psychiatric education and research. **Publication(s):** *American Journal of Psychiatry,* monthly. • *Hospital and Community Psychiatry,* monthly. • *Membership Directory,* biennial. • *Psychiatric News,* semimonthly.

American Public Health Association (APHA)

1015 15th St., NW
Washington, DC 20005
Phone: (202)789-5600
Fax: (202)789-5681

Membership: Professional organization of physicians, nurses, educators, academicians, environmentalists, epidemiologists, new professionals, social workers, health administrators, optometrists, podiatrists, pharmacists, pharmacy assistants, dentists, dental assistants, nutritionists, health planners, health care workers, other community and mental health specialists, and

interested consumers. Activities: Sponsors job placement service. Seeks to protect and promote personal, mental, and environmental health. Services include: promulgation of standards; establishment of uniform practices and procedures; development of the etiology of communicable diseases; research in public health; exploration of medical care programs and their relationships to public health. Presents Award for Excellence to individuals for outstanding contributions to the improvement of public health; also bestows the Drotman Award to a young health professional who demonstrates potential in the health field and Sedgwick Memorial Medal to those who have advanced public health knowledge and practices. Maintains Action Board and Program Development Board.

> **G**rowth in employment is only one source of job openings. In fact, most openings arise because of the need to replace workers who transfer to other occupations or leave the labor force.
>
> Source: *Occupational Outlook Quarterly*

American School Health Association (ASHA)

7263 State Rt. 43
PO Box 708
Kent, OH 44240
Phone: (216)678-1601
Fax: (216)678-4526

Membership: School physicians, dentists, nurses, nutritionists, health educators, dental hygienists, and public health workers. Activities: Maintains placement service. Formed to promote comprehensive and constructive school health programs including the teaching of health, health services, and promotion of a healthful school environment. Offers a professional referral service, classroom teaching aids, and professional reference materials. Conducts research programs; compiles statistics. Sponsors annual foreign travel study tour. Bestows William A. How Award annually for distinguished service in school health.

American Society of Anesthesiologists (ASA)

515 Busse Hwy.
Park Ridge, IL 60068-3189
Phone: (708)825-5586
Fax: (708)825-1692

Membership: Professional society of physicians specializing or interested in anesthesiology. Activities: Maintains placement service. Seeks 'to develop and further the specialty of anesthesiology for the general elevation of the standards of medical practice.' Encourages education, research, and scientific progress in anesthesiology. Conducts refresher courses and other postgraduate educational activities. Operates library.

American Society of Colon and Rectal Surgeons (ASCRS)

800 E. Northwest Hwy.
Ste. 1080
Palatine, IL 60067
Phone: (708)359-9184

Membership: Professional society of surgeons specializing in the diagnosis and treatment of diseases of the colon, rectum, and anus. Activities: Offers placement service; bestows awards; conducts research programs.

American Society of Handicapped Physicians (ASHP)

105 Morris Dr.
Bastrop, LA 71220
Phone: (318)281-4436

Membership: Handicapped physicians and others concerned with the problems faced by handicapped physicians. Activities: Operates placement service. Acts as a forum to address the needs of physically disabled physicians. Works against discrimination of the handicapped and serves as a support group and legal and career counselor. Disseminates information about resources for handicapped physicians. Plans to offer rehabilitation services. Bestows awards; maintains speakers' bureau; compiles statistics; offers specialized education.

American Society for Health Care Marketing and Public Relations (ASHCMPR)

American Hospital Assn.
840 N. Lake Shore Dr.
Chicago, IL 60611
Phone: (312)280-6359
Toll-free: 800-621-6712
Fax: (312)280-5923

Membership: Persons in hospitals, hospital councils or associations, hospital-related schools, and health care organizations responsible for marketing and public relations. **Purpose:** Bestows awards including the Touchstone Award for excellence in hospital public relations and marketing. **Publication(s):** *Directory of Hospital Marketing, Planning, and Public Relations Consultants,* annual. • *Hospital Marketing and Public Relations,* bimonthly. • *Membership Directory of the American Society for Hospital Marketing and Public Relations,* annual.

American Society of Hospital Pharmacists (ASHP)

4630 Montgomery Ave.
Bethesda, MD 20814
Phone: (301)657-3000
Fax: (301)652-8278

Membership: Professional society of pharmacists employed by hospitals and related institutions. Activities: Provides personnel placement service for members. Sponsors professional and personal liability program. Conducts educational and exhibit programs. Maintains library of medical and pharmacy journals. Presents Harvey A.K. Whitney Lecture Award. Has 25 practice interest areas, 11 specialty practice groups, and research and education foundation.

American Society of Internal Medicine (ASIM)

1101 Vermont Ave., Ste. 500
Washington, DC 20005-3457
Phone: (202)289-1700
Fax: (202)682-8659

Membership: Professional society of physicians specializing in internal medicine. **Purpose:** Concerned with the social, economic, and political factors affecting the delivery of high quality care. Focuses on the delivery and financing of medical care in areas including access to care, appropriate reform of American health care system, medical and public education, issues affecting the elderly, private and public sector, health insurance and reimbursement, managed care, documentation of physician performance, and medical technology and computerization aimed at maintaining and promoting high quality medical care at a reasonable cost. **Publication(s):** *Contracting and Negotiations Update,* bimonthly. • *Directory,* biennial. • *The Internist: Health Policy in Practice,* 10/year. • *Internist's Intercom,* monthly.

American Society of Outpatient Surgeons (ASOS)

3960 Park Blvd., Ste. E
San Diego, CA 92103
Phone: (619)692-9918
Fax: (619)692-3143

Membership: Surgeons with various specialties who practice surgery in an office-based setting; anesthesiologists. **Purpose:** Seeks to provide improved surgical care at lower costs and further education of surgeons. Makes patients and insurers aware of the benefits of office-based surgery. Conducts surveys and prepares statistical reports. Conducts seminars on office-based surgery. **Publication(s):** *Membership Directory,* annual. • *Monitor,* quarterly.

American Surgical Association (ASA)

c/o George F. Sheldon, M.D.
Univ. of North Carolina at Chapel Hill
136 Burnett-Womack
Box CB 7245
Chapel Hill, NC 27500-7245
Phone: (919)966-4320
Fax: (919)966-6009

Membership: Surgeons organized to promote the science and art of surgery. **Publication(s):** *Annals of Surgery,* monthly. • *Transactions,* annual.

Association for Academic Surgery (AAS)

Duke University Medical Center
Box 3123
Durham, NC 27710
Phone: (919)681-5078

Membership: Surgeons with backgrounds in all surgical specialities in academic surgical cen-

ters at chief resident level or above. Activities: Maintains placement service; bestows awards. Encourages young surgeons to pursue careers in academic surgery; supports them in establishing themselves as investigators and educators by providing a forum in which senior surgical residents and junior faculty members may present papers on subjects of clinical or laboratory investigations; promotes interchange of ideas between senior surgical residents, junior faculty, and established academic surgeons; facilitates communication among academic surgeons in all surgical fields.

Association for the Advancement of Health Education

1900 Association Dr.
Reston, VA 22091
Phone: (703)476-3437

Membership: Professionals who have responsibility for health education in schools, colleges, communities, hospitals and clinics, and industries. **Purpose:** Advancement of health education through program activities and federal legislation; encouragement of close working relationships between all health education and health service organizations. **Publication(s):** *Directory of Institutions Offering Specialization in Health Education,* biennial. • *HE-XTRA,* semimonthly. • *Journal of Health Education,* bimonthly.

Whether you're looking for your next job or your first job, networking must be a key element of your search. More jobs are found by networking than through any other source.

Source: *Business Monday/Detroit Free Press*

Association for the Advancement of Medical Instrumentation (AAMI)

3330 Washington Blvd.
Ste. 400
Arlington, VA 22201-4598
Phone: (703)525-4890
Fax: (703)276-0793

Membership: Clinical engineers, biomedical equipment technicians, physicians, hospital administrators, consultants, engineers, manufacturers of medical devices, and others interested in medical instrumentation. Activities: Maintains placement service. Purpose is to improve the quality of medical care through the application, development, and management of technology. Bestows awards.

Association of African Physicians in North America (AAPNA)

2031 Brooks Dr.
No. 225
Forestville, MD 20747

Membership: Practicing physicians and dentists, lay people, medical and dental students, residents, and fellows; other health and business professionals and organizations. Activities: Offers placement services. Unites African physicians and dentists both in practice and training in North America. Goals are to: organize efforts and mobilize African physicians and dentists abroad and in Africa; facilitate the smooth transition from the training and practice of medicine in North America to the African setting; help African physicians see health problems in Africa as their responsibility rather than the responsibility of developed countries or the wealthy; facilitate the exchange of health information among African nations, and between African nations and industrialized nations. Collects medication, medical supplies, and equipment for use in needy parts of Africa; attempts to bridge the gap between modern medicine and traditional medicine in Africa; helps Africans develop a better cultural, social, and racial image, especially as it relates to health. Helps African nations develop better working relationships with other nations; works to facilitate the return of African physicians to their homeland. Provides expert and consultant services to African institutions in research, licensure, and training of medical support personnel. Maintains liaison with professional African medical associations and other organizations providing services for the welfare of Africa. Awards scholarships and grants; maintains speakers' bureau and data base. Sponsors student exchange between American and African medical schools and competitions. Compiles statistics and conducts research, "African Night" events, telephone hot line programs, fundraising events, charitable programs, and an African Experience Program, which sends qualified individuals to Africa for firsthand experience. Promotes the principles of the World Health Organization. Publishes *Job Opportunities in Africa.*

Association of American Medical Colleges (AAMC)

2450 N St., NW
Washington, DC 20037
Phone: (202)828-0400
Fax: (202)828-1125

Membership: Medical schools, graduate affiliate medical colleges, affiliate medical colleges, academic societies, teaching hospitals, and individuals interested in the advancement of medical education, biomedical research, and healthcare. **Purpose:** Provides centralized application service. Offers management education program for medical school deans, teaching hospital directors, department chairmen, and service chiefs of affiliated hospitals. Develops and administers the Medical College Admissions Test (MCAT) and Medical Science Knowledge Profile test (MSKP). Operates student loan program. Maintains information management system and institutional profile system. Bestows awards; compiles statistics. **Publication(s):** *Academic Medicine*, monthly. • *Curriculum Directory*, annual. • *Directory of American Medical Education*, annual. • *Medical School Admission Requirements*, annual. • *The Reporter.* • Also publishes annual and semiannual data reports.

Association of Black Nursing Faculty in Higher Education (ABNF)

5823 Queens Cove
Lisle, IL 60532
Phone: (708)969-3809
Fax: (708)810-0128

Membership: Black nursing faculty teaching in baccalaureate and higher degree programs accredited by the National League for Nursing. Activities: Operates placement services and is establishing a computer-assisted job bank. Fosters networking and guidance in employment and recruitment activities. Works to promote health-related issues and educational concerns of interest to the black community and ABNF. Serves as a forum for communication and the exchange of information among members; develops strategies for expressing concerns to other individuals, institutions, and communities. Assists members in professional development; develops and sponsors continuing education activities. Promotes health-related issues of legislation, government programs, and community activities. Supports black consumer advocacy issues. Encourages research. Maintains speakers' bureau, hall of fame, and biographical archives. Offers charitable program. Sponsors competitions; bestows awards; compiles statistics; plans to develop bibliographies related to research groups.

Association of Mental Health Practitioners With Disabilities (AMHPD)

3 E. 10th St.
Ste. 4B
New York, NY 10003
Phone: (212)673-4284

Membership: Disabled psychiatrists, social workers, psychologists, psychiatric nurses, other mental health practitioners, and students. Activities: Offers job information and referral services. Formed in response to complaints of discrimination by disabled colleagues who have been rejected by training institutes and in career opportunities. Devoted to the education, research, training, and advocacy of all areas affecting the clinical practice and professional advancement of members. Offers peer supervision, consultation, and education on the impact of the practitioner's disability on training and patient treatment. Explores how the patient's reaction to a disability can be used in treatment. Works with mental health agencies and educational and training institutes. Sponsors conferences, workshops, and seminars.

Association of Operating Room Nurses (AORN)

10170 E. Mississippi Ave.
Denver, CO 80231
Phone: (303)755-6300
Fax: (303)752-0299

Membership: Registered professional nurses engaged in perioperative (operating room) nursing on supervisory, teaching, or staff levels. **Purpose:** Aims to improve standards of periop-

erative nursing care through increased understanding, knowledge, and skills of personnel; fosters leadership qualities in members. Sponsors national and regional institutes and scholarships. Maintains library; compiles statistics; conducts research; bestows awards. **Publication(s):** *AORN Journal,* monthly. • Also publishes books and pamphlets.

Association of Part-Time Professionals

Crescent Plaza
7700 Leesburg Pike
No. 216
Falls Church, VA 22043
Phone: (703)734-7975

Activities: Promotes employment opportunities for qualified men and women interested in part-time professional positions. Primary goals are to upgrade the status of part-time employment by providing a professional association that represents all part-time professionals, permanent part-timers, job-sharers, free-lancers, and consultants; to educate employers, employees, and the community about the advantages of increased flexibility in working patterns; to advocate prorated benefits for part-timers and a work environment responsive to individual and family needs. Works to develop a constituency of professional men and women nationwide who want the part-time employment option available to them. Operates as an information resource center; conducts research and workshops; maintains speakers' bureau.

Association of Philippine Physicians in America

2717 W. Olive Ave.
Ste. 200
Burbank, CA 91505
Phone: (818)843-8616

Membership: Individuals from the Philippines who are licensed to practice medicine in the U.S. Activities: Provides medical residency program placement service. Seeks to: render free medical care to indigent persons; establish a continuing medical education program for physicians; provide aid for education of physicians; support medical research. Sends medical missions to the Philippines. Bestows awards; maintains speakers' bureau; compiles statistics.

Association of Physician Assistant Programs (APAP)

950 N. Washington St.
Alexandria, VA 22314-1552
Phone: (703)684-1924

Membership: Educational institutions with training programs for assistants to primary care and surgical physicians. **Purpose:** Assists in the development and organization of educational curricula for physician assistant (PA) programs to assure the public of competent PAs; contributes to defining the roles of PAs in the field of medicine to maximize their benefit to the public; serves as a public information center on the profession; coordinates program logistics such as admissions and career placements. Sponsors Annual Survey of Physician Assistant Educational Programs in the United States. Maintains library of 200 volumes on books and articles. Conducts research projects; compiles statistics. **Publication(s):** *Annual Report on Physician Assistant Education in the U.S.* • *APAP Update*, monthly. • *National Directory of Physician Assistant Programs*, biennial. • *Proceedings of the Annual Meeting of the Association of Physician Assistant Programs.* • Also publishes *Physician Assistant Profession Bibliography.*

This year's 1992 new grads should be prepared to work harder to find their first jobs. "Be flexible enough to consider a move, or part-time employment, or skilled nursing facilities," advises Niki O'Keeffe, president of the National Association for Health Care Recruitment.

Source: *American Journal of Nursing*

Association of Physician's Assistants in Cardio-Vascular Surgery (APA-CVS)

2000 Tate Springs Rd.
PO Box 2242
Lynchburg, VA 24501-2242
Phone: 800-528-1506

Membership: Physician's assistants who work with cardiovascular surgeons. Activities: Offers placement service. Objective is to assist in defining the role of physician's assistants in the field of cardiovascular surgery through educational forums. Compiles statistics.

Association of Rehabilitation Nurses (ARN)

5700 Old Orchard Rd., 1st Fl.
Skokie, IL 60077
Phone: (708)966-3343
Fax: (708)966-9418

Membership: Registered nurses concerned with or actively engaged in the practice of rehabilitation nursing; others interested in rehabilitation. **Purpose:** To advance the quality of rehabilitation nursing service through educational opportunities and to facilitate the exchange of ideas. **Publication(s):** *ARN Newsletter*, bimonthly. • *Membership Directory*, annual. • *Rehabilitation Nursing Journal*, bimonthly. • Also publishes *Standards of Rehabilitation Practice, Rehabilitation Nursing: Concepts and Practices - A Core Curriculum, Application of Rehabilitation Concepts to Nursing Practice: Self-Study Program, Rehabilitation Nursing: Scope of Practice*, and *Process and Outcome Criteria for Selected Diagnoses.*

Association for Research in Vision and Ophthalmology (ARVO)

9650 Rockville Pike
Bethesda, MD 20814
Phone: (301)571-1844
Fax: (301)571-8311

Membership: Professional society of researchers in vision and ophthalmology. Activities: Operates placement service. Organized to encourage ophthalmic research in the field of blinding eye disease. Issues four awards annually for significant research. Administers Fight for Sight research grant program.

Association of Schools of Public Health (ASPH)

1015 15th St. NW, Ste. 404
Washington, DC 20005
Phone: (202)842-4668

Membership: Accredited graduate schools of public health. **Purpose:** Provides focus for the enhancement of academic public health programs. Serves as an information center for governmental and private groups, and individuals whose concerns overlap those of higher education for public health. **Publication(s):** *Public Health Career Information, Gerontology Programs and Curricula in U.S. Schools of Public Health, Reach*, and other materials.

Association of University Programs in Health Administration (AUPHA)

1911 N. Ft. Myer Dr., Ste. 503
Arlington, VA 22209
Phone: (703)524-5500

Membership: Universities offering graduate and undergraduate study in health services and hospital administration. **Purpose:** To improve the quality of education in health services administration. Undertakes research and educational programs, such as studies of the criteria used for selection of students and curriculum patterns adopted by various universities. Conducts faculty institutes on topics relating to health administration. Compiles statistics; sponsors competitions; bestows distinguished service awards. Maintains biographical archives and 2000 volume library of texts, journals, and monographs on health services administration and related subjects. **Publication(s):** *Health Services Administration Education,* biennial. • *Journal of Health Administration Education,* quarterly. • *Staff Report,* bimonthly.

Chinese American Medical Society (CAMS)

c/o Dr. H.H. Wang
281 Edgewood Ave.
Teaneck, NJ 07666
Phone: (201)833-1506

Membership: Physicians of Chinese origin residing in the U.S. and Canada. Activities: Maintains placement service. Purposes are: to advance medical knowledge, scientific research, and interchange of information among members; to establish scholarship and endowments in medical schools and hospitals of good standing; to hold periodic meetings for professional purposes. Conducts educational meetings; supports research. Grants scholarships; bestows Scientific Award annually to member with highest scholastic achievements. Sponsors limited charitable program.

Christian Medical Foundation International (CMF)

7522 N. Hines Ave.
Tampa, FL 33614
Phone: (813)932-3688

Membership: Physicians, nurses, clergy, and laity. Activities: Offers placement service. Seeks to: investigate and promote the Christian spiritual care of those who are ill; educate doctors, nurses, and medical students regarding Christian medical and ethical principles. Bestows awards. Maintains speakers' bureau, biographical archives, and 2500 volume library.

Clinical Ligand Assay Society (CLAS)

3139 S. Wayne Rd.
PO Box 67
Wayne, MI 48184
Phone: (313)722-6290

Membership: Clinical laboratory directors and doctors, hospital technologists, private laboratories, industry, and other individuals interested in ligand assays. (Ligand assay is a quantitative clinical laboratory technique for a specific area of diagnostic testing which measures proteins, peptides, or haptens and deals with methods such as radioimmunoassay, florescenceimmunoassay, and receptor assay.) Activities: Sponsors job placement service. Objectives are to: improve, maintain, and support diagnostic and investigative use of ligand assays and related health science methods; further educational achievements and improve teaching methods and applications; encourage research; advance standards of ligand assay practice as applied to physiology in the prevention, diagnosis, and treatment of disease. Conducts symposia and workshops.

College of American Pathologists (CAP)

325 Waukegan Rd.
Northfield, IL 60093-2750
Phone: (708)446-8800
Fax: (708)446-8807

Membership: Physicians practicing the specialty of pathology (diagnosis, treatment, observation, and understanding of the progress of disease or medical condition) obtained by morphologic, microscopic, chemical, microbiologic, serologic, or any other type of laboratory examination made on the patient. Activities: Provides placement service for members. Fosters improvement of education, research, and medical laboratory service to physicians, hospitals, and the public. Conducts laboratory accreditation program and laboratory proficiency testing

239

surveys. Maintains speakers' bureau; compiles statistics.

Committee on Allied Health Education and Accreditation (CAHEA)

515 N. State St.
Chicago, IL 60610
Phone: (312)464-5830
Fax: (312)464-4184

Purpose: Serves as an accrediting agency for 2885 allied health programs in 28 occupational areas. Sponsored by the American Medical Association. Compiles statistics on enrollment and graduates of CAHEA-accredited allied health education programs. **Publication(s):** *Allied Health Education Directory*, annual. • *Allied Health Education Newsletter*, bimonthly.

By the end of this decade, 85 percent of all new entrants into the workforce will be women, minorities and immigrants, and they will bring with them very different cultures and values.

Source: *Television Quarterly*

Congress of Neurological Surgeons

c/o Thomas G. Saul, M.D.
506 Oak St.
Cincinnati, OH 45219
Phone: (513)872-2657
Fax: (513)872-2597

Membership: Professional society of neurological surgeons in the U.S. and 55 other countries. Activities: Provides placement service. Facilitates exchange of professional and technical information and experience; promotes the interests of neurological surgeons in their practice. Bestows annual award.

Council on Medical Education of the American Medical Association (CME-AMA)

515 N. State St.
Chicago, IL 60610
Phone: (312)464-5000

Purpose: Participates in the accreditation of and provides consultation to medical school pro-

grams, graduate medical educational programs, and educational programs for several allied health occupations. Provides information on medical and allied health education at all levels. Bestows Physicians Recognition Award. **Publication(s):** *Allied Health Education Directory*, annual. • *Annual Report of Medical Education in the Journal of the AMA*. • *Continuing Education Courses for Physicians Supplement to the Journal of the AMA*, semiannual. • *Directory of Graduate Medical Education Programs*, annual.

Federation of American Health Systems (FAHS)

1405 N. Pierce, No. 311
Little Rock, AR 72207
Phone: (501)661-9555
Fax: (501)663-4903

Membership: Privately- or investor-owned (for-profit) hospitals. **Publication(s):** *Annual Report*. • *Directory of Investor-Owned Hospitals, Residential Treatment Facilities and Centers, Hospital Management Companies, and Health Systems*, annual. • *FAHS Review*, bimonthly. • *Federation of American Health Systems Hotline*, biweekly. • *State-to-State Report*, periodic.

Foundation for Hospice and Homecare (FHHE)

519 C St., NE
Stanton Park
Washington, DC 20002
Phone: (202)546-4759
Fax: (202)547-3540

Purpose: Established to improve the quality of life of American citizens, with particular emphasis on the needs of the dying, the disabled, the disadvantaged, and the elderly. Promotes high standards of patient care for hospice and home care services; develops and fosters mechanisms for assuring the proper preparation of hospice and home care staff and volunteers; conducts research related to health services, aging, and social policies. Promotes the development of a comprehensive continuum of health care; provides a forum for public comment on social and health policy issues; educates and informs the public concerning matters of health and social policy. Seeks to reverse negative stereotypes associated with age and physical impairment. Accredits homemaker-home health aides; sponsors projects on subjects of importance to health care including Alzheimer's Disease, cancer care, and chronic pediatric health problems. Presents Lifetime Achievement Award. **Publication(s):** *Annual Report.* • *Directory of Accredited Homemaker-Home Health Aide Services,* semiannual. • *Foundation News,* quarterly. • Also publishes *All About Homecare—A Consumer's Guide* (booklet), *Model Curriculum and Teaching Guide for the Instruction of the Homemaker-Home Health Aide* (in conjunction with the U.S. Public Health Service), educational manuals, and brochures; produces documentaries.

Health Sciences Communications Association (HESCA)

6105 Lindell Blvd.
St. Louis, MO 63112
Phone: (314)725-4722
Fax: (314)721-6675

Membership: Media managers, graphic artists, biomedical librarians, producers, faculty members of health science and veterinary medicine schools, health professional organizations, and industry representatives. Activities: Offers placement service. Acts as a clearinghouse for information used by professionals engaged in health science communications. Coordinates Media Festivals Program which recognizes outstanding media productions in the health sciences. Sponsors workshops and competitions; bestows awards.

Healthcare Information and Management Systems Society (HIMSS)

840 N. Lake Shore Dr.
Chicago, IL 60611
Phone: (312)280-6147
Fax: (312)280-4152

Membership: Persons who, by education and/or appropriate experience, are professionally qualified to engage in the analysis, design, and operation of hospital telecommunications, management, and information systems. **Purpose:** Works to enhance telecommunications, management, and information systems while striving for high quality levels of patient care at lowest practical costs. **Publication(s):** *Healthcare Information Management,* quarterly. • *Healthcare Information and Management Systems Society—Membership Directory,* annual. • *HIMSS News,* monthly.

Institute for Hospital Clinical Nursing Education (IHCNE)

American Hospital Association
Center for Nursing
840 N. Lakeshore Dr.
Chicago, IL 60611
Phone: (312)280-6432
Fax: (312)280-5995

Membership: Hospital schools for nursing. **Purpose:** Provides support for issues common to hospital schools of nursing and promotes advancement of schools through educational programs and other activities. **Publication(s):** *Institute Communique,* quarterly newsletter. • *Directory of Program Offerings and Curriculum Characteristics,* periodic.

Institute on Hospital and Community Psychiatry (IHCP)

1400 K St., NW
Washington, DC 20005
Phone: (202)682-6174

Membership: Open to employees of all psychiatric and related health and educational facilities. Activities: Maintains placement service. Includes lectures by experts in the field and workshops and accredited courses on problems, programs, and trends. Presents awards for outstanding programs in the mental health field. Organizes scientific exhibits. Annual forum sponsored by the American Psychiatric Association.

International College of Surgeons (ICS)

1516 N. Lake Shore Dr.
Chicago, IL 60610
Phone: (312)642-3555
Fax: (312)787-1624

Membership: General surgeons and surgical specialists in 111 countries maintaining official relations with the World Health Organization. **Purpose:** Promotes the universal teaching and advancement of surgery and its allied sciences. Maintains International Museum of Surgical Sciences and hall of fame containing specialty rooms showing the growth and perfection of many surgical specialties and unique national exhibits tracing the development of surgery within each country. Maintains library open to researchers, individuals working in the profession, and the public. Organizes postgraduate clinics around the world; conducts lecture series and periodic congresses; offers grants, scholarships, and loans for residencies, research, and advanced study in surgery. Sends surgical teaching teams to developing countries. Bestows honorary fellowship. **Publication(s):** *International College of Surgeons Newsletter,* 3/year. • *International Surgery,* quarterly. • *Membership Directory,* every 2-3 years.

International Society for Clinical Laboratory Technology (ISCLT)
818 Olive St., Ste. 918
St. Louis, MO 63101-1598
Phone: (314)241-1445
Fax: (314)241-1449

Membership: Clinical laboratory technologists and technicians; physician's office laboratory technicians. **Purpose:** Conducts educational programs, workshops, and seminars. Presents awards and scholarships; maintains placement service; offers specialized education. **Publication(s):** *ISCLT Newsletter,* bimonthly.

When training is unavailable free on the job, the next cheapest way to acquire new skills may be right in the back yard. The majority of Americans live within 30 miles of one of the nation's nearly 1,200 community and technical colleges, which are rapidly gaining importance as centers of retraining.

Source: *U.S. News & World Report*

International Society of Healthcare Executives (ISHE)
Address unknown since 1992.

Membership: Executives of small practices; hospitals and organizations. **Purpose:** To advance the delivery of health care by improving administration. Seeks to help its members succeed in the health care management field. Offers management consulting services. Sponsors research and development activities and educational programs. Provides placement service. Maintains library resource center. **Publication(s):** *Executive Update,* monthly. • *Healthcare Management,* bimonthly. • *ISHE Directory,* annual.

Intersociety Committee on Pathology Information (ICPI)
4733 Bethesda Ave., Ste. 700
Bethesda, MD 20814
Phone: (301)656-2944
Fax: (301)656-3179

Membership: One representative from each sponsoring society: American Society for Investigative Pathology; American Society of Clinical Pathologists; Association of Pathology Chairmen; College of American Pathologists; U.S. & Canadian Academy of Pathology. **Purpose:** Disseminates information about the medical practice and research achievements of pathology. Produces career information and supplies it to schools and students; assists writers and editors in preparing articles about pathology. **Publication(s):** *Directory of Pathology Training Programs: Anatomic, Clinical, Specialized,* annual. • Also publishes career brochures.

Islamic Medical Association (IMA)
4121 Fairview
Ste. 203
Downers Grove, IL 60515
Phone: (312)852-2122

Membership: Muslim physicians and allied health professionals. Activities: Sponsors placement service. Organized to unite Muslim physicians and allied health professionals in the U.S. and Canada for the improvement of professional and social contact; to provide assistance to Muslim communities worldwide. Charitable programs include: scholarships awarded to needy students; donation of books, journals, and educational and research materials to medical institutions; donation of medical supplies and equipment to charitable medical institutions in Muslim countries. Maintains speakers' bureau to present Islamic viewpoints on medical topics; offers assistance in orientation. Organizes conferences, seminars, and workshops to be held regularly in Muslim countries.

Joint Council of Allergy and Immunology (JCAI)
PO Box 4620
Arlington Heights, IL 60006
Phone: (708)359-3090

Membership: Physicians specializing in allergy

or clinical immunology. Members must belong to the American Academy of Allergy and Immunology or the American College of Allergists. Activities: Maintains clearinghouse for young physicians wishing to join practices and older physicians wishing to sell practices.

Medical Library Association (MLA)

6 N. Michigan Ave., Ste. 300
Chicago, IL 60602
Phone: (312)419-9094
Fax: (312)419-8950

Membership: Librarians and others engaged in professional library or bibliographical work in medical and allied scientific libraries. **Purpose:** To promote the educational and professional growth of health science librarians, and to exchange medical literature among members. Offers continuing education courses, certification and recertification programs, and placement service. Bestows scholarships, fellowships, and continuing education awards; compiles statistics. 24-hour jobline and infoline, (312)553-INFO. **Publication(s):** *Bulletin of the Medical Library Association*, quarterly. • *Current Catalog Proof Sheets*, weekly. • *Directory of the Medical Library Association*, annual. • *MLA News*, 10/year. • *Salary Survey*, triennial. • Also publishes monographs including *Handbook of Medical Library Practice* (three volumes), *Hospital Library Management, Introduction to Reference Sources in the Health Sciences, Medline: A Basic Guide to Searching, Drug Information: A Guide to Current Resources, Educational Services in Special Libraries, Challenge to Action: Planning and Evaluation Guide for Academic Health Sciences Libraries*, and other administrative publications.

NAACOG: The Organization for Obstetric, Gynecologic, and Neonatal Nurses

409 12th St., SW
Washington, DC 20024
Phone: (202)638-0026

Membership: Registered nurses and allied health workers with an interest in obstetric, gynecologic, and neonatal (OGN) nursing. **Purpose:** Promotes and establishes the highest standards of OGN nursing practice, education, and research; cooperates with all members of

the health team; stimulates interest in OGN nursing. Sponsors educational meetings and continuing education courses. **Publication(s):** *Journal of Obstetric, Gynecologic, and Neonatal Nursing*, bimonthly. • *NAACOG Newsletter*, monthly.

National Association for Healthcare Recruitment (NAHCR)

PO Box 5769
Akron, OH 44372
Phone: (216)867-3088
Fax: (216)867-1630

Membership: Individuals employed directly by hospitals and other health care organizations which are involved in the practice of professional health care recruitment. **Purpose:** Promotes sound principles of professional health care recruitment. Conducts regional seminars, symposia, and workshops. Provides financial assistance to aid members in planning and implementing regional educational programs. Offers technical assistance and consultation services. **Publication(s):** *Annual Recruitment Survey*. • *New Recruiter's Handbook*, periodic. • *Recruitment Directions*, 10/year. • *Who's Who in Recruitment Resources*, annual.

National Association of Pediatric Nurse Associates and Practitioners

1101 Kings Hwy. N.
No. 206
Cherry Hill, NJ 08034
Phone: (609)667-1773
Fax: (609)667-7187

National Association of Physician Nurses (NAPN)

900 S. Washington St., No. G-13
Falls Church, VA 22046
Phone: (703)237-8616

Membership: Physicians' nurses. **Purpose:** To bring added stature and purpose to their profession and to create for themselves the benefits normally limited to members of specialized professional and fraternal groups. Awards scholarships. **Publication(s):** *The Nightingale*, monthly. • *Salary Survey Report*, biennial. • Also publishes special reports.

National Association for Practical Nurse Education and Service (NAPNES)

1400 Spring St., Ste. 310
Silver Spring, MD 20910
Phone: (301)588-2491
Fax: (301)588-2839

Membership: Licensed practical/vocational nurses, registered nurses, physicians, hospital and nursing home administrators, and interested others. **Purpose:** Provides consultation service to advise schools wishing to develop a practical/vocational nursing program on facilities, equipment, policies, curriculum, and staffing. Promotes recruitment of students through preparation and distribution of recruitment materials. Sponsors seminars for directors and instructors in schools of practical/vocational nursing and continuing education programs for LPNs/LVNs; approves continuing education programs and awards contact hours; holds national certification courses in pharmacology and gerontics. Maintains a library of nursing and health publications. Compiles statistics. **Publication(s):** *Journal of Practical Nursing,* quarterly. • *NAPNES Forum,* 8/year. • Also publishes brochures, pamphlets, and reprints.

Much faster than average employment growth is expected for registered nurses, due to the overall growth in health care and the number of complex medical technologies. Hospitals in many parts of the country report shortages of RN's. However, increasing enrollments in nursing programs may result in a balance between job seekers and openings.

Source: *Occupational Outlook Quarterly*

National Association of Registered Nurses (NARN)

1520 Huguenot Rd., Ste. 116
Midlothian, VA 23113
Phone: (804)794-6513
Fax: (804)379-7698

Purpose: Seeks to offer nurses the opportunity to plan and create a financially sound future through financial management programs. Provides financial products, consultation, and services including Individual Retirement Accounts, full investment services, and group life insurance. Conducts seminars and educational programs. **Publication(s):** *Newsletter,* periodic. • Also publishes brochures.

National Association of School Nurses (NASN)

Lamplighter Ln.
PO Box 1300
Scarborough, ME 04078
Phone: (207)883-2117
Fax: (207)883-2683

Membership: School nurses who conduct comprehensive school health programs in public and private schools. Objectives are: to provide national leadership in the promotion of health services for schoolchildren; to promote school health interests to the nursing and health community and the public; to monitor legislation pertaining to school nursing. Provides continuing education programs at the national level and assistance to states for program implementation. Operates the National Board for Certification of School Nurses and certifies school nurses. Has established workshops and grants for study of child and drug abuse, the female body, and skin care. Bestows the annual School Nurse of the Year and Lillian Wald Research awards. **Publication(s):** *NASNewsletter,* quarterly. • *School Nurse,* quarterly. • Also publishes *Guidelines for a Model School Nurse Services Program, Hearing Screening Guidelines for School Nurses,* and vision guidelines.

National Black Nurses Association (NBNA)

PO Box 1823
Washington, DC 20013-1823
Phone: (202)393-6870

Membership: Registered nurses, licensed practical nurses, licensed vocational nurses, and student nurses. **Purpose:** Functions as a professional support group and as an advocacy group for the black community and their health care. Recruits and assists blacks interested in pursuing nursing as a career. Presents scholarships to student nurses, including the Dr. Lauranne Sams and Ambi scholarships. Compiles statistics; maintains biographical archives and charitable program. **Publication(s):** *Annual Report.* • *Journal of Black Nurses Association,* semiannual. • *National Black Nurses Association— Proceedings,* periodic. • *NBNA Newsletter,* quarterly.

National Commission on Certification of Physician Assistants (NCCPA)

2845 Henderson Mill Rd. NE
Atlanta, GA 30341
Phone: (404)493-9100
Fax: (404)493-7316

Purpose: Certifies physicians' assistants at the entry level and for continued competence. Has certified 19,000 physicians' assistants. **Publication(s):** *Directory of Physician's Assistants - Certified*, annual.

National Council of State Boards of Nursing (NCSBN)

676 N. St. Clair St., Ste. 550
Chicago, IL 60611
Phone: (312)787-6555

Purpose: Assists member boards in administering the National Council Licensure Examinations for Registered Nurses and Practical Nurses and works to insure relevancy of the exams to current nursing practice. Aids boards in the collection and analysis of information pertaining to the licensure and discipline of nurses. Provides consultative services, conducts research, develops model nursing legislation and administrative regulations, and sponsors educational programs. **Publication(s):** *National Council of State Boards of Nursing Issues*, bimonthly. • *National Council of State Boards of Nursing Newsletter to the Member Boards*, biweekly. • *State Nursing Legislation Quarterly*. • Also publishes research results and monographs.

National Environmental Health Association (NEHA)

720 S. Colorado Blvd., Ste. 970, S. Tower
Denver, CO 80222
Phone: (303)756-9090
Fax: (303)691-9490

Membership: Professional society of persons engaged in environmental health and protection for governmental agencies, public health and environmental protection agencies, industry, colleges, and universities. **Purpose:** Conducts national professional registration program and continuing education programs. Provides self-paced learning modules for field professionals. Offers placement service; bestows awards; compiles statistics. Maintains speakers' bureau, biographical archives and 1,000 volume library on environmental health and protection. **Publication(s):** *Directory of Local Health Departments*, annual. • *Journal of Environmental Health*, bimonthly. • *National Environmental Health Association—Membership Directory*, annual. • *NEHA Member Mailing List*, bimonthly. • Also publishes manuals and reports.

National Federation of Licensed Practical Nurses (NFLPN)

PO Box 18088
Raleigh, NC 27619
Phone: (919)781-4791
Toll-free: 800-999-4791

Membership: Federation of state associations of licensed practical and vocational nurses. **Purpose:** Aims to preserve and foster the ideal of comprehensive nursing care for the ill and aged; improve the standards of practice; secure the education of LPNs. Acts as a clearinghouse for information on practical nursing and cooperates with other groups concerned with better patient care. Maintains loan program. **Publication(s):** *Licensed Practical Nurse*, quarterly. • *LPN*, quarterly. • *The NFLPN Update*, 8/year.

National Federation of Specialty Nursing Organizations (NFSNO)

875 Kings Hwy., Ste. 200
West Deptford, NJ 08096
Phone: (609)848-5932
Fax: (609)853-0411

Membership: Nursing specialty organizations representing approximately 370,000 individuals. **Purpose:** Provides a forum for the discussion of issues of mutual concern to members; attempts to gain more input in the establishment of nursing standards. Sponsors Nurse in Washington Internship.

National League for Nursing (NLN)

350 Hudson St.
New York, NY 10014
Phone: (212)989-9393
Toll-free: 800-NOW-1NLN
Fax: (212)989-3710

Membership: Individuals and leaders in nursing and other health professions, and community members interested in solving health care problems; also agencies, nursing educational institutions, departments of nursing in hospitals and related facilities, and home and community health agencies. **Purpose:** Works to assess nursing needs, improve organized nursing services and nursing education, and foster collaboration between nursing and other health and community services. Provides tests used in selection of applicants to schools of nursing; also prepares tests for evaluating nursing student progress and nursing service tests. Holds seminars and workshops. Nationally accredits nursing education programs and community health agencies. Collects and disseminates data on nursing services and nursing education. Conducts studies and demonstration projects on community planning for nursing and nursing service and education. Bestows awards for excellence and achievement in nursing education and service. **Publication(s):** *Newsletter*, periodic. • *Nurse Faculty Census*, biennial. • *Nursing Data Review*, annual. • *Nursing and Health Care*, 10/year. • *Nursing Student Census*, annual. • *Public Policy Bulletin*, periodic. • *State Approved Schools of Nursing - LPN*, annual. • *State Approved Schools of Nursing - RN*, annual. • Also publishes memos to members, reports, manuals, curriculum and evaluation guides, career guidance materials, and 25 books on health policy, administration, management, and education; produces educational videotapes.

Four out of five companies say their employees can't write well. But only 21 percent of corporate training aims at writing skills.

Source: *U.S. News & World Report*

National Medical Association (NMA)
1012 10th St., NW
Washington, DC 20001
Phone: (202)347-1895
Fax: (202)842-3293

Membership: Professional society of black physicians. Activities: Plans to establish physician placement service and library. Bestows awards. Maintains 19 sections representing

major specialties of medicine. Conducts symposia and workshops.

National Medical Fellowships (NMF)
254 W. 31st St., 7th Fl.
New York, NY 10001
Phone: (212)714-0933
Fax: (212)239-9718

Purpose: Promotes education of minority students in medicine. Conducts financial assistance program for first- and second-year minority medical students who are U.S. citizens. Conducts workshops in financial planning and management for medical and premedical students, administrators, and parents. Bestows awards and provides special recognition for third- and fourth-year medical students. **Publication(s):** *Annual Report.* • *NMF Update*, biennial. • *Special Report*, annual. • Also publishes *Informed Decision Making* and booklets.

National Mental Health Association (NMHA)
1021 Prince St.
Alexandria, VA 22314-2971
Phone: (703)684-7722
Fax: (703)684-5968

Purpose: Consumer advocacy organization devoted to fighting mental illnesses and promoting mental health. Advocates funding for research to discover new and better ways to treat and prevent mental illness; supports community mental health center program; engages in visitations to hospitals, nursing homes, board and care homes, and centers to assess adequacy of care; works with mental hospitals, government agencies, and private organizations for the rehabilitation of recovered patients; serves as central national source for educational materials on mental illness and mental health; conducts public education on mental illness and the need for public action through newspapers, magazines, radio, and television. Presents numerous awards annually including: Clifford W. Beers Award; Katherine Hamilton Volunteer of the Year Award; Media Awards. **Publication(s):** *NMHA Focus*, 4/year. • Also issues leaflets, pamphlets, and reports.

National Podiatry Medical Association (NPMA)

c/o Raymond E. Lee, D.P.M.
1638 E. 87th St.
Chicago, IL 60617
Phone: (312)374-1616

Membership: Minority podiatrists, predominantly black. **Purpose:** Promotes the science and art of podiatry. Seeks to: improve public health; raise the standards of the podiatric profession and education; stimulate a favorable relationship between all podiatrists; nurture growth and diffusion of podiatric information; stimulate public education concerning public health and features of podiatric medicine. Sponsors proposal of podiatric laws; works to eliminate religious and racial discrimination and segregation in American medical institutions. **Publication(s):** *Annual Seminar Ad Book.* • *National Podiatric Medical Association—Newsletter,* annual.

National Rehabilitation Association (NRA)

633 S. Washington St.
Alexandria, VA 22314
Phone: (703)836-0850
Fax: (703)836-2209

Membership: Physicians, counselors, therapists, disability examiners, vocational evaluators, and others interested in rehabilitation of persons with disabilities. Activities: Maintains Job Placement Division. Sponsors Graduate Literary Awards Contest. Conducts legislative activities; develops accessibility guidelines; offers specialized education.

National Rural Health Association (NRHA)

301 E. Armour Blvd.
Ste. 420
Kansas City, MO 64111
Phone: (816)756-3140
Fax: (816)756-3144

Membership: Administrators, physicians, dentists, nurses, physician assistants, health planners, academicians, and others interested or involved in rural health care. Activities: Provides placement services. Purpose is to: create a better understanding of health care problems unique to rural areas; utilize a collective approach in finding positive solutions; articulate and represent the health care needs of rural America; supply current information to rural health care providers; serve as a liaison between rural health care programs throughout the country. Offers continuing education credits for medical, dental, nursing, and management courses. Bestows awards.

National Student Nurses' Association (NSNA)

555 W. 57th St., Ste. 1325
New York, NY 10019
Phone: (212)581-2211
Fax: (212)581-2368

Membership: Students enrolled in state-approved schools for the preparation of registered nurses. **Purpose:** Seeks to aid in the development of the individual nursing student and to urge students of nursing, as future health professionals, to be aware of and to contribute to improving the health care of all people. Encourages programs and activities in state groups concerning nursing, health, and the community. Cooperates with nursing organizations in recruitment of nurses and in professional, community, and civic programs. Awards annual scholarships; sponsors writing contest for members; holds careers workshops. **Publication(s):** *Career Planning Guide,* annual. • *Dean's Notes,* 6/year. • *Imprint,* 5/year. • *NSNA News,* 6/year. • Also publishes *Convention News,* manuals, guides, and handbooks.

Oncology Nursing Society (ONS)

501 Holiday Dr.
Pittsburgh, PA 15220
Phone: (412)921-7373
Fax: (412)921-6565

Membership: Registered nurses interested in oncology. **Purpose:** Seeks to promote high professional standards in oncology nursing; provide a network for the exchange of information, resources, and peer support; encourage nurses to specialize in oncology; promote and develop educational programs in oncology nursing extending through the graduate level; identify, encourage, and foster nursing research in improving the quality of patient care. Conducts instructional and abstract sessions. Bestows research awards; compiles statistics. **Publication(s):** *Oncology Nursing Forum,* bimonthly. • *Oncology Nursing Society— Membership Directory*, annual. • *Oncology Nursing Society—Proceedings of Annual Congress.* • *ONS News*, monthly. • Also publishes *Standards of Cancer Nursing Practice: Education.*

Pathology Practice Association (PPA)

1301 Connecticut Ave., NW, 7th Fl.
Washington, DC 20036
Phone: (202)659-4593

Membership: Pathologists (individuals who study the effects of disease). **Purpose:** Provides an arena for communication among pathologists. Represents the views of members on legislative issues. **Publication(s):** *Pathology PAC Update*, annual. • *PPA Legislative Alert*, periodic. • *PPA Newsletter*, bimonthly.

Society for Advancement in Nursing (SAN)

Box 307, Cooper Sta.
11th St. & 4th Ave.
New York, NY 10003
Phone: (212)998-5335

Membership: Nurses having earned a minimum of a baccalaureate degree in nursing. **Purpose:** Seeks to make a distinction between educational preparation and practice toward professional and technical careers in nursing. Promotes establishment of new licensure procedures for professional practice that differ from current registered nurse licensure. Strives to serve as a unified voice promoting relevant issues in nursing and health. Maintains speakers' bureau.

Society of University Surgeons (SUS)

c/o Linda M. Graham
PO Box 7069
New Haven, CT 06519
Phone: (203)932-0541

Membership: Professional society of surgeons connected with university teaching. **Purpose:** To advance the art and science of surgery by encouraging original investigations both in the clinic and in the laboratory and by developing methods of graduate teaching of surgery with particular reference to the resident system.

Ukrainian Medical Association of North America (UMANA)

2320 W. Chicago Ave.
Chicago, IL 60622
Phone: (312)323-6970

Membership: Physicians, surgeons, dentists, and persons in related professions who are of Ukrainian descent. Activities: Maintains placement service. Provides assistance to members; sponsors lectures. Maintains museum, biographical and medical archives, and library of 1800 medical books and journals in Ukrainian. Bestows awards.

Visiting Nurse Associations of America (VNAA)

3801 E. Florida
Ste. 206
Denver, CO 80210
Phone: (303)753-0218
Fax: (303)753-0258

Membership: Voluntary, nonprofit home health care agencies. Activities: Offers placement service for those seeking employment with VNAA. Develops competitive strength among voluntary nonprofit health care agencies; works to strengthen business resources and economic programs through marketing and contracting. Issues radio and television public service announcements. Offers workshops and training programs.

Employment Agencies and Search Firms

Academy Medical Personnel Services

571 High St.
Worthington, OH 43085
Phone: (614)848-6011

Employment agency. Fills openings on a regular or temporary basis.

Consult One, Inc.

10291 N. Meridan St.
Ste. 325
Indianapolis, IN 46290
Phone: (317)573-2025
Fax: (317)573-2035

Executive search firm.

Davis-Smith Medical Employment Service, Inc.

24725 W. 12 Mile Rd.
No. 2302 Lockdale Office Plaza
Southfield, MI 48034
Phone: (313)354-4100

Employment agency. Executive search firm.

Durham Medical Search, Inc.

6300 Transit
Depew, NY 14043
Phone: (716)681-7402

Employment agency.

Eden Personnel, Inc.

280 Madison Rd.
Rm. 202
New York, NY 10016
Phone: (212)685-8600

Employment agency. Places individuals in regular or temporary positions.

Executive Medical Recruiters

221 E. 4th St.
PO Box 83
Waterloo, IA 50704
Phone: (319)232-6641

Employment agency.

Focus: Healthcare

129 N. Adams St.
Louisville, KY 40206

Executive search firm.

Harper Associates-Detroit, Inc.

29870 Middlebelt
Farmington Hills, MI 48334
Phone: (313)932-1170

Employment agency.

Phyllis Hawkins and Associates

3550 N. Central Ave.
Ste. 1400
Pheonix, AZ 85012
Phone: (602)263-0248
Fax: (602)263-1016

Executive search firm.

C iticorp is changing the way it uses interns, as are other companies. Instead of providing opportunities for students to examine various career paths, employers are taking a closer look at them as potential full-time employees. This means giving interns more responsibility.

Source: *Fortune*

Health and Science Center

PO Box 213
Lima, PA 19037
Phone: (215)891-0794

Employment agency. Executive search firm.

Robert William James and Associates

PO Box 8136
Waco, TX 76714
Phone: (817)776-7782

Employment agency.

Janamar Nurses

1200 N. Eldorado Pl.
D-430
Tucson, AZ 85715
Phone: (602)722-2600

Employment agency. Provides regular or temporary placement of staff.

Kimberly Quality Care

4010 DuPont Cir.
Ste. 275
Louisville, KY 40207
Phone: (502)893-8888

Employment agency. Provides temporary staffing for some positions.

Massachusetts Medical Bureau
101 Tremont St.
Boston, MA 02108
Phone: (617)842-2400
Fax: (617)482-7290

Employment agency. Executive search firm.

Medical Personnel Pool
Ala Moana Bldg.
Ste. 1320
1441 Kapiolani Bldg.
Honolulu, HI 96814
Phone: (808)955-1102

Offices throughout the continental U.S. as well. Provides temporary staffing assistance.

> The forces that will produce the new jobs of the 1990s are already in place. Information services will generate new hiring as the computer revolution rolls on. The graying of America will mean strong job growth in health care and leisure activities.
>
> Source: *Business Week*

Medical Personnel Service
4801 Woodway
333 West
Houston, TX 77056
Phone: (713)623-2200

Employment agency.

Medical Personnel Services, Inc.
1899 L St., NW
Ste. 705
Washington, DC 20036
Phone: (202)466-2955
Fax: (202)452-1818

Employment agency.

Midwest Medical Consultants
8910 Purdue Rd.
Ste. 200
Indianapolis, IN 46268-1155
Phone: (317)872-1053

Employment agency. Executive search firm.

Ocean Personnel Agency
PO Box 698
Malibu, CA 90265
Phone: (213)451-8183

Employment agency.

Pasadena Nurses Registry
1000 E. Walnut St.
Ste. 212
Pasadena, CA 91106
Phone: (818)792-2103

Employment agency.

Physicians Search Associates Agency, Inc.
500 N. State College Blvd.
Ste. 870
Orange, CA 92668
Phone: (714)978-6899
Fax: (714)978-2654

Executive search firm. Affiliate office in Spokane, WA.

Professional Placement Associates, Inc.
11 Rye Ridge Plaza
Port Chester, NY 10573
Phone: (914)939-1195
Fax: (914)939-1959

Employment agency.

Putzek Medical Search
4150 Falcon Dr.
Austell, GA 30001
Phone: (404)941-3339

Employment agency.

Ranier Home Health Care
1530 S. Union
Ste. 10
Tacoma, WA 98405
Phone: (206)759-8060

Employment agency.

Retail Recruiters/Spectra Professional Search

1 Bala Cynwyd Plaza
Ste. 217
Bala Cynwyd, PA 19004
Phone: (215)667-6565
Fax: (215)667-5323

Employment agency. Affiliate offices in many locations across the country.

Oliver Scott and Associates, Inc.

16 Shawmut St.
Boston, MA 02116
Phone: (617)357-7333
Fax: (617)482-9399

Executive search firm.

Shiloh Careers International, Inc.

PO Box 831
Brentwood, TN 37024-0831
Phone: (615)373-3090

Employment agency.

Team Placement Service, Inc.

5113 Leesburg Pike
Ste. 510
Falls Church, VA 22041
Phone: (703)820-8618
Fax: (703)820-3368

Employment agency.

Travcorps, Inc.

40 Eastern Ave.
Malden, MA 02148
Phone: (617)322-2600

Places staff in temporary assignments.

Underhill Personnel Service

1147 S. Edgewood Ave.
Jacksonville, FL 32205
Phone: (904)388-7645

Employment agency. Handles temporary and regular placement of staff.

Weatherby Healthcare

25 Van Zant St.
Norwalk, CT 06855
Phone: (203)866-1144
Fax: (203)853-3154

Executive search firm. Branch office in Fairfax, VA.

The 100 Best Companies to Work for in America

Signet/NAL Penguin
1633 Broadway
New York, NY 10019

Levering, Robert, Moskowitz, Milton, and Katz, Michael. 1985. $5.95. 477 pages. Describes the best companies to work for in America, based on such factors as salary, benefits, job security, and ambience. The authors base their 'top 100' rating on surveys and personal visits to hundreds of firms.

The United States economy is projected to provide 24 million more jobs in 2005 than it did in 1990, an increase of 20 percent.

Source: *Occupational Outlook Quarterly*

120 Careers in the Health Care Field

U.S. Directory Service, Publishers
121 Chalon Rd.
PO Box 68-1700
New Providence, FL 07974
Phone: (305)769-1700

Stanley Alperin. Second edition, 1989.

A-Job Hunting We Will Go

McGraw Hill Book Company
Continuing Education Program
1221 Avenue of the Americas
New York, NY 10020
Phone: (212)997-6572

Video cassette. 3/4' U-matic. 21 minutes. Part of a ten-part series entitled *The Career Development Video Series*, which offers a step-by-step approach to finding a job and planning a career.

The AJN Guide to Nursing Career Opportunities

American Journal of Nursing Co.
555 W. 57th St.
New York, NY 10019
Phone: (212)582-8820

Annual. Gives career planning, self-assessment,

and job hunting advice. This is primarily a listing of hospitals and health centers. Profiles on each hospital describe the facilities, professional climate, and benefits.

The AJN Guide to Nursing Career Opportunities

American Journal of Nursing Co.
555 W. 57th St.
New York, NY 10019
Phone: (212)582-8820

Annual. Gives career planning, self-assessment, and job hunting advice. This is primarily a listing of hospitals and health centers. Profiles on each hospital describe the facilities, professional climate, and benefits.

One way to improve your chances in the job hunt is to define "you" as broadly as possible . . . . Defining yourself in terms of your skills rather than your job history is the key.

Source: *Business Monday/Detroit Free Press*

The American Almanac of Jobs and Salaries

Avon Books
1350 Avenue of the Americas
New York, NY 10019
Phone: (212)261-6800
Toll-free: 800-238-0658

John Wright, editor. Revised and updated, 1990. A comprehensive guide to the wages of hundreds of occupations in a wide variety of industries and organizations.

Arming Yourself for a Part-Time or Summer Job

Olympus Publishing Company
1670 East 13th St., S.
Salt Lake City, UT 84105

Nadler, Burton Jay. 1982. $4.95. 100 pages.

Being a Long-Term Care Nursing Assistant

Prentice Hall
Rte. 9W
Englewood Cliffs, NJ 07632
Phone: (201)592-2000
Toll-free: 800-638-0220

Connie A. Will. 1983.

The Berkeley Guide to Employment for New College Graduates

Ten Speed Press
PO Box 7123
Berkeley, CA 94707
Phone: (415)845-8414

Briggs, James I. $7.95. 256 pages. Basic job-hunting advice for the college student.

The Best Companies for Women

Simon and Schuster
Simon and Schuster Bldg.
1230 Avenue of the Americas
New York, NY 10020

1989. $8.95.

Best of the National Business Employment Weekly

Consultants Bookstore
Templeton Rd.
Fitzwilliam, NH 03447
Phone: (603)585-2200
Fax: (603)585-9555

$5.00/booklet. Booklets summarizing the best articles from the *National Business Employment Weekly* on a variety of job hunting topics.

The Career Fitness Program: Exercising Your Options

Gorsuch Scarisbrick, Publishers
8233 Via Paseo del Norte
Ste. F-400
Scottsdale, AZ 85258

Sukiennik et al. 1989. $16.00. 227 pages. Textbook, with second half devoted to the job search process.

The Career Guide—Dun's Employment Opportunities Directory

Dun's Marketing Services
Dun and Bradstreet Corp.
3 Sylvan Way
Parsippany, NJ 07054-3896
Phone: (201)605-6000

Annual, December. $450.00; $385.00 for public libraries (lease basis). Covers: More than 5,000 companies that have a thousand or more employees and that provide career opportunities in sales, marketing, management, engineering, life and physical sciences, computer science, mathematics, statistics planning, accounting and finance, liberal arts fields, and other technical and professional areas; based on data supplied on questionnaires and through personal interviews. Also covers personnel consultants; includes some public sector employers (governments, schools, etc.) usually not found in similar lists. Entries include: Company name, location of headquarters, and other offices of plants; entries may also include name, title, address, and phone of employment contact; disciplines or occupational groups hired; brief overview of company; discussion of types of positions that may be available; training and career development programs; benefits offered. Arrangement: Companies are alphabetical; consultants are geographical. Indexes: Geographical, Standard Industrial Classification code.

Career Information System (CIS)

National Career Information System
1787 Agate St.
Eugene, OR 97403
Phone: (503)686-3872

Includes information on job search techniques and self-employment options. Also provides extensive career planning information.

Career Ladders: An Approach to Professional Productivity and Job Satisfaction

American Nurses Association Cabinet on Nursing Services
600 Maryland Ave., SW, Ste. 100, W.
Washington, DC 20024-2571
Phone: (202)554-4444
Fax: (202)554-2262

American Nurses' Association, Cabinet on Nursing Services. 1984.

Career Opportunities

Quanta Press, Inc.
1313 5th St. SE, Ste. 223A
Minneapolis, MN 55414
Phone: (612)379-3956

CD-ROM (Compact Disc-Read Only Memory) database that provides job titles and job descriptions and information on education levels, chances for advancement, average salaries, and working conditions.

Career Placement Registry (CPR)

Career Placement Registry, Inc.
302 Swann Ave.
Alexandria, VA 22301
Phone: (703)683-1085
Fax: (703)683-0246

Contains brief resumes of job candidates currently seeking employment. Comprises two files, covering college and university seniors and recent graduates, and alumni, executives, and others who have already acquired substantial work experience. Entries typically include applicant name, address, telephone number, degree level, function, language skills, name of school, major field of study, minor field of study, occupational preference, date available, city/area preference, special skills, citizenship status, employer name, employer address, description of duties, position/title, level of education, civil service register, security clearance type/availability, willingness to relocate, willingness to travel, salary expectation, and overall work experience. Available online through DIALOG Information Services, Inc.

Although the pipeline supplying the field of neuroscience starts out with lots of women in it, it is leaking—like a sieve. "We are losing women all along the way," says Linda Spear, psycho-pharmacologist at the State University of New York. Although roughly 45% of the students entering neuroscience graduate programs for the past decade have been women, last year's survey showed only 38% of Ph.D.s going to women.

Source: *Science*

Career Planning: Nurse's Guide to Career Advancement

National League for Nursing (NLN)
350 Hudson St.
New York, NY 10014
Phone: (212)989-9393
Toll-free: 800-NOW-1NLN

Patricia Winstead-Fry. 1990. This is a guide to career planning and self assessment. Describes opportunities in nurse-midwifery, independent practice, community health, administration, research and education. Gives advice on getting into the field and acquiring the education needed.

Career Planning in Nursing

J. B. Lippincott Co.
PO Box 600
Hagerstown, MD 21741
Phone: (215)238-4200
Toll-free: 800-441-4526

Janie B. Nowak and Cecelia G. Grindel. 1984. Includes bibliographies and an index.

Career Strategies—From Job Hunting to Moving Up

Association for Management Success
2360 Maryland Rd.
Willow Grove, PA 19090

Six video cassettes. Kennedy, Marilyn Moats. $36.95/each. $203.70/set. 30 minutes each. Covers the following topics: planning the job hunt, networking, resumes, interviewing, negotiating salaries and benefits, and moving up on the job.

Careering and Re-Careering for the 1990's

Consultants Bookstore
Templeton Rd.
Fitzwilliam, NH 03447
Phone: (603)585-6544
Fax: (603)585-9555

Krannich, Ronald. 1989. $13.95. 314 pages. Details trends in the marketplace, how to identify opportunities, how to retrain for them, and how to land jobs. Includes a chapter on starting a business. Contains index, bibliography, and illustrations.

Careers

National Textbook Co.
4255 W. Touhy Ave.
Lincolnwood, IL 60646
Phone: (312)679-5500
Toll-free: 800-323-4900

1990. Includes a bibliography and an index.

Careers and the College Grad

Bob Adams, Inc.
260 Center St.
Holbrook, MA 02343
Phone: (617)767-8100
Fax: (617)767-0994

Ranno, Gigi. 1992. $12.95. 64 pages. An annual resource guide addressing the career and job-hunting interests of undergraduates. Provides company profiles and leads.

Careers in Health Care

Chelsea House Publishers
1974 Sproul Rd., Ste. 400
PO Box 914
Broomall, PA 19008
Phone: (212)683-4400
Toll-free: 800-848-2665
Fax: (215)359-1439

Rachel S. Epstein. 1989.

Careers in Health Services: Opportunities for You

Cambridge Career Products
90 MacCorkle Ave., SW
South Charleston, WV 25311
Phone: (304)744-9323

Videocassette. 1989. 30 mins. This program shows the range of career opportunities in health care fields.

Careers in Medicine: Traditional and Alternative Opportunities

Garrett Park Press
PO Box 190
Garrett Park, MD 20096
Phone: (301)946-2553

T. Donald Rucker and Martin D. Keller. Revised edition, 1990. Written for college students who are considering applying to medical school, for medical students attempting to select a specialty, and for physicians who want to explore non-clinical work. Gives an overview and the employment outlook for the medical profession, and lists 900 job titles of persons with medical training.

Change Your Job to Change Your Life

Lorimar Home Video
17942 Cowan Ave.
Irvine, CA 92714

Video cassette. Beta, VHS. 1986. 60 minutes. This tape outlines strategies, tips, and tactics in job hunting, including interviewing, resume writing and career planning.

Changing Patterns in Nursing Education

National League for Nursing (NLN)
350 Hudson St.
New York, NY 10014
Phone: (212)989-9393
Toll-free: 800-NOW-1NLN

Joanna Rhode, editor. 1987. Discusses the issues of change in nursing education, practice, and research.

Choosing a School of Nursing: Questions for You to Answer

American Hospital Association
840 N. Lake Shore Dr.
Chicago, IL 60611
Phone: (312)280-6000

This two-page pamphlet outlines the questions to ask about cost, financial aid, curriculum, and extracurricular activities when considering a school of nursing.

Chronicle Career Index

Chronicle Guidance Publications
PO Box 1190
Moravia, NY 13118-1190
Phone: (315)497-0330

Annual. $14.25. Provides bibliographic listings of career and vocational guidance publications and other resources. Arrangement: Alphabetical by source. Indexes: Occupation; vocational and professional information.

Code for Nurses With Interpretative Statements

American Nurses' Association
600 Maryland Ave., SW, Ste. 100, W.
Washington, DC 20024-2571
Phone: (202)554-4444
Fax: (202)554-2862

1985.

Come Alive

Great Plains National Instructional Television Library (GPN)
University of Nebraska at Lincoln
PO Box 80669
Lincoln, NE 68501-0669

Video cassette. Beta, VHS, 3/4' U-matic. 1981. 30 minutes. A series of 6 cassettes that take a look at the job market and offer guidance on career and life planning. Program titles: 1. Need

a Paycheck? 2. Half of Your Life! 3. It's Your Choice! 4. I Can! 5. To Market, to Market! 6. Hidden Jobs!

Commonly Asked Questions About Nursing

American Hospital Association
840 N. Lake Shore Dr.
Chicago, IL 60611
Phone: (312)280-6000
Toll-free: 800-242-2626

This three-page pamphlet offers such information as the number of nurses in the profession and the locations of jobs.

> **A**s much as half of the impression you make on a prospective employer may have to do with your general knowledge of issues in your profession as well as issues in the industry in which you currently work or the industry in which you want to work. Subscribe to the journals in your field and industry, and don't forget to stay on top of the broader picture of the national and world economies.
>
> Source: *Working Woman*

Company Connections, The Cover Letter

Cambridge Career Products
723 Kanawha Blvd., E.
Charleston, WV 25301

1986. Contains two programs. Company Connections is a directory of company names, addresses, and phone numbers, and professional associations for a variety of career fields. The Cover Letter addresses the content and format of cover letters and guides the user through completion of a sample letter.

Compensation Report on Hospital-Based and Group Practice Physicians

Hospital Compensation Service
John R. Zabka Associates, Inc.
69 Minnehaha Blvd.
PO Box 376
Oakland, NJ 07436
Phone: (201)405-0075

1989. Describes compensation and benefits for

the chief of staff or medical director, staff physicians, and heads of departments. Includes information on bonuses, base salary, number of hours worked annually by each physician, housing and meal allowances, hospital bed size, group practice organization size, and governmental and nongovernmental facilities.

Competencies of the Associate Degree Nurse on Entry Into Practice

National League for Nursing (NLN)
350 Hudson St.
New York, NY 10014
Phone: (212)989-9393
Toll-free: 800-NOW-1NLN

Prepared by the NLN Council of AD Programs. 1978. Describes the scope and roles of practice and competencies of nurse graduating from an associate degree program.

S ome handy books to help you contemplate the job change process: *Switching Gears: How to Master Career Change and Find the Work That's Right for You,* by Carole Hyatt; *Congratulations! You've Been Fired,* by Emily Knoltnow; and *How to Get the Job You Want,* by Melvin Danaho and John L. Meyer.

Source: *Better Homes and Gardens*

Competencies of the Associate Degree Nurse: Valid Definers of Entry-Level Nursing Practice

National League for Nursing (NLN)
350 Hudson St.
New York, NY 10014
Phone: (212)989-9393
Toll-free: 800-NOW-1NLN

Verle Waters and Sharlene Limon. 1987. This book is an outcome of a study that clarifies the working skills or competencies of AD graduates.

Competencies of Graduates of Nursing Programs

National League For Nursing (NLN)
350 Hudson St.
New York, NY 10014
Phone: (212)989-9393
Toll-free: 800-NOW-1NLN

Report of the NLN Task Force on Competencies of Graduates of Nursing Programs. 1982. Presents the commonalities among the statements of competencies by the various types of nursing education and the problems arising from these statements and their use.

The Complete Job Search Book

John Wiley and Sons
General Books Division
605 3rd Ave.
New York, NY 10158

Beatty, Richard H. 1988. $12.95. 256 pages.

The Complete Job-Search Handbook

Consultants Bookstore
Templeton Rd.
Fitzwilliam, NH 03447
Phone: (603)585-6544
Fax: (603)585-9555

Figler, Howard. 1988. $12.95. 366 pages. Contains information on how to look for career opportunities every day. Focuses on 20 life skills in self-assessment, detective work, communication skills, and selling oneself. Includes skill-building exercises.

Compu-Job

Cambridge Career Products
723 Kanawha Blvd., E.
Charleston, WV 25301

Menu-driven program designed to take the user through the job search process, from determining career alternatives to identifying openings, applying for employment, and interviewing.

The Corporate Directory of U.S. Public Companies

Gale Research Inc.
835 Penobscot Bldg.
Detroit, MI 48226
Phone: (313)961-2242
Fax: (313)961-6241

1991. $325.00. Provides information on more than 9,500 publicly-traded firms having at least $5,000,000 in assets. Entries include: General background, including name, address and phone, number of employees; stock data; description of areas of business; major subsidiaries; officers; directors; owners; and financial data. Indexes: Officers and directors, owners, subsidiary/parent, geographic, SIC, stock exchange, company rankings, and newly registered corporations.

CSI National Career Network

Computer Search International Corporation (CSI)
7926 Jones Branch Dr.
Ste. 120
McLean, VA 22102
Phone: (302)749-1635

Contains job listings from potential employers and candidate resumes from executive recruiting firms. Covers more than 40 technical and managerial job categories.

Developing Your Career in Nursing

Routledge, Chapman & Hall
29 W. 35th St.
New York, NY 10001
Phone: (212)244-3336
Fax: (212)563-2269

Desmond F.S. Cormack, editor. 1990.

The Discipline of Nursing: An Introduction

Appleton and Lange
25 Van Zant St.
East Norwalk, CT 06855
Phone: (203)838-4400
Fax: (203)854-9486

Margaret O'Bryan, Christina B. Cook, and Mary C. Stopper. Second edition, 1987. Includes bibliographies and an index.

Doctor of Podiatric Medicine: Partner for Health

American Podiatric Medical Association
9312 Old Georgetown Rd.
Bethesda, MD 20814-1621
Phone: (301)571-9200

1986. Pamphlet describing the profession, practice, educational background, and responsibilities of podiatrists.

Effective Job Search Strategies

Robert Ehrmann Productions
4741 Calle Camarada
Santa Barbara, CA 93110

Video casssette. $150.00. 26 minutes. Two college seniors, one of whom is handicapped, are advised of job search strategies and resources by a college job counselor.

The Elements of Job Hunting

Bob Adams, Inc.
260 Center St.
Holbrook, MA 02343
Phone: (617)767-8100
Fax: (617)767-0994

Noble, John. $4.95. Concisely focuses on the key components of job hunting.

General practitioners have grown scarcer and scarcer as physicians have specialized and subspecialized; a new government study says the nation is short by as many as 100,000 generalists. One reason is that a heightened emphasis on preventive care is sending more people in for checkups.

Source: *U.S. News & World Report*

Employability Inventory

Education Associates, Inc.
PO Box Y
8 Crab Orchard Rd.
Frankfort, KY 40602
Phone: (502)227-4783

1984. This program allows the user to test his/her knowledge of job hunting and employment protocol, by taking the user through a series of questions on everything from developing a resume to maintaining a job.

The Encyclopedia of Career Choices for the 1990s: A Guide to Entry Level Jobs

Walker and Co.
720 5th Ave.
New York, NY 10019
Phone: (212)265-3632
Toll-free: 800-289-2553

1991. Describes entry-level careers in a variety of industries. Presents qualifications required, working conditions, salary, internships, and professional associations.

The Encyclopedia of Careers and Vocational Guidance

J. G. Ferguson Publishing Co.
200 W. Monroe, Ste. 250
Chicago, IL 60606
Phone: (312)580-5480

William E. Hopke, editor-in-chief. Eighth edition, 1990. Four-volume set that profiles 900 occupations and describes job trends in 71 industries.

Fastest growing US counties, 1989-2000

1. Orange County, CA, with 674 thousand new jobs
2. Los Angeles County, CA, 652
3. Harris County, TX, 452
4. Maricopa County, AZ, 434
5. San Diego County, CA, 420
6. Dallas County, TX, 371
7. Santa Clara County, CA, 304
8. Fairfax/Fairfax City/Falls Church County, VA, 258
9. King County, WA, 253
10. Broward County, FL, 246

Source: *American Demographics*

Entering and Moving in the Professional Job Market: A Nurse's Resource Kit

American Nurses' Association (ANA)
600 Maryland Ave. SW, Ste. 100 W.
Washington, DC 20024
Phone: (202)554-4444

Lyndia Flanagan. 1988. Contains one booklet and five brochures.

The Experienced Hand: A Student Manual for Making the Most of an Internship

Carroll Press
43 Squantum St.
Cranston, RI 02920
Phone: (401)942-1587

Stanton, Timothy, and Ali, Kamil. 1987. $6.95. 88 pages. Guidance for deriving the most satisfaction and future benefit from an internship.

Exploring Careers in Medicine

Rosen Publishing Group, Inc.
29 E. 21st St.
New York, NY 10010
Phone: (212)777-3017
Toll-free: 800-323-4900

Alan Ralph Bleich. Revised edition, 1991. Covers medical school, internships, and licensure. Separate chapters discuss specialties in medicine such as obstetrics, pediatrics, and family medicine. Describes the day-to-day work, employment outlook. Gives a worldwide list of medical schools.

Exploring Careers in Nursing

Rosen Publishing Group, Inc.
29 E. 21st St.
New York, NY 10010
Phone: (212)777-3017
Toll-free: 800-237-9932
Fax: (212)777-0277

Jackie Heron. Revised edition, 1990. $13.95 per volume; $125.55 per set. Part of a 9 volume set of career titles that describes the nursing profession; discusses educational requirements and how to find a job. Covers different opportunities for nurses in hospitals.

Exploring Nontraditional Jobs for Women

Rosen Publishing Group, Inc.
29 E. 21st St.
New York, NY 10010
Phone: (212)777-3017
Toll-free: 800-237-9932
Fax: (212)777-0277

Rose Neufeld. Revised edition. 1989. $13.95 per volume; $139.50 per set. Part of a 10 volume set that describes occupations where few women are found, including the job of camera operator. Covers job duties, training routes, where to apply for jobs, tools used, salary, and advantages and disadvantages of the job.

Family Practice Physician

Vocational Biographies, Inc.
PO Box 31
Sauk Centre, MN 56378-0031
Phone: (612)352-6516
Toll-free: 800-255-0752
Fax: (612)352-5546

1988. $2.00. Four-page pamphlet containing a personal narrative about a worker's job, work likes and dislikes, career path from high school to the present, education and training, the rewards and frustrations, and the effects of the job on the rest of the worker's life. The data file portion of this pamphlet gives a concise occupational summary, including work description, working conditions, places of employment, personal characteristics, education and training, job outlook, and salary range.

Finding and Following-Up on Job Opportunities: Job World Series
Career Aids
Dept. SPB
8950 Lurine Ave.
Chatsworth, CA 91311

1984. Tests the user's knowledge of help-wanted information sources, including want ads, employment agencies, placement services, job lead files, and others.

Get a Better Job!
Peterson's
PO Box 2123
Princeton, NJ 08543-2123
Phone: (609)243-9111

Rushlow, Ed. 1990. $11.95. 225 pages. Counsels the reader on job search techniques. Discusses how to win the job by bypassing the Personnel Department and how to understand the employer's system for screening and selecting candidates. Written in an irreverent and humorous style.

Get That Job!
Consultants Bookstore
Templeton Rd.
Fitzwilliam, NH 03447
Phone: (603)585-6544
Fax: (603)585-9555

Camden, Thomas. 1981. $24.95. Two 30-minute cassettes supplemented by a 45-page booklet that include dramatizations of interviews, cover what questions to expect, and how to respond to them. Provides sample resumes and letters.

Getting Hired: How to Sell Yourself
Carolina Pacific Publishing
7808 SE 28th Ave.
PO Box 02399
Portland, OR 97202

Costanzo, W. Kenneth. 1987. $8.95. 103 pages.

Getting to the Right Job
Workman Publishing
708 Broadway
New York, NY 10003
Phone: (212)254-5900

Cohen, Steve, and de Oliveira, Paulo. 1987. $6.95. 288 pages.

Go Hire Yourself an Employer
Doubleday and Company, Inc.
666 5th Ave.
New York, NY 10103
Phone: (212)984-7561

Irish, Richard K. 1987. $9.95. 312 pages.

Guerilla Tactics in the Job Market
Bantam Books
666 5th Ave.
New York, NY 10103
Phone: (212)765-6500

Jackson, Tom. 1987. $4.50. 384 pages. Provides 79 action-oriented tips for getting the job or changing jobs.

The Guidance Information System
Houghton Mifflin Company
Educational Software Division
1 Memorial Dr.
Cambridge, MA 02142
Phone: (617)252-3000

Online database that contains a series of files covering occupations, two- and four-year colleges, graduate schools, and sources of scholarships and financial aid.

The Health Care Worker: An Introduction to Health Occupations
Prentice-Hall, Inc.
200 Old Tappan Rd.
Old Tappan, NJ 07675
Phone: (201)767-5937

Shirley A. Badasch and Doreen S. Chesebro. Second edition, 1988. Includes a bibliography and an index.

Health Career Planning: A Realistic Guide
Human Sciences Press
233 Spring St.
New York, NY 10013-1578
Phone: (212)620-8000
Toll-free: 800-221-9369

Ellen F. Lederman. 1988.

Health Careers Today

C.V. Mosby Co.
11830 Westline Industrial Dr.
St. Louis, MO 63146
Phone: (314)872-8370
Toll-free: 800-325-4177

Judith A. Gerdin. 1991. Surveys health occupations. Includes information on basic health care skills and careers.

The Hidden Job Market

Peterson's
PO Box 2123
Princeton, NJ 08543-2123
Phone: (609)243-9111

1992. $16.95. Subtitled *A Job Seeker's Guide to America's 2,000 Little-Known but Fastest-Growing High-Tech Companies*. Listing of high technology companies in such fields as environmental consulting, genetic engineering, home health care, telecommunications, alternative energy systems, and others.

> **W**hen zapped by a tough question, men tend to clasp their hands in front of them in a "fig leaf" position, and women cross their arms over their chests, according to Karen Berg of CommCore, a New York-based consulting firm. Both are signals of feeling attacked, she points out and the person you're talking with will sense, on a subliminal level, that you're experiencing stress. When the tough interview questions pop up, remember to lower your physical guard and keep looking in control.
>
> Source: *Working Woman*

High-Impact Telephone Networking for Job Hunters

Bob Adams, Inc.
260 Center St.
Holbrook, MA 02343
Phone: (617)767-8100
Fax: (617)767-0994

Armstrong, Howard. 1992. $6.95. Examines the challenges associated with phone networking, shows the reader how to use "positive errors" to generate referrals, and offers hints on how to deal with "getting the runaround". Includes advice on how to ask for the meeting and addresses long-distance job searches by phone.

Hot Tips, Sneaky Tricks and Last-Ditch Tactics

John Wiley and Sons, Inc.
605 3rd Ave.
New York, NY 10158
Phone: (212)850-6000

Speck, Jeff B. 1989. $10.95. Subtitled: *An Insider's Guide to Getting Your First Corporate Job*. Gives an inside glimpse of the recruiting process and provides tips on using this knowledge to get the interview or the job.

How to Find and Get the Job You Want

Johnson/Rudolph Educational Resources, Inc.
1004 State St.
Bowling Green, KY 42101

1989. $20.50. 160 pages. Aimed at the college student.

How to Get a Better Job in This Crazy World

Crown Publishers, Inc.
225 Park Ave., S.
New York, NY 10003
Phone: (212)254-1600

Half, Robert. $17.95.

How to Get and Get Ahead on Your First Job

VGM Career Horizons
4255 West Touhy Ave.
Lincolnwood, IL 60646-1975
Phone: (708)679-5500

Bloch, Deborah Perlmutter. 1988. $7.95. 160 pages. Details in step-by-step ways how to go about finding that first job, apply for it, write the winning resume, and manage the successful interview.

How to Get a Good Job and Keep It

VGM Career Horizons
4255 W. Touhy Ave.
Lincolnwood, IL 60646-1975
Phone: (708)679-5500

Bloch, Deborah Perlmutter. 1993. $7.95. Aimed at the recent high school or college graduate, this guide provides advice on finding out about jobs, completing applications and resumes, and managing successful interviews.

How to Get Hired Today!

VGM Career Horizons
4255 W. Touhy Ave.
Lincolnwood, IL 60646-1975
Phone: (708)679-5500

Kent, George, E. 1991. $7.95. Directed at individuals who know the type of job they are looking for. Focuses the reader on activities that are likely to lead to a job and eliminates those that won't. Shows how to establish productive contacts and discover, evaluate, and pursue strong job leads.

How to Get Interviews from Job Ads

Elderkin Associates
PO Box 1293
Dedham, MA 02026

Elderkin, Kenton W. 1989. $19.50. 256 pages. Outlines how to select and follow up ads to get the job. Includes unique ways to get interview offers and how to incorporate the use of a computer and a fax machine in arranging interviews. Illustrated.

How to Get a Job

Cambridge Career Products
723 Kanawha Blvd. E.
Charleston, WV 25301

Video cassette. Beta, VHS, 3/4' U-matic. 1986. 60 minutes. An instructional survey of the job search and acquisition process.

How to Get a Job

Business Week Careers
PO Box 5810
Norwalk, CT 06856-9960

Video cassette. $34.95. 70 minutes. Job search skills presented from the viewpoint of career planning and placement professionals, CEOs, and others.

How to Land a Better Job

VGM Career Horizons
4255 West Touhy Ave.
Lincolnwood, IL 60646-1975
Phone: (708)679-5500

Lott, Catherine S., and Lott, Oscar C. 1989. $7.95. 160 pages. Tells the job seeker how to enhance his or her credentials, overcome past weaknesses, uncover job leads, get appointments, organize an appealing resume, and score

points in interviews. A special section devoted to getting a better job without changing companies covers the process of transferring departments and gives pointers on moving up to the boss's job.

How to Locate Jobs and Land Interviews

The Career Press, Inc.
180 5th Ave.
PO Box 34
Hawthorne, NJ 07507

French, Albert L. $9.95. Shows readers how to tap into the unadvertised, hidden job market and guides them through the resume, cover letter, and interview preparation process.

> Over the last year, companies in sectors as diverse as software, skiing, hospitals, and private bus services have added a total of 600,000 jobs, even while overall employment was sinking.
>
> Source: *Business Week*

How to Market Your College Degree

VGM Career Horizons
4255 W. Touhy Ave.
Lincolnwood, IL 60646-1975
Phone: (708)679-5500

Rogers, Dorothy, and Bettinson, Craig. 1992. $12.95. Provides a guide to self-marketing as a key component of an effective job search. Helps job seekers to develop a strategic marketing plan that targets niches with needs that match their skills, differentiate themselves from the competition by positioning themselves against other candidates, evaluate their potential worth from the employer's perspective, and manage their careers as they move up the career ladder or into another field.

How to Seek a New and Better Job

Consultants Bookstore
Templeton Rd.
Fitzwilliam, NH 03447
Phone: (603)585-6544
Fax: (603)585-9555

Gerraughty, William. 1987. $5.95. 64 pages.

Presents information on cover letters, resumes, and mailings. Includes a self-analysis, fifty-six questions asked by interviewers, and a variety of forms and lists.

I Got the Job!
Crisp Publications, Inc.
95 1st St.
Los Altos, CA 94022

Chapman, Elwood N. 1988. $7.95. 80 pages. Provides case studies and demonstrates how to plan a targeted job search.

There are two types of ads: open (the company identified) and blind. Open ads are great for job-hunters. They give you the opportunity to do some investigation on the firm. Be sure to tailor your cover letter with your knowledge of the company. If you're lucky, you may uncover a contact.

Source: *Business Monday/Detroit Free Press*

Inside Doctoring: Stages and Outcomes in the Professional Development of Physicians
Greenwood Publishing Group, Inc.
88 Post Rd., W., Box 5007
Westport, CT 06881
Phone: (203)226-3571
Toll-free: 800-225-5800

Robert H. Coombs, D. Scott May, and Gary W. Small, editors. 1986. Includes bibliographies and an index.

International Directory for Youth Internships
Council on International and Public Affairs
777 United Nations Plaza
Ste. 9A
New York, NY 10017
Phone: (212)972-9877

Irregular; latest edition spring 1990. $5.75, plus $2.80 shipping. Covers: United Nations agencies and nongovernmental organizations offering intern and volunteer opportunities. Entries include: Agency, organization, or office name, address, description of internship. Arrangement: Classified by type of organization.

Internship and Job Opportunities in New York City and Washington, D.C.
The Graduate Group
86 Norwood Rd.
West Hartford, CT 06117

$27.50.

Internships Leading to Careers
The Graduate Group
86 Norwood Rd.
West Hartford, CT 06117

$27.50. Covers a variety of paid and voluntary internships that can lead to professional opportunities.

Internships: On-the-Job Training Opportunities for All Types of Careers
Peterson's Guides, Inc.
20 Carnegie Center
PO Box 2123
Princeton, NJ 08543-2123
Phone: (609)243-9111
Fax: (609)243-9150

Annual, December. $27.95, plus $3.00 shipping. Covers: 850 corporations, social service organizations, government agencies, recreational facilities (including parks and forests), entertainment industries, and science and research facilities which offer about 50,000 apprenticeships and internships in 23 different career areas. Entries include: Organization name, address, name of contact; description of internship offered, including duties, stipend, length of service; eligibility requirements; deadline for application and application procedures. Arrangement: Classified by subject (arts, communications, business, etc.). Indexes: Subject/organization name, geographical.

Introduction to the Health Professions
Jones and Bartlett Publishers, Inc.
1 Exeter Plaza
Boston, MA 02116
Phone: (617)859-3000
Toll-free: 800-832-0034

Peggy Stanfield. 1990.

Issues in Graduate Nursing Education

National League for Nursing (NLN)
350 Hudson St.
New York, NY 10014
Phone: (212)989-9393
Toll-free: 800-NOW-1NLN

Sylvia E. Hart, editor. 1987. Discusses the growing number of graduates of master and doctoral degrees in nursing, and how they should be utilized.

The Job Bank Series

Bob Adams, Inc.
260 Center St.
Holbrook, MA 02343
Phone: (617)767-8100
Fax: (617)767-0994

$12.95/volume. There are 18 volumes in the Job Bank Series, each covering a different job market. Volumes exist for the following areas: Atlanta, Boston, Chicago, Dallas/Fort Worth, Denver, Detroit, Florida, Houston, Los Angeles, Minneapolis, New York, Ohio, Philadelphia, Phoenix, San Francisco, Seattle, St. Louis, and Washington D.C. Each directory lists employers and provides name, address, telephone number, and contact information. Many entries include common positions, educational backgrounds sought, and fringe benefits provided. Cross-indexed by industry and alphabetically by company name. Profiles of professional associations, a section on the region's economic outlook, and listings of executive search and job placement agencies are included. Features sections on conducting a successful job search campaign and writing resumes and cover letters.

Job and Career Building

Ten Speed Press
PO Box 7123
Berkeley, CA 94707
Phone: (415)845-8414

Germann, Richard, and Arnold, Peter. $7.95. 256 pages.

Job Hunt

AIMS Media Inc.
6901 Woodley Ave.
Van Nuys, CA 91406-4878

Video cassette. Beta, VHS, 3/4' U-matic. 15 minutes. The do's and don'ts of seeking and getting a job.

The Job Hunt

Ten Speed Press
PO Box 7123
Berkeley, CA 94707
Phone: (415)845-8414

Nelson, Robert. $3.95. 64 pages. A compact guide with a direct, question-and-answer format with space for notations.

Jeffrey A. Sonnenfeld, an Emory University management professor, divides US corporations into 4 categories: the Baseball Team—advertising, entertainment, investment banking, software, biotech research, and other industries based on fad, fashion, new technologies, and novelty; the Club—utilities, government agencies, airlines, banks, and other organizations that tend to produce strong generalists; the Academy—manufacturers in electronics, pharmaceuticals, office products, autos, and consumer products; and the Fortress—companies in fields such as publishing, hotels, retailing, textiles, and natural resources.

Source: *Fortune*

The Job Hunter's Final Exam

Surrey Books, Inc.
230 E. Ohio St.
Ste. 120
Chicago, IL 60611
Phone: (312)661-0050

Camden, Thomas. 1990. $10.95. 140 pages. Helps job seeker quiz self about resumes, interviews, and general job-hunting strategies.

Job Hunters Survival Kit

The Guidance Shoppe
2909 Brandemere Dr.
Tallahassee, FL 32312
Phone: (904)385-6717

Includes two interactive software programs: *The Skill Analyzer* and *The Resume Writer*. $149.95. Compatible with Apple II-plus, IIe, IIc; TRS—80 III/4; and IBM.

The Job Hunter's Workbook

Peterson's Career Guides, Inc.
PO Box 2123
Princeton, NJ 08543-2123
Phone: (609)243-9111

Taggart, Judith, Moore, Lynn, and Naylor, Mary. $12.95. 140 pages. Deals with such job-seeking topics as assessing personal strengths, networking, interviewing and answering interview questions, dealing with salaries and benefits, and preparing resumes, cover letters, and portfolios. A combination of self-assessment exercises, work sheets, checklists, and advice.

Job Hunting for Success

Ready Reference Press
PO Box 5249
Santa Monica, CA 90409
Phone: (213)474-5175

Set of three video cassettes. Aimed at the student job hunter. Focuses on the importance of knowing yourself, your interests, aptitudes, and other characteristics. Describes job openings in a variety of areas, including apprenticeship, clerical, on-the-job training, and summer employment. Helps prepare the student for the career planning and job search process.

Job Search: Career Planning Guidebook, Book II

Brooks/Cole Publishing Company
Marketing Dept.
511 Forest Lodge Rd.
Pacific Grove, CA 93950

Lock. 1992. 248 pages. Assists the reader in a production job search.

The Job Search Companion: The Organizer for Job Seekers

The Harvard Common Press
535 Albany St.
Boston, MA 02118
Phone: (617)423-5803

Wallach and Arnold. 1987. $7.95. 160 pages. An organizer with resources and forms to assist in and direct the job search process.

The Job Search Handbook

Bob Adams, Inc.
260 Center St.
Holbrook, MA 02343
Phone: (617)767-8100
Fax: (617)767-0994

Noble, John. $6.95. 144 pages. Identifies and provides advice on the essential elements of the job search, including networking, cover letters, interviewing, and salary negotiation. Aimed at first-time entrants to the job market, those looking for a job in a new field, and middle-level professionals looking to take their next step up.

The Job Search Organizer

Consultants Bookstore
Templeton Rd.
Fitzwilliam, NH 03447
Phone: (603)585-2200
Fax: (603)585-9555

O'Brien, Jack. 1990. $14.95. A combination job search manual/workbook/organizer to help the reader plan and manage the job campaign.

Job Search: The Total System

Consultants Bookstore
Templeton Rd.
Fitzwilliam, NH 03447
Phone: (603)585-6544
Fax: (603)585-9555

Dawson, Kenneth, and Dawson, Sheryl. 1988. $14.95. 244 pages. A guide that shows how to link networking, resume writing, interviewing, references, and follow-up letters to land the job. Thirty resumes are included.

The Job Search Videotape Series

Tucker Associates
10521 Elmenden Ct.
Oakton, VA 22124

Set of three video cassettes. 1986. $129.00/each. $499.00/set. Covers the job search, successful interviewing, and negotiating the job offer.

Job Seeker's Guide to Private and Public Companies

Gale Research Inc.
835 Penobscot Bldg.
Detroit, MI 48226
Phone: (313)961-2242
Fax: (313)961-6241

Annual. Four volumes. $95.00 per volume;

$350.00 per set. Covers over 15,000 employers in all industries. Each volume covers a specific regional area. Entries include: Company name, address, phone, fax; number of employees; company history; description; main products, services, or accounts; parent company; names and titles of key personnel; employee information; job titles; benefits and features of employment; human resources contacts; and application procedures. Arrangement: Geographical by state, then by city. Indexes: Industry, cumulative corporate name index.

Job Seeking

Great Plains National Instructional Television
Library (GPN)
University of Nebraska at Lincoln
PO Box 80669
Lincoln, NE 68501-0669

Video cassette. Beta, VHS, 3/4' U-matic. 1980. 15 minutes. An eight-program career education series for students and adults, dealing with resumes, letters, applications, appearance of a job candidate, and how to handle oneself on an interview.

Jobs Rated Almanac: Ranks the Best and Worst Jobs by More Than a Dozen Vital Criteria

World Almanac
200 Park Ave.
New York, NY 10166
Phone: (212)692-3830

Les Krantz. 1988. Ranks 250 jobs by environment, salary, outlook, physical demands, stress, security, travel opportunities, and geographic location. Includes jobs the editor feels are the most common, most interesting, and the most rapidly growing.

Jobs! What They Are—Where They Are—What They Pay

Simon & Schuster, Inc.
Simon & Schuster Bldg.
1230 Avenue of the Americas
New York, NY 10020
Phone: (212)698-7000
Toll-free: 800-223-2348

Robert O. Snelling and Anne M. Snelling. Third edition, 1992. Describes duties and responsibilities, earnings, employment opportunities, training, and qualifications.

Journeying Outward: A Guide to Career Development

Delmar Publishers, Inc.
2 Computer Dr., W.
PO Box 15015
Albany, NY 12212-5015
Phone: (518)459-1150
Fax: (518)459-3552

Lynton, Jonathan. 1989. 224 pages. Examines the correct way to present oneself in the job search, covering appearance, interviewing, writing a resume, and completing a job application. Resume writing section illustrates models of various resume formats. Includes sections on planning the job search and working the plan.

Normal hiring patterns seem to be holding firmest in the South and the Midsouth, especially in rural communities and at hospitals that are expanding or have no affiliation with a school. Georgia, Texas and Tennessee hospitals are among those searching hardest for nurses.

Source: *American Journal of Nursing*

Just Around the Corner: Jobs and Employment

Cambridge Career Products
723 Kanawha Blvd. E.
Charleston, WV 25301

Videocassette. Beta, VHS, 3/4' U-matic. 30 minutes. The many different aspects of work are explored in this series of eight cassettes. Tips on good and bad job habits are given, how to fill out a job application, and how to act on a job interview are explained. Program titles: 1. Effective Job Behavior I. 2. Effective Job Behavior II. 3. Employment Agencies I. 4. Employment Agencies II. 5. Job Interviews I. 6. Job Interviews II. 7. Equal Employment Opportunity/Discrimination I. 8. Equal Employment Opportunity/Discrimination II.

Joyce Lain Kennedy's Career Book

VGM Career Horizons
4255 West Touhy Ave.
Lincolnwood, IL 60646-1975
Phone: (708)679-5500

Kennedy, Joyce Lain. Co-authored by Dr. Darryl

Laramore. 1992. $17.95 paperback. $29.95 hardcover. 448 pages. Guides the reader through the entire career-planning and job-hunting process. Addresses how to find the kinds of jobs available and what to do once the job is secured. Provides a number of case histories to give examples.

Making It Work

Magna Systems Inc.
W. Countyline 95
Barrington, IL 60010
Phone: (708)382-6477

Video cassette. Beta, VHS, 3/4' U-matic. 1983. 12 minutes. A series of 12 programs which focus on the characteristics that employers consider most important in hiring and keeping employees. Program titles: 1. How Do I Find a Job? 2. Opening Doors. 3. The Application. 4. Tests and Stress. 5. The Interview. 6. Learning by Experience. 7. You Have a Job Offer - Now What? 8. I'm Here to Work - What Now? 9. Say That One More Time. 10. Practical Planning. 11. Making the Most of Yourself. 12. How Am I Doing? Programs in this series are also available individually.

People assume that they get better within their careers over time, that growth is a step-by-step improvement. Studies have shown that growth occurs in episodic movement, often triggered by a small event. People tend to remain at a uniform level until some change propels them toward a new level of performance.

Source: *The Canadian Nurse*

Managing Your Career in Nursing

Addison-Wesley Publishing Co., Inc.
Rte. 128
Reading, MA 01867
Phone: (617)944-3700
Toll-free: 800-447-2226

Frances C. Henderson and Barbara O. McGettigan. 1986. Includes a bibliography and an index.

Martin's Magic Formula for Getting the Right Job

St. Martin's Press
Special Sales Dept.
175 5th Ave.
New York, NY 10010
Phone: (212)674-5151

Martin, Phyllis. 1987. $7.95. 192 pages. A comprehensive approach to the job campaign.

Merchandising Your Job Talents

Superintendent of Documents
U.S. Government Printing Office
Washington, DC 20402

Booklet. 21 pages. General advice for job seekers. Illustrated.

Moonlighting: A Complete Guide to Over 200 Exciting Part-Time Jobs

McGraw-Hill, Inc.
1221 Avenue of the Americas
New York, NY 10020
Phone: (212)512-2000

Davidson, Peter. 1983. 260 pages. Includes index.

Mosby's Tour Guide to Nursing School: A Student's Road Survival Kit

C. V. Mosby Co.
11830 Westline Industrial Dr.
St. Louis, MO 63146
Phone: (314)872-8370
Toll-free: 800-325-4177

Melodie Chenevert. 1991.

National Commission on Nursing Implementation Project: Models for the Future of Nursing

National League for Nursing (NLN)
350 Hudson St.
New York, NY 10014
Phone: (212)989-9393
Toll-free: 800-NOW-1NLN

1988.

National Directory of Internships

National Society for Internships and
Experiential Education
3509 Haworth Dr.
Ste. 207
Raleigh, NC 27609
Phone: (919)787-3263

Biennial, fall of odd years. $22.00, plus $2.50
shipping. Covers: Over 30,000 educational
internship opportunities in 75 fields with over
2,650 organizations in the United States for
youth and adults. Entries include: Organization
name, address, phone, contact name, description of internship opportunities, including application procedures and deadlines, remuneration,
and eligibility requirements. Arrangement:
Classified by type of organization. Indexes:
Geographical, organization name, career field.

Network Your Way to Job and Career Success

Consultants Bookstore
Templeton Rd.
Fitzwilliam, NH 03447
Phone: (603)585-6544
Fax: (603)585-9555

Krannich, Ron and Krannich, Caryl. 1989.
$11.95. 180 pages. Based on a comprehensive
career planning framework, each chapter outlines the best strategies for identifying, finding,
and transforming networks to gather information and obtain advice and referrals that lead to
job interviews and offers. Includes exercises,
sample interviewing dialogues, and a directory
of organizations for initiating and sustaining networking activities.

New Careers in Hospitals

Rosen Publishing Group, Inc.
29 E. 21st St.
New York, NY 10010
Phone: (212)777-3017
Toll-free: 800-237-9932
Fax: (212)777-0277

Siegel, Lois S. Revised edition. 1990. $13.95 per
volume; $125.55 per set. Part of a 9 volume set
that describes a variety of hospital positions,
including careers in public relations. Covers
background, professional preparation, functions,
salary, and job outlook.

New Careers in Nursing

Prentice Hall General Reference Travel
15 Columbus Circle
New York, NY 10023
Phone: (212)373-8368
Fax: 800-223-2348

Florence Downs and Dorothy Brooten. 1983.

The New Quick Job-Hunting Map

Ten Speed Press
PO Box 7123
Berkeley, CA 94707
Phone: (415)845-8414

Bolles, Richard N. $3.95. 64 pages. Trade ver-
sion of *The Quick Job-Hunting Map* in *What
Color Is Your Parachute?* Provides a personal
blueprint for the job search.

> **T**echniques for winning people over to your team when you're new on the job and change is in your pro-gram: make sure those who work for you see your vision as clearly as you do; listen to your critics—if you respect their work, they probably have good advice; make it clear that you're not on a power trip—be honest and don't promise what you can't deliver; get people involved in dif-ferent aspects of the business so they know how every-thing works.
>
> Source: *Working Woman*

Nurse-Midwife

Vocational Biographies, Inc.
PO Box 31
Sauk Centre, MN 56378-0031
Phone: (612)352-6516
Toll-free: 800-255-0752
Fax: (612)352-5546

1988. $2.00. Four-page pamphlet containing a
personal narrative about a worker's job, work
likes and dislikes, career path from high school
to the present, education and training, the
rewards and frustrations, and the effects of the
job on the rest of the worker's life. The data file
portion of this pamphlet gives a concise occupational summary, including work description,
working conditions, places of employment, personal characteristics, education and training, job
outlook, and salary range.

Nurse Oncologist

Vocational Biographies, Inc.
PO Box 31
Sauk Centre, MN 56378-0031
Phone: (612)352-6516
Toll-free: 800-255-0752
Fax: (612)352-5546

1988. $2.00. Four-page pamphlet containing a personal narrative about a worker's job, work likes and dislikes, career path from high school to the present, education and training, the rewards and frustrations, and the effects of the job on the rest of the worker's life. The data file portion of this pamphlet gives a concise occupational summary, including work description, working conditions, places of employment, personal characteristics, education and training, job outlook, and salary range.

Nurse Power: New Vistas in Nursing

Dutton Child Books
375 Hudson St.
New York, NY 10014-3657
Phone: (212)366-2000

Diane Seide. 1986. Describes qualifications and education needed, specialty areas, career ladders, unionization, and trends in nursing. Gives advice on getting the first job.

Nurse, Registered

Careers, Inc.
PO Box 135
Largo, FL 34649-0135
Phone: (813)584-7333
Toll-free: 800-726-0441

1988. Eight-page brief offering the definition, history, duties, working conditions, personal qualifications, educational requirements, earnings, hours, employment outlook, advancement, and careers related to this position.

Nurse's Aide

Vocational Biographies, Inc.
PO Box 31, Dept. VF10
Sauk Centre, MN 56378
Phone: (612)352-6516
Toll-free: 800-255-0752
Fax: (612)352-5546

1988. $2.00. This pamphlet profiles a person working in the job. Includes information about job duties, working conditions, places of employ-ment, educational preparation, labor market outlook, and salaries.

Nurses, Registered Professional

Chronicle Guidance Publications, Inc.
66 Aurora St. Extension
PO Box 1190
Moravia, NY 13118-1190
Phone: (315)497-0330
Toll-free: 800-622-7284

1991. Career brief describing the nature of the job, working conditions, hours and earnings, education and training, licensure, certification, unions, personal qualifications, social and psychological factors, location, employment outlook, entry methods, advancement, and related occupations.

Nursing Assistants

Chronicle Guidance Publications, Inc.
PO Box 1190
Moravia, NY 13118-1190
Phone: (315)497-0330
Toll-free: 800-622-7284

1987. This career brief describes the nature of the work, working conditions, hours and earnings, education and training, licensure, certification, unions, personal qualifications, social and psychological factors, employment outlook, entry methods, advancement, and related occupations.

Nursing Assistants & the Long-Term Health Care Facility

J. B. Lippincott Co.
227 E. Washington Sq.
Philadelphia, PA 19106-3780
Phone: (215)238-4200
Toll-free: 800-441-4526

Lorna Hanebuth. 1977.

The Nursing Experience: Trends, Challenges, and Transitions

McGraw-Hill, Inc.
1221 Avenue of the Americas
New York, NY 10020
Phone: (212)512-2000
Toll-free: 800-722-4726

Lucie Y. Kelly. Edited by Madeline R. Turkeltaub. 1987. Includes a bibliography and an index.

Nursing: From Education to Practice

Appleton and Lange
PO Box 5630
Norwalk, CT 06856
Phone: (203)838-4400
Toll-free: 800-423-1359

Helen Frishe Hodges, et al. 1988. Practical guide designed to help nursing students and registered nurses reentering the workforce make the transition to a clinical setting. Covers diagnostic related groups, ethics, and professional liability. Gives tips on time management, conflict management, and evaluating employers.

Nursing Home Salary and Benefits Report

Hospital Compensation Service
John R. Zabka Associates, Inc.
69 Minnehaha Blvd.
PO Box 376
Oakland, NJ 07436
Phone: (201)405-0075

Annual. Gives salaries and fringe benefits for registered and licensed practical nurses. Lists salaries by the annual gross revenue of the nursing home, bed size, and profit and nonprofit status.

The One Day Plan for Jobhunters

Prakken Publications, Inc.
PO Box 8623
416 Longshore Dr.
Ann Arbor, MI 48107

Segalini and Kurtz. 1988. $9.95. 100 pages.

Online Hotline News Service

Information Intelligence, Inc.
PO Box 31098
Phoenix, AZ 85046
Phone: (602)996-2283

Online database containing five files, one of which is Joblines, which features listings of employment and resume services available in voice, print, and online throughout North America. Joblines focuses on the online, library automation, and information-related fields.

The Only Job Hunting Guide You'll Ever Need

Poseidon Press
Simon and Schuster Bldg.
1230 Avenue of the Americas
New York, NY 10020
Phone: (212)698-7290

Petras, Kathryn, and Petras, Ross. 1989. $10.95. 318 pages. Covers the full range of the job search process.

Only You Can Decide: The First Key to Career Planning and Job Hunting

McGraw Hill Book Company
Continuing Education Program
1221 Avenue of the Americas
New York, NY 10020
Phone: (212)997-6572

Video cassette. 3/4' U-matic. 28 minutes. Part of a ten-part series entitled *The Career Development Video Series*, which offers a step-by-step approach to finding a job and planning a career.

Average teachers' salaries rose only 3.6 percent during the 1991-92 school year, their smallest increase in 27 years, according to the American Federation of Teachers. Physical therapists, pharmacists and nurses, by contrast, enjoyed raises of up to 7.3 percent.

Source: *U.S. News & World Report*

Operating Room Laser Nurse

Vocational Biographies, Inc.
PO Box 31
Sauk Centre, MN 56378-0031
Phone: (612)352-6516
Toll-free: 800-255-0752
Fax: (612)352-5546

1987. Four-page pamphlet containing a personal narrative about a worker's job, work likes and dislikes, career path from high school to the present, education and training, the rewards and frustrations, and the effects of the job on the rest of the worker's life. The data file portion of this pamphlet gives a concise occupational summary, including work description, working conditions, places of employment, personal characteristics, education and training, job outlook, and salary range.

Opportunities in Fitness Careers

National Textbook Co.
4255 W. Touhy Ave.
Lincolnwood, IL 60646
Phone: (312)679-5500
Toll-free: 800-323-4900

Jean Rosenbaum. 1991. Surveys fitness related careers, including the career of physician. Describes career opportunities, education and experience needed, how to get into entry-level jobs and what income to expect. Schools are listed in the appendix.

Interview proactively. Make a list of questions you'd like answered. Target the company's current and future plans, the job and where it could lead. You'll have the chance to ask most of them if you tie them into the answers you give on similar topics.

Source: *Business Monday/Detroit Free Press*

Opportunities in Nursing Careers

VGM Career Horizons
4255 W. Touhy Ave.
Lincolnwood, IL 60646
Phone: (312)679-5500

Keville Frederickson. 1984.

Osteopathic Physician

Careers, Inc.
PO Box 135
Largo, FL 34649-0135
Phone: (813)584-7333
Toll-free: 800-726-0441

1990. Eight-page brief offering the definition, history, duties, working conditions, personal qualifications, educational requirements, earnings, hours, employment outlook, advancement, and careers related to this position.

Out of Work But Not Alone

Self-Help Clearinghouse
Publications Dept.
St. Clares - Riverside Medical Center
Pocono Rd.
Denville, NJ 07834
Phone: (201)625-9565

1984. $9.00.

The Overnight Job Change Strategy

Ten Speed Press
PO Box 7123
Berkeley, CA 94707
Phone: (415)845-8414

Asher, Donald. 1993. Subtitled *How to Plan a Comprehensive, Systematic Job Search in One Evening.* Incorporates sales and marketing techniques into a six-stage job search process.

PA Fact Sheet. The Physician Assistant Profession

American Academy of Physician Assistants
950 N. Washington St.
Alexandria, VA 22314-1534
Phone: (703)836-2272

1991. This sheet describes what a physician assistant does, training and education required, prerequisites for entering a training program, certification, specialties, salaries, and the future of the profession.

Part-Time Professional

Acropolis Books
2400 17th St., NW
Washington, DC 20009
Phone: (202)387-6805

Rothberg, Diane S., and Cook, Barbara Ensor. 1985. 158 pages. Includes index.

The Perfect Job Reference

Consultants Bookstore
Templeton Rd.
Fitzwilliam, NH 03447
Phone: (603)585-2200
Fax: (603)585-9555

Allen, Jeffrey, G. 1990. $9.95. Step-by-step methods for securing a written or verbal recommendation.

Peterson's Career Planning Service

Peterson's
PO Box 2123
Princeton, NJ 08543-2123
Phone: (609)243-9111

Diskette database that contains information on occupations, related jobs, and training requirements. Software is designed to assist users in making career decisions. Users complete personal assessment exercises in such areas as general, academic, and work-related interests; general abilities and aptitudes; values; work environment preferences; data, people, and thing preferences. Based on the exercises, the system provides information on suggested careers.

Physician Assistant

Careers, Inc.
PO Box 135
Largo, FL 34649-0135
Phone: (813)584-7333
Toll-free: 800-726-0441

1992. Two-page occupational summary card describing duties, working conditions, personal qualifications, training, earnings and hours, employment outlook, places of employment, related careers, and where to write for more information.

The Physician Assistant in a Changing Health Care Environment

Aspen Publishers, Inc.
200 Orchard Ridge Dr., Ste. 200
Gaithersburg, MD 20878
Phone: (301)417-7500
Toll-free: 800-638-8437

Gretchen Engle Schafft, and James F. Cawley. 1987. Covers the development of the physician assistant profession and the profession's place in the current health care environment.

The Physician Assistant Up Close

Pennsylvania Society of Physician Assistants
PO Box 8988
Pittsburgh, PA 15221-8988
Phone: (412)371-2205

1989. Eight-panel brochure explaining education, credentials, and roles of physician assistants.

Physician Assistants

Chronicle Guidance Publications, Inc.
Aurora St. Extension
PO Box 1190
Moravia, NY 13118-1190
Phone: (315)497-0330
Toll-free: 800-622-7284

1988. Career brief describing the nature of the job, working conditions, hours and earnings, education and training, licensure, certification, unions, personal qualifications, social and psy-

chological factors, location, employment outlook, entry methods, advancement, and related occupations.

Physician Power: New Vistas for Women in Medicine

Dutton Children's Books
375 Hudson St.
New York, NY 10014-3657
Phone: (212)366-2000

Diane Seide. 1989. Interviews three women physicians and includes information on early preparation, education and scholarships.

Physicians (Medical and Osteopathic)

Chronicle Guidance Publications, Inc.
Aurora St. Extension
PO Box 1190
Moravia, NY 13118-1190
Phone: (315)497-0330
Toll-free: 800-622-7284

1987. Career brief describing the nature of the job, working conditions, hours and earnings, education and training, licensure, certification, unions, personal qualifications, social and psychological factors, location, employment outlook, entry methods, advancement, and related occupations.

Podiatric Medicine: The Profession, the Practice

American Podiatric Medical Association
9312 Old Georgetown Rd.
Bethesda, MD 20814-1621
Phone: (301)571-9200
Fax: (301)530-2752

1991. This eight-page booklet outlines preprofessional, professional, postdoctoral and continuing education for podiatrists; describes the profession, and discusses practice in hospitals, public health, and federal service. Lists colleges of podiatric medicine and organizations for the profession.

Podiatrist

Careers, Inc.
PO Box 135
Largo, FL 34649-0135
Phone: (813)584-7333
Toll-free: 800-726-0441

1990. Two-page occupational summary card

describing duties, working conditions, personal qualifications, training, earnings and hours, employment outlook, places of employment, related careers, and where to write for more information.

Podiatrists

Chronicle Guidance Publications, Inc.
Aurora St. Extension
PO Box 1190
Moravia, NY 13118-1190
Phone: (315)497-0330
Toll-free: 800-622-7284

1989. Career brief describing the nature of the job, working conditions, hours and earnings, education and training, licensure, certification, unions, personal qualifications, social and psychological factors, location, employment outlook, entry methods, advancement, and related occupations.

A ccording to the Bureau of Labor Statistics, the rapid growth of women entering the workforce—about 2.3% per year from 1975 to 1990—is expected to slow, growing at a rate of 1.6% per year in the next fifteen years. By 2005, minorities are expected to account for more than 25% of all working people in the US, with the fastest growth occurring among Hispanics, who will make up over 11% of the workforce by 2005.

Source: *Forbes*

Preparing for the Future: Questions and Answers About Trends in Nursing Education

American Nurses' Association (ANA)
2420 Pershing Rd.
Kansas City, MO 64108
Phone: (816)474-5720
Fax: (202)554-4444

1985. This eight-page booklet gives an overview of the profession's future, anticipated effect of trends on health care work, how these are being reflected in health care job market, and ANA's position on their four-year degree as a requirement for future licensing of professional nurses.

Professional's Job Finder

Planning/Communications
7215 Oak Ave.
River Forest, IL 60305-1935
Phone: (708)366-5297

$15.95. Discusses how to use sources of private sector job vacancies in a number of specialties and state-by-state, including job-matching services, job hotlines, specialty periodicals with job ads, salary surveys, and directories. Covers a variety of fields from health care to sales. Includes chapters on resume and cover letter preparation and interviewing.

Profiles of the Newly Licensed Nurse

National League for Nursing (NLN)
350 Hudson St.
New York, NY 10014
Phone: (212)989-9393
Toll-free: 800-NOW-1NLN

Peri Rosenfeld. 1989. This book is based on a survey of over 38,000 recently licensed registered nurses, describing their background, professional activities, compensation, and likes and dislikes. Also gives data such as age, region, program type, length of time it took to find a job, and salaries.

Psychiatric Aide

Careers, Inc.
PO Box 135
Largo, FL 34649-0135
Phone: (813)584-7333

1988. Two-page job guide card describing duties, working conditions, personal qualifications, training, earnings and hours, employment outlook, places of employment, related careers and where to write for more information.

Psychiatric Aides and Technicians

Chronicle Guidance Publications, Inc.
PO Box 1190
Moravia, NY 13118-1190
Phone: (315)497-0330
Toll-free: 800-622-7284

1988. This career brief describes the nature of the work, working conditions, hours and earnings, education and training, licensure, certification, unions, personal qualifications, social and psychological factors, employment outlook, entry methods, advancement, and related occupations.

Q: How Do I Find the Right Job? A: Ask the Experts.
Consultants Bookstore
Templeton Rd.
Fitzwilliam, NH 03447
Phone: (603)585-2200
Fax: (603)585-9555

Bowman, David, and Kweskin, Ronald. 1990. $10.95. Based on interviews with human resource directors at Fortune 500 companies.

Q: What Kind of a Nurse Would Work in a Nursing Home?
American Health Care Association
1201 L St., NW
Washington, DC 20005-4014
Phone: (202)842-4444
Toll-free: 800-321-0343

1987. This six-panel pamphlet describes the work of a nurse in a nursing home.

Rejection Shock
McGraw Hill Book Co.
Continuing Education Program
1221 Avenue of the Americas
New York, NY 10020
Phone: (212)997-6572

Video cassette. 3/4' U-matic. 28 minutes. Part of a 10-part series entitled *The Career Development Video Series*, which offers a step-by-step approach to finding a job and planning a career. Provides viewers with ways to handle frustration, anxiety, and despair in job hunting.

Resume Writing for the Professional Nurse
Continuing Education Systems, Inc.
112 S. Grant St.
Hinsdale, IL 60521
Phone: (312)654-2596

Nancy Kuzmich. 1988. Self-study guide written for the professional nurse on how to set career goals, interview for a job, and select the best job offer. Includes sample resumes and cover letters.

The Right Place at the Right Time
Ten Speed Press
PO Box 7123
Berkeley, CA 94707
Phone: (415)845-8414

Wegmann, Robert G. $11.95. 192 pages. A comprehensive approach to career planning and job seeking developed to find the right job in the new economy.

The Role of the Clinical Nurse Specialist
American Nurses' Association
2420 Pershing Rd.
Kansas City, MO 64108
Phone: (816)474-5720

1986.

> **P**athologists fare best in the Southeast, where a relative scarcity of managed health care programs such as health maintenance organizations means doctors are freer to set their fees. In the Northeast, where companies have embraced managed care, participating doctors typically are limited in what they can charge.
>
> Source: *U.S. News & World Report*

San Francisco Bay Area and Silicon Valley Internship Directory
University Resources Services
PO Box 3722
Stanford, CA 94309

1989. $45.00. Lists hundreds of internship opportunities in binder format to allow for adding updated information as it becomes available.

Secrets of the Hidden Job Market
Betterway Publications, Inc.
White Hall, VA 22987
Phone: (804)823-5661

Rodgers, Bob; Johnson, Steve; and Alexander, Bill. 1986.

The Self-Directed Job Search
Cambridge Career Products
723 Kanawha Blvd. E.
Charleston, WV 25301

Video cassette. Beta, VHS. 1986. 90 minutes. An

instructional tape on searching out and acquiring job positions.

The Self-Help Bridge to Employment

Employment Support Center (ESC)
900 Massachusetts Ave. NW
Ste. 444
Washington, DC 20001
Phone: (202)783-4747

Manual.

Selecting a boss who is a good match for your work style can be critical to your job success. The mismatched, or wrong boss, can make your work life miserable, as well as significantly damage your career.

Source: *The Detroit News*

Skills in Action: A Job-Finding Workbook

University of Akron
Adult Resource Center
Akron, OH 44325

Selden, J.H. $5.50. 75 pages. Workbook format; aimed at job seekers looking for initial or transitional employment.

Strategic Career Planning and Development for Nurses

Aspen Publishers, Inc.
200 Orchard Ridge Dr., Ste. 200
Gaithersburg, MD 20878
Phone: (301)417-7500
Toll-free: 800-638-8437

Russell C. Swansburg and Phillip W. Swansburg. 1984. Includes a bibliography and an index.

Strategic Job Search

Creative Alliance
108 Ross Creek Ct.
Los Gatos, CA 95032

Two video cassettes. Gordon, John. 25 minutes each. Video 1 covers the development of job leads through a variety of sources such as networks, placement services, publications; video 2 covers the interviewing process.

The Student's Guide to Finding a Superior Job

Slawson Communications
165 Vallecitos de Oro
San Marcos, CA 92069

Cohen, William A. 1987. $9.95. Aimed at the new college graduate.

The Successful Job Hunter

American Media Inc.
1454 30th St.
West Des Moines, IA 50265
Phone: (515)224-0919

Video cassette. Beta, VHS, 3/4' U-matic. 1984. 30 minutes. Series of 4 programs which serves as the complete job placement program for placement upon termination and initial job hunting. Combines job counseling and personal marketing techniques. Program titles: 1. Introduction - Developing Your Image. 2. Coordinating a Promotional Package. 3. Generating Multiple Contacts. 4. Interviewing and Negotiating.

The Successful Job Hunter's Handbook

Johnson/Rudolph Educational Resources, Inc.
1004 State St.
Bowling Green, KY 42101

1987. $12.95. 150 pages.

Suggestions for Career Exploration and Jobseeking

New York State Department of Labor
Division of Research and Statistics
NY-SOICC
Rm. 488, Bldg. 12, State Office Bldg.
Campus
Albany, NY 12240
Phone: (518)457-3800

Brochure. 1989. Free. Prepared for New York State labor market. Includes roster of state Job Service offices. English/Spanish version available.

Super Job Search: The Complete Manual for Job-Seekers and Career-Changers

Jamenair Ltd.
PO Box 241957
Los Angeles, CA 90024
Phone: (213)470-6688

Studner, Peter. $22.95. 352 pages. A step-by-step

guidebook for getting a job, with sections on getting started, how to present accomplishments, networking strategies, telemarketing tips, and negotiating tactics.

The Temp Worker's Handbook: How to Make Temporary Employment Work for You

AMACOM
135 W. 50th St.
New York, NY 10020
Phone: (212)903-8087

Lewis, William, and Schuman, Nancy. 1988. Discusses the advantages and disadvantages of temporary work, where the jobs are, and how to work with a temporary employment agency. Lists members of the National Association of Temporary Services and the National Association of Personnel Consultants who place temporary workers.

U.S. Employment Opportunities: A Career News Service

Washington Research Associates
7500 E. Arapaho Plaza
Ste. 250
Englewood, CO 80112
Phone: (303)756-9038
Fax: (303)770-1945

Annual; quarterly updates. $184.00. List of over 1,000 employment contacts in companies and agencies in the banking, arts, telecommunications, education, and 14 other industries and professions, including the federal government. Entries include: Company name, name of representative, address, description of products or services, hiring and recruiting practices, training programs, and year established. Classified by industry. Indexes: Occupation.

What Color Is Your Parachute?

Ten Speed Press
PO Box 7123
Berkeley, CA 94707
Phone: (415)845-8414

Bolles, Richard N. 1993. $12.95 paperback. $18.95 hardcover. Subtitled: *A Practical Manual for Job-Hunters and Career-Changers.* Provides detailed and strategic advice on all aspects of the job search.

What Everyone Should Know About Osteopathic Physicians

Channing L. Bete Co., Inc.
200 State Rd.
South Deerfield, MA 01373
Phone: (413)665-7611

1987. Booklet describing osteopathic physicians, their views about health care, where they work, and their education and training.

What Is a D.O.? What Is an M.D.?

American Osteopathic Assocation
142 E. Ontario St.
Chicago, IL 60611
Phone: (312)280-5800

1991. This six-panel brochure compares and contrasts medical doctors and osteopathic physicians.

> A powerful combination of workers who equip themselves to be competitive and employers who provide them with challenging jobs can help businesses stay on top. But to mesh these elements managers must give employees a voice in their jobs and enable workers to develop new skills throughout their careers. Workers must get as much schooling as possible, demand broader duties on the job, and take on more responsibility for the company's success.
>
> Source: *Business Week*

When Can You Start? How to Get the Interview, How to Get the Job

John Wiley and Sons
General Books Division
605 3rd Ave.
New York, NY 10158

Audio cassette. Artise, John. 1986. $8.95.

Where Do I Go from Here with My Life?

Ten Speed Press
PO Box 7123
Berkeley, CA 94707
Phone: (415)845-8414

Crystal, John C. and Bolles, Richard N. $11.95. 272 pages. A planning manual for students of all ages, instructors, counselors, career seekers, and career changers.

Where the Jobs Are

Magna Systems Inc.
W. Countyline 95
Barrington, IL 60010
Phone: (708)382-6477

Video cassette. Beta, VHS, 3/4' U-matic. 1982. 30 minutes. A half-hour 'talk show' for college students who are concerned with making career decisions and with gaining employment upon graduation. Program titles: 1. The Value of an MBA. 2. Preparing for the Interview. 3. The Job Outlook for Technical Graduates. 4. How to Size Up the Interviewer. 5. Making Liberal Arts a Plus. 6. Setting Career Goals.

"**M**edicine is changing faster than ever and changing in more significant ways," says Lowell S. Levin, Ed.D., professor of public health at Yale University School of Medicine. Dr. Levin points not only to the millions of pages of research published in medical journals each year, but also to recent breakthroughs in fields such as genetics that are changing some of our basic notions about health.

Source: *Glamour*

Where the Jobs Are: A Comprehensive Directory of 1200 Journals Listing Career Opportunities

Garrett Park Press
PO Box 190
Garrett Park, MD 20896
Phone: (301)946-2553

1989. $15.00; $14.00, prepaid. Contains list of approximately 1,200 journals that publish advertisements announcing job opportunities. Arranged alphabetically. Indexes: Occupational field.

Where the Jobs Are: The Hottest Careers for the '90s

The Career Press, Inc.
180 5th Ave.
PO Box 34
Hawthorne, NJ 07507

Satterfield, Mark. 1992. $9.95. Provides a look at current trends in the job market and the industries that offer the greatest opportunity for those entering the work force or making a career change. Contains advice on career pathing opportunities and breaking into the field.

Where to Start Career Planning

Peterson's
PO Box 2123
Princeton, NJ 08543-2123
Phone: (609)243-9111

Lindquist, Carolyn Lloyd and Miller, Diane June. 1991. $17.95. 315 pages. Lists and describes the career-planning publications used by Cornell University's Career Center, one of the largest career libraries in the country. Covers more than 2,000 books, periodicals, and audiovisual resources on topics such as financial aid, minority and foreign students, overseas employment and travel, resources for the disabled, second careers, study-and-work options, summer and short-term jobs, women's issues, and careers for those without a bachelor's degree. Includes a bibliographic title index.

Who's Hiring Who

Ten Speed Press
PO Box 7123
Berkeley, CA 94707
Phone: (415)845-8414

Lathrop, Richard. $9.95. 268 pages. Provides advice on finding a better job faster and at a higher rate of pay.

Winning at Job Hunting

Consultants Bookstore
Templeton Rd.
Fitzwilliam, NH 03447
Phone: (603)585-2200
Fax: (603)585-9555

Video cassette. Schnapper, Mel. $59.95. Combines with a workbook approach to help the reader make the connection between accomplishments and employer needs. Demonstrates how to sell accomplishments in the interview.

Work in the New Economy: Careers and Job Seeking into the 21st Century

The New Careers Center
1515 23rd St.
Box 297-CT
Boulder, CO 80306

1989. $15.95.

Work and You Series

Barr Films
3490 E. Foothill Blvd.
PO Box 5667
Pasadena, CA 91107
Phone: (213)681-2165

Video cassette. Beta, VHS, 3/4' U-matic. 14 minutes. This six-part series helps the job seeker confront common problems and situations. Programs are available individually. Program titles: 1. What Is Business? 2. The Work Prejudice Film. 3. Work and You. 4. I Want to Work for Your Company. 5. The Interview Film. 6. Your New Job.

Work Your Way Around the World

Peterson's Guides, Inc.
20 Carnegie Center
PO Box 2123
Princeton, NJ 08543-2123

Biennial, February of odd years. $17.95. Covers: Temporary employment opportunities worldwide. Entries include: Name and address of employer, description of position. Arrangement: Geographical.

A Working Solution

Walter J. Klein Company, Ltd.
Box 2087
6311 Carmel Rd.
Charlotte, NC 28247

Filmstrip. 1988. $290.000. (Video cassette - $217.50.) 15 minutes. Addresses how to obtain temporary and part-time work.

Worldwide Jobs

Peterson's
PO Box 2123
Princeton, NJ 08543-2123
Phone: (609)243-9111

1993. $19.95. Profiles international companies offering opportunities in a variety of areas. Describes hiring practices, qualifications, and training, internship, and summer employment opportunities. Provides key contacts.

Your Career in Nursing

National League for Nursing (NLN)
350 Hudson St.
New York, NY 10014
Phone: (212)989-9393
Toll-free: 800-NOW-1NLN

Lila Anastas. Second edition, 1988. Describes types of nursing schools, salaries, specialties, opportunities, issues, and trends. Includes statistical information on nursing practice and education, graduate nursing, continuing education, and career mobility.

Your Podiatrist Talks About Podiatric Medicine

American Podiatric Medical Association (APMA)
9312 Old Georgetown Rd.
Bethesda, MD 20814-1621
Phone: (301)571-9200

1991. This pamphlet describes career opportunities, educational preparation, and financial aid for potential podiatrists. Lists accredited colleges of podiatric medicine.

You . . . The Doctor: Challenges and Opportunities in the Medical Profession

American Medical Association
515 N. State St.
Chicago, IL 60610
Phone: (312)464-5000
Toll-free: 800-621-8335

1987. This 35-page booklet describes the practice of medicine, high school and college educational preparation, applying to medical school, cost, financing a medical education, and getting an M.D. license. An appendix lists medical schools.

Professional and Trade Periodicals

AACN's Clinical Issues in Critical Care Nursing

J.B. Lippincott Co., Periodicals Div.
227 E. Washington Sq.
Philadelphia, PA 19106-3780
Phone: (215)238-4200

Quarterly. An official publication of the American Association of Critical Care Nurses (AACN).

ACEP News

American College of Emergency Physicians
(ACEP)
PO Box 619911
Dallas, TX 75261-9911
Phone: (214)550-0911
Fax: (214)580-2816

Editor(s): Earl Schwartz, M.D. Monthly. Informs emergency physicians of socioeconomic issues affecting the specialty of emergency medicine. Contains information on medical practice management, pertinent federal and state legislation, and College activities and services.

AHANews (AHA)

American Hospital Association (AHA)
840 N. Lake Shore Dr.
Chicago, IL 60611
Phone: (312)280-6000
Toll-free: 800-242-2626

Weekly.

Students with the luxury of a couple of years until graduation should start plotting for that first job and snagging some experience *now*. But with many employers reluctant to pay even the modest salary of an internship, getting actual business experience is increasingly difficult. One strategy: Try a so-called externship, typically a one-week, unpaid stint at a company that provides a snapshot of various careers and a chance to network with insiders. Externships can be particularly useful for liberal-arts majors without a clear career track.

Source: *U.S. News and World Report*

American Academy of Podiatry Administration—Newsletter

American Academy of Podiatry
Administration
2737 E. Oakland Park Blvd.
Fort Lauderdale, FL 33306
Phone: (305)561-3338

Steven E. Tager, D.P.M., editor. Quarterly. Supplies management information for Academy members. Covers such subjects as investments, advertising and marketing, and tax planning.

American Association of Senior Physicians—Newsletter

American Association of Senior Physicians
(AASP)
515 N. State St., 14th Fl.
Chicago, IL 60610
Phone: (312)464-2460

Editor(s): Gerald L. Farley. Bimonthly. Focuses on successful retirement for physicians. Supplies information on finances, social security, taxes, residence relocation, closing a medical practice, travel opportunities, estate considerations, and related subjects.

American Journal of Medicine

Cahners Publishing Co.
249 W. 17th St.
New York, NY 10011
Phone: (212)463-6463
Fax: (212)463-6470

Claude Bennett, M.D., editor. Monthly. $66/year.

American Journal of Nursing

American Journal of Nursing Co.
555 W. 57th
New York, NY 10019
Phone: (212)582-8820
Fax: (212)586-5462

Mary Mallison, R.N., editor. Monthly. Journal for staff nurses, nurse managers, and clinical nurse specialists. Focuses on patient care in hospitals, hospital ICUs and homes. Provides news coverage of health care from the nursing perspective.

American Medical News

American Medical Association
515 N. State St.
Chicago, IL 60610
Phone: (312)464-4440
Fax: (312)464-4814

Robert L. Kennett, publisher. 48x/year. $45/year.

The American Nurse

American Nurses Assn.
600 Maryland Ave., Sw, Ste. 100, W.
Washington, DC 20024-2571
Phone: (202)544-4444
Fax: (202)554-2262

Patricia McCarty, editor. Ten issues/year. Newspaper for the nursing profession.

American Organization of Nurse Executives—Newsletter

American Organization of Nurse Executives
AHA Bldg.
840 N. Lake Shore Dr.
Chicago, IL 60611
Phone: (312)280-5213

Editor(s): Debra Stock. Monthly. Discusses all aspects of improving the management and administration of nursing service in health care institutions. Disseminates information on administrative problems and profiles successful operations.

American Society of Ophthalmic Registered Nurses—Insight

American Society of Ophthalmic Registered Nurses
PO Box 3030
San Francisco, CA 94119
Phone: (415)561-8513

Bimonthly. Designed to facilitate continuing education of registered nurses through the study, discussion, and exchange of knowledge, experience, and ideas in the field of ophthalmology. Features news of research and innovations in the field.

APMA News

American Podiatric Medical Association (APMA)
9312 Old Georgetown Rd.
Bethesda, MD 20814-1621
Phone: (301)571-9200
Fax: (301)530-2752

David Zych, editor. Monthly. Covers news of the association as well as reporting on bylaws and on regulations that affect the profession.

Association of Schools—Trends

1101 Connecticut Ave., NW, Ste. 700
Washington, DC 20036
Phone: (202)857-1150
Toll-free: 800-879-2724
Fax: (202)223-4579

Editor(s): Thomas W. Elwood. Monthly. Discusses the educational programs, grants and funding, and employment opportunities available to those employed in allied health professions. Examines the achievements of allied health professionals as well as the effects and implications of their work.

Breathline

American Society of Post Anesthesia Nurses
11512 Allecingie Pkwy.
Richmond, VA 23235
Phone: (804)379-5516
Fax: (804)379-1386

Editor(s): Nancy Burden, R.N. Bimonthly. Publishes news of the Society, which is "an organization of licensed nurses engaged in the practice of post anesthesia patient care." Carries legislative updates, scientific articles, and state component society information. Discusses patient care standards, new drugs and treatments, and clinical issues relating to anesthesia and surgery. Recurring features include a calendar of events and columns titled Comment, Profiles, Keeping Up, Resource Review, President's Message, and Other PACU's.

Clinical Laser Monthly

American Health Consultants, Inc.
3525 Piedmont Rd., NE
Bldg. 6, No. 400
Atlanta, GA 30305
Phone: (404)262-7436

Editor(s): Steve Frandzel. Monthly. Concerned with topics related to lasers in surgery and medicine in general. Considers safety, legal issues, reimbursement, cost containment, and new products and procedures. Recurring features include news of research and conferences, a calendar of events, guest columns, and laser practice reports.

Cooperative Connection

Nurse Healers-Professional Associates, Inc.
85 Hawthorne Rd.
Williamstown, MA 01267
Phone: (413)458-9181

Editor(s): Susan Wright. Quarterly. Discusses holistic treatment, healing techniques, and other health issues. Promotes the sharing of healing experiences among health practitioners.

Corhealth

American Correctional Health Services
Association
11 W. Monument Ave., Ste. 510
PO Box 2307
Dayton, OH 45401
Phone: (513)223-9630
Fax: (513)223-6307

Editor(s): Rebecca Craig and Janis James.

Bimonthly. "Dedicated to improving correctional health services." Covers news of the association and its chapters and affiliates, who administer and monitor efficiency of health care in correctional institutions. Concerned with the multidisciplinary approach to nursing, dentistry, medicine, surgery, and medical administration. Recurring features include editorials, news of members, statistics, publications available, calls for papers, abstracts, book reviews, and a calendar of events.

Nothing can be more frustrating than getting typecast at work. You can get typecast in a certain job or image. Then, when you're ready to move up or into a different area of expertise, you can't get anyone to see you in a different way . . . . One technique to change your image is to dress in a more professional manner. You must also position yourself with people who can help you. One good way is to become active in a professional group, which also can provide you with good contacts and news of opportunities throughout your industry.

Source: *Business Monday/Detroit Free Press*

The D.O.: A Publication for Osteopathic Physicians and Surgeons

American Osteopathic Association (AOA)
142 E. Ontario St.
Chicago, IL 60611-2864
Phone: (312)280-5800

Thomas Allen, editor. Monthly. Contains news of the profession and its members, articles of professional and personal interest to practicing physicians, legislative developments, reports of meetings, and coming events.

The Family Physician

Illinois Academy of Family Physicians
1101 Perimeter Dr.
Schaumburg, IL 60173
Phone: (312)574-8502
Toll-free: 800-826-7944

Editor(s): Ernest P. Pessel. Six issues/year. Provides news and information of interest to medical doctors in family practice.

Geriatric Nursing, American Journal of Care for the Aging

American Journal of Nursing Co.
555 W. 57th St.
New York, NY 10019
Phone: (212)582-8820
Fax: (212)586-5462

Bimonthly. $23/year. Magazine for nurses in geriatric and gerontologic nursing practice. Provides news on issues affecting elders and clinical information on techniques and procedures.

Health Labor Relations Reports

Interwood Publications
PO Box 20241
Cincinnati, OH 45220
Phone: (513)221-3715

Editor(s): Frank J. Bardack. Biweekly. Focuses on employee and labor relations in the health care field. Reports on court and National Labor Relations Board (NLRB) decisions in the areas of wrongful discharge, employment-at-will, discrimination, and union organizing. Also notifies readers of arbitration awards and contract settlements.

Health Professions Report

Whitaker Newsletters, Inc.
313 South Ave.
Fanwood, NJ 07023-0340
Phone: (908)889-6336
Fax: (908)889-6339

Editor(s): Arne C. Bittner. Twenty-six issues/year. Tracks statistics on enrollment and educational costs, reports on relevant legislative and regulatory changes, and announces conferences, workshops, and other educational opportunities.

Healthwire

Federation of Nurses and Health Professionals
American Federation of Teachers
555 New Jersey Ave. NW
Washington, DC 20001
Phone: (202)879-4430

Editor(s): Priscilla M. Nemeth. 6/yr. Explores national news and issues affecting health care workers. Discusses general union developments as well as labor and union concerns specific to the health care field. Recurring features include local member news, book reviews, news of research, and columns titled Clipboard, Pulse Points, Stethescope, Second Opinion, and Making Rounds.

Hospitals (AHA)

American Hospital Association (AHA)
840 N. Lake Shore Dr.
Chicago, IL 60611
Phone: (312)280-6000

Biweekly.

Imprint

National Student Nurses Assn., Inc.
555 W. 57th St.
New York, NY 10019
Phone: (212)581-2211
Fax: (212)581-2368

Caroline Jaffe, editor. Five issues/year. Magazine for nursing students, focusing on issues and trends in nursing education.

Internal Medicine World Report

Medical World Business Press, Inc.
322-D Englishtown Rd., Ste. 201
Oak Bridge, NJ 08857
Phone: (201)251-9400

21x/year. Trade journal.

The Journal of the American Academy of Nurse Practitioners

J.B. Lippincott Co., Periodical Div.
E. Washington Sq.
Philadelphia, PA 19105
Phone: (301)824-7300
Fax: (301)824-7398

Jan Towers and Donna G. Nativio, editors. Quarterly. The official publication of the American Academy of Nurse Practitioners.

Journal of the American Osteopathic Association

American Osteopathic Assn.
142 E. Ontario St.
Chicago, IL 60611-2864
Phone: (312)280-5800
Fax: (312)280-5893

Thomas Wesley Allen, D.O., editor. Monthly. Osteopathic clinical journal.

The Journal of Family Practice

Appleton & Lange
25 Van Zant St.
PO Box 5630
East Norwalk, CT 06856
Phone: (203)838-4400
Fax: (203)854-9486

Paul Fischer, M.D., editor. Twelve issues/year. Journal covering clinical, family practice, and osteopathic medicine.

The Lancet (North American Edition)

Williams & Wilkins
428 E. Preston St.
Baltimore, MD 21202
Phone: (301)528-4227
Fax: (301)528-8596

Robin Fox, M.D., editor. Weekly. Medical journal.

> If the current trend holds, men may soon constitute a more substantial portion of the nursing workforce, to judge by the latest report from the American Association of Colleges of Nursing . . . . Though only 3% of today's RNs are men, 9.5% of the entry-level students and 5.2% of RNs returning for degrees were men.
>
> Source: *American Journal of Nursing*

Medical Decision Making

Hanley & Belfus, Inc.
210 S. 13th St.
Philadelphia, PA 19107
Phone: (215)546-0313
Fax: (215)790-9330

Robert Beck, M.D., editor. Quarterly. $82/year, $24 single issue.

Medical Staff News

American Hospital Association (AHA)
737 N. Michigan Ave., Ste. 700
Chicago, IL 60611
Phone: (312)440-6800
Toll-free: 800-621-6902
Fax: (312)944-4232

Monthly. Devoted to specific and common concerns of medical staff and hospital administration. Recurring features include articles on joint ventures, ethics, legislation, malpractice, and medical by-laws.

The Nightingale

National Association of Physicians' Nurses
900 S Washington St., No. G13
Falls Church, VA 22046-4020
Phone: (703)237-8616
Fax: (703)533-1153

Editor(s): Sue Young. Monthly. Presents items on "medical and personal subjects pertaining to office nurses and other staff."

The Nurse Practitioner

Vernon Publications Inc.
3000 Northup Way, Ste. 200
PO Box 96043
Bellevue, WA 98009
Phone: (206)827-9900
Fax: (206)822-9372

Linda J. Pearson, editorial director. Monthly. $36.00/year; $52.00/year for institutions; $5.00/issue. Magazine presenting clinical information to nurses in advanced primary care practice. Also covers legal, business, economic, ethical, research, pharmaceutical, and theoretical issues.

Nursing Outlook

Mosby Publishing Co.
11830 W. Line Industrial Dr.
St. Louis, MO 63146
Phone: (314)872-8370
Toll-free: 800-325-4177

Lucie Kelly, R.N., editor. Six issues/year. Official magazine of the American Academy of Nursing, reporting on trends and issues in nursing.

Nursing Research

American Journal of Nursing Co.
555 W. 57th St.
New York, NY 10019-2961
Phone: (212)582-8820
Fax: (212)586-5462

Florence Downs, R.N., editor. Six issues/year. Magazine focusing on nursing research.

Physicians' Newsletter

Blue Shield of California
Two N Point
San Francisco, CA 94133
Phone: (415)445-5090

Editor(s): Ken Duchscherer. Bimonthly. Provides information pertaining to Blue Shield of California's private healthcare plans in the areas of new coverage, expenditures, policy guidelines, and items of general healthcare financing affecting physicians in California.

Political Stethoscope

American Medical Political Action Committee
1101 Vermont Ave., NW
Washington, DC 20005
Phone: (202)789-7400

Editor(s): Nancy Warren. Quarterly. Serves to ensure that the physician's voice is heard in state and federal legislatures. Monitors legislation affecting the medical field and suggests ways individual physicians can affect the outcome of this legislation through letter-writing, telephone calls, and political campaigning.

The Practice Builder

Alan Bernstein
2755 Bristol, Ste. 100
Costa Mesa, CA 92626
Phone: (714)545-8900

Editor(s): Alan Bernstein. Offers marketing strategies to small health care practices.

Provider: For Long Term Care Professionals (AHCA)

American Health Care Association (AHCA)
1201 L St. NW
Washington, DC 20005
Phone: (202)842-4444
Toll-free: 800-321-0343

Monthly. Free to long-term health care professionals; Magazine; includes buyers' guide, news reports, advertisers' index, a listing of new products and services, and calendar of events.

Quickening

American College of Nurse-Midwives
1522 K St. NW, Ste. 1120
Washington, DC 20005
Phone: (202)347-5445

Editor(s): Mickey G. Nall. Bimonthly. Promotes the training and certification of nurse-midwives.

Recurring features include membership, board and convention news, announcements of relevant meetings and workshops, help-wanted items, and lists of significant publications.

RN Magazine

Medical Economics Co., Inc.
5 Paragon Dr.
Montvale, NJ 07645
Phone: (201)358-7200
Fax: (201)573-0440

Marianne Dekker Mattera, editor. Monthly. Magazine for registered nurses.

Vital Signs

710 Higgins Rd.
Park Ridge, IL 60068-5765
Phone: (708)823-5169
Fax: (708)823-0458

Editor(s): Linda Miceli. Quarterly. Contains information related to the certification, training, and responsibilities of Registered Medical Assistants. Highlights continuing education programs available and promotes high standards in the field.

Basic Reference Guides

300 New Ways to Get a Better Job

Bob Adams, Inc.
260 Center St.
Holbrook, MA 02343
Phone: (617)767-8100
Fax: (617)767-0994

Baldwin, Eleanor. $7.95. Advocates a job search approach designed to meet the changing nature of the job market.

850 Leading USA Companies

Jamenair Ltd.
PO Box 241957
Los Angeles, CA 90024
Phone: (213)470-6688

Studner, Peter K. $49.95. Compatible with IBM and IBM-compatibles.

AAFP Membership Directory

American Academy of Family Physicians
8880 Ward Pkwy.
Kansas City, MO 64114
Phone: (816)333-9700

Triennial.

AAGP Membership Directory

American Association for Geriatric Psychiatry (AAGP)
PO Box 376-A
Greenbelt, MD 20768
Phone: (301)220-0952
Fax: (301)220-0941

Annual.

> **T**o gain more control over your career, develop strong communications skills, both listening and talking. This means understanding and being able to translate what corporate goals are, and being able to talk to management. Actively solicit feedback.
>
> Source: *Dallas Morning News*

AAI Directory

American Association of Immunologists (AAI)
9650 Rockville Pike
Bethesda, MD 20014
Phone: (301)530-7178
Fax: (301)571-1816

Periodic.

AAMD — Registry of Members

American Academy of Medical Directors (AAMD)
1 Urban Center
Ste. 648
Tampa, FL 33609
Phone: (813)287-2000

Annual. Free to members.

AAMI Directory of Members

Association for the Advancement of Medical Instrumentation (AAMI)
3330 Washington Blvd.
Ste. 400
Arlington, VA 22201-4598
Phone: (703)525-4890
Fax: (703)276-0793

Biennial.

AAN Membership Directory

American Academy of Neurology (AAN)
2221 University Ave., SE
Ste. 335
Minneapolis, MN 55414
Phone: (612)623-8115

Annual.

AANP Roster of Members

American Association of Neuropathologists
(AANP)
c/o Reid R. Heffner, Jr., M.D.
Buffalo Medical School/ SUNY
Department of Pathology
204 Farber Hall
Buffalo, NY 14214
Phone: (716)898-3114

Annual.

W hat is underway in the 1990s is more than a massive corporate restructuring or a one-time adjustment. It's an overhaul of the US labor force, a sea change in the kinds of jobs and the type of work that will be available. Workers in this new era will have to be more flexible, more willing to move cross-country for a job, more willing to go back to school. Today's college graduate can expect 12 to 13 jobs in three to four different careers over her or his lifetime.

Source: *USA Today*

AANPA Membership Directory

Association of African Physicians in North
America (AAPNA)
2031 Brooks Dr.
No. 225
Forestville, MD 20747

Periodic.

AAOS Directory

American Association of Osteopathic
Specialists (AAOS)
804 Main St.
Ste. D
Forest Park, GA 30050
Phone: (404)363-8263
Fax: (404)361-2285

Annual. Free to members. Provides alphabetical
and geographical list of members.

AAPA Membership Directory

American Association of Pathologists'
Assistants (AAPA)
c/o Leo J. Kelly
Dept. of Pathology
VA Medical Center
West Haven, CT 06516
Phone: (203)932-5711

Biennial.

AAPA Membership Directory

American Academy of Physician Assistants
(AAPA)
950 N. Washington St.
Alexandria, VA 22314
Phone: (703)836-2272
Fax: (703)684-1924

Annual.

ACCP Membership Directory

American College of Clinical Pharmacy
(ACCP)
3101 Broadway
Ste. 380
Kansas City, MO 64111
Phone: (816)531-2177

Annual. Free to members; $30.00/copy for non-
members.

ACHA Membership Profile Directory

American College Health Association
(ACHA)
1300 Piccard Dr.
Ste. 200
Rockville, MD 20850
Phone: (301)963-1100
Fax: (301)330-6781

Periodic.

ACOI Directory

American College of Osteopathic Internists
(ACOI)
300 5th St.
Washington, DC 20002
Phone: (202)546-0095
Fax: (202)543-5584

Annual.

ACOS Membership Directory and By-laws

American College of Osteopathic Surgeons (ACOS)
123 N. Henry St.
Alexandria, VA 22314
Phone: (703)684-0416

Annual. Free to members.

ACPE Membership Directory

American College of Physician Executives (ACPE)
4890 W. Kennedy Blvd.
Ste. 200
Tampa, FL 33609
Phone: (813)287-2000
Fax: (813)287-8993

Annual. Free to members.

ACR Directory

American College of Radiology (ACR)
1891 Preston White Dr.
Reston, VA 22091
Phone: (703)648-8900

Annual.

ACSM Membership Directory

American College of Sports Medicine (ACSM)
PO Box 1440
Indianapolis, IN 46206-1440
Phone: (317)637-9200
Fax: (317)634-7817

Annual. Free to members; $30.00/copy for non-members. Arranged alphabetically and geographically.

AFS Membership Directory

American Fertility Society (AFS)
2140 11th Ave., S.
Ste. 200
Birmingham, AL 35205-2800
Phone: (205)933-8494
Fax: (205)930-9904

Biennial. Free to members. Arranged alphabetically and geographically.

AGA Membership Roster

American Gastroenterological Association (AGA)
6900 Grove Rd.
Thorofare, NJ 08086
Phone: (609)848-9218
Fax: (609)853-5991

Annual.

AGPA Directory

American Group Practice Association (AGPA)
1422 Duke St.
Alexandria, VA 22314
Phone: (703)838-0033

Annual, January. $125.00. Covers: About 300 private group medical practices and their professional staffs, totalling about 23,000 physicians. Entries include: Group member name, address, phone, names of administrator and other executives, names of physicians listed by medical specialties. Arrangement: Alphabetical. Indexes: Group location, personal name.

> E ach year about 2,400 organizations offer more than 30,000 courses for the nation's physicians, on topics ranging from sports medicine to the prevention of breast cancer.
>
> Source: *Glamour*

AHSM Membership Directory

Academy for Health Services Marketing (AHSM)
c/o American Marketing Association
250 S. Wacker Dr.
Ste. 200
Chicago, IL 60606
Phone: (312)648-0536

Annual.

American Academy of Optometry—Geographical Directory of Members

American Academy of Optometry (AAO)
5530 Wisconsin Ave., NW
Ste. 1149
Washington, DC 20815
Phone: (301)652-0905

Biennial.

American Academy of Psychiatrists in Alcoholism and Addictions—Membership Directory

American Academy of Psychiatrists in
Alcoholism and Addictions
PO Box 376
Greenbelt, MD 20768
Phone: (301)220-0951

Periodic.

American Association of Certified Orthoptists—Directory

American Association of Certified Orthoptists
(AACO)
Hermann Eye Center
6411 Fannin
Houston, TX 77030-1697
Phone: (713)797-1777

Annual. Free to members.

A computer can make it easier to customize your resume. If you store your resume on a computer disk, you can copy it and rearrange it by skills, job chronology or almost any other method, customizing it for each job you apply for.

Source: *Business Monday/Detroit Free Press*

The American Association of Nurse Attorneys—Membership Directory

The American Association of Nurse Attorneys
(TAANA)
720 Light St.
Baltimore, MD 21230-3816
Phone: (301)752-3318
Fax: (301)752-8295

Annual.

American Board of Neurological and Orthopaedic Medicine and Surgery Journal

American Board of Neurological and
Orthopaedic Medicine and Surgery
(ABNOMS)
2320 Rancho Dr.
Ste. 108
Las Vegas, NV 89102-4592
Phone: (702)385-6886

Quarterly. $30.00/year. Includes annual membership directory.

American Hospital Association - Guide to the Health Care Field

American Hospital Association (AHA)
840 N. Lakeshore Dr.
Chicago, IL 60611
Phone: (312)280-5957

Annual, July. $195.00; payment with order. Covers: 7,000 hospitals, long-term care facilities, and multihospital systems; individual members; and 1,800 health-related organizations. Entries include: For hospitals - Facility name, address, phone, administrator's name, number of beds, facilities and services, other statistics. For multi-hospital systems -Headquarters name, address, phone, chief executive. Arrangement: Hospitals are geographical; members are alphabetical. Indexes: Subject.

American Journal of Nursing Directory of Nursing Organizations Issue

American Journal of Nursing Company
555 W. 57th St.
New York, NY 10019
Phone: (212)582-8820
Fax: (212)586-5462

Annual, April. $4.00. Publication includes: Directory of nursing organizations and agencies. Entries include: Name, address, names of officers or nursing representative. Arrangement: Classified by type of organization.

American Osteopathic Hospital Association Directory

American Osteopathic Hospital Association
5301 Wisconsin Ave. NW
Ste. 630
Washington, DC 20015-2015
Phone: (202)686-1700

Annual, April. $125.00; payment must accompany order. Covers: About 150 osteopathic hospitals. Includes list of individuals and institutional members; also lists osteopathic colleges and state osteopathic hospital associations. Entries include: For hospitals - Name of hospital, name of chief executive officer, address, phone, number of beds and other hospital data, including multi-hospital systems. Similar data given for other lists. Arrangement: Geographical.

America's Fastest Growing Employers

Bob Adams, Inc.
260 Center St.
Holbrook, MA 02343
Phone: (617)767-8100
Fax: (617)767-0994

Smith, Carter. 1992. $14.95. Identifies firms with the most rapid growth in employment opportunities. Provides contact information, recent sales figures, current employees, and a breakdown of common positions sought by the firms profiled.

AMPRA Membership Directory

American Medical Peer Review Association (AMPRA)
810 1st St., NE
Ste. 410
Washington, DC 20002
Phone: (202)371-5610

Annual.

AOA Yearbook and Directory

American Osteopathic Association (AOA)
142 E. Ontario St.
Chicago, IL 60611
Phone: (312)280-5800
Fax: (312)280-5893

AOCP Directory

American Osteopathic College of Pathologists (AOCP)
c/o Joan Gross
12368 NW 13th Ct.
Pembroke Pines, FL 33026
Phone: (305)432-9640

Annual.

APACVS Membership Directory

Association of Physician's Assistants in Cardio-Vascular Surgery (APACVS)
2000 Tate Springs Rd.
PO Box 2242
Lynchburg, VA 24501-2242
Phone: 800-528-1506

Annual.

APMA Desk Reference

American Podiatric Medical Association (APMA)
9312 Old Georgetown Rd.
Bethesda, MD 20814
Phone: (301)571-9200
Fax: (301)530-2752

Annual. 1991.

APPA Directory of Physicians

Association of Philippine Physicians in America (APPA)
2717 W. Olive Ave.
Ste. 200
Burbank, CA 91505
Phone: (818)843-8616

Biennial.

> Companies are forgoing the old five-year plan method of strategic planning for a new, everyday outlook: strategic thinking. This describes what a company does in becoming smart, targeted, and nimble enough to prosper in an era of constant change. The key words for the 1990s are focus and flexibility.
>
> Source: *Fortune*

ASA Directory of Members

American Society of Anesthesiologists (ASA)
515 Busse Hwy.
Park Ridge, IL 60068
Phone: (708)825-5586
Fax: (708)825-1692

Annual.

ASHP Directory

American Society of Handicapped Physicians (ASHP)
105 Morris Dr.
Bastrop, LA 71220
Phone: (318)281-4436

Annual.

Association of Black Nursing Faculty in Higher Education—Membership Directory

Association of Black Nursing Faculty in Higher Education (ABNF)
5823 Queens Cove
Lisle, IL 60532
Phone: (708)969-3809

Annual.

Billian's Hospital Blue Book

Billian Publishing Co.
2100 Powers Ferry Rd.
Ste. 300
Atlanta, GA 30339
Phone: (404)955-5656

Annual, spring. $95.00, plus $4.50 shipping. Covers more than 7,100 hospitals. Entries include name of hospital, accreditation, mailing address, phone, number of beds, type of facility (nonprofit, general, state, etc.); list of administrative personnel and chiefs of medical services, with titles.

CAMS Membership Directory

Chinese American Medical Society (CAMS)
c/o Dr. H.H. Wang
281 Edgewood Ave.
Teaneck, NJ 07666
Phone: (201)833-1506

Biennial.

Canada Nursing Job Guide Directory

Prime National Publishing Corporation
470 Boston Post Rd.
Weston, MA 02193
Phone: (617)899-2702

$50.00. Directory of Canadian hospitals.

CAP Directory

College of American Pathologists (CAP)
325 Waukegan Rd.
Northfield, IL 60093-2750
Phone: (708)446-8800
Fax: (708)446-8807

Annual. Free to members.

CLAS Membership Directory

Clinical Ligand Assay Society (CLAS)
3139 S. Wayne Rd.
PO Box 67
Wayne, MI 48184
Phone: (313)722-6290

The Clinical Career Ladder: Planning and Implementation

Springer Publishing Co.
536 Broadway
New York, NY 10012
Phone: (212)431-4370

Laura R. Merker, Kathleen Mariak, and Diana W. Dwinnells. 1985. Includes a bibliography and an index.

A Clinical Manual for Nursing Assistants

Jones & Bartlett Publishers, Inc.
1 Exeter Plaza
Boston, MA 02116
Phone: (617)859-3900

Sharon McClelland. 1985.

Clinician's Pocket Reference

Appleton and Lange
25 Van Zant St.
East Norwalk, CT 06855
Phone: (203)838-4400
Toll-free: 800-423-1359

Leonard G. Gomella, G. Richard Braen, and Michael Olding, editors. Sixth edition, 1989. Covers procedures, techniques, and patient care information; features many charts and tables for quick and easy reference. Gives common lab values, medication actions, and dosages. Explains intravenous therapy, emergency care, operating room procedures, and suturing techniques.

CNS U.S. and Canada Directory

Congress of Neurological Surgeons (CNS)
c/o Thomas G. Saul, M.D.
506 Oak St.
Cincinnati, OH 45219
Phone: (513)872-2657
Fax: (513)872-2597

Annual.

Coming Alive from Nine to Five
Mayfield Publishing
1240 Villa St.
Mountain View, CA 94041

Micheolzzi, Betty N. 1988. $12.95. In addition to general job-hunting advice, provides special information for women, young adults, minorities, older workers, and persons with handicaps.

Conn's Current Therapy: Latest Approved Methods of Treatment for the Practicing Physician
W. B. Saunders Co.
Curtis Center
Independence Ave.
Philadelphia, PA 19106
Phone: (215)238-7800

Howard F. Conn; edited by Robert E. Rakel. Annual. Presents current recommended therapy.

CPC Annual
College Placement Council
62 Highland Ave.
Bethlehem, PA 18017

Annual, fall. Provides a directory of opportunities and employers in many fields, including health, engineering, sciences, computer fields, administration, and business. Offers job-hunting guidance.

Directory of the American Academy of Dermatology
American Academy of Dermatology (AAD)
1567 Maple Ave.
PO Box 3116
Evanston, IL 60201-3116
Phone: (708)869-3954
Fax: (708)869-4382

Biennial.

Directory of Career Training and Career Development Programs
Ready Reference Press
PO Box 5249
Santa Monica, CA 90409
Phone: (213)474-5175

$98.00. Provides details on hundreds of professional career training programs offered by some of America's top corporations. Each company profile contains type of training, length of training, and qualifications.

Directory of Corporate Affiliations
National Register Publishing Company
Macmillan Directory Division
3004 Glenview Rd.
Wilmette, IL 60091
Phone: (708)933-3322

Annual. $687.00. Covers: 5,000 parent companies; 500 privately owned companies; and about 45,000 domestic divisions, subsidiaries, joint ventures, and/or affiliates. Entries include: Name of parent company, address, phone, assets, earnings, liabilities, net worth, type of business, approximate annual sales, number of employees, corporate headquarters address, alphabetical listing of subsidiaries, divisions, and affiliates; names, titles, address, phone of key personnel. Arrranged alphabetically by parent company name; geographical; by Standard Industrial Classification (SIC) code. Indexes: Alphabetical, SIC code, geographical, personal name.

I t can honestly be said that nursing is unique in that no one has to step on anyone else to get ahead. The field is wide open, with multiple opportunities within easy reach of any able, career-minded professional.

Source: *Journal of Professional Nursing*

Directory of Drug Stores & HBA Chains
Chain Store Guide Information Services
3922 Coconut Palm Dr.
Tampa, FL 33619
Phone: (813)664-6700

Annual, December. $260.00, plus $5.00 shipping. Covers: Approximately 1,850 drug store chains operating over 31,000 drug and HBA (health and beauty aid) stores, 120 drug wholesalers and their 257 divisions. Also covers over 10,500 key personnel in the industry. Entries include: For drug store chains -Company name, address, phone, fax, product lines, annual sales volume, computerized RX indicator, distribution center, percentage of sales that are prescription sales, store names, number of prescriptions filled daily, number of pharmacies, and names and titles of key personnel. For drug wholesalers - Company name, address, phone, fax, product line, sales history, percentage of sales from prescription sales, number of stores served, and names and titles of key personnel. Arrangement: Separate geographical sections for chains and wholesalers; shows are chronological. Indexes: Top 100 drug store chains ranked by sales (with number of stores); chain headquarters. Regional editions available.

Directory of Hospital Marketing, Planning, and Public Relations Consultants

American Society for Health Care Marketing and Public Relations (ASHCMPR)
c/o American Hospital Association
840 N. Lake Shore Dr.
Chicago, IL 60611
Phone: (312)280-6359

Annual. Free to members; $40.00/single issue for nonmembers.

E very resume should pass the "so what?" test. It's not enough to simply list your accomplishments. You need to demonstrate the impact of your actions on your department or the company at large. Beverly Robsham, president of Robsham & Associates, an outplacement firm in Boston, MA, advocates the "PAR" approach when delineating accomplishments: "Specify the *problem*, the *actions* you took, and the *results* for the company."

Source: *Working Woman*

Directory of Hospital Personnel

Medical Device Register
5 Paragon Dr.
Montvale, NJ 07645-1725

Annual. $279.00, plus $5.00 shipping. Covers: 50,000 executives at hospitals with more than 200 beds. Entries include: Name of hospital, address, phone, number of beds, type of hospital, names and titles of key department heads and staff. Arrangement: Geographical. Indexes: Hospital name, personnel, hospital size.

Directory of International Internships

Career Development and Placement Services
Michigan State University
113 Student Services Bldg.
East Lansing, MI 48824

1990. $20.00.

Directory of Internships

Ready Reference Press
PO Box 5249
Santa Monica, CA 90409
Phone: (213)474-5175

$95.00. Lists internship opportunities in many fields of interest, including, but not limited to arts, journalism, public relations, education, law, environmental affairs, business, engineering, and computer science. In addition, cites summer internship opportunities, work/study programs, and specialized opportunities for high school and undergraduate students. Indexed by subject, geography, and program.

Directory of Leading Private Companies

National Register Publishing Company
Reed Reference Publishing
121 Chanlon Rd.
New Providence, NJ 07974
Phone: (908)464-6800

Annual, March. $529.00, plus $8.75 shipping. Covers: Over 7,800 privately owned companies. Entries include: Company name, address, phone, telex, year founded, financial assets and liabilities, net worth, approximate sales, names and titles of key personnel, number of employees, number of U.S. and foreign offices, and other information. Arrangement: Alphabetical. Indexes: Geographical, parent company, Standard Industrial Classification number.

Directory of Nursing Homes

Oryx Press
4041 N. Central
No. 700
Phoenix, AZ 85012
Phone: (602)265-2651
Fax: (602)253-2741

Reported as triennial; latest edition August 1991.

$225.00. Covers: 16,259 state-licensed long-term care facilities. Entries include: Name of facility, address, phone, licensure status, number of beds; many listings also include name of administrator and health services supervisor; number of nursing, dietary, and auxiliary staff members; availability of social, recreational, and religious programs; and medicaid/medicare certification status. Arrangement: Geographical. Indexes: Facility name.

Directory of Overseas Summer Jobs

Peterson's Guides, Inc.
PO Box 2123
Princeton, NJ 08543
Phone: (609)243-9111

Annual, January. $12.95. Covers: More than 30,000 jobs, worldwide. Entries include: Name of employer, address, length of employment, number of positions available, pay rates, how and when to apply, name of contact. Arrangement: Geographical, then by type of job.

Directory of Physicians Assistants - Certified

National Commission on Certification of Physician Assistants (NCCPA)
2845 Henderson Mill Rd., NE
Atlanta, GA 30341
Phone: (404)493-9100

Annual.

Directory of Special Programs for Minority Group Members: Career Information Services, Employment Skills Banks, Financial Aid Sources

Garrett Park Press
PO Box 190 C
Garrett Park, MD 20986-0190
Phone: (301)946-2553

Johnson, Willis L. 1990. $30.00. 348 pages. Cites thousands of job training opportunities, talent banks, summer jobs, internships, assistantships, employment services, fellowships, scholarships, loan programs, and useful publications to aid minorities.

Directory of Student Placements in Health Care Settings in North America

Association for the Care of Children's Health
7910 Woodmont Ave.
Ste. 300
Bethesda, MD 20814
Phone: (301)654-6549

Irregular; latest edition 1985. $7.50, plus $2.50 shipping. Covers: Nearly 150 internships, fellowships, and other practical teaching experiences in hospitals for students of 'child life activity.' Entries include: Facility name, address, phone, name of individual in charge of the practicum; number of hours and number of weeks for practicum; beginning dates, if specified; number of students accepted each term; total number of students accepted for year; colleges from which students are generally referred; areas of study from which students generally come; fees; stipend and other benefits; prerequisites; whether application is to be made to college or hospital; level of student generally accepted; practicum experiences available; form of evaluation. Arrangement: Geographical.

Top traits of superior leaders
1. Honest
2. Competent
3. Forward-looking
4. Inspiring
5. Intelligent
6. Fair-minded
7. Broad-minded
8. Courageous
9. Straightforward
10. Imaginative

Source: Business Credit

Directory of Washington, D.C. Internships

University Resource Services
PO Box 3722
Stanford, CA 94309
1990. $45.00.

Diseases

Springhouse Corp.
1111 Bethlehem Pike
Springhouse, PA 19477
Phone: (215)646-8700

Fourth edition, 1992. Includes bibliographies an index.

Dorland's Illustrated Medical Dictionary

W. B. Saunders Co.
Curtis Center
Independence Sq.,W.
Philadelphia, PA 19106
Phone: (215)238-7800

27th edition. 1988.

Dun and Bradstreet Million Dollar Directory

Dun's Marketing Services
Dun and Bradstreet Corporation
Three Sylvan Way
Parsippany, NJ 07054-3896
Phone: (201)605-6000
Fax: (201)605-6911

Annual, February. $1,250.00. Covers: 160,000 businesses with a net worth of $500,000 or more, including industrial corporations, utilities, transportation companies, bank and trust companies, stock brokers, mutual and stock insurance companies, wholesalers, retailers, and domestic subsidiaries of foreign corporations. Entries include: Company name, state of incorporation, address, phone, annual sales, number of employees, parent company name; names, titles, and functions of principal executives; other data. Arranged alphabetically. Indexes: Geogrpahical, product.

Duncan's Dictionary for Nurses

Springer Publishing Co.
536 Broadway
New York, NY 10012
Phone: (212)431-4370
Fax: (212)941-7842

Helen A. Duncan. Second edition, 1989.

Encyclopedia and Dictionary of Medicine, Nursing, and Allied Health

W. B. Saunders Co.
Curtis Center
Independence Sq., W.
Philadelphia, PA 19106-3399
Phone: (215)238-7800

Benjamin F. Miller and Claire B. Keane. Fourth edition, 1989.

Financial World—500 Fastest Growing Companies

Financial World Partners
1328 Broadway
New York, NY 10001
Phone: (212)594-5030

Annual, August. $3.95. Lists of 500 United States firms showing greatest growth in net earnings for the year. Entries include: Company name, rank, net earnings for two previous years, total assets, other financial and statistical data. Arrangement: Main list arranged by net earnings, other lists arranged by return on equity and other measures and by industry.

Financial World America's Top Growth Companies Directory Issue

Financial World Partners
1328 Broadway
New York, NY 10001
Phone: (212)594-5030

Annual, May. $3.00. List of companies selected on the basis of earnings per share growth rate over 10 year period ending with current year; minimum growth rate used is 5%. Entries include: Company name, current and prior year's ranking, earnings growth rate, and other financial data. Classified by sales and earnings growth rate. Indexes: Company ranked within industry.

Forbes Up-and-Comers 200: Best Small Companies in America

Forbes, Inc.
60 5th Ave.
New York, NY 10011
Phone: (212)620-2200
Fax: (212)620-1863

Annual, November. $4.00. List of 200 small companies judged to be exceptionally fast-growing on the basis of 5-year return on equity and other qualitative measurements. Entries include:

Company name, address; biographical data for chief executive officer; financial data. Arranged alphabetically. Indexes: Ranking.

Fortune Directory

Time, Inc.
Time and Life Bldg.
Rockefeller Center
New York, NY 10020
Phone: (212)586-1212

Annual, August. $25.00; payment must accompany order. Covers: Combined, in a fall reprint, 500 largest United States industrial corporations (published in an April issue each year) and 500 largest United States non-industrial corporations, the Service 500 (published in a June issue). The Service 500 comprises 100-company rankings of each of the largest diversified financial, diversified service, and commercial banking companies, and 50-company rankings each of the largest life insurance, retailing, transportation, and utility companies. Entries include: Company name, headquarters city, sales, assets, and various other statistical and financial information. Classified by annual sales, where appropriate; otherwise by assets. Indexes: Separate alphabetical indexes for industrials and service companies. Send orders to: Fortune Directory, 229 W. 28th St., New York, NY 10001.

Freestanding Outpatient Surgery Center Directory

SMG Marketing Group, Inc.
1342 N. LaSalle Dr.
Chicago, IL 60610
Phone: (312)642-3026
Fax: (312)642-9729

Annual, June. $395.00. Covers: More than 1,200 ambulatory surgical centers that are not affiliated with a hospital or medical center. Entries include: Facility name, address, phone, ownership; number of operating suites, number of surgeries performed each year and types of surgery performed. Arrangement: Geographical.

From Campus to Corporation

The Career Press, Inc.
180 5th Ave.
PO Box 34
Hawthorne, NJ 07507

Strasser, Stephen, and Sena, John. Helps job-

seekers negotiate the obstacles from classroom to career and beyond.

Geriatric Nursing Assistants: An Annotated Bibliography with Models to Enhance Practice

Greenwood Publishing Group, Inc.
88 Post Rd., W.
PO Box 5007
Westport, CT 06881
Phone: (203)226-3571
Toll-free: 800-225-5800
Fax: (202)222-1502

George H. Weber. 1990. Part of Bibliographies & Indexes in Gerontology Series.

N ursing is a valid career choice for everyone, and a progressive career. It offers different avenues of employment and holds the potential for academic and practical growth. The key is career planning.

Source: *The Canadian Nurse*

Health Sciences Communications Association—Who's Who

Health Sciences Communications Association (HESCA)
6105 Lindell Blvd.
St. Louis, MO 63112
Phone: (314)725-4722
Fax: (314)721-6675

Annual. Free to members. Membership directory.

HMO/PPO Directory

Medical Device Register(AMCRA)
655 Washington Blvd.
Stamford, CT 06901
Phone: (203)348-6319

Annual. $129.00. Covers 600 health maintenance organizations (HMOs) and 400 preferred provider organizations (PPOs). Entries include: Name of organization, address, phone, number of members, geographical area served, parent company, average fees and copayments, and cost control practices.

Hospital Market Atlas

SMG Marketing Group, Inc.
1342 N. LaSalle Dr.
Chicago, IL 60610
Phone: (312)642-3026
Fax: (312)642-9729

Biennial. $595.00, postpaid; payment with order. Covers: Over 8,200 hospitals, clinical laboratories, hospital systems, group purchasing organizations, health maintenance organizations, outpatient surgery centers, and diagnostic imaging centers. Entries include: Hospital or organization name, address, phone, management, type of hospital service, number of beds, admissions, surgical operations, and emergency room visits. Arrangement: Geographical.

H ospitals are paying their top nurses more to assume increasing responsibilities . . . growing numbers of chief nurse execs are overseeing ORs, ERs, outpatient services, and social services.

Source: *American Journal of Nursing*

Hospitals Directory

American Business Directories, Inc.
American Business Information, Inc.
5711 S. 86th Circle
Omaha, NE 68127
Phone: (402)593-4600
Fax: (402)331-1505

Annual. $415.00, payment with order. Number of listings: 10,020. Entries include: Name, address, phone (including area code), year first in 'Yellow Pages.' Arrangement: Geographical.

How to Get a Better Job Quicker

Taplinger Publishing Company, Inc.
132 W. 22nd St.
New York, NY 10011
Phone: (212)877-1040

Payne, Richard A. 1987. $16.95. 217 pages.

Inc.—The Inc. 100 Issue

The Goldhirsh Group
38 Commercial Wharf
Boston, MA 02110
Phone: (617)248-8000
Fax: (617)248-8090

Annual, May. $3.50. List of 100 fastest-growing

publicly held companies in manufacturing and service industries which had revenues greater than $100,000 but less than $25 million five years prior to compilation of current year's list. Entries include: Company name, headquarters city, type of business, date incorporated, number of employees, sales, and net income five years earlier and currently, and five-year growth rate. Arranged by sales growth.

Inc.—The Inc. 500 Issue

The Goldhirsh Group
38 Commercial Wharf
Boston, MA 02110
Phone: (617)248-8000
Fax: (617)248-8090

Annual, October. $3.50. List of 500 fastest-growing privately held companies in service, manufacturing, retail, distribution, and construction industries, based on percentage increase in sales over the five-year period prior to compilation of current year's list. Entries include: Company name, headquarters city, type of business, year founded, number of employees, sales five years earlier and currently, profitability range, and growth statistics. Arranged by sales growth.

Internships for College Students Interested in Law, Medicine and Politics

The Graduate Group
86 Norwood Rd.
West Hartford, CT 06117

$27.50.

The Lippincott Manual of Nursing Practice

J. B. Lippincott Co.
227 East Washington Sq.
East Washington Sq., PA 19106
Phone: (215)238-4200

Lillian Sholtis Burnner. Fourth edition, 1986.

Medical and Health Information Directory

Gale Research Inc.
835 Penobscot Bldg.
Detroit, MI 48226
Phone: (313)961-2242
Fax: (313)961-6241

Three volumes. Each volume published separately on a biennial basis; volume 1, latest edition 1991; volume 2, latest edition 1992; volume 3, latest edition 1992. $195.00 per volume; $480.00 for the three-volume set. Covers: In volume 1, medical and health oriented associations, organizations, institutions, and government agencies, including health maintenance organizations (HMOs), preferred provider organizations (PPOs), insurance companies, pharmaceutical companies, research centers, and medical and allied health schools. In volume 2, medical book publishers; medical periodicals, review serials, etc.; audiovisual producers and services, medical libraries and information centers, and computerized information systems and services. In volume 3, clinics, treatment centers, care programs, and counseling/diagnostic services for 30 subject areas (drawn from specialized lists published by governments and associations). Entries include: Institution, service, or firm name, address, phone; many include names of key personnel and, when pertinent, descriptive annotation. Arrangement: Classified by activity, service, etc. Indexes: Each volume has a complete master name and keyword index.

Medical Marketing and Media Healthcare Agency Profiles Issue

CPS Communications, Inc.
7200 W. Camino Real
Ste. 215
Boca Raton, FL 33433
Phone: (407)368-9301
Fax: (407)368-7870

Annual, December. $7.00. Publication includes: List of about 130 health care advertising agencies. Entries include: Company name, address, phone, key personnel, financial revenue, market breakdown, current accounts, number of employees, year established, and other information. Arrangement: Alphabetical.

Medical Research Centres

Gale Research Inc.
835 Penobscot Bldg.
Detroit, MI 48226
Phone: (313)961-2242
Fax: (313)961-6241

Ninth edition, 1990. Two volumes; $470.00/set. Covers medical and biochemical research conducted in over 100 countries. Entries include information on industrial enterprises, research laboratories, universities, societies, and professional associations engaged in research in medicine and related subjects like dentistry, nursing, pharmacy, psychiatry, and surgery.

The Merck Manual of Diagnosis and Therapy

Merck and Co., Inc.
PO Box 2000
Rahway, NJ 07065
Phone: (908)750-7470
Toll-free: 800-999-3633

Fifthteenth edition, 1987. Describes symptoms to facilitate diagnosis; explains recommended treatment.

"**W**e've run counter to the modern demands for more general physicians by allowing specialists in neurology to become superspecialists in particular groups of diseases, such as movement disorders, neuromuscular diseases and problems involving dementia. The amount of knowledge available is so huge that people have to focus if they're going to be on the front lines," advises Lewis Rowland, chief of neurology, Columbia-Presbyterian Medical Center.

Source: *U.S. News & World Report*

Moody's Corporate Profiles

Moody's Investors Service, Inc.
Dun and Bradstreet Company
99 Church St.
New York, NY 10007
Phone: (212)553-0300
Fax: (212)553-4700

Provides data on more than 5,000 publicly held companies listed on the New York Stock Exchange or the American Stock Exchange or NMS companies traded on the National Association of Securities Dealers Automated Quotations. Typical record elements: Company name, address, phone, D-U-N-S number, Moody's number, stock exchange, line of business analysis, annual earnings and dividends per share, and other financial and stock trading data. Available through DIALOG Information Services, Inc.

Mosby's Fundamentals of Medical Assisting: Administrative and Clinical Theory and Technique

C. V. Mosby Co.
11830 Westline Industrial Dr.
St. Louis, MO 63146
Phone: (314)872-8370
Toll-free: 800-325-4177

Margaret A. Shea and Sharron M. Zakus. 1990.
Includes a bibliography and an index.

Mosby's Medical Dictionary

C. V. Mosby Co.
11830 Westline Industrial Dr.
St. Louis, MO 63146
Phone: (314)872-8370
Toll-free: 800-325-4177

Walter D. Glanze, Kenneth N. Anderson, and
Lois E. Anderson, editors. Revised second edition, 1987.

Mosby's Pharmacology in Nursing

C. V. Mosby Co.
11830 Westline Industrial Dr.
St. Louis, MO 63146
Phone: (314)872-8370
Toll-free: 800-325-4177
Fax: (314)432-1380

Anne Burgess Hahn, et al., editors. 18th edition,
1992. This textbook contains information for
nurses on drug therapy.

Mosby's Textbook for Nursing Assistants

Mosby Year Book, Inc.
11830 Westline Industrial Dr.
St. Louis, MO 63146
Phone: (314)872-8370
Toll-free: 800-325-4177

Sorrentino. Third edition, 1991.

National Directory of Addresses and Telephone Numbers

Omnigraphics, Inc.
2500 Penobscot Bldg.
Detroit, MI 48226
Phone: (313)961-1340

Annual. Covers about 223,000 corporations, federal, state, and local government offices, banks, colleges and universities, associations, labor unions, political organizations, newspapers, magazines, television and radio stations, foundations, postal and shipping services, hospitals, office equipment suppliers, airlines, hotels and motels, accountants, law firms, computer firms, foreign corporations, overseas trade contacts, and other professional services. Entries include company, organization, agency, or firm name, address, phone, fax, toll-free phone.

National Directory of Minority-Owned Business Firms

Gale Research Inc.
835 Penobscot Bldg.
Detroit, MI 48226
Phone: (313)961-2242
Fax: (313)961-6241

January, 1990. $195.00. Covers: Over 35,000 minority-owned businesses. Entries include: Company name, address, phone, name and title of contact, minority group, number of employees, description of products or services, sales volume. Arrangement: Alphabetical. Indexes: Standard Industrial Classification (SIC) Code, geographical.

National Directory of Nonprofit Organizations

Gale Research Inc.
835 Penobscot Bldg.
Detroit, MI 48226
Phone: (313)961-2242
Fax: (313)961-6241

Annual. $225.00. Covers: Over 210,000 nonprofit organizations with incomes over $100,000. Entries include: Organization name, address, phone, annual income, IRS filing status, activity description. Arrangement: Alphabetical. Indexes: Area of activity, income, geographical.

National Directory of Women-Owned Business Firms

Gale Research Inc.
835 Penobscot Bldg.
Detroit, MI 48226
Phone: (313)961-2242
Fax: (313)961-6241

January, 1990. $195.00. Covers: Over 20,000 women-owned businesses. Entries include: Company name, address, phone, name and title of contact, number of employees, description of products or services, sales volume. Arrangement: Alphabetical. Indexes: Standard Industrial Classification (SIC) code, geographical.

The New American Medical Dictionary and Health Manual

New American Library
375 Hudson St.
New York, NY 10014-3657
Phone: (212)366-2000
Toll-free: 800-526-0275

Robert E. Rothenberg. 6th edition, 1992.

Nurses and Nurses Registries

American Business Directories, Inc.
American Business Information, Inc.
5711 S. 86th Circle
Omaha, NE 68127
Phone: (402)593-4600
Fax: (402)331-1505

Annual. $450.00, payment with order. Number of listings: 12,049. Entries include: Name, address, phone (including area code), year first in 'Yellow Pages.' Arrangement: Geographical.

Nursing

Springhouse Corp.
1111 Bethlehem Pike
Springhouse, PA 19477
Phone: (215)646-8700

Maryanne Wagner, editor. Monthly. Practical nursing journal focusing on hospital nurses; includes articles for critical-care nurses and nurse managers.

Nursing Career Directory

Springhouse Corporation
1111 Bethlehem Pike
Springhouse, PA 19477
Phone: (215)646-8700

Annual, January. Free; restricted circulation. Covers: Nonprofit and investor-owned hospitals and departments of the United States government which hire nurses. Does not report specific positions available. Entries include: Unit name, location, areas of nursing specialization, educational requirements for nurses, licensing, facilities, benefits, etc. Arrangement: Geographical.

The Nursing Clinics of North America

W. B. Saunders Co.
Curtis Center
Independence Sq., W.
Philadelphia, PA 19106
Phone: (215)238-7800
Toll-free: 800-654-2452
Fax: (407)363-9661

Carol Wolfe, editor. Quarterly.

The Nursing Process: Assessing, Planning, Implementing, Evaluating

Appleton and Lange
PO Box 5630
Norwalk, CT 06855
Phone: (203)838-4400
Toll-free: 800-423-1359

Helen Yura and Mary B. Walsh. Fifth edition, 1988. Covers nursing research, computers in nursing, and the future of nursing. Includes nursing diagnosis and case studies.

Hospitals and universities may offer clinical ladders and courses, but the nurse must show the initiative to use these resources. Networking is an important tool in professional development. It allows for self-promotion, sharing of ideas and opinions, and allows you to keep aware of the happenings within the field.

Source: *The Canadian Nurse*

Nursing World Journal—Nursing Job Guide

Prime National Publishing Corporation
470 Boston Post Rd.
Weston, MA 02193
Phone: (617)899-2702
Fax: (617)899-4361

Annual, January. $85.00. Covers: Over 7,000 hospitals and medical centers, infirmaries, government hospitals, and other hospitals in the United States; in tabular format, provides information about each facility which would be of interest to nurses considering employment there, but does not list specific openings. Entries include: Hospital name, address, phone, name of nurse recruiter; number of beds, number of admissions, number of patient days, type of control, whether a teaching institution; nurses salary range; nursing specialties utilized; list of fringe benefits; whether relocation assistance is given; educational opportunities; special programs. Arrangement: Geographical.

Occupational Outlook Handbook

Bureau of Labor Statistics
441 G St., NW
Washington, DC 20212
Phone: (202)523-1327

Biennial, May of even years. $22.00 hardcover. $17.00 paperback. Contains profiles of various occupations, which include description of occupation, educational requirements, market demand, and expected earnings. Also lists over 100 state employment agencies and State Occupational Information Coordinating Committees that provide state and local job market and career information; various occupational organizations that provide career information. Arranged by occupation; agencies and committees are geographical. Send orders to: Superintendent of Documents, U.S. Government Printing Office, Washington, D.C. 20402 (202-783-3238).

> **N**ever in our history have we had more or better opportunities to make a difference for patients and for health care. But, we need a great number of committed professionals to successfully meet these challenges.
>
> Source: *Journal of Professional Nursing*

Operating Room Nursing Handbook

Warren H. Green, Inc.
8356 Olive Blvd.
St. Louis, MO 63132
Phone: (314)991-1335
Toll-free: 800-537-0655

Nancy Girard. 1991.

Osteopathic Medicine: An American Reformation

American Osteopathic Association (AOA)
142 E. Ontario St.
Chicago, IL 60611-2864
Phone: (312)280-5800
Fax: (312)280-5893

George W. Northup, editor-in-chief. Third edi-

tion, 1987. Provides an overview of osteopathic medicine, its history and theory, and a picture of the past and present of the profession.

Osteopathic Research: Growth and Development

American Osteopathic Association (AOA)
142 E. Ontario St.
Chicago, IL 60611-2864
Phone: (312)280-5800

George W. Northup, editor. 1987. Traces the development of osteopathic research.

The Oxford Companion to Medicine

Oxford University Press, Inc.
200 Madison Ave.
New York, NY 10016
Phone: (212)679-7300
Toll-free: 800-334-4249

John Walton, Paul B. Beeson, and Ronald Bodley Scott, editors. 1986. This two-volume set contains articles covering the theory and practice of medicine, medical terminology, and medical biography.

PDR: Physicians' Desk Reference

Medical Economics Books
680 Kinderkamack Rd.
Oradell, NJ 07649
Phone: (201)358-7200
Toll-free: 800-223-0581

Barbara B. Huff, et al., editors. Annual. Forty-sixth edition, 1992. Contains descriptions of drugs including medical indications, pharmacological actions, and adverse reactions.

Pharmaceutical Products- Wholesalers & Manufacturers

American Business Directories, Inc.
American Business Information, Inc.
5711 S. 86th Circle
Omaha, NE 68127
Phone: (402)593-4600
Fax: (402)331-1505

Annual. $125.00, payment with order. Number of listings: 2,679. Entries include: Name, address, phone (including area code), year first in 'Yellow Pages.' Arrangement: Geographical.

Physician's Handbook

Appleton and Lange
25 Van Zant St.
East Norwalk, CT 06855
Phone: (203)838-4400
Toll-free: 800-423-1359

Marcus A. Krupp, et al. Twenty-first edition, 1985. Contains information on diagnosis.

Podiatric Medicine

Williams and Wilkins
428 E. Preston St.
Baltimore, MD 21202
Phone: (410)528-4000

Irving Yale. Second edition, 1980. Includes a bibliography and an index.

Podiatrists Directory

American Business Directories, Inc.
American Business Information, Inc.
5711 S. 86th Circle
Omaha, NE 68127
Phone: (402)593-4600
Fax: (402)331-1505

Annual. $660.00, payment with order. Number of listings: 20,481. Entries include: Name, address, phone (including area code), year first in 'Yellow Pages.' Arrangement: Geographical.

The Principles and Practice of Medicine

Appleton and Lange
25 Van Zant St.
East Norwalk, CT 06855
Phone: (203)838-4400
Toll-free: 800-423-1359

Harvey A. McGehee, et al., editors. Twenty-second edition, 1988. Practical guide to diagnosis and treatment.

Professional Guide to Diseases

Springhouse Corp.
1111 Bethlehem Pike
Springhouse, PA 19477
Phone: (215)646-8700
Toll-free: 800-346-7844

Fourth edition, 1991. An encyclopedia of illnesses, disorders, injuries, and their treatments. Includes bibliographies and an index.

Quick Reference to Medical-Surgical Nursing

J. B. Lippincott Co.
227 E. Washington Sq.
Philadelphia, PA 19106
Phone: (215)238-4200

Ellen B. Raffensperger, Mary L. Zusy, and Lynn Marchesseault. 1983. Includes bibliographies and indexes.

Relative Values for Physicians

McGraw-Hill, Inc.
1221 Avenue of the Americas
New York, NY 10020
Phone: (212)512-2000
Toll-free: 800-722-4726

Compiled by the Relative Value Studies, Inc., staff. Second edition, 1986. Lists 6000 medical procedures with relative value units provided to indicate the comparative difficulty of each procedure as an aid to help physicians set their fees.

Standard and Poor's Register of Corporations, Directors and Executives

Standard and Poor's Corp.
25 Broadway
New York, NY 10004
Phone: (212)208-8283

Annual, January; supplements in April, July, and October. $550.00, lease basis. Covers: Over 55,000 corporations in the United States, including names and titles of over 500,000 officials (Volume I); 70,000 biographies of directors and executives (Volume 2). Entries include: For companies—Name, address, phone, names of principal executives and accountants; number of employees, estimated annual sales, outside directors. For directors and executives—Name, home and principal business addresses, date and place of birth, fraternal organization memberships, business affiliations. Arranged alphabetically. Indexes: Volume 3 indexes companies geographically, by Standard Industrial Classification number, and by corporate family groups.

Successful Nurse Aide Management in Nursing Homes
Oryx Press
4041 N. Central Ave., Ste. 700
Phoenix, AZ 85012-3397
Phone: (602)265-2651
Toll-free: 800-279-6799
Fax: (602)253-2741

Joann M. Day, editor. 1989.

The University of Pennsylvania's Linda Aiken emphasized that healthcare is expanding faster than any other industry and that hospitals have kept adding nursing positions even though the number of patients has dropped. "Nurses have fared well in recent years compared to other Americans. Not that they made unreasonable gains, but everybody else's income was standing still."

Source: *American Journal of Nursing*

Taber's Cyclopedic Medical Dictionary
F. A. Davis Co.
1915 Arch St.
Philadelphia, PA 19103
Phone: (215)568-2270
Toll-free: 800-523-4049

Clarence W. Taber. Edited by Clayton L. Thomas. Sixteenth edition, 1989. Includes an index.

Taking Charge of Your Career Direction
Brooks/Cole Publishing Company
Marketing Dept.
511 Forest Lodge Rd.
Pacific Grove, CA 93950

Lock. 1992. 377 pages. Provides guidance for the job search process.

U.S. Medical Directory
U.S. Directory Service, Publishers
655 NW 128th St.
PO Box 68-1700
Miami, FL 33168
Phone: (305)769-1700
Fax: (305)769-0548

Latest edition 1989. $150.00, plus $5.00 shipping. Covers: Medical doctors, hospitals, nursing facilities, medical research laboratories, poison control centers, medical schools and libraries, and other medical services, organizations, facilities, and institutes.

Veterinary and Human Toxicology
American Academy of Clinical Toxicology (AACT)
Kansas State University
Comparative Toxicology Laboratories
Manhattan, KS 66506-5606
Phone: (913)532-4334
Fax: (913)532-4481

Bimonthly. $50.00/year. Includes annual directory.

Ward's Business Directory of U.S. Private and Public Companies
Gale Research Inc.
835 Penobscot Bldg.
Detroit, MI 48226
Phone: (313)961-2242
Fax: (313)961-6241

1991. Four volumes. Volumes 1-3 lists companies alphabetically and geographically; $930.00/set. Volume 4 ranks companies by sales with 4-digit SIC code; $655.00. $1,050.00/complete set. Contains information on over 85,000 U.S. businesses, over 90% of which are privately held. Entries include company name, address, and phone; sales; employees; description; names of officers; fiscal year end information; etc. Arrangement: Volume 1 and 2 in alphabetic order; Volume 3 in zip code order within alphabetically arranged states.

Who's Who in American Nursing
Society of Nursing Professionals
3004 Glenview Rd.
Wilmette, IL 60091
Phone: (708)441-2387

Biennial, March of odd years. $69.95. Covers: Approximately 30,000 nursing professionals, including educators, administrators, deans of nursing, directors of nursing, nurse practitioners, clinical supervisors, and others. Entries include: Name, address, personal history, area of specialization, professional experience, education, professional organization membership, and other data. Arrangement: Alphabetical. Indexes: Geographical, specialization.

Who's Who among Human Services Professionals

National Reference Institute
3004 Glenview Rd.
Wilmette, IL 60091
Phone: (708)441-2387

Biennial, February of even years. $69.95. Covers: Nearly 20,000 human service professionals, in such fields as nursing, counseling, social work, psychology, audiology, and speech pathology. Entries include: Name, address, education, work experience, professional association memberships. Arrangement: Alphabetical. Indexes: Geographical, field of specialization.

MASTER INDEX

Master Index

The Master Index provides comprehensive access to all four sections of the Directory by citing all subjects, organizations, publications, and services listed throughout in a single alphabetic sequence. The index also includes inversions on significant words appearing in cited organization, publication, and service names. For example, "Ward's Business Directory of U.S. Private and Public Companies" could also be listed in the index under "Companies; Ward's Business Directory of U.S. Private and Public."